rebecca robb benne

jon hird

move

advanced

coursebook
with CD-ROM

MACMILLAN

move advanced contents map

Module 1 Individuals

Module 2 Pairs

Module 3 Groups

Unit	Topic	Language study	Vocabulary	Main skills
1 **Living together** pages 66–69	• Happy families (Britain's biggest family) • A social experiment (living in an alternative community)	• Ellipsis and substitution	• Family relationships • Community organisation	• **Reading:** understanding gist; understanding vocabulary in context • **Speaking:** discussing cultural values and family relationships; discussing the aims of non-traditional living communities • **Listening:** identifying key information • **Writing:** an online advert
2 **Talk talk** pages 70–73	• World languages (Are fewer languages better?) • Language learning (attitudes to learning English and other foreign languages)	• Forming adjectives from verbs and nouns (adjective suffixes)	• Sensitive language (euphemisms)	• **Reading:** predicting; understanding main information and vocabulary in context • **Speaking:** evaluating the cultural and practical value of languages; using sensitive language and softeners to avoid offence • **Listening:** identifying key information • **Pronunciation:** sentence stress
3 **Net value** pages 74–77	• Is the Internet a good thing? • Are you addicted to email? (survey report)	• Using vague language	• Phrasal verbs: communication • Surveys	• **Listening:** understanding gist and key information; understanding vocabulary in context • **Speaking:** discussing the Internet; clarifying information and checking understanding; talking about email addiction; conducting a survey • **Pronunciation:** stress and weak forms • **Reading:** understanding key information • **Writing:** a survey report
4 **Team spirit** pages 78–81	• Team building • Are you a team player?	• Dependent prepositions	• World of work	• **Reading:** predicting information; checking key information and vocabulary in context • **Speaking:** discussing work practices and leadership styles; describing college- or work-related problems and giving advice • **Listening:** identifying key information; understanding vocabulary in context • **Writing:** a programme script

5 **Review unit** pages 82–85
- **Extra practice** pages 86–89 • **Grammar reference and wordlist** pages 90–92 • **Listening scripts** pages 94–95 • **Communication activities** pages 93, 96
- **Use CD2 for listening activities in this module.**

CD-ROM

Location	• Modules 1–3
Activities for each unit	• Language activity • Vocabulary activity • Common European Framework linked activity • Language game
Features	• Markbook – helps you to record and update your marks. • Bookmark – helps you to save your favourite activities. • Wordlist – helps you to create your own wordlists. • You can back up, restore and print out your Markbook, Bookmarks and Wordlists. You can also send saved files as emails. • For more information use the Help feature.

In the Coursebook:

three 32-page modules

On the CD-ROM:

48 language activities and games, a help section and markbook, wordlist and bookmark features

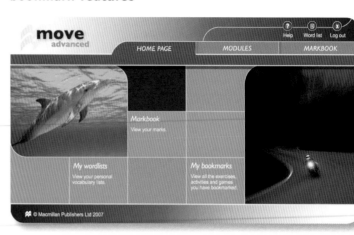

In each module:

four main units

a review unit

four extra practice pages

five reference pages: grammar, wordlist and listening scripts

two communication activity pages

Module 1
Individuals

Unit	Topic	Language study	Vocabulary	Main skills
1 Behave! pages 2–5	• Eccentrics • Are you a nonconformist?	• Contrast (discourse markers)	• Behavioural traits (adjectives and their collocations) • Taking turns in a discussion	• **Reading:** predicting and checking; summarising information • **Speaking:** discussing types of behaviour; discussing pressure to conform in different countries; taking turns and interrupting • **Listening:** identifying main information • **Pronunciation:** stress and intonation in discussions
2 Form and function pages 6–9	• Modern wonders (buildings and design) • Your workspace and you	• Describing buildings, places and objects (structures used to describe nouns)	• Compound adjectives • Expressing sympathy and annoyance	• **Reading:** understanding gist • **Speaking:** discussing architecture and design preferences; sympathising and expressing annoyance; talking about workspaces • **Writing:** a description of your favourite place • **Listening:** understanding gist and identifying key topics; understanding vocabulary in context
3 It's up to you! pages 10–13	• Moments in time (the best day of my life) • Changing the world (supporting causes by wearing wristbands)	• Adding emphasis	• Social issues and direct action	• **Listening:** understanding gist and key information; understanding vocabulary in context • **Speaking:** describing one of the best days of your life; talking about social issues and direct action • **Reading:** understanding main information • **Writing:** a message board thread and comments
4 No pain, no gain pages 14–17	• Getting to the top (life of a sumo wrestler) • What motivates you?	• Three-part phrasal verbs	• Proverbs and idioms: success • Motivation	• **Reading:** identifying key information • **Speaking:** talking about success, motivation and overcoming problems; explaining causes and results; discussing an autobiography • **Listening:** understanding gist and key information • **Writing:** a blurb for a biography

5 Review unit pages 18–21
Extra practice pages 22–25 • **Grammar reference and wordlist** pages 26–28 • **Listening scripts** pages 30–31 • **Communication activities** pages 29, 32

1 Behave!

Eccentrics

Lead-in

1 Work in groups. Which of the people in the box are in the photos? What do you know about these six people? What is / was strange or different about them?

> Björk   Salvador Dalí   Albert Einstein
> Frida Kahlo   Ozzy Osbourne   Vincent van Gogh

2 There are many famous male eccentrics, but few female. Why do you think this is so?

3 Read this quote by American author Michael J. Gelb. Do you agree?

Crazy people who are productive are geniuses.
Crazy people who are rich are eccentric.
Crazy people who are neither productive nor rich are just plain crazy.

Reading

1 Do you think these statements are true or false? Discuss them with a partner.

1 Eccentrics are generally optimistic and interested in finding out about things.
2 Most eccentrics don't mind being made fun of.
3 Eccentricity is something which people have no control over.

2 🔊 **01** Read the magazine interview on page 3. Find the answers to Ex 1.

3 Is David Weeks positive or negative about eccentricity? Write a paragraph (60–80 words) and summarise his main results and opinions.

4 Compare your summaries with a partner. Have you included similar information?

5 Look at this scale from conformity (1) to individuality (5). Where are you on the scale? Why? Explain this to a partner.

conformity ⟵ 1   2   3   4   5 ⟶ individuality

Vocabulary and speaking

1 Look at these words from the text. Underline the main stressed syllable.

> conventional   curious   gloomy   intelligent   mischievous   opinionated
> rebellious   unorthodox

2 💿 **02** Listen and check your answers.

HW
Synonyms + antonyms

3 Work with a partner. Agree which words in Ex 1 have positive meanings and which have negative meanings. Think of words with similar and opposite meanings.

ss think of famous people with these traits (dead or alive).

4 Tell a partner which of the adjectives in Ex 1–3 apply to you. Explain why or give examples of specific situations.

Example:
I am quite opinionated. I have very strong opinions about things like religion and politics, and I often get into arguments about them.

5 Complete these sentences with the words in the box to make collocations. Check your answers in the text.

> collector   imagination   outlook   side   traits

1 Anna has a vivid ___imagination___.

2 Tom is an obsessive ___collector___.

3 Jack's got a strong creative ___side___.

4 Sara's got a few eccentric ___traits___.

5 Rick has an optimistic ___outlook___ on life.

6 Replace the names in Ex 5 with the names of people you know. Work with a partner and tell your partner about these people.

7 Which of these adjectives can be used with which nouns in Ex 5? Do you know any other nouns which collocate with these words? Example: *avid collector*

> avid   dark   fertile   feminine   gloomy   keen   overactive   positive   serious   sympathetic   unconventional

An interview with David Weeks, author of *Eccentrics, a study of sanity and strangeness*

According to David Weeks, eccentrics like Mr Christmas 'don't give a damn what the rest of the world thinks of them'. Mr Christmas (real name Andy Park) has celebrated Christmas with Christmas dinner and presents every day for twelve years.

Happy, healthy and *odd!*

Q: What prompted you to make a scientific study of eccentricity?

A: Psychologists have undertaken exhaustive studies of every personality type under the sun, yet somehow we have completely overlooked eccentrics. And psychiatry, on the other hand, tends only to take an interest in those who seek treatment, and since eccentrics rarely do so, they have been overlooked. I thought it might contribute something important to our understanding of the mind if we had a better understanding of the thought processes of those who regard themselves and who are regarded by others as eccentric.

Q: Can you give us a description of the eccentric?

A: The eccentric is very creative and curious and has vivid visual imagination in the daytime and vivid dreams at night. Eccentrics are intelligent, opinionated, and frequently have a mischievous sense of humour. Many of them are loners, and they often have unorthodox living arrangements.

Q: For example?

A: We have several men who lived in caves. Women eccentrics tend to be obsessive collectors and renovators. One woman in our study has 7,500 garden gnomes on her lawn.

Q: You found in your study that eccentrics are happier and healthier than the rest of us.

A: We did meet a few gloomy eccentrics, but most of the subjects in our study had a refreshingly sunny outlook on life. There is also pretty solid proof that eccentrics are healthier than the norm. In Great Britain the average person goes to the doctor twice a year, while eccentrics will typically go for eight or nine years without seeking medical help. It's not that they're avoiding doctors or don't believe in conventional medicine. They just don't need it much.

Q: How do you explain this?

A: It's a combination of an optimistic outlook and low stress, due to the fact that eccentrics don't feel the need to conform. Eccentrics don't give a damn what the rest of the world thinks of them; if someone makes fun of them, instead of getting angry or embarrassed, they regard the other person as the one with a problem.

Q: What makes a person an eccentric? After all, everyone has some unusual habits or traits.

A: Eccentricity is a choice. It's quite true that everyone has eccentric traits, but as we grow older, most of us learn to conform, to blend in – the process we call socialisation. But the eccentric says, 'No, thank you,' and chooses not to conform.

Q: Are men or women more likely to be eccentric?

A: The incidence of eccentricity is about the same, but it manifests itself in different ways. Society has always been more tolerant of aberrant behaviour in men than in women. If a man gets into a fight with a colleague or goes off on a drinking spree, we might overlook it, but if a woman does the same thing it's considered scandalous. A woman sometimes becomes eccentric later in life: she conforms in her youth, marries and has children, but once the kids have left home, she leaves her husband and lets her eccentric, creative side take over.

Q: Dr Weeks, are you eccentric?

A: I would say that I may have always been slightly eccentric, perhaps a little rebellious. I do, however, admire the authentic, life-long eccentrics. I think we can all learn a lot from them about holding onto the dreams and curiosity we had as children.

start here 21/7/10

LANGUAGE STUDY

Contrast

1 Underline the four other contrastive discourse markers in these sentences.

   a *Psychologists have studied every personality type, yet somehow we have overlooked eccentrics. And psychiatry, on the other hand, tends only to take an interest in those who seek treatment.*

   b *We did meet a few gloomy eccentrics, but most of the subjects had a refreshingly sunny outlook on life.*

   c *In Great Britain the average person goes to the doctor twice a year, while eccentrics will typically go for eight or nine years without seeking medical help.*

   d *I would say that I may have always been slightly eccentric, perhaps a little rebellious. I do, however, admire the authentic, life-long eccentrics.*

2 Contrastive discourse markers most commonly go between the ideas they are contrasting, but there are other possible positions. Complete the table with the discourse markers from Ex 1.

Must always go between the ideas they are contrasting	Can also go before the first idea they are contrasting	Can also go in various positions in the second sentence
yet but	even though whereas while	nevertheless ✓
		OTOH

3 What is the function of the verb *do* in sentences 'b' and 'd'?

Grammar reference page 26

Aux. verb 'do' emphasises contrast. - There were thousands of people there, but we did see the celebrity
- I do believe you, honestly.

4 Look at these biography extracts. Combine each sentence 1–5 with one of the sentences a–e in **two** different ways using appropriate discourse markers.

   Example:
   nTL
   but
   *Van Gogh was a truly great artist, **yet** he only sold one painting in his lifetime.*
   ***Even though** Van Gogh was a truly great artist, he only sold one painting in his lifetime.*
   while   V.G. . . . .

   1 c David Bowie has created some of the most colourful personas in popular music.
   2 d The young Einstein couldn't read or write until he was eight years old.
   3 a Most people get into the music business to actively seek fame and fortune.
   4 e At school Gaudí did rather badly in most subjects.
   5 b Dalí based his appearance on the fashion style of a century earlier.

   3 a *Nirvana* front man Kurt Cobain found the invasion of his privacy all too much.
   5 b His paintings were anything but retrospective.
   1 c He has been virtually colour blind since a childhood accident.
   2 d He went on to become perhaps the greatest scientist of the 20th century.
   4 e He did excel in geometry, which inspired his lifetime's work.

5 Join the two sentences using *but* and the auxiliary verb *do* to emphasise contrast.

   Example: I enjoyed the meal. The service wasn't too good.
   I did enjoy the meal, but the service wasn't too good.

   1 I wanted to go. It was just impossible.
   2 I like them. I've just listened to them too much.
   3 I enjoyed it. I was glad to get home.
   4 I agree I should do it more. Sometimes I just can't be bothered.
   5 We liked each other. It just wasn't to be.
   6 I felt for them. There was nothing I could do to help.

6 Work with a partner. Explain situations in your life to which some of the sentences in Ex 5 could apply.

   Example: *I went to that new café near the school yesterday. I did enjoy the meal, but the service was a bit slow.*

*Pics
Punk   Skater
Goth   surfer
Grunge chav*

Are you a nonconformist?

Listening and speaking

1 Discuss and agree on a definition of a nonconformist.

2 🔘 **03** Listen to the classroom discussion about nonconformists. Explain these statements by Alex, Mette and Natsuko talking about their country.

People have lots of different lifestyes.

If you don't like spending time with other people, you've had it.

The nail that sticks out gets hammered down.

3 Discuss the opinions in Ex 2 in groups. Are any of these things true about your country? How much pressure is there to conform in your country in terms of dress, behaviour and lifestyle?

Vocabulary and pronunciation

Taking turns in a discussion

1 Listen again. Pay attention to stress and intonation, and write the phrases used when …

1 Alex takes up his point after interruption by Mette. *Er, yeah . anyway*
2 Mette interrupts Alex the second time. *That reminds me of*
3 Natsuko interrupts Mette. *Sorry ..to interrupt*
4 Natsuko prevents Mette from interrupting. *Wait .a minute*
5 Natsuko prevents Alex interrupting. *Just .let me finish*
6 Mette takes up an earlier point again. *To get back to what I was saying*

2 Put the phrases from Ex 1 in the correct place in the table. Then work with a partner and add the phrases in the box to the table.

> Before you comment, can I just … By the way … Can I add something?
> Can I finish what I was saying? Hang on! Incidentally … Where was I?

Interrupting	Preventing interruption	Returning to a topic	Changing the topic
TRMOf	Just wait		BTW
STIBut	Just let me finish	Er, yeah … Anyway,	Incidentally
CIASth	Byou comment...	TGB2WIWS	
	Can I fin?what Hang on!	Where was I	

Speaking

1 Work in groups. Look at the discussion circle and add two topics of your own.

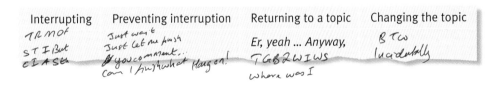

1 *We will all end up following in our parents' footsteps.*

2 _____

3 *Uniforms (at school and at work) infringe people's right to express their individuality.*

4 _____

5 *It's better to live in an anonymous city than in a close-knit village.*

2 Working individually, note down two arguments for and against each topic.

3 Your group has ten minutes to discuss all the topics. Start by discussing topic 1. Then in turns, change the topic to the next one in the circle until you return to the first topic.

CD-ROM For more activities go to **Individuals Unit 1**

2 Form and function

> **LEARNING AIMS**
>
> - Can describe buildings, places and objects
> - Can talk about workspaces
> - Can sympathise with problems

Modern wonders

Lead-in

1 These photos were on a shortlist for a competition to find the New Seven Wonders of the World. Do you know the names of the buildings and monuments? Or do you know where they are? (You can check with the list on page 29.)

2 What makes a building or monument a modern wonder? Discuss your ideas with the class, and make a list of your criteria.

3 Work in groups. Use the shortlist and agree on your New Seven Wonders of the World.

Reading and speaking

1 Work in groups. Look at the adjectives in the box and add other adjectives that can describe a building.

| functional | modern | 19th century | three-storey | smart | well-maintained |

2 Think about the building where you have your English classes and discuss these questions.
 1 What is it like inside? Is it a good environment for learning English?
 2 What's the building like outside?

3 ⊙ **04** Read the article on page 7. Does the author like the building? Why / Why not?

4 Answer these questions.
 1 What's the official name of the building? What's its nickname and why?
 2 What other metaphors have been used to describe it? Looking at the photo, which do you think is the most appropriate?
 3 What do people in London think of it?
 4 What special features does the building have?

5 Work in groups and discuss these statements.
 1 Ultramodern buildings should not be built next to old buildings.
 2 A company's building says a lot about the company itself.

A brilliant new skyscraper

At just 180 metres and 40 stories, the new skyscraper officially known as 30 St. Mary Axe is less than half the height of the world's ten tallest buildings, and not even the tallest building in London. But it draws instant attention because of its unique shape, which has been variously compared to a cigar, a rocket, a bullet, a lipstick, a Zeppelin airship, a lava lamp, a bandaged finger, and – most frequently – a gherkin. Its architect, Norman Foster, prefers the metaphor of a pine cone or pineapple, since they do more justice to the building's shape.

The Gherkin has rapidly become a well-known contemporary icon and much-loved tourist attraction. Most Londoners appreciate the novelty and sophistication of the building. Some despise it for desecrating the ancient City of London; but the quaint character of the City was pretty well desecrated decades ago by uninspired postwar rebuilding. The shape is a bit frivolous-looking for a building whose original owner was Swiss Re, a sober and respectable Zurich-based insurance company. But the sparkling glass surfaces covering the entire outside (made of 5,500 triangular windows, many of which open) and calm gray* walls inside the building are ultrachic and ultramodern.

unworthy of attention / silly

The building is round in floor plan to reduce the high winds generated at street level by tall rectangular buildings. On each of the office levels (floors 2–34), six pie-shaped pieces have been cut out from the plan, with elevators* and other service facilities at the center*. These six open cuts allow natural daylight to penetrate far back towards the elevator core and add desirable window-facing working space.

Swiss Re is seriously concerned about the possible financial costs to its clients of such things as global warming, and was determined to make its London headquarters a model of environment-friendly, energy-saving design. Genuine fresh air from outside can be guided about and used to reduce the need for mechanical air conditioning. In the basement there are no spaces for cars, but there are racks for bicycles and showers for cyclists.

London's new symbol is a sparkling, sensuous but profoundly sensible tower.

Glossary
*gray, elevator, center = American English for 'grey', 'lift' and 'centre'

Vocabulary

1 Look at these compound adjectives from the text. What do they describe in the article, and what do they mean?

1	well-known	4	Zurich-based	7	environment-friendly
2	much-loved	5	pie-shaped	8	energy-saving
3	frivolous-looking	6	window-facing		

2 Look at these compound adjectives. Which compound adjective in each set is not a correct collocation? What things could the other two words in each set describe?

Example:
best-known *singer in the world*   little-known *area*   terribly known [X]

1   well-loved   badly loved✗   much-loved
2   rainy-looking✗   expensive-looking   tasty-looking
3   American-based   London-based   Britain-based✗
4   sky-shaped✗   heart-shaped   crescent-shaped
5   south-facing   sea-facing   room-facing✗
6   world-friendly✗   child-friendly   tourist-friendly
7   time-saving   food-saving✗   money-saving

3 What other *-looking* compounds can you think of? *good funny odd expensive cheap forward*

4 Rewrite these sentences using compound adjectives.

Example: I live in that building *with the bright colour* next to the market.
I live in that brightly coloured building next to the market.

1   That building *really catches your eye.*
2   I rent a flat *on the third floor.*
3   It's a flat *where you can't smoke.*
4   I have a flat *with two bedrooms.*
5   The cupboards *were made badly* and don't open properly.
6   There's a good café nearby where you can get a great breakfast *all day.*

5 Describe the place where you live to a partner. Use at least three compound adjectives.

Example: *I live in a three-roomed flat in an old four-storey building. The building has an elegant-looking entrance and beautiful windows. Our flat has a small south-facing balcony…*

NOTE

Most compound adjectives have hyphens when they come before the noun, but when the first word ends in -ly there is no hyphen.
Examples:
Well-known,
badly dressed

[handwritten: noun + adj = noun phrase / rel. clause / phrase]

LANGUAGE STUDY

Describing buildings, places and objects

1 Look at these extracts from the text on page 7 and the structures that describe the nouns in **bold**. Find other examples in the extracts.

1 adjectives   *unique*

[handwritten: glass, floor] 2 nouns used as adjectives   *tourist*

[handwritten: whose orig owner was] 3 relative clauses   *which has been variously compared to a cigar, a rocket ...*

[handwritten: generated at st level] 4 clauses beginning with a present (*-ing*) or past participle   *covering the entire outside ...*

[handwritten: from outside] 5 phrases beginning with a preposition   *inside the building ...*

a *But it draws instant attention because of its <u>unique</u> **shape**, <u>which has been variously compared to a cigar, a rocket</u> ...*

b *The Gherkin has rapidly become a well-known contemporary **icon** and much-loved <u>tourist</u> **attraction**.*

c *The shape is a bit frivolous-looking for a **building** <u>whose original owner was Swiss Re</u>.*

d *But the sparkling glass **surfaces** <u>covering the entire outside</u> and calm gray **walls** <u>inside the building</u> are ultrachic and ultramodern.*

e *The building is round in floor **plan** to reduce the high **winds** generated at street level.*

f *Genuine fresh **air** from outside can be guided about.*

2 Which of the structures in Ex 1 go before the noun and which go after the noun?

[handwritten: adj, nouns as adj]

[handwritten: After   rel clause, clause beginning w participle, phrase beginning with preposition]

Grammar reference page 27

3 Use one word or phrase from each column to describe four of the buildings and monuments from page 6.

Example:
It's a redbrick cathedral with multi-coloured domes standing in Red Square in Moscow.

	redbrick	pyramid	of a woman	~~standing in Red Square~~	in Egypt
	ruined	statue	discovered in 1908	at the entrance to the harbour	in Peru
It's a	4,500-year-old	city	made of two million blocks of stone	perched high in the Andes plateau	~~in Moscow~~
	copper	~~cathedral~~	~~with multi-coloured domes~~	rising 150 metres out of the desert	in New York

4 Complete the descriptions of the nouns in **bold** by adding the words and phrases in *italics* in the most natural order.

1 My favourite place to eat is a **restaurant**.
   family-run   just round the corner from my house   pizza   called Luigi's

2 My favourite item of clothing is a **jacket**.
   with a hole in the sleeve   I've had since I was in my teens   old   denim   faded

3 My favourite film is No way out. It's a **thriller**.
   starring Kevin Costner   with a great twist at the end   fast-paced

4 My favourite place anywhere in the world is Pushkar in India. It's a **town**.
   with over 400 temples   chilled-out   surrounding a holy lake   small

5 Adapt the sentences in Ex 4 to talk about your favourite place, etc.

Writing

1 Look at the competition and write your entry.

2 Read other students' entries. Which of the other places sound particularly interesting? Why? Choose the competition winner.

COMPETITION

Tell us about your favourite place in the world and win an all-expenses paid weekend in New York. Write about 200 words describing your favourite city, town, area or building and say why it is special to you.

[handwritten: split class / HO pics to each side / work from home/office.]

Your workspace and you

Listening and vocabulary

1 Do you enjoy studying or working at home? What are the advantages and disadvantages? *[handwritten: for each focus]*

2 🔘 **05** Listen to the conversation and tick the things that Kyle talks about.

work and free time ☑ his business ☑ work colleagues ☑ girlfriends ☐

his social life ☑ office politics ☐ technical problems ☐ communication ☑

commuting ☐ independence ☑

3 Is Kyle positive or negative about working from home? Why? *[handwritten: -ve / no free time / isolated lonely / likes uncle but misses his social life]*

4 Match Kyle's sentence beginnings to the endings. <u>Underline</u> the words that express dissatisfaction or annoyance.

1 I'm getting a bit sick   *4* with being on my own.
2 I don't even have time to have lunch   *5* it's driving me mad.
3 I miss   *1* of sitting at my desk every day.
4 I'm fed up   *2* let alone watch TV.
5 I get a new email every ten minutes and   *3* the drinks after work with the lads.

5 Put these phrases into two lists: *sympathising* and *expressing annoyance*.

[handwritten: note. Sympc = Ex]

> *S* Come on, it can't be that bad.   *Ex* Stop moaning!   *Ex* Oh, just shut up!   *S* Oh, poor you!
> *S* What a shame!   *S* Oh, dear, I'm sorry.   *Ex* Oh, change the record!   *Ex* Put a sock in it!
> *S* How awful!   You're not the only one with problems, you know. *Ex*   Cheer up! *S*

6 Listen to the conversation again and tick the phrases in Ex 5 that Nicola uses. Pay attention to stress and intonation.

[handwritten: HO cards]

7 Work with a partner. Student A look at page 29. Student B look at page 32. Review the phrases in this section for expressing dissatisfaction, sympathy and annoyance before you begin.

Reading and speaking

1 Complete the questionnaire. Then follow the instructions on page 32.

What does your workspace say about you?

1 How tidy is your workspace?
a It's overflowing with all sorts of stuff.
b There isn't a paperclip out of place.
c You can usually find most things (fingers crossed!)

2 What about the personal items (photos, cuddly toys, magazines, etc) in your workspace?
a What personal items? Your desk is for work, not fun.
b There aren't many – you adhere to the minimalist approach.
c They'd fill a small removal van.

3 How do you keep track of your appointments?
a Make a mental note and hope it doesn't slip your mind.
b Enter them in your computer calendar or diary as soon as they're scheduled.
c Stick a post-it on your computer monitor, along with all the others.

4 Your computer wallpaper is …
a an abstract pattern in soothing tones.
b a motif from nature: a tropical beach, a lush forest, exotic flowers.
c a picture of a universally-acclaimed member of the opposite sex.

5 You're feeling peckish while working, do you …
a eat a piece of fruit from the bowl on your desk?
b rummage through your desk drawer and hope something turns up?
c have a snack away from your workspace to protect your keyboard from crumbs?

CD-ROM For more activities go to **Individuals Unit 2**

3 It's up to you!

▲ Martin Luther King

Def: Civil Rights on WB

Moments in time

Lead-in 1 Work with a partner. Talk about what the people in the photos did to earn a place in the world's history books. Use the words in the box to help you.

> apartheid   civil rights movement   democratic rule
> equality   independence injustice   military rulers
> non-violent protest   peace   segregation

▲ Nelson Mandela

Listening 1 🔘 **06** Listen to Jodie talking about one of the best days of her life. Make notes on these points.

The event: (What? Why? Where?) *Live 8, Cheer up,*
London Hyde Park

Jodie's feelings at the start of the concert: (How did she feel? Why?) *Vast crowd   laid back*
crowd lapping msg up
a bit hollow

▲ Aung San Suu Kyi

How the concert changed Jodie's life: (What happened? How did her outlook on life change?) _____
Buzz - special day momentous anything possible
Own experiences trivial - fail exams, breakups of
Trivia -
Huge turning point in my life

2 Listen again and complete the words and phrases describing the feelings and reactions of Jodie and the crowd.

1 There was a great feeling, really *laid back*.
2 The crowd was *lapping it all up*, but all the speeches rang a bit *hollow* to me somehow.
3 The mood in the crowd seemed to *intensify*. There was this fantastic *buzz*.
4 It was like everyone's hope *was embodied* in this one man.
5 It was an absolute *revelation* to me then, at that moment in time.
6 That day was a huge *turning point* in my life.

▲ Gandhi

3 Explain what the words and phrases in Ex 2 mean in this context.

Speaking 1 Think about these situations and make notes if necessary. Then tell your partner.

1 A time when you were in a crowd at a special event. What was the event? What was the mood? Did you feel part of the crowd or apart from it?
2 A revelation or turning point in your life. What led up to it? What happened? What were the consequences?

2 Discuss these questions with your class.

1 Is music a good way to create interest in a problem or raise money? What other ways can you think of drawing attention to a good cause or of raising money to help other people?
2 Do you think Bob Geldof will / should take a place in history in the same way as the people in the photos on this page? Think of arguments for and against.

LANGUAGE STUDY

Adding emphasis

1 Look at these extracts from Listening Ex 1–2 on page 10. Which include examples of:

1 adding emphasis to a noun? [a] [e]

2 adding emphasis to an adjective? [d] [f]

3 adding emphasis to a verb or verb clause? [c]

4 using a phrase to add emphasis to what you are saying in general? [b]

a *The sun was blazing down and this **vast** crowd of people was chilling out.*

b *It was as if anything was possible, that music really could change the world, **you know**.*

c *I **just** realised that my own experiences were so trivial.*

d *It's probably **even** harder to understand what it was like if you weren't there.*

e *It was an **absolute** revelation to me then, at that moment in time.*

f *This was a **very** special day.*

Grammar reference page 27

2 Match the words in **bold** to functions 1–4 in Ex 1.

a It's (1) **without doubt** the most amazing place I've (2) **ever** been to.

b The (3) **entire** event was a (4) **complete** waste of time.

c It was (5) **so** peaceful. We didn't see a (6) **single** person (7) **at all**.

d The house was (8) **absolutely** immaculate (9) **from top to bottom**. It was (10) **totally** spotless.

3 Put the words in *italics* in an appropriate position in the sentence to add emphasis.

Example: We didn't want the day to end. *just you know*
We just didn't want the day to end, you know.

1 I couldn't believe it. I was speechless. *just totally*

2 It was good to see them again after all that time. *so you know*

3 It was a shock. I had no idea what they'd been planning. *complete at all*

4 It took us an age to get to the top, but it was worth it. The views were stunning.
absolute well absolutely

5 The day was amazing. It was better than I'd dared imagine. *whole from start to finish even*

6 It was the best moment of my life. *without doubt single entire*

4 🔊 **07** Listen and check your ideas for Ex 3. Notice how the voice adds emphasis and enthusiasm.

5 Could any of the sentences in Ex 2 and 3 describe any moments or days in your life? Tell your partner.

Example: *One time we just didn't want the day to end was the other month when …*

6 You are going to tell a partner about one of the best days in your life. Think about these questions and spend a few minutes preparing what you are going to say. Be as emphatic as you can.

When was it?	Did you know what was going to happen?
Where were you?	What happened to make it such a good day?
Who was with you?	How did you feel at different parts of the day?
What events led up to this day?	What was the single most important moment?
How did the day start?	Do you have any special mementos of that day?

Warmer: Ways of showing support for sth.   T shirts   logo/motto   wristbands
Tattoos

Changing the world

Reading

1   Look at the photo. Which of these issues can you see on the wristbands?

> cancer   anti-bullying   help for poor countries   racism in football

2   Are you wearing or have you worn a wristband? Are wristbands still a popular way to show public support for campaigns?

3   📀 **08**   Read the message board comments. Are these statements true or false? Correct the false ones.

1   According to Jack, wristbands show you belong to a community. *T*
2   Jack thinks it's important to know what message a wristband carries. *F*
3   In Alina's opinion wristbands are just fashion accessories. *F*
4   Fernando thinks supporting a cause is the most important thing. *T*
5   Camille wants people to use more indirect methods of protest and support. *F*
6   Camille thinks people often use donations to charities and campaigns to make them feel good about themselves. *T*

On the bandwagon

Do you support important causes by wearing wristbands? Do you think they're an effective way of raising awareness about important issues? Or do you think most people just wear wristbands as a fashion accessory and don't care too much about what they stand for?

I think wristbands are a great way to support a cause. They raise money and they also raise awareness of what that cause is all about. It's like meeting an old friend when you see somebody with the same wristband because you know it means they share the same values as you. But even if other people don't know what a particular wristband represents, it can be a great conversation starter.

Jack, UK

Most people wear wristbands just because they're trendy. They probably don't really care much about the cause, they're just following the crowd. But that still raises awareness of the issue, so if wristbands help spread the word about something, maybe it doesn't matter if they're basically a fashion accessory.

Alina, Romania

I wear a white wristband to express solidarity with a campaign that wants to eradicate poverty. Actually, I don't like wearing things on my wrist but I'm making an exception for this as I think the issue is just so important. Generally, I think it's essential to show commitment to a cause and not just jump on any old bandwagon because it happens to be fashionable.

Fernando, Mexico

Some people use wristbands to say 'Hey look, I've given money to charity, I'm a good person.' Instead of feeling smug because they've done nothing but donate a small amount of money, they should get out on the streets and protest properly for change. That's what we do in France when we want to do something about something. Armchair protests like wristbands, text message campaigns and online petitions don't get you anywhere at all. They just ease your guilty conscience.

Camille, France

4   What do you think? Whose comments do you most agree or disagree with? Why?

Example:

I strongly disagree with Camille's comments. Advances in technology and the importance of global issues mean that newer forms of protest like online petitions are more effective because more people all over the world can participate in them.

5   In your country is it usual to actively support change or raise awareness by protesting in some way? How? What role do mobile phones and the Internet play?

Example:

I come from a country where the government controls the media. The Internet is important because it is an independent source of information. Organising protests by SMS has also become very popular.

Vocabulary and speaking

1 Match the verbs and the nouns. Then check your answers in the text on page 12.

do	express	eradicate
give	raise	raise
show	spread	support

9 a cause 6 awareness 7 commitment 5 money
4 money to charity 3 poverty 2 solidarity
1 something about something 8 the word

2 Work in groups and discuss these questions.

Have you ever …
… raised money for a cause? How?
… given money to charity? Which charity? Why?
… spread the word about a cause? How?

Do you currently actively support any causes? Which ones and why?

3 Replace the underlined words with words or phrases from the message board on page 12.

1 Inequality and forms of oppression are topics most people feel strongly about.
2 I've no idea what the letters in UNICEF represent.
3 A current political topic is always a good way of getting a discussion going.
4 It's easier to do what the majority do than swim against the tide.
5 It's unfair to call people self-satisfied just because they try to help.
6 I often have a bad feeling about the fact that we have such easy lives compared to many people in the world.

4 Work with a partner. You are going to discuss an issue using the vocabulary from Ex 1 and Ex 3. Student A, look at page 29. Student B, look at page 32.

Writing

1 Look at the message board discussion topics in the box. Which one do you find most interesting?

animal testing   censorship and state control   computer games and violence
fair trade   gun control   illegal music downloads   private healthcare
sex discrimination

2 Think of other possible message board topics with the class.

3 Work in groups. You are going to start your own message boards and write comments on them. Choose a topic and write a brief 'thread' or starting comment (two or three sentences – as in the one in the reading text) on a piece of paper. Make it as interesting and / or controversial as possible and end it with a question.

4 Pass your thread to the person in the group on your right. Respond to the thread you have been given by writing a paragraph. Make sure you put your opinion across clearly.

5 When the 'message boards' have been round the whole group, stop the activity. Read the comments on your board and sum up the general attitude and reactions to your starting comment for the group.

CD-ROM   For more activities go to **Individuals Unit 3**

4 No pain, no gain

Proverbs
Ex from own L into Eng

Getting to the top

Lead-in

1 Work with a partner. Look at these proverbs.
Do you have similar proverbs in your language?

a Rome wasn't built in a day.
b Where there's a will, there's a way.
c All work and no play makes Jack a dull boy.
d Look before you leap.
e There's no time like the present.

2 Which of the proverbs in Ex 1 best sums up your attitude to life?

Reading and speaking

1 Work with a partner and discuss these questions.

- What do you know about sumo wrestling? Do you ever watch it?
- What do you think of the sport? What problems might be associated with it?
- What do you think is essential for sumo wrestlers to become champions?

2 09 Read the article on page 15. What problem did Mainoumi have to overcome in order to become a sumo champion? How did he manage it?

3 Which of these things does the article mention? Tick them. Then check your answers in the text and note the adjectives used to describe them.

Mainoumi's speed [✓] *dazzling*   his build [✓] *puny*   his weight [✓] *puny*   his diet [ ]

his family [ ]   his command of conventional techniques [✓] *supreme*

his tricks and manoeuvres [✓] *dizzying*   his friend [✓] *close*   his training [ ]   his injuries [✓] *terrible*

4 What other words would you use to describe Mainoumi? What do you think of his actions and achievements?

Vocabulary and speaking

1 Explain the meaning of these idioms from the text.

1 make it big (paragraph 2)
2 by hook or by crook (paragraph 2)

2 Match the idioms to the correct meanings.

1 They got off to a flying start. *c*
2 She won hands down. *h*
3 I passed with flying colours. *g*
4 I was fighting a losing battle. *e*
5 I sailed through it. *f*
6 They stole the show. *a*
7 He decided to throw in the towel. *b*
8 It was a case of sink or swim. *d*

a attracted the most attention
b stopped trying to do something
c began something very well
d being left on one's own to succeed or fail
e trying to do something that would probably fail
f dealt with something very easily
g achieved something with great success
h won very easily

3 Work with a partner. Think about situations involving yourself or people you know which match the idioms in Ex 2. Tell your partner about these situations.

Example:

My driving test got off to a flying start. My parking was excellent and I did a great emergency stop. Unfortunately it was downhill from then on. I saw a car too late at a roundabout and nearly hit it. And then I scraped my wing-mirror on a parked car. I failed the test.

Sports idioms ws

4 In the article, Mainoumi's sumo bouts were described as 'must-see events'. What does *must-see* mean?

5 Work in groups and discuss these questions.

Over the last few years, what have been …

1 the must-see films and TV programmes?
2 the must-see events (sports competitions, matches, concerts, etc)?
3 the must-have gadgets and accessories?
4 the must-have CDs, in your opinion?

A head start for Mainoumi?

'Where there's a will there's a way' is an extremely trite phrase, but in this case, it's hard to think of a more succinct summary. Mainoumi was one of the smallest sumo wrestlers ever, weighing in at 98 kg and 169 cm, only reaching the 173 cm required to wrestle by having an extremely painful silicone implant embedded under his scalp. He was also one of the most exciting wrestlers ever, making up for his pint-sized build with a dizzying array of tricks and manoeuvres that made his bouts the must-see events of his era.

Born Nagao Shuhei in 1967, Mainoumi was a talented sumo wrestler at Nihon University, but knew he could never join the pro ranks because he was too short. Instead, he decided to become a high school teacher, and channelled his love of sumo into mentoring a close friend to become a sumo champion. His friend showed much promise, but during their senior year, the friend died suddenly of an illness. Nagao was heartbroken, and gave up sumo entirely for a few months. But after some reflection, he decided that the best way to honour his friend's memory was to make it big in pro sumo himself, by hook or by crook.

And that is what he did, eventually rising to become the fifth-ranked wrestler in all of sumo. The first challenge was to come up with a way to increase his height from 169 cm to the required 173 cm. After making several inquiries, he finally found a doctor who agreed to implant a sack under his scalp and gradually inject silicone into it over a period of several months. The stretching of his scalp to increase his height by four centimetres meant that Mainoumi had to put up with incredible discomfort, such that he would sometimes throw up or pass out from the pain during his everyday activities. But nevertheless he wrestled throughout his career with the implant, which altogether required four different operations to maintain.

In the ring Mainoumi was nothing short of a sensation. To compensate for his small size, the quick-thinking Mainoumi used dazzling speed, supreme command of conventional techniques, and a willingness to try anything and everything to achieve victory when conventional techniques failed. Perhaps most impressive of all was that Mainoumi was wrestling some of the most massive sumo wrestlers ever. Mainoumi became the ultimate underdog, and a hero to sumo fans everywhere, standing up for the supremacy of wits and technique over size and brute force. Some of the most memorable sumo bouts of the 1990s involved the puny 98 kg Mainoumi facing off against 239 kg Akebono or 275 kg Konishiki.

One of these fights, memorable for all the wrong reasons, was a bout in 1996 when, in a match which Mainoumi actually won, all 275 kilograms of Konishiki came crashing down on Mainoumi's knee, shredding it completely. It took Mainoumi more than a year and a half to make his way back to the ring. He finally made it back in 1999 before a new spate of terrible injuries forced him to retire once and for all at age 32.

Sumo wrestlers must agree to follow the strict rules of their sport.

LANGUAGE STUDY

Three-part phrasal verbs

1 Look at these sentences. <u>Underline</u> the three-part phrasal verbs and match each one with its meaning a–d. The first one has been done for you.

1 Mainoumi **made up for** his pint-sized build with a dizzying array of tricks and manoeuvres.
2 The first challenge was to come up with a way to increase his height from 169 cm to the required 173 cm.
3 He had to put up with incredible discomfort.
4 Mainoumi stood up for the supremacy of wits and technique over size and brute force.

a tolerate ☐ b compensate for [1] c defend ☐ d think of ☐

2 All three-part phrasal verbs must have an object. In which position do you always put the object?

Grammar reference page 27

3 Match the beginnings and endings of these quotes. Check your answers on page 32.

1 Too many people **run out of** ideas
2 If your children **look up to** you, .
3 I take a simple view of life:
4 The way I see it, if you want the rainbow,
5 It takes a great deal of courage to **stand up to** your enemies,
6 You need to feel good about yourself. The motivation has to come from within.

a but even more to **stand up to** your friends.   JK Rowling, author
b You have nobody to **fall back on** except yourself.   Dana Hill, actress
c you gotta **put up with** the rain.   Dolly Parton, singer
d long before they **run out of** words.   Anonymous
e you've made a success of life's biggest job.   Anonymous
f keep your eyes open and **get on with** it.   Sir Laurence Olivier, actor

4 What is the meaning of the phrasal verbs in **bold** in Ex 3?

5 Which quotation in Ex 3 do you like the best? Compare your ideas with a partner.

6 Complete the extracts with an appropriate form of the phrasal verbs in the box.

> come back from   ~~come up against~~   come up with   drop out of
> face up to   put up with   stand up to

1 In the 2005 European Cup final, Liverpool *came up against* a rampaging AC Milan. Liverpool _____ being 3–0 down to win on penalties.
2 After being diagnosed with cancer in 1996, world champion cyclist Lance Armstrong had to _____ the possibility that he would never compete again. He went on to win the *Tour de France* a record seven consecutive times.
3 Bill Gates first _____ the idea of setting up a software company while he was a student at Harvard. Against all advice he _____ university to set up the Microsoft Corporation. He was a billionaire by the time he was 30.
4 On 1st December 1955, after _____ years of racial abuse and segregation, Rosa Parks _____ the driver of the bus she was travelling on and refused to give up her seat for a white passenger. She became known as the 'Mother of the modern-day civil rights movement.'

7 Think of someone you know or a famous person who has had to overcome the odds to succeed. Tell your partner.

What motivates you?

Listening

1 🔘 **10** Listen to four young people talking about their motivation to succeed. Choose the reason for each person's motivation.

| a famous person   a friend   an inspirational book   an inspirational family member |
| a person in history   competition   failure   praise |

1 Max _____   3 Tom _____

2 Chloe _____   4 Ellen _____

2 Listen again and answer the questions.

1 What are the positive and negative results of the way Max was brought up?
2 Why was Chloe feeling down?
3 How was Chloe motivated after she watched TV?
4 Why were Tom's parents initially disappointed in him?
5 What was the reaction of Tom's parents to his choice of career?
6 How did Ellen's mother react to getting divorced?

Vocabulary

1 Listen again and complete these sentences. Then check your answers in the listening script on page 31.

1 I think my motivation _____ my childhood.

2 My confidence today is definitely _____ the way I was brought up.

3 It's all _____ Kylie!

4 I love what I'm doing – and that _____ to try and be better.

5 All my life I've had a very strong _____.

6 I _____ everything to my mum.

2 Work in small groups. Talk about what motivates you. Think about these things.

1 Is the source of your motivation something recent or something deeply rooted?
2 Is your motivation the result of a particular experience? Was it positive or negative?
3 Is a particular person responsible for inspiring or motivating you?

Speaking and writing

1 Find the meaning of these words in a dictionary.

| cherished   genocide   huddle   machete   rip   slaughter   spree |

2 Read the summary of an autobiography. Do you think the book would be inspiring? Why? / Why not? Discuss your ideas with a partner.

3 Choose an inspiring person. Find out information about them and write a blurb of about 120 words for the back cover of a biography of their life.

Left to tell by Immaculée Ilibagiza

Immaculée Ilibagiza grew up in a country she loved, surrounded by a family she cherished. But in 1994 her idyllic world was ripped apart as Rwanda descended into bloody genocide. Immaculée's family was brutally murdered during a killing spree that lasted three months and claimed the lives of nearly a million Rwandans. Incredibly, Immaculée survived the slaughter. For 91 days, she and seven other women huddled silently together in the cramped bathroom of a local pastor, while hundreds of machete-wielding killers hunted for them. The triumphant story of this remarkable young woman's journey through the darkness of genocide will inspire anyone whose life has been touched by fear, suffering, and loss.

Foreword by Dr Wayne W. Dyer

LEFT TO TELL
One woman's story of surviving the Rwandan holocaust

'gripping'
Independent on Sunday

IMMACULÉE ILIBAGIZA
with Steve Erwin

CD-ROM For more activities go to **Individuals Unit 4**

5 Review

Lead-in 1 Are there any websites that you visit regularly or that you really like? Which websites do you have bookmarked in your 'favourites'?

Million dollar boy

1 Look at the photo of the Million Dollar homepage. Can you guess what it consists of?

2 11 Listen to the news story and check your ideas in Ex 1.

3 What do the figures represent? Listen again and check.

Example: 100,000 – *He made £100,000 during the first week at university.*

1	a million ☐	2	2005 ☐	3	100 ☐	4	6,400 ☐	5	21 ☐

6 40,000 and 60,000 ☐   7 1000 and 38 ☐   8 tens of thousands ☐

4 Complete these extracts with an appropriate form of the three-part phrasal verbs in the box.

> be down to   come up with   drop out of   fall back on   get on with   run out of

1 While most of his fellow students were already _____ what little cash they had during fresher's week, Nottingham University student Alex Tew made over £100,000.

2 Alex Tew _____ the idea one night in August 2005.

3 The fees and accommodation for the first year alone were starting to look daunting, and with no finances to _____ Alex was dreading running up huge debts.

4 Alex immediately _____ setting up the website.

5 And not for one minute did Alex consider _____ university.

6 Experts agree that the Million Dollar Homepage's success _____ three things: the power of word of mouth, that it's the rags-to-riches story of an ordinary student and that it was a truly innovative yet simple idea.

5 Look at this summary of the story of the Million Dollar Homepage. Complete the descriptions of the nouns in **bold** by adding the words and phrases in *italics* in an appropriate order.

Example:
Alex Tew was accepted on a **course**.   *degree   which started in September 2005 at Nottingham University   business management*

Alex Tew was accepted on a business management degree course at Nottingham University, which started in September 2005.

1 He was worried about his **situation** and the **debts**.
that he would be running up   huge   financial

2 He came up with the **idea** of a **website**. *that he would sell to advertisers for a dollar a pixel   made up of a million pixels   consisting of just one page   ingenious*

3 Alex decided the web page would need a **name**. He thought of and bought the **name** 'milliondollarhomepage.com' that **evening**. *same   memorable   domain   that would capture the imagination*

4 Most of the **companies** reported an **increase** in the number of **hits** as well as **sales**. *increased   immediate   that bought webspace   on their websites*

5 **Websites** copied Alex's idea, but none achieved anything like the **success**. *of the Million Dollar Homepage   numerous other   phenomenal*

6 The chart shows the results of an internet survey. What is your opinion and why?

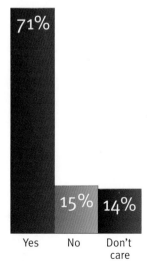

Does Alex Tew deserve his million dollars?

71%

15%   14%

Yes   No   Don't care

Innovation

1 Choose the correct alternative in these extracts from an article called 'Beds in the boardroom'.

1 We tend to associate lying down with being tired and emptying the mind, *on the other hand / nevertheless / yet* research has shown that we think more clearly and innovatively when lying down.

2 When we are standing, the brain produces more of the chemical noradrenalin, which slows brain activity. When we are lying down, *however / while / yet*, production of noradrenalin is reduced and thinking speeds can increase by 10%.

3 *But / However / While* meetings are where ideas are supposed to be generated, about 80% of us have our best work-related ideas outside the workplace and one in five of us when we're lying in bed.

4 *Even though / On the other hand / Yet* there is evidence supporting the idea of making meetings more informal and relaxed, we are still a long way from beds in the boardroom.

5 Business managers believe that sitting upright makes people get to the point quicker, *yet / whereas / on the other hand* they fear that a more relaxed atmosphere could make meetings drag on.

2 Where do you do your best thinking and have your best ideas?

3 Are you an innovator or more suited to turning other people's ideas into a success? Complete the questionnaire.

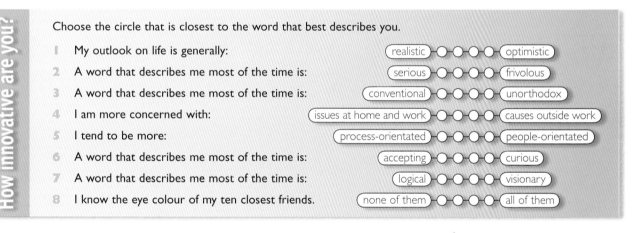

How innovative are you?

Choose the circle that is closest to the word that best describes you.

1 My outlook on life is generally: realistic –O–O–O–O– optimistic
2 A word that describes me most of the time is: serious –O–O–O–O– frivolous
3 A word that describes me most of the time is: conventional –O–O–O–O– unorthodox
4 I am more concerned with: issues at home and work –O–O–O–O– causes outside work
5 I tend to be more: process-orientated –O–O–O–O– people-orientated
6 A word that describes me most of the time is: accepting –O–O–O–O– curious
7 A word that describes me most of the time is: logical –O–O–O–O– visionary
8 I know the eye colour of my ten closest friends. none of them –O–O–O–O– all of them

4 Add up your score from the questionnaire (from left to right score 1, 2, 3, 4) and read the analysis.

Your final score: 25–32
You're a **right-brain** thinker, meaning you tend to draw on your emotional, creative side the most. You are curious, with a vivid imagination and you have innovative ideas. But you need to be partnered by a left-brainer who can help you bring your ideas to fruition.

Your final score: 17–24
You're a **whole-brain** thinker, meaning you have easy access to both sides of your brain. This allows you to come up with great new ideas and put them into action. Whole-brainers tend to be natural innovators and entrepreneurs who can often go it alone.

Your final score: 8–16
You're a **left-brain** thinker. Left-brainers are logical, analytical, and organised, and are well suited for turning a good idea into a reality. Your ideal partner is a right-brain visionary who will help you look at situations creatively and provide you with initial ideas.

5 Discuss these questions with a partner.

1 Are you a right-, left- or whole-brain thinker? Is the analysis of you accurate?
2 Do you think Alex Tew is a right-, left- or whole-brain thinker?
3 Which famous people do you think are right-, left- and whole-brain thinkers?

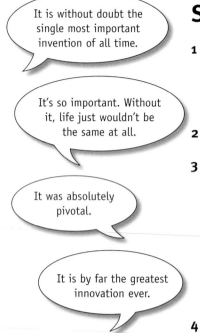

It is without doubt the single most important invention of all time.

It's so important. Without it, life just wouldn't be the same at all.

It was absolutely pivotal.

It is by far the greatest innovation ever.

Speaking

1 A recent survey asked people to vote for the greatest 'everyday' innovation in each of the following categories. Work in groups and discuss what you think the winners should be.

Communications	Household	The arts and music	Transport

2 Turn to page 29 to see which innovation won each category.

3 You are going to give a brief presentation. Follow these instructions.

- Work in groups of four. Each person selects a different innovation from the category winners on page 29.
- Prepare a two-minute presentation explaining why your innovation should win. Be as emphatic as you can. Use the ideas in the speech bubbles and the Language study on page 11 to help you.
- Take turns to give your presentations.
- When you have all spoken, vote for the winner. You can't vote for your innovation.

4 Look at page 32 to see which innovation was the overall winner in the survey.

Vocabulary

1 Read how to play 'Win hands down' and then play the game.

Win hands down

How to play

1 Play in two teams of two or three players each.
2 Team A chooses a sentence for team B. If team B thinks the sentence is correct they 'keep it' and if they think it is incorrect they 'give it' to team A. Cross off this sentence so it cannot be used again.
3 Team B then chooses a sentence for team A and so on. Keep a record of which team has which sentences.
4 When all the sentences have been used, check the answers on page 32. You get one point for each correct sentence you have. The team with the highest score wins.

1 They got off to a flying start.	**2** She's a bit of loser.	**3** I really look up at her.	**4** It's quite cheap-looking.	**5** They came up against a lot of opposition.	**6** He's rather inorthodox.
7 It's driving me mad.	**8** It was must-watching TV.	**9** It was a non-violent protest.	**10** She's got an avid imagination.	**11** She's very softly-spoken.	**12** They are fighting a lose battle.
13 It's very bright-coloured.	**14** He followed in his father's footprints.	**15** I'm fed up with it.	**16** It's a time-saving device.	**17** It's bad-made.	**18** He did a lot to raise the word.
19 They stole the show.	**20** It's got an oval-shape window.	**21** They ran out with good ideas.	**22** I think they'll make it big.	**23** It's not very children-friendly.	**24** He should throw in the towel.
25 He did a lot for civilian rights.	**26** It's just a fashion accessory.	**27** She supports a lot of causes.	**28** He's an obsessing collector.	**29** It's the current must-have CD.	**30** I passed with flying colour.

2 Can you think of someone or something that can be described by each of the sentences in the game? Share your ideas.

Song

1 Read the factfile about KT Tunstall and answer these questions.
   1 What is her musical background?
   2 What prejudice did she face getting a record deal?
   3 What was the turning point in her career?

factfile

KT Tunstall was born in 1975 to a Chinese mother and Irish father, but was adopted as a baby by a Scottish couple and raised in St Andrews in Scotland. She was musical from an early age, learning to play piano, flute and guitar as a teenager.

KT spent some time studying in the USA and then returned to the UK to do a music course at Royal Holloway College in London, before moving back to St Andrews. She became involved in the local music scene, where she served her musical apprenticeship before moving back to London to start her solo career. Her attempts to get a record deal were thwarted by constantly being told that at 25 she was too old to start a successful career as a recording artist. KT's big break came when she appeared on a TV show as a last-minute replacement for another act. She brought the house down and was suddenly in great demand. Her first album *Eye to the telescope*, which includes the song *Suddenly I see*, was released in 2004 to great critical acclaim.

2 **12** Listen to the song *Suddenly I see* and read the lyrics.
   1 What does she 'suddenly see'?
   2 Who do you think she is singing about?

3 Look at the picture and read the quote on page 29 to check your answers to Ex 2.

4 Listen to the song again. How do you interpret these lyrics?
   1 Her face is a map of the world
   2 I feel like walking the world
   3 She likes to leave you hanging on a word
   4 She makes me feel like I could be a tower

5 Are you, or were you, inspired in any way by someone famous? Tell a partner.

Suddenly I see

Her face is a map of the world, is a map of the world
You can see she's a beautiful girl, she's a beautiful girl
And everything around her is a silver pool of light
People who surround her feel the benefit of it
It makes you calm
She holds you captivated in her palm

Chorus

Suddenly I see
This is what I wanna be
Suddenly I see
Why the hell it means so much to me

And I feel like walking the world, like walking the world
And you can hear she's a beautiful girl, she's a beautiful girl
She fills up every corner like she's born in black and white
Makes you feel warmer when you're trying to remember
What you heard
She likes to leave you hanging on a word

Chorus

And she's taller than most and she's looking at me
I can see her eyes looking from the page in a magazine
She makes me feel like I could be a tower, big strong tower, yeah
The power to be, the power to give, the power to see, yeah yeah

Suddenly I see
She got the power to be
The power to give
The power to see yeah yeah

Chorus

Extra practice

Unit 1

1 Complete the puzzle with the character and behaviour adjectives. Do you agree with the advice in the shaded column?

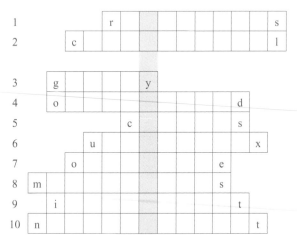

1			r							s
2	c									l
3	g				y					
4	o						d			
5				c			s			
6		u					x			
7	o					e				
8	m				s					
9	i					t				
10	n						t			

1 opposing authority or the accepted rules of society.

2 following the usual and accepted opinions and ways of behaving, especially without questioning them.

3 feeling sad and without hope.

4 having very strong opinions and refusing to change them even when they are clearly unreasonable.

5 wanting to find out about things.

6 not following the usual rules or beliefs of your religion, society, etc.

7 always thinking about someone or something that is important to you, in a way that seems extreme to other people.

8 enjoying having fun by causing trouble, used especially to describe a child.

9 good at thinking clearly and quickly, at understanding difficult ideas and subjects, and at gaining and using knowledge.

10 different from the way most people usually think or behave.

2 Which noun from the box collocates with each set of adjectives?

> collector   imagination   outlook   side   traits

1 positive / gloomy / sunny   _____

2 avid / keen / obsessive   _____

3 unusual / unorthodox / eccentric _____

4 dark / funny / creative   _____

5 fertile / overactive / vivid   _____

3 Read the article and complete it by putting an appropriate contrastive discourse marker in each space. Choose from those in the box and use each at least once.

> even though   however   nevertheless
> whereas / while   yet

Japanese inventor Dr NakaMats has been officially recognised as one of the five most influential scientists in history, (1) _____ his accomplishments are all-too-often overlooked and people tend to focus instead on his unique lifestyle and somewhat eccentric personality.

Dr NakaMats holds the all-time record for patents with over 3,200 inventions to date, surpassing the great inventor Thomas Edison. And (2) _____ many of Edison's patents were for already existing inventions to which Edison simply put his name, Dr NakaMats' patents are all his own work. His inventions include the digital watch, the floppy disk and the less notable and yet-to-catch-on 'Bouncing Shoes'.

According to Dr NakaMats, in order to be a great inventor, you must be born with special abilities. He believes that (3)_____ engineers and researchers generally find their solutions through trial and error, the inventor will, at some point during the invention process, experience a flash of revelation. 'If a team of engineers works hard enough and long enough, they will eventually be able to make small improvements in technology. (4) _____, only true inventors are able to devise breakthroughs that change the world overnight,' Dr NakaMats explains. He firmly believes that (5) _____ engineering can be learned, inventing is an innate ability that people are born with.

(6) _____ most people of Dr NakaMats' age (he was born in 1928) are enjoying their twilight years, he works out lifting weights on a daily basis, stays away from doctors and conventional medicine and confidently predicts he will live to 144. And (7) _____ he eats only one meal a day (of 700 calories) and sleeps exactly four hours a night (from 4am to 8am) he is (8) _____ in perfect health.

Unit 2

1 Rewrite these newspaper extracts to include one or more compound adjectives so that the meaning is the same.

Example:
The main course was followed by a selection of fruit that made the mouth water.

The main course was followed by a selection of mouth-watering fruit.

1
> The family escaped the blaze by jumping out of a window on the second floor.

The family escaped the blaze by jumping out of
_____.

2
> **All their products are made by hand.**

All their products _____.

3
> **She was wearing a black and gold dress that caught the eye.**

She was wearing _____
_____.

4
> **It is one of the records in sport that has stood for the longest.**

It is one of _____
_____.

2 Make compound adjectives.

1	well- / badly	a	coloured
2	good- / expensive-	b	known
3	well- / little-	c	day
4	smartly / casually	d	paid
5	heart- / diamond-	e	shaped
6	broad- / open-	f	looking
7	environment- / child-	g	spoken
8	well- / softly	h	based
9	multi- / brightly	i	minded
10	European- / Tokyo-	j	friendly
11	energy- / time-	k	dressed
12	all- / modern-	l	saving

3 Write six more compound adjectives that include some of the words in Ex 2.

Example: *poorly paid, strange-looking*

4 Look at the example and write similar one-sentence descriptions of the famous people, places and things.

Example:
He's a businessman. He's American. He was born in 1955. He dropped out of Harvard University. He went on to become a billionaire before he was 30.

He's an American businessman born in 1955, who dropped out of Harvard University, and who went on to become a billionaire before he was 30.

1 It's a device. It's hand-held. It allows you to talk to other people wherever you are.

_____
_____

2 It's a mode of transport. It's two-wheeled. It was invented by a Scotsman in the mid-1800s.

_____
_____

3 It's a statue. It's of a human figure. It's got outstretched arms. It overlooks Rio de Janeiro in Brazil.

_____
_____

4 He's an actor. He's American. He was born in 1963. He is of British, German and Cherokee Indian descent.

_____
_____

5 Which people, places and things are described in Ex 4? Check your answers at the bottom of the page.

6 Complete the mini-dialogues with the words in the box.

> alone   bad   fed up   mad   moaning
> poor   problems   sick   sock

1 **A:** I'm totally _____ of this dreadful weather.
   B: Oh, stop _____ about it! Anyway, it's going to be nicer tomorrow.

2 **A:** I can't even afford new socks let _____ a new pair of shoes.
   B: Come on, it can't be that _____.

3 **A:** I've had this awful cold for days now. I just can't get anything done. It's driving me _____.
   B: Oh, _____ you! Are you taking anything for it?

4 **A:** I'm totally _____ with absolutely everything at the moment. If it's not one thing, it's another.
   B: Oh, put a _____ in it. You're not the only one with _____, you know.

7 Complete these sentences so they are true for you.
1 I'm sick and tired of _____.
2 I'm fed up with _____.
3 _____ drives me mad.

Example: Bill Gates   1 mobile phone   2 bicycle   3 statue of Christ the Redeemer   4 Johnny Depp

Unit 3

1 Complete the newspaper headlines with the words and phrases in the box. The country and date in brackets will help you.

> apartheid   civil rights movement
> democratic rule   equality   military rulers
> non-violent protest   segregation

1
> Civil Rights Act outlaws all racial
> _____.
> (USA, 1964)

2
> Four students killed as national
> guardsmen open fire on _____
> (Ohio, USA, 1970)

3
> _____ restored after 17 years as
> _____ stand down
> (Chile, 1990)

4
> _____ for all as _____
> officially ended
> (South Africa, 1994)

5
> 'Mother of the modern _____'
> Rosa Parks dies.
> (USA, 2005)

2 Rewrite these sentences putting the words in *italics* in an appropriate position to add emphasis.

1 They are the greatest band. *by far ever*

   _____

2 It was a mistake. It looks worse than before.
   huge even

   _____

3 There's no chance of it happening in the near future. *absolutely at all*

   _____

4 They are cheaper than when they came out.
   loads first

   _____

5 I don't understand what they were thinking of. It's ugly. *just so*

   _____

6 The thing was a disaster.
   whole total from start to finish

   _____

3 Think of something or someone that each of the sentences in Ex 2 could be describing.

1 *Sugababes*   4 _____

2 _____ 5 _____

3 _____ 6 _____

4 Complete the website forum using the words and phrases in the boxes.

> by far   single   vast

Buffet $37 billion giveaway

The second richest man in the world, investor Warren Buffet, has announced that he is going to donate the (1) _____ majority of his wealth, namely $37 billion, to charity. Buffet's donation is (2) _____ the (3) _____ biggest philanthropic act in history. <u>Click here</u> to have your say on this great giveaway.

> anywhere   awesome   simply

I applaud Mr Buffet for his (4) _____ generosity, but everyone knows that the vast proportion of money donated 'disappears' and (5) _____ doesn't get to the people who actually need it. After Live Aid 80% of the money didn't get (6) _____ near those who needed it.

Russ, Sheffield, UK

> at all   highly   just   much   real   very

While the money Mr Buffet has given away is indeed (7)_____ commendable, I think it's a (8)_____ shame that it took him so long to do so. After all, he's been a multi-billionaire for a (9)_____ long time now. Also, I remember Mr Buffet once saying that he believed that educating a person goes (10)_____ farther than giving away cash. So, why is he doing the opposite? I (11)_____ don't understand it (12)_____.

Jakob, Berlin

5 Complete the sentences with the verbs in the box.

> eradicate   express   raise   show   spread

1 The demonstration was to _____ solidarity with the sacked workers and to inform the board and shareholders alike that the dismissals will not be taken lying down.

2 With 15% of the world's population going hungry every day, the need to _____ poverty is as great today as it has ever been.

3 The campaign is designed to _____ awareness among primary-aged schoolchildren of the need to eat sensibly.

4 To _____ support for the worldwide 'kindness' day, people are being asked to wear something with a heart on it.

5 Environmentalists were distributing 'If you care, car share' car stickers to _____ the word about the campaign to cut congestion.

Unit 4

1 Match the two halves of these proverbs.

1	Where there's a will,	a	like the present.
2	All work and no play	b	in a day.
3	Rome wasn't built	c	leap.
4	Look before you	d	there's a way.
5	There's no time	e	makes Jack a dull boy.

2 Complete these sports headlines with the idioms in the box.

> flying colours   flying start   hands down
> sail through   sink or swim   steals the show

1   Woods off to a _____ with six birdies and an eagle in first round of US open

2   Tampa Bay Buccaneers _____ to next round with 75-6 win

3   Jian _____ at World Championships with perfect 10 for floor routine

4   Palmer wins _____, 6-1, 6-0

5   All Blacks pass first test match with _____.

6   It's _____ for 'The Mariners' as League One relegation battle looms

3 Complete these newspaper extracts with an appropriate form of the three-part phrasal verbs in the box.

> come back from   come up against
> face up to   ~~get on with~~   look up to
> make up for   put up with   run out of

1
'We've just got to (1) *get on with it* and go out on Saturday and win the game. Our destiny is in our own hands,' says goalkeeper Tom MacAlister. 'Last season we (2) _____ being five points adrift at the foot of the table with only three games to go and managed to avoid relegation. I'm confident we can do so again.'

2
Tiger's opening round of 63 and 6-stroke first-day lead will go a long way in (3) _____ his disappointment at finishing in tenth place in last year's event.

3
The American absolutely dominated the match, which lasted a mere 36 minutes. It seemed that opponent Kuchova simply (4) _____ energy and motivation mid-way through the second set, in which she didn't win a single game.

4
The British Lions (5) _____ a rampaging New Zealand in Christchurch yesterday and could do little but watch as the All Blacks ran in nine tries. 'We need to (6) _____ the reality that we were simply second-best in the game and we have a long way to go,' said coach Andrew Robinson.

5
The Miami Dolphins had to (7) _____ driving rain as well as a rampant Tampa Bay as they were well and truly beaten by 11 touchdowns to one.

6
'We've always (8) _____ Russia and other Eastern European nations, and we still do, but now we are competing with them as equals.' said the gold-medal winning Chinese gymnast.

4 Match the sports with the headlines in Ex 2 and the extracts in Ex 3.

	Sport	Headline	Extract
1	football	6	1
2	American football		
3	golf		
4	gymnastics		
5	rugby		
6	tennis		

5 Complete these extracts with an expression using *must-* and the words in the box.

> have (x2)   see   visit   watch   win

1   For its first few series after it was first broadcast in 1999, *Big Brother* was without doubt the _____ programme of its day.

2   Argentina go into their _____ match against Germany with a number of injury worries.

3   Every Harry Potter release was the _____ film of the year for the majority of under-twelves, and many adults alike.

4   Making the Walkman and portable CD player almost redundant overnight, the iPod instantly became the _____ gadget for any self-respecting teenager and twenty-something.

5   Poll after poll puts *What's going on?* by Marvin Gaye as the number one _____ album of all time.

6   Whether passing through in a day or on holiday, Central Park, the Empire State Building and Fifth Avenue are the _____ places when in New York.

Grammar reference

Unit 1

Contrast

The most common contrastive linkers (discourse markers) are:

but

But is the most common contrastive linker in English.

You can use *but* in conjunction with other contrastive linkers. For example, *but nevertheless ..., but whereas ...*

You use *but* between two contrasting ideas.
*It was sunny, **but** a bit cold.*
*Jane knows all about the party, **but** please don't tell her you know.*
*We were exhausted, **but nevertheless** we continued.*

yet

Yet emphasises that something is surprising.

You use *yet* between the two contrasting ideas in a sentence.

*He is colour blind, **yet** his paintings are full of colour.*

however

However is more formal than *but* and can suggest that something is surprising or unexpected.

You use *however* at the beginning of the second sentence, after the subject in the second sentence or at the end of the second sentence.
*I'm terrible at remembering names. **However**, I never forget a face.*
*He was confident he had the right credentials. His interviewers, **however**, were not impressed.*

on the other hand

On the other hand balances two ideas that contrast but do not contradict. You can use it when you are trying to be fair and moderate.

You use *on the other hand* at the beginning of the second sentence, after the subject in the second sentence or at the end of the second sentence.
*She tends to keep herself to herself. Her sister, **on the other hand**, is very outgoing.*

whereas / while

Whereas and *while* balance two ideas that contrast, but do not contradict. The meaning of *whereas* and *while* is basically the same.

You use *whereas* and *while* before the first or second idea in the sentence.
*Top players' wages have risen astronomically, **whereas** those in the lower leagues have seen little rise in pay, at all.*
***While** it hasn't yet been officially announced, it is believed the president has offered his resignation.*

nevertheless

Nevertheless expresses that something happens when something else makes it seem unlikely. It is quite formal.

You use *nevertheless* at the beginning of the second sentence, after the subject in the second sentence or at the end of the second sentence.
*E-commerce is a difficult area to do well in. **Nevertheless**, tens of thousands of new businesses start up every year.*
*He was advised against making a formal complaint. He went ahead and did it **nevertheless**.*

even though / although / despite / in spite of

Even though | although | despite | in spite of express that something happens when something else makes it seem unlikely.

You use *even though | although | despite | in spite of* at the beginning of the subordinate clause (the idea that makes the other seem unlikely).
*They carried on walking **even though** the rain was pouring down.*
***Although** sales aren't what we'd been hoping for, they're quite encouraging.*
*Most of the people I spoke to had never seen the film. **Despite** this, everyone seemed familiar with its content.*

Auxiliary *do*

You can use the auxiliary verb *do* to show and emphasise contrast.
*It rained all day, but we **did** have a good time.*
*I **do** agree, honest.*

Unit 2

Describing buildings, places and objects

You can add descriptive detail to nouns by adding:
* adjectives – including present and past participles used as adjectives, and nouns used as adjectives (defining nouns)
* relative clauses
* clauses beginning with a present or past participle (participle clauses)
* phrases beginning with a preposition.

Adjectives, present and past participles used as adjectives, and nouns used as adjectives come before the noun.
*It was a **lovely** day.*
*The **twisting** road stretched for miles.*
*There are lots of **recently built** apartments.*
*She lost her **wedding** ring.*
*We stayed in a **tiny beach** hut.*

Relative clauses, clauses beginning with a present or past participle and phrases beginning with a preposition come after the noun.
*We went to that restaurant **that your sister recommended**.*
*Is this the book **you were talking about**?*
*The man **standing over there** is the new sales manager.*
*That's the hotel **featured in the paper** the other day.*
*The café **next to the park** has good coffee.*

Unit 3

Adding emphasis

You can add emphasis in many different ways. Some of the more common ways are as follows. Note that you can use some words (*just*, *even*, etc) in more than one way.

You can add emphasis to nouns using certain adjectives:
*I have a **terrible** cold.*
*The **vast** majority disagreed with the proposal.*
*It's an **absolute** disgrace.*
*That's the **single** most disgusting thing I've ever eaten.*
*The **whole** day was brilliant.*
*It was a **total** waste of time.*

You can add emphasis to adjectives using certain adverbs:
*She was **absolutely** delighted.*
*It's **really** great to see you.*
*The film was **just** amazing.*
*It was **even** better than we'd imagined.*
*It's **so** difficult to know what to do.*
*It's **by far** the most amazing place I've been to.*
*He was **all** alone.*

You can add emphasis to verbs or verb clauses using certain adverbs:
*We **just** stood there in amazement.*
*I **really** couldn't believe it.*
*I didn't **even** have time to say hello.*

You can add more general emphasis to what you are saying using certain phrases, which usually occur at the beginning or end of a clause:
*I couldn't hear anything **at all**.*
*It was **without doubt** her best film to date.*
*It was great **from start to finish**.*
*I didn't regret it **for a moment**.*

When speaking you can use the phrase *you know* to add emphasis. This is quite informal, but very common.
*It was unbelievable, **you know**.*
***You know**, I've never seen anything like it.*

Unit 4

Three-part phrasal verbs

Form

Three-part phrasal verbs comprise a verb with two particles.
> *to put up with*
> *to run out of*

Three-part phrasal verbs are transitive and therefore must always take an object. The object always goes after the second particle.
*I'll get back to **you** later.* (not: ~~I'll get back you to later~~ or ~~I'll get you back to later~~.)

Use and meaning

The meaning of a three-part phrasal verb is not the same as the independent meaning of the verb and particles. Most three-part phrasal verbs have only one meaning (unlike many two-part phrasal verbs which can have multiple meanings).

Here are some common three-part phrasal verbs (and their meanings).
catch up with (reach the same level or position), *come back from* (to be successful after being in a bad situation), *come back to* (return to), *come down with* (become ill with), *come out with* (say), *come up with* (think of), *cut down on* (reduce), *drop out of* (leave something, such as a course, before you have finished it), *fall back on* (use when other things have failed), *get away with* (avoid discovery), *get back to* (to phone, write or speak to somebody at a later time), *get on with* (do), *get round to* (find time to do), *get up to* (do), *look up to* (respect), *keep up with* (stay at the same level as), *look down on* (think you are better than), *look forward to* (feel excited about something that is going to happen), *make up for* (compensate for), *put up with* (tolerate), *run out of* (have no more of / use all of), *stand up for* (defend), *stand / face up to* (face)

*My printer has **run out of** ink.*
*I need to **catch up with** the work I missed last week.*
*I'm so **looking forward to** the end of term.*
*Is there anything you can **fall back on**?*

Wordlist

*** the 2,500 most common English words, ** very common words, * fairly common words

Unit 1

aberrant *adj* /æˈberənt/
avid *adj* /ˈævɪd/
Before you comment, can I just ... *phr* /bɪˈfɔː juː ˈkɒment kən aɪ dʒʌst/
By the way ... *expr* /baɪ ðə ˈweɪ/
Can I add something? *phr* /kən aɪ ˈæd ˌsʌmθɪŋ/
Can I finish what I was saying? *phr* /kən aɪ ˌfɪnɪʃ ˌwɒt aɪ wəz ˈseɪɪŋ/
collector *n* /kəˈlektə/
colour blind *adj* /ˈkʌlə ˌblaɪnd/ **
conformity *n* /kənˈfɔːməti/
conventional *adj* /kənˈvenʃnəl/ ***
creative *adj* /kriˈeɪtɪv/ **
curious *adj* /ˈkjʊəriəs/ **
dark *adj* /dɑːk/ ***
eccentric *adj* /ɪkˈsentrɪk/
eccentricity *n* /ˌeksenˈtrɪsəti/
Er, yeah ... Anyway *expr* /ˌɜː jeə... ˈeniweɪ/
excel (in) *v* /ɪkˈsel (ɪn)/
exhaustive *adj* /ɪgˈzɔːstɪv/
feminine *adj* /ˈfemənɪn/ *
fertile *adj* /ˈfɜːtaɪl/ *
gloomy *adj* /ˈgluːmi/ *
Hang on! *expr* /hæŋ ˌɒn/
incidence *n* /ˈɪnsɪdəns/ *
Incidentally *expr* /ˌɪnsɪˈdentli/ *
individuality *n* /ˌɪndɪˌvɪdʒʊˈæləti/
invasion *n* /ɪnˈveɪʒn/ **
Just let me finish, please *phr* /ˌdʒʌst let miː ˈfɪnɪʃ ˌpliːz/
keen *adj* /kiːn/ ***
manifest itself *v* /ˈmænɪfest ɪtˌself/ *
mischievous *adj* /ˈmɪstʃɪvəs/
obsessive *adj* /əbˈsesɪv/
opinionated *adj* /əˈpɪnjəˌneɪtɪd/
optimistic *adj* /ˌɒptɪˈmɪstɪk/ **
outlook *n* /ˈaʊtlʊk/ *
overactive *adj* /ˌəʊvərˈæktɪv/
persona *n* /pəˈsəʊnə/
positive *adj* /ˈpɒzətɪv/ ***
privacy *n* /ˈprɪvəsi/ *
rebellious *adj* /rɪˈbeljəs/
retrospective *adj* /ˌretrəʊˈspektɪv/ *
scandalous *adj* /ˈskændələs/
side *n* /saɪd/ ***
Sorry to interrupt *phr* /ˌsɒri tuː ˌɪntəˈrʌpt/
sympathetic *adj* /ˌsɪmpəˈθetɪk/ **
That reminds me ... *phr* /ˌðæt rɪˈmaɪndz ˌmiː/
To get back to what I was saying before *phr* /tə ˌget bæk tə ˌwɒt aɪ wəz ˌseɪɪŋ bɪˈfɔː/
trait *n* /treɪt/ *
unconventional *adj* /ˌʌnkənˈvenʃnəl/
unorthodox *adj* /ʌnˈɔːθəˌdɒks/ *
vivid *adj* /ˈvɪvɪd/ *
Wait a minute! *phr* /ˈweɪt ə ˌmɪnɪt/
Where was I? *expr* /ˌweə ˈwɒz ˌaɪ/

Unit 2

adhere to *v* /ədˈhɪə tuː/
(Zurich)-based *adj* /(ˈzjʊərɪk) ˌbeɪst/
Cheer up! *expr* /ˌtʃɪər ˈʌp/
Come on, it can't be that bad. *expr* /ˈkʌm ˌɒn ɪt ˌkɑːnt biː ˌðæt ˌbæd/
copper *n* /ˈkɒpə/ **
crumb *n* /krʌm/
desecrate *v* /ˈdesɪˌkreɪt/
desirable *adj* /dɪˈzaɪrəbl/ **
despise *v* /dɪˈspaɪz/
dome *n* /dəʊm/
drive sb mad *expr* /draɪv ... ˈmæd/
(window)-facing *adj* /(ˈwɪndəʊ) ˌfeɪsɪŋ/
fed up with (+ -ing) *expr* /fed ˈʌp wɪð/
(environment)-friendly *adj* /(ɪnˈvaɪrənmənt) ˌfrendli/
functional *adj* /ˈfʌŋkʃnəl/ **

How awful! *expr* /haʊ ˈɔːfl/
let alone *expr* /let əˌləʊn/
(frivolous)-looking *adj* /(ˈfrɪvələs) ˌlʊkɪŋ/
(much)-loved *adj* /(ˈmʌtʃ) ˌlʌvd/
make a mental note *expr* /meɪk ə ˌmentl ˈnəʊt/
miss *v* /mɪs/ ***
motif *n* /məʊˈtiːf/ *
multi-coloured *adj* /ˌmʌlti ˈkʌləd/
novelty *n* /ˈnɒvlti/ *
Oh, change the record! *expr* /əʊ ˈtʃeɪndʒ ðə ˌrekɔːd/
Oh, dear, I'm sorry. *expr* /əʊ ˌdɪə ˌaɪm ˈsɒri/
Oh, just shut up. *expr* /əʊ ˌdʒʌst ˈʃʌt ʌp/
Oh, poor you! *expr* /əʊ ˈpʊə ˌjuː/
overflowing (with) *adj* /ˌəʊvəˈfləʊɪŋ (wɪð)/
peckish *adj* /ˈpekɪʃ/
penetrate *v* /ˈpenətreɪt/ **
perched *adj* /pɜːtʃt/
plateau *n* /ˈplætəʊ/
postwar *adj* /ˌpəʊstˈwɔː/ *
Put a sock in it! *expr* /ˌpʊt ə ˈsɒk ɪn ɪt/
quaint *adj* /kweɪnt/
rebuilding *n* /ˌriːˈbɪldɪŋ/ **
redbrick *adj* /ˈredˌbrɪk/
ruined *adj* /ˈruːɪnd/ **
rummage *v* /ˈrʌmɪdʒ/
(energy)-saving *adj* /(ˈenədʒi) ˌseɪvɪŋ/
schedule *v* /ˈʃedjuːl/ **
sensuous *adj* /ˈsensjuəs/
(pie)-shaped *adj* /(ˈpaɪ) ʃeɪpt/
sick of (+ -ing) *expr* /ˈsɪk əv/
smart *adj* /smɑːt/ **
soothing *adj* /ˈsuːðɪŋ/
sophistication *n* /səˌfɪstɪˈkeɪʃn/
sparkling *adj* /ˈspɑːklɪŋ/
Stop moaning! *expr* /ˌstɒp ˈməʊnɪŋ/
(three)-storey *adj* /(ˈθriː) ˌstɔːri/ *
ultra *adv* /ˈʌltrə/
universally-acclaimed *adj* /ˌjuːnɪˌvɜːsəli əˌkleɪmd/
well-known *adj* /ˌwel ˈnəʊn/ **
well-maintained *adj* /ˌwel meɪnˈteɪnd/
What a shame! *expr* /ˌwɒt ə ˈʃeɪm/
workspace *n* /ˈwɜːkspeɪs/

Unit 3

a single person (at all) *expr* /ə ˈsɪŋgl ˌpɜːsn (ət ˈɔːl)/
absolute *adj* /ˈæbsəluːt/ **
absolutely *adv* /ˈæbsəluːtli/ ***
anti-bullying *n* /ˈænti ˈbʊliɪŋ/
apartheid *n* /əˈpɑːtheɪt; əˈpɑːthaɪd/
break the spell *phr* /breɪk ðə ˈspel/
cancer *n* /ˈkænsə/ ***
civil rights movement *n* /ˌsɪvl ˈraɪts ˌmuːvmənt/
conversation starter *n* /ˌkɒnvəˈseɪʃn ˌstɑːtə/
democratic rule *n* /ˌdeməkrætɪk ˈruːl/
donation *n* /dəʊˈneɪʃn/ ***
ease sb's guilty conscience *expr* /ˌiːz ... ˌgɪlti ˈkɒnʃəns/
entire *adj* /ɪnˈtaɪə/ ***
equality *n* /ɪˈkwɒləti/ **
eradicate poverty *phr* /ɪˌrædɪkeɪt ˈpɒvəti/
express solidarity *phr* /ɪkˌspres ˌsɒlɪˈdærəti/
fashion accessory *n* /ˈfæʃn əkˌsesəri/ **
from top to bottom *expr* /frəm ˌtɒp tə ˈbɒtəm/
give money to charity *phr* /ˌgɪv ˌmʌni tə ˈtʃærəti/
go mad *expr* /ˌgəʊ ˈmæd/
immaculate *adj* /ɪˈmækjʊlət/
injustice *n* /ɪnˈdʒʌstɪs/
jump on (the) bandwagon *expr* /ˌdʒʌmp ɒn (ðə) ˈbændˌwægən/
make an exception *phr* /ˌmeɪk ən ɪkˈsepʃn/

military ruler *n* /ˌmɪlɪtri ˈruːlə/
non-violent protest *n* /ˌnɒn ˌvaɪələnt ˈprəʊtest/
peace *n* /piːs/ ***
physical *adj* /ˈfɪzɪkl/ ***
poverty *n* /ˈpɒvəti/ **
racism *n* /ˈreɪsɪzm/ *
raise awareness *phr* /ˌreɪz əˈweənəs/
raise money *phr* /ˌreɪz ˈmʌni/
segregation *n* /ˌsegrɪˈgeɪʃn/
show commitment *phr* /ˌʃəʊ kəˈmɪtmənt/
smug *adj* /smʌg/
spread the word *phr* /ˌspred ðə ˈwɜːd/
stillness *n* /ˈstɪlnəs/
support a cause *phr* /səˌpɔːt ə ˈkɔːz/
waste of time *phr* /ˌweɪst əv ˈtaɪm/
without doubt *phr* /wɪˌðaʊt ˈdaʊt/
wristband *n* /ˈrɪstˌbænd/

Unit 4

all down to sb *phr* /ˈɔːl daʊn tə/
array *n* /əˈreɪ/ *
be rooted in *phr* /bɪ ˈruːtɪd ɪn/
by hook or by crook *expr* /baɪ ˈhʊk ɔː baɪ ˌkrʊk/
cherished *adj* /ˈtʃerɪʃt/
come back from *phr* /ˌkʌm ˈbæk frəm/
come up against *phr* /ˌkʌm ˈʌp əˌgenst/
come up with *phr* /ˌkʌm ˈʌp wɪð/
compensate for *v* /ˈkɒmpənseɪt fə/
dazzling *adj* /ˈdæzlɪŋ/
dizzying *adj* /ˈdɪziɪŋ/
drop out of *phr* /drɒp ˈaʊt əv/
due to *phr* /ˈdjuː tə/
face up to *phr* /ˌfeɪs ˈʌp tə/
fall back on *phr* /ˌfɔːl ˈbæk ɒn/
fight a losing battle *phr* /ˌfaɪt ə ˌluːzɪŋ ˈbætl/
get off to a flying start *expr* /get ˌɒf tuː ə ˌflaɪɪŋ ˈstɑːt/
get on with *phr* /ˌget ˈɒn wɪð/
heartbroken *adj* /ˈhɑːtˌbrəʊkən/
huddle *n, v* /ˈhʌdl/
look up to *phr* /ˌlʊk ˈʌp tuː/
machete *n* /məˈʃeti/
make it big *expr* /ˌmeɪk ɪt ˈbɪg/
make up for *phr* /ˌmeɪk ˈʌp fə/
must-see *adj* /ˈmʌst ˌsiː/
overcome the odds *phr* /ˌəʊvəkʌm ði ˈɒdz/
owe everything to *phr* /əʊ ˈevriθɪŋ tə/
pass with flying colours *phr* /ˌpɑːs wɪð ˌflaɪɪŋ ˈkʌləz/
pint-sized *adj* /ˈpaɪnt ˌsaɪzd/
puny *adj* /ˈpjuːni/
put up with *expr* /ˌpʊt ˈʌp wɪð/
quick-thinking *adj* /ˌkwɪk ˈθɪŋkɪŋ/
rip *v* /rɪp/ **
role model *n* /ˈrəʊl ˌmɒdl/ *
run out of *phr* /ˈrʌn ˌaʊt əv/
sail through it *phr* /ˈseɪl ˌθruː ɪt/
shred *v* /ʃred/
sink or swim *expr* /sɪŋk ɔː ˈswɪm/
slaughter *n, v* /ˈslɔːtə/ *
spate *n* /speɪt/
spree *n* /spriː/
spur sb on to do sth *phr* /ˌspɜː ... ɒn tə ˈduː .../
stand up for *expr* /ˌstænd ˈʌp fə/
stand up to *expr* /ˌstænd ˈʌp tə/
steal the show *phr* /ˌstiːl ðə ˈʃəʊ/
succinct *adj* /səkˈsɪŋkt/
supreme *adj* /sʊˈpriːm/ **
throw in the towel *expr* /ˌθrəʊ ɪn ðə ˈtaʊəl/
tolerate *v* /ˈtɒləreɪt/
trite *adj* /traɪt/
underdog *n* /ˈʌndəˌdɒg/
win hands down *expr* /ˌwɪn ˌhændz ˈdaʊn/

Communication activities

Unit 2, Lead-in Ex 1 page 6

a The Acropolis, Athens, Greece.
b Alhambra, Granada, Spain
c Angkor, Cambodia
d Colosseum, Rome, Italy
e The Statue of Liberty, New York City, USA
f Eiffel Tower, Paris, France
g The Great Wall of China, China
h Hagia Sophia, Istanbul, Turkey
i The Kremlin, St Basil's Cathedral, Moscow, Russia
j Machu Picchu, Peru
k Petra, Jordan
l The Pyramids of Giza, Egypt
m Statues of Easter Island, Easter Island
n Sydney Opera House, Australia
o The Taj Mahal, Agra, India

Unit 2, Listening and vocabulary Ex 6 page 9

Student A

Rolecard
You have a lot of problems. You've just lost your job as a trainee journalist on a local newspaper because the newspaper has had to make cutbacks and you haven't got much prospect of getting another position locally. You've been feeling depressed about this and it has affected your relationship with your girlfriend / boyfriend: she / he has asked for a cooling off period as your constant moaning is getting her / him down. Losing your job also means you can't afford the rent on your new flat and will have to move somewhere smaller and cheaper. All in all, you're feeling pretty sorry for yourself and take every opportunity to tell other people how hard done by you are. By chance you have just met Student B in the shopping centre. He / she is a school friend who you haven't seen for a long time, and you are now in a café talking. Tell him / her about your problems.

Unit 3, Vocabulary and speaking Ex 4 page 13

Read the rolecard and prepare your arguments.

Rolecard
You're collecting money for children orphaned by AIDS in Africa. They need money for food, health care and education and you also want to raise awareness in Africa about AIDS. You knock at Partner B's door. Convince him / her to give money by appealing to his / her conscience.

Unit 5, Speaking Ex 2 page 20

The category winners were: Communications – World Wide Web, Household – electric light, The arts and music – the piano, Transport – bicycle

Unit 5, Song Ex 3 page 21

'*Suddenly I See* is about the fact that singer Patti Smith looks great on the cover of her record *Horses* and I wanted to be like that.' (KT Tunstall)

Listening scripts

Unit 1 Behave!

🔊 Listening script 01

Reading text from page 3

🔊 Listening script 02

Vocabulary and speaking Ex 1 from page 2

🔊 Listening script 03

(T= Teacher, A= Alex, a student from Germany, M= Mette, a student from Denmark, N= Natsuko, a student from Japan)

T: Right, we're going to talk a bit about nonconformism. Er … Alex, what about you? Are you a nonconformist? Do you follow society's rules for behaviour, dress and things like that, or don't you care what other people think of you?

A: Er, well, I suppose I'm quite conventional really. I don't think I deliberately try to be different for the sake of it. In some ways I don't actually want to stand out. Probably because I'm too lazy. I think you have to have time to think about projecting an alternative image. You have to, er, work at being different. I'm not bothered about standing out from the crowd.

T: Is it difficult to be a nonconformist in Germany?

A: Well, it depends where you live. Germany's such a big country. If you live in a small village in the south, I don't think people perhaps are as tolerant about people being different. But I come from Berlin so for me …

M: Berlin? Great city!

A: Er, yeah, … Anyway, in a big city like Berlin there are lots of people from different countries, and lots of different lifestyles. There's no one norm that everyone follows, so it's harder to say what conformism and nonconformism is. On the whole, German people are quite individual and …

M: That reminds me of a trip I took to, er, Berlin last year. I was just amazed, you know, how individual people were there. Everybody looked so different. In my town people all dress the same way.

T: So is there a lot of pressure to conform in Denmark, then, Mette?

M: Definitely. It's a small country and it's like, everybody thinks the same. People tend to do everything in groups. In kindergarten, you have to have the whole class to your birthday and then in school you have to do endless cooperative projects. If you don't like spending time with other people, you've had it, you don't fit in and er …

N: Sorry to interrupt, but, Denmark sounds a lot like Japan with the group … er … mentality, you know. We have a saying in Japanese, in English it's something like 'The nail that sticks out gets hammered down …'. People don't like you being different. You're made to conform in school and at work.

A: I've never … er … been to Japan but I've seen some Japanese TV shows on TV in Germany. They're wild, there's just no limits to what people do on those shows. That doesn't fit with conformism.

M: And you look quite unconventional, don't you? You know your clothes and …

N: Wait a minute! Just because I like wearing unusual clothes doesn't mean I'm a nonconformist. In fact in Tokyo I don't look 'unconventional'! All my friends dress like this. I think …

A: And don't people in Japan …

N: Just let me finish, please. I think nonconformism has more to do with personality and how you view other people.

M: Yeah, you have to be very tolerant towards other people and also be quite thick-skinned yourself … To get back to what I was saying before, I like doing things by myself. I've always liked doing my own thing. I suppose other people would say I'm a loner. Some people say I'm stuck up. A lot of people don't like it if you don't follow the crowd. They feel threatened somehow.

A: Talking of threatening situations …

Unit 2 Form and function

🔊 Listening script 04

Reading text from page 7

🔊 Listening script 05

(K=Kyle, N=Nicola)

K: Hello, 6431845?

N: Hi Kyle. How's it going?

K: Oh, hi Nicola. It's going OK but I'm getting a bit sick of sitting at my desk every day. This isn't what I expected working at home would be like!

N: Come on, it can't be that bad. This is your dream job, remember? No 9 to 5, no boss, no boring meetings … I bet you're still in your pyjamas right now watching the daytime soaps!

K: Yeah, I wish! I've got so much work I don't even have time to have lunch, let alone watch TV. I'm just up to my eyes in paper and more paper. I can't see my desk for work.

N: Oh, poor you! But I suppose that's good news, isn't it? It means your company is doing well.

K: Yes, it is. I've been inundated with great projects, which is, pretty amazing after such a short time. It usually takes a while to get the quality of work I've been getting, so of course, I'm really pleased it's worked out. I just never realised how little time I'd have. Basically I'm just at work all the time – all day and then usually most of the evening as well. But I must admit, I miss the drinks after work with the lads and the office gossip. I felt I saw my colleagues a bit too much outside work when I had my office job, but now I'm fed up with being on my own and looking at the same four walls all day.

N: Well, I can imagine it's a bit lonely at times. I certainly want a job where I work with other people. Perhaps not in an office, but definitely with other people … But, Kyle, you must talk to people on the phone, at least?

K: Sometimes, of course. But most people do business by email. I know it's cheaper than phoning but it's just so anonymous. And people send me mails about every little thing. I get a new email every ten minutes and it's driving me mad. I just can't get anything done.

N: Oh dear, I'm sorry. I thought you'd be happy working for yourself at home. You certainly whinged enough about your office job!

K: Yeah, I suppose on balance, working at home is still better than working in an office. It's great that I decide what I do with my time rather than someone else – even if I do end up deciding to work all the time. Anyway, sorry, Nicola, I know I'm being a pain in the neck going on like this. I'll stop moaning now!

N: Well, the good news is I'm coming up to the city tomorrow. So cheer up! You can take me out for a drink – just pretend I'm one of the lads!

Unit 3 It's up to you!

🔊 Listening script 06

It was my sister who got tickets for the Live 8 concert in London – one of the concerts that Bob Geldof organised for 'Make Poverty History'. She thought it might cheer me up because I'd had a terrible year and I was feeling a bit depressed. Yeah, so there we were in Hyde Park, and the sun was blazing down and this vast crowd of people was chilling out, enjoying the music and, there was a … a great feeling, really laid-back. Everyone on stage was talking about the message, the meaning of … of the concert, that it was a political event not a party. The crowd was lapping it all up but the speeches rang a bit hollow to me somehow.

But, then … er … Bob Geldof came on stage and he … er … sang one of my favourite songs, *I don't like Mondays*. It was magical. And with him up there singing on stage, the mood in the crowd seemed to intensify. There was this fantastic buzz, a feeling that this was a very special day … that … that something momentous was taking place. It was as if anything was possible, that music really could change the world, you know. It's hard to describe now, such a long time after the event, and it's probably even harder to understand what it was like if you weren't there. It was like everyone's hope was embodied in this one man. The whole crowd was on a high. And then I just realised that my own experiences were so … so trivial, compared to what's happening in other parts of the world. I failed my exams and broke up with my boyfriend – well, so what? People are dying of hunger, it's things like that that are important. You can't just live your life for yourself, everyone has a responsibility to other people. I know it sounds, well, trite, now, when I put it like that, but it was an absolute revelation to me then, at that moment in time. That day was a huge turning point in my life.

🔊 Listening script 07

1 I just couldn't believe it. I was totally speechless.
2 It was so good to see them again after all that time, you know.
3 It was a complete shock. I had no idea what they'd been planning, at all.
4 It took us an absolute age to get to the top, but it was well worth it. The views were absolutely stunning.

5 The whole day was amazing, from start to finish. It was even better than I'd dared imagine.

6 It was without doubt the single best moment of my entire life.

Listening script 08

Reading texts from page 12

Unit 4 No pain, no gain

Listening script 09

Reading text from page 15

Listening script 10

Max

What motivates me? Well, I think my motivation is rooted in my childhood. I was an only child and my parents thought everything I did was fantastic. For example, when I built something with building blocks, they'd praise me so much you'd think I'd built the Taj Mahal! And when we played games, they always let me win hands down and told me how clever I was. My confidence today is definitely due to the way I was brought up. And today I'd have to say that it's still praise that motivates me to do things. The downside is, though, that I just can't put up with criticism. I try not to show it but even the slightest hint of negativity makes me feel quite vulnerable.

Chloe

Last year I was feeling quite depressed. The stupid thing was that there was no particular reason for it. I'd passed my exams with flying colours and had started college, training to be a physiotherapist, my dream job. And I just felt so down. Maybe it was the anti-climax after studying so hard for exams and the high of getting through them. But suddenly I just couldn't see a reason to get out of bed in a morning. Then … well, I hate to admit this because it sounds so corny, but I was encouraged to get on with my life after seeing Kylie Minogue on TV. It was just after she'd had breast cancer, she'd been through chemotherapy and lost her hair. And suddenly there she was in New York looking so full of life. And I thought: 'What's up with you? If she can get on with life, you can'. So I really made an effort and now I feel great. And it's all down to Kylie!

Tom

My motivation? Well, I haven't always been as motivated as I am now. My parents are real high-fliers. They're both architects. They always put pressure on me to do well at school and they were quite disappointed that I was just average. Anyway, when I was 16, I decided to throw in the towel at school. I suppose you could say failure forced me to do something different. I dropped out of school – much to my parents' disappointment – and I concentrated on what I really enjoyed: art. I'm a freelance artist now. To be honest, I don't think I'll ever make it big as an artist, but I love what I'm doing – and that spurs me on to try and be better. And because my parents can see I'm happy, they've accepted what I do and are even quite proud of the fact that I stood up for what I wanted.

Ellen

I know I'm going to be successful simply because I know I can achieve whatever I want to achieve. And I think this is because, er, all my life I've had a very strong role model. My mother got divorced when I was two and was left to look after three small children on her own. She also worked part-time as a doctor. When I was older, my mum told me she knew it was a sink or swim moment in her life. And she didn't want to sink, she wanted to show everybody she could manage her family life and be successful at the same time. She was just determined to do it, you know – by hook or by crook. I've sort of inherited the same … er, determination and strong belief in myself. I owe everything to my mum.

Unit 5 Review

Listening script 11

(SP = Presenter, P = Paul, A = Alex, C = Chris)

SP: While most of his fellow students were already running out of what little cash they had during fresher's week, Nottingham University student Alex Tew made over £100,000. The 21-year-old undergraduate then went on to net more than a million dollars during his first term at university. So what was the secret of Alex's sudden wealth? Our business correspondent Paul Benn takes up the story.

P: Alex Tew came up with the idea one night in August 2005 while he was contemplating the financial consequences of starting a university course. The fees and accommodation for the first year alone were starting to look daunting and with no finances to fall back on Alex was dreading running up huge debts. As Alex tells us himself …

A: I've always been an ideas sort of person and I like to brainstorm at night before I go to sleep – it's my most productive time. So I wrote down 'How can I become a millionaire before I go to university?' It was a rather ambitious question, but I went with it. Then I wrote down the attributes that this idea would need: it had to be simple to understand and to set up; it had to attract a lot of media interest: and it needed a good name. After I wrote down those three things, the idea just popped into my head. I'd like to say it was more dramatic than that, but it wasn't.

P: Alex's idea was to design a web page consisting of exactly one million pixels, the dots which make up a computer screen, and to sell those pixels as advertising space, costing a dollar per pixel. Clicking on that space would take you to the buyer's website. Alex immediately got on with setting up the website and he bought the domain name 'milliondollarhomepage.com' that same evening. To get things up and running, he sold his first block of 100 pixels, which is the minimum number the eye can read, to his brothers and some friends. He then used that money to pay for a press release and that's when the site really took off. Advertisers were attracted to it by its novelty and by the curiosity factor, and with people flocking to take a look at the website that made the advertising good value for money. Chris Magras, Chief Executive of engineseeker.com, an Arizona-based company, bought 6,400 pixels as soon as he heard about the Million Dollar Homepage.

C: It was ingenious. It is easy to make money on the Internet, but it is very difficult to have a unique idea, and this was. The results for us were amazing. We used to get 40,000 visitors a day to our site – that's now up to 60,000.

P: And back in his student digs, when he wasn't catching up with course work or attending lectures, Alex managed to keep track of the money rolling in, which it did at the rate of tens of thousands of pounds per week. And not for one minute did Alex consider dropping out of university. And in a final typically inventive money-spinning twist, Alex sold the last 1000 pixels for 38 times their face value via an ebay auction at the beginning of his second university term. As seems to be the norm with internet-based business, the Million Dollar Homepage rapidly spawned hundreds of copycat sites, but none were anywhere near as successful as Alex's. Experts agree that the Million Dollar Homepage's success is down to three things: the power of word of mouth, that it's the rags-to-riches story of an ordinary student, and that it was a truly innovative yet simple idea. Expect to hear more from Alex Tew in the near future.

Listening script 12

Song from page 21

Communication activities

Unit 2, Listening and vocabulary Ex 6 page 9

Student B

Rolecard
You've just met Student A, an old school friend who you haven't seen for a long time, in the shopping centre and invited him / her for a cup of coffee to catch up on old times. You ask how Student A is doing. You are sympathetic at first, but gradually get annoyed at his / her attitude.

Unit 2, Reading and speaking Ex 1 page 9

1 Calculate your score and read the analysis. Compare your answers with a partner. Do you agree with the analysis?

2 Work in small groups. What do you think is the ideal workspace?

3 Present your ideas to the rest of the class.

Quiz score

1	a 1	b 5	c 3
2	a 5	b 3	c 1
3	a 1	b 5	c 3
4	a 5	b 3	c 1
5	a 3	b 1	c 5

Analysis

20+: You're conscientious and you're good at getting things sorted out. However, you're cautious when it comes to making big changes or decisions and can be inflexible. Learn to loosen up and let your creative side take over.

10–19: You have a balanced attitude to work: you get things done but you're not chained to your workspace. When it comes to other areas of your life, though, you may sit on the fence. Take opportunities with both hands – and don't think too much about the consequences.

5–9: You pride yourself on your individuality and a stimulating, creative workspace is important to you. But your creativity may be getting in the way of your efficiency. Clear up and try not to get distracted from the real issues.

Unit 3, Vocabulary and speaking Ex 4 page 13

Read the rolecard and prepare your arguments.

Rolecard
Somebody is collecting money for charity. You never give money to charities because you think it's the government's job to supply aid. You also think giving money isn't a good idea. People need to be trained to help themselves. It is more important to provide help with learning skills and professional competence.

Unit 4, Language study Ex 3 page 16

The complete quotations are as follows:

1 Too many people run out of ideas long before they run out of words. *Anonymous*

2 If your children look up to you, you've made a success of life's biggest job. *Anonymous*

3 I take a simple view of life: keep your eyes open and get on with it. *Sir Laurence Olivier, actor*

4 The way I see it, if you want the rainbow, you gotta put up with the rain. *Dolly Parton, singer*

5 It takes a great deal of courage to stand up to your enemies, but even more to stand up to your friends. *JK Rowling, author*

6 You need to feel good about yourself. The motivation has to come from within. You have nobody to fall back on except yourself. *Dana Hill, actress*

Unit 5, Speaking Ex 4 page 20

The overall winner was the bicycle.

Unit 5, Game Ex 1 page 20

Answers for the game are as follows:
Correct sentences, numbers 1, 4, 5, 7, 9, 11, 15, 16, 19, 22, 24, 26, 27, 29

Incorrect sentences and correct answers as follows:
2 She's a bit of a loser.   3 I really look up to her.
6 He's rather unorthodox.   8 It was must-watch TV.
10 She's got a vivid imagination.   12 They are fighting a losing battle.   13 It's very brightly coloured.   14 He followed in his father's footsteps.   17 It's badly made.
18 He did a lot to spread the word.   20 It's got an oval-shaped window.   21 They ran out of good ideas.
23 It's not very child-friendly.   25 He did a lot for civil rights.   28 He's an obsessive collector.   30 I passed with flying colours.

1 Telling tales

LEARNING AIMS

- Can discuss literary texts
- Can connect events using the perfect
- Can write a fictional narrative using dramatic and descriptive effects

Lead-in 1 What do you know about the famous couples in the photos?

2 What other famous couples can you think of? Think about contemporary couples, couples in history, and couples in literature and films.

A chance encounter

Reading and speaking

1 🔊 13 Read the novel extract on page 35 from *An equal music* by the contemporary Indian-born novelist Vikram Seth. Did you enjoy reading it? What impact did the extract have on you? Note down adjectives which describe how it made you feel.

2 Work with a partner. Speculate about the extract. Refer to the text to support your ideas.

1 Where does this extract take place? *Oxford Circus*
2 How do the characters feel when they see each other on the bus?
3 What is / was their relationship?
4 How do you think the narrator feels at the end of the extract?

3 Find examples of these features in the text and discuss the effect they create with the class.

- short sentences
- the present simple used for narrative
- repetition
- descriptive verbs

4 What did you think of the outcome of this encounter? Would you have preferred a different outcome?

5 What do you think happens in the novel after this meeting? Write a paragraph explaining how you think the story of Michael and Julia ended.

Vocabulary 1 Look at the words in the table. Add the missing nouns or adjectives. Then check in the text on page 35.

pron

Feelings	alarm	desperation					*perplexity*	annoyance	
How you feel	*alarmed*		hesitant	astonished	dismayed	perplexed			hopeful

2 What feelings in Ex 1 do these sentences express?

    1   Oh no! What have I done?

    2   What the hell did you do that for?

    3   Even if he hasn't rung, I think he'll turn up later.

    4   Yes, I'm afraid it's true. She isn't coming.

    5   I'm not sure I want to get back together with her.

    6   What are you talking about? I don't understand.

    7   Really? Are you absolutely sure about that?

    8   You have to help me! I don't know what to do.

3 Find synonyms for the adjectives in Ex 1.

4 Look at the example situations in the box. Think of similar situations, or other situations where you have experienced some of the feelings in Ex 1. Tell a partner.

> a friend lied to you   you broke or lost a valuable item   you got an unexpected text message or email   you had a job interview   you won something

Example:
I was quite hesitant about meeting my girlfriend's parents for the first time last week.

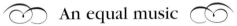

An equal music

In the bus directly opposite, at the window directly opposite is Julia. Her bus has stopped at the traffic light.

I begin to pound the window and shout, 'Julia! Julia! Julia! Julia!'

She cannot hear me. We are in separate worlds.

Stop reading, Julia. Look. Look out of the window. Look at me. Oh God.

Around me the passengers stop talking. In the bus opposite no one seems to notice. I keep pounding the window. At any moment her bus or mine could move off.

A man sitting behind her notices me and the commotion that has resulted. He looks mystified but not alarmed. I gesticulate and point desperately – and with great hesitation, he taps Julia on the shoulder and points at me.

Julia looks at me, her eyes opening wide in what? Astonishment? Dismay? Recognition? I must look wild – my face red – my eyes filled with tears – my fists still clenched – I am a decade older.

I rummage around in my satchel for a pen and a piece of paper, write my telephone number in large digits and hold it against the glass.

She looks at it, then back at me, her eyes full of perplexity.

Simultaneously both buses begin to move.

My eyes follow her. Her eyes follow me.

I look for the number that's on the back of the bus. It is 94.

I get to the stairs. I am given a wide berth. The conductor is coming up the stairs. I can't get past him. I am losing time, I am losing it.

Finally I get down, push my way past a couple of people, and jump off the moving bus.

Weaving across the traffic, I get to the other side. I have lost too much time. Her bus has moved away.

I try to push through the crowd, but it is too thick. I will never catch up.

A taxi lets out a passenger. A young woman, her hands full of shopping, is about to grab it, when I interpose myself. 'Please,' I say. 'Please.'

She takes a step back and stares at me.

I get into the cab. To the taxi-driver I say: 'I want to catch up with the Number Ninety-Four in front.'

We move forward. The lights turn yellow against us. He stops.

'Couldn't you go through?' I plead. 'It's not red yet.'

'I'll get my licence taken away,' he says, annoyed. 'What's the hurry anyway? You won't save much time.'

'It's not that,' I blurt out. 'There's someone on that bus I haven't seen for years. I've got to catch it.'

'Take it easy, mate,' says the driver. But he tries his best.

After one more tricky feat of overtaking the driver says: 'Look mate, I'm nearer but, to be quite honest, I won't make it. Your best bet now is to get out and run for it.'

'You're right. Thanks.'

'That's two pounds sixty.'

I only have a five-pound note in my wallet. I tell him to keep it and grab my satchel.

I know I have no chance against the crowds on the pavement. My one hope is to run between the opposing streams of traffic.

Sweating, diesel-gassed, unable to see clearly through my most inconvenient tears, I run and gasp and run.

I catch up with the bus a little before Oxford Circus. I try to run up the stairs but can't. I walk up slowly, in hope and in dread.

Julia is not there. I go to the very front and look back at every face. I go downstairs, I look at every face. She is not there.

[handwritten top margin:] Post Perf 1 To connect a past sit'n with sth that happened or started happening at an earlier time in the past
Fut P 2 future — will happen or will start happening — future
Pres Perf 3 pres — happened or started happening at a time in the past.

LANGUAGE STUDY

Connecting events using the perfect

[handwritten:] To present a sit? + connect with sth that happened, or started to happen, in the past.

1 What is the function of the present perfect in these extracts from the text on page 35?

1 In the bus directly opposite, at the window directly opposite is Julia. Her bus **has stopped** at the traffic light. _[hw:] Bus is there now, had stopped_

2 Weaving across the traffic, I get to the other side. I **have lost** too much time. Her bus **has moved** away. _[hw:] Wasn't have enough time to reach the bus as he lost time in the past._ _[hw right:] No longer there as bus has moved away_

3 There's someone on that bus I **haven't seen** for years. I've got to catch it. _[hw:] Situation of not seeing the woman exists now even though it started a long time ago._

2 Look at these sentences and answer the questions.

[hw left margin:] start

a They**'d been chatting** all night and **had lost** all sense of time. _[hw:] Pres Perf C_ _[hw:] past PPS_ _Future PS_

b We**'ll have been** together for two years next month. _[hw:] Past Perf Simp_

c We**'ve been seeing** a lot of each other lately. I'd say we**'ve become** quite close. _[hw:] Future Perf Simple_

1 What is the name of each the perfect tenses in the sentences?

2 What is the function of each perfect tense in the sentences? _[hw:] To connect a past sit'n with sth that happened or started happening past / earlier; will happen or will start" "future; pres; happened started happening in the past._

3 Which form, simple or continuous, do you generally use with the perfect to emphasise a) activity or duration and b) completion or result?

[hw:] cont.   Simple.

Grammar reference page 58

3 Complete the first part of the article by putting the verbs into an appropriate perfect form. Where both simple or continuous are possible, what is the difference in emphasis?

[hw left margin:] 2 1,8,9 -
[hw:] where 2 As emphasises activity + repetition + emphasises result + sit'n as a whole.

Bad habits
can ruin
romance

Fiddling with the controls of the car stereo or stealing chips from your partner's plate may seem minor niggles but they could ruin a relationship. Researchers, who over the last few months (1 delve) _have been delving / have delved_ into the private lives of 500 couples, (2 identify) _have identified_ a list of the most annoying habits that can cause rifts between couples. One couple even split up after one partner (3 finally / have) _had finally had_ enough of publicly being referred to as 'honeybunny' or 'bunnyboo'.

The study (4 find) _has found_ that the smallest of irritations can provoke the most extreme

of reactions in a partner. 'We (5 look) _have been looking_ at how relatively minor behavioural quirks can affect a partner's emotions,' said researcher Mike Harold, 'While bickering (6 always / be) _has always been_ a natural feature of relationships, over time minor irritations can sometimes take on unmanageable proportions and it's possible that by then the behaviour in question (7 become) _modal: have become_ a major issue in the relationship.' 'Irritating habits (8 come up) _have been coming / have come_ a lot recently as an issue in relationship problems,' said therapist Philippa Hills, from YouRelate. 'Over the last couple of years we (9 see) _have been seeing / have seen_ more and more couples who (10 develop) _have developed_ issues concerning each other's habits.'

4 Complete the rest of the article using an appropriate perfect form of these verbs.

> be   do   get   know   lose   remind

Couples generally agree that finding their other half annoying is part of life. John Mitchell, 29, said of his girlfriend Susan Thomas, 'It's a mystery how she can take so long to get ready. She always (1) _has done_ . And I get very frustrated with her map reading. I (2) _have lost count_ count of the number of times she (3) _has got_ us lost.' John of course has his faults too according to Susan.

'He always leaves his clothes lying around, even though I (4) _have reminded_ him about it a thousand times,' she says. Nevertheless, the couple, who next month (5) _will have been_ together for five years, say they are still blissfully happy. 'Even if we (6) _had known_ about each other's annoying habits before we got together, we'd still have done so,' Susan added.

5 What do you think are the top ten most annoying habits according to the research in Ex 3? Turn to page 61 to find out. Which of the habits do you, or would you, find annoying?

The end of a nightmare

Listening 1 　🔘 **14** Listen to the first part of an extract from Dermot Healy's *A goat's song*. Choose the correct answers.

Main character: *male / female*　　Background: *start / break up* of a relationship

Mood: *hope / desperation*　　Setting: *urban / rural*

The main character's work: *farmer and fisherman / author and fisherman*

2 　🔘 **15** Listen to the second part of the extract and make notes about what happens.

* Work with a partner. Tell the story to your partner in your own words, using your notes. Your partner listens and points out any differences from his / her notes.
* Discuss the ending of the story – is it a happy one?

3 Use a dictionary to check the meaning of these literary techniques.

> alliteration　　metaphor　　simile　　use of a highly descriptive adjective / verb

4 Match the phrases in **bold** from the listening script, with the techniques in Ex 3.

1 He knew, with a sense of **furious sadness**, that this would be followed by another minute.

2 On the radio various voices of other fishermen were **cajoling**, **complaining**, **cursing**, talking of the forthcoming storms.

3 Her voice, filled with static, **cut through** the quiet.

4 A sound **like a strimmer** went through the airwaves.

5 He **threw open** the door of the lightkeeper's house.

6 I'm trusting you, **treading on thin ice** in the hope that someday we'll be **skating along** without fear.

Literature and you

Speaking and vocabulary
1 Do you enjoy reading for pleasure? Do you read mainly for college or work? What do you read or have to read? Tick the words in the lists. Then tell a partner.

Fiction: chick lit, classics, detective stories, historical novels, modern fiction, poetry, thrillers.

Non-fiction: blogs, chat room discussions, biographies / autobiographies, cookery books, daily or weekly newspapers, guidebooks, magazines, professional journals or articles, self-help manuals, message boards, textbooks.

2 Tell a partner about something memorable you have read recently. Use these words and phrases to help you.

> a load of rubbish　a real tearjerker　a slow-starter　badly written　controversial disappointing　entertaining　hilarious　in-depth　informative　inspiring monotonous　moving　poetic　superficial　trashy　unputdownable

Writing
1 You are going to write a 300–400 word short story for a competition. Choose one of these titles: A chance encounter, The end of a nightmare

2 Make notes for your story. You can draw on your own experiences if you wish. Think about the key events, the main characters' feelings and relationships, and how the story ends.

3 Write your story. Then read other students' stories. Say what you enjoyed, what could be improved on and how they made you feel.

CD-ROM　　For more activities go to **Pairs Unit 1**

2 A perfect world

LEARNING AIMS

- Can focus attention on important information
- Can comment on current affairs
- Can express surprise or indifference

Seeking perfection

Lead-in **1** How did this sheep bring scientists 'closer to perfection'? Check your ideas on page 61.

Reading and vocabulary **1** Replace the underlined phrases with phrases from the box. Make any changes necessary.

▲ Dolly, 1996–2003

cause concern	create controversy	inspire sympathy	make headlines
rekindle debate	set a precedent		

1 What has renewed discussion about genetic screening?
2 Why did Adam Nash's birth become a big newspaper story?
3 What aspect of the case aroused compassion?
4 Why has the case given rise to worry?
5 This is the first case of its kind. What is its importance for future cases?
6 How did a US entrepreneur provoke debate and disagreement?

2 🔘 **16** Read the article on page 39 and answer the questions in Ex 1.

3 Discuss these questions with your class.

1 Did reading about this case inspire sympathy in you or cause concern? Why?
2 Do you know if the topic of genetic screening has also created controversy in your country? If so, what has been the outcome of the discussion?
3 Plastic surgery is widely used today. To what extent is selling the embryos of models a logical further step?
4 What do you think would be 'perfect offspring'?
5 Is it possible to achieve perfection? Is it a worthwhile goal?

4 How do you think the debate on genetic screening will pan out? Does the responsibility for the use of genetic screening lie with scientists, parents or governments?

5 Work with a partner. Look at the questions and the content of each paragraph of the text on page 39. Identify the purpose of each paragraph. For example: *Paragraph 1 introduces and summarises the controversy*. Compare your ideas and establish a structure model.

6 Read this article about a report on genetically modified foods. Choose the correct meaning of the underlined phrasal verbs.

GM food has made headlines again. The renewed focus on GM foods has (1) come about because of new evidence concerning the approval of seven GM foods by the European Commission. A new report by the environmental groups *Friends of the Earth* and *Greenpeace* (2) spells out the uncertainty surrounding the dangers of GM foods. The report also (3) touches on the fact that lack of data means that certain issues relating to GM foods, such as the risk of cancer and allergies, haven't been studied at all. According to the report, the Commission (4) played down the risks and approved the foods, despite not (5) ruling out the possibility that a study to support their decision was scientifically flawed. Given the high emotions surrounding this issue, the controversy is unlikely to (6) die down in the near future.

1 happened / continued
2 hints / clearly explains
3 mentions / ignores
4 emphasised / minimised
5 dismissing / acknowledging
6 become more intense / become less intense

7 How do you feel about the growing of genetically modified crops?

Designer **babies**

1 The first 'designer baby' has rekindled furious debate about the ethical issues of using genetics to select the attributes of babies. Genetic screening was used so that the test-tube baby Adam Nash could become a donor for his six-year-old sister Molly, who has a rare and fatal genetic disease. But whilst the case has inspired sympathy, it has also increased fears of babies becoming 'commodities' where intelligence and athletic prowess are bought.

2 **What is a 'designer baby'?**
Adam Nash, whose birth in America made headlines all over the world, is the first known designer baby. What was revolutionary about Adam's birth was that scientists genetically selected his embryo so that he would have the right cells to save the life of his dying sister. Normally, there would be a very high chance that any baby Adam's parents had would also have the disease. After Adam's birth, he became a donor to his sister and there was a blood transfusion which has more than doubled her survival chances.

3 **If he saves his sister's life, why the concern?**
Although the parents' dilemma inspired sympathy, there are those who believe it is intrinsically wrong to bring a human being into the world for any purpose other than living their own life. But, in the main, it is the precedent that this birth sets that is causing concern: the technique could be extended to allow parents to 'design' children with a variety of genetic traits.

4 **What would be available to parents deciding to have a 'designer baby'?**
Eye colour, athletic ability, beauty, intelligence, height, stopping a tendency towards obesity, guaranteeing freedom from certain mental and physical illnesses. All of these could in the future be determined by genetic science. Even characteristics such as sexuality could be selected. The problem for many is that the frontiers of what is now genetically possible are being pushed back so quickly that the ethical debate can't keep up.

5 **Who are the people worried about genetics?**
Some scientists have voiced concerns, although many echo the views of Dr John Wagner, who carried out the Nash operation. He said he was just trying to save the girl's life. The anti-abortion charity, *Life*, said selecting top quality embryos was more akin to the farmyard and that one child should not be used to save the life of another. Groups worried about social injustices, and the gap between rich and poor, are also concerned about a future where the wealthy can purchase a perfect offspring. Last year, related controversy was created when a US entrepreneur started a website offering the embryos of models.

6 **How will the debate pan out?**
As the knowledge of what each gene does grows it will become possible to predict most, if not all diseases and details of other characteristics before birth. The key issue is how parents respond to the increasing possibilities that will be offered to them.

Writing

1 Think about an issue that has been the subject of debate in your country recently and make notes, using the structure model you discussed in Reading and vocabulary Ex 5.

2 Write an article about your issue, using your notes. Introduce your paragraphs with questions similar to those in the text. Use the phrases and the phrasal verbs in Reading and vocabulary Ex 1 and 6 to help you.

3 Swap articles with a partner. Ask your partner for his / her opinion and comments.

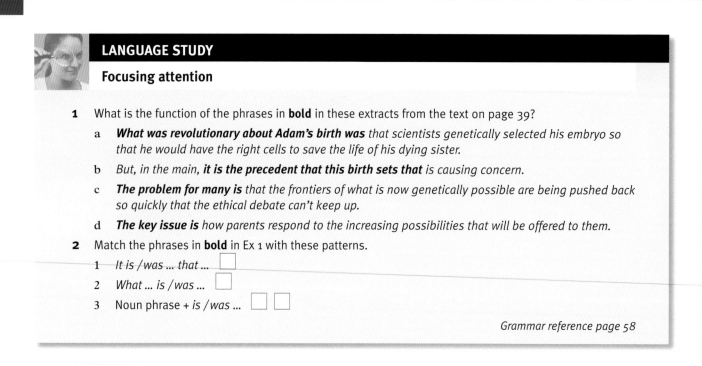

LANGUAGE STUDY

Focusing attention

1 What is the function of the phrases in **bold** in these extracts from the text on page 39?

  a *__What was revolutionary about Adam's birth was__ that scientists genetically selected his embryo so that he would have the right cells to save the life of his dying sister.*

  b *But, in the main, __it is the precedent that this birth sets that__ is causing concern.*

  c *__The problem for many is__ that the frontiers of what is now genetically possible are being pushed back so quickly that the ethical debate can't keep up.*

  d *__The key issue is__ how parents respond to the increasing possibilities that will be offered to them.*

2 Match the phrases in **bold** in Ex 1 with these patterns.

  1 *It is / was ... that ...* ☐

  2 *What ... is / was ...* ☐

  3 Noun phrase + *is / was ...* ☐ ☐

Grammar reference page 58

3 Rephrase each sentence in <u>two</u> ways to focus attention more. Use (a) *It is / was ... that ...* and (b) *What ... is / was ...*

Example:
How on earth they came up with the idea in the first place amazes me.
*(a) **It's** how on earth they came up with the idea in the first place **that** amazes me.*
*(b) **What** amazes me **is** how on earth they came up with the idea in the first place.*

  1 The clarity of the images amazes me.
  2 What they will come up with next really frightens me.
  3 I can't get my head round the distances involved.
  4 Watching it live on TV really brought it home.
  5 Not knowing what the long-term dangers are worries me.
  6 I just don't understand how so much can be stored on something so small.

4 What phenomena could each of the sentences in Ex 3 be referring to?

5 Match the beginnings to the endings of the sentences.

  1 What really irritates me about TV is   a never having any money.
  2 The best thing about the Internet is   b all the adverts every few minutes.
  3 What I'd really love is to be able to   c the Himalayas.
  4 One thing I really object to is   d people smoking in public places.
  5 The worst thing about being a   e take a year off and go
     student is   travelling.
  6 A place I'd really love to visit is   f their obsession with celebrity.
  7 What never ceases to amaze me   g meeting people from all over the
     about the press is   world.
  8 One thing that's great about studying   h being able to download music for
     English is   free.

6 Use the sentence beginnings in Ex 5 to write your own ideas. Read your sentences to a partner and discuss some of your ideas.

Example:
A: *What really irritates me about TV is all the reality shows.*
B: *Really? I think they're a bit of a laugh. They're ...*

Did they win?
We'll find out after the break.

Nobody's perfect

Listening and speaking

1 Before you listen, think about you and your parents. What have you got in common personality-wise?

2 🔘 **17** Listen to the conversation. What have Ellie and her mum got in common?

3 These characteristics are typical of perfectionists. Listen again and tick the ones that apply to Ellie's mum.

1 is afraid of disapproval ☐

2 likes things to be just so ☐

3 is fussy ☐

4 is extremely competitive ☐

5 is self-critical ☐

6 has high expectations ☐

7 is indecisive ☐

8 is intolerant of mistakes ☐

4 Work with a partner. Look at the list of characteristics in Ex 3.

1 Do you know people who are perfectionists and have the characteristics in Ex 3? What positive traits do they have?
2 Do any of the things in Ex 3 apply to you? Are you a perfectionist?
3 Extreme perfectionists can suffer from illnesses such as depression, eating disorders, and addictions such as alcoholism. Why do you think this is so?

Vocabulary and pronunciation

1 How does Zoe react …

1 … when she finds Ellie hoovering?
2 … when Ellie says she might clean the fridge before she goes to bed?
How does she express these feelings? Check in the listening script on page 62.

2 Which of these phrases express surprise (S)? Which express indifference (I)? Mark them.

1 You're kidding me, aren't you?
2 So what?
3 Are you having me on?
4 Who cares?
5 It doesn't matter.

6 No way!
7 Whatever.
8 What?
9 If you like.
10 Never!

3 🔘 **18** Listen and repeat the phrases. Pay attention to stress and intonation.

4 Work with a partner. Student A look at page 61. Student B respond to student A's statements with a phrase from Ex 2 and continue the conversation. Use as many phrases from Ex 2 as possible. When student A has finished, swap roles. Student B look at page 64.

Example:
A: *I found a £20 note on the street today.*
B: *No way! Some people have all the luck. I never find anything.*
A: *Do you think I should take it to the police?*
B: *Are you having me on? Why would you want to do that?*

CD-ROM For more activities go to **Pairs Unit 2**

3 Modern-day icons

PAIRS

LEARNING AIMS

- Can use spoken phrases with *say* and *speak*
- Can talk about popular icons and celebrity culture
- Can contrast British and American English pronunciation

Lead-in **1** An English proverb says 'Imitation is the sincerest form of flattery'. Discuss what this means. When does it go too far?

Keeping a legend alive

Listening and speaking **1** Tribute artists and bands where singers impersonate famous performers are big business. Why do you think these acts are so popular? What age group do they appeal to? Why do you think people want to be in tribute bands?

2 🔘 **19** Listen to an interview with Shawn Klush, an Elvis tribute artist. Make notes on the following:
  a his expectations about the concert in Switzerland
  b his feelings before going on stage
  c the audience and how it affected him
  d what the concert shows about Elvis and his music

3 Compare your notes with a partner. Listen again if necessary.

4 What impressions do you get of Shawn Klush? How would you describe his attitude towards his work?

5 Work with a partner and discuss these questions.
  1 What do you think of Elvis and his music? Why was and is he popular?
  2 Elvis is a 20th-century legend. Who else would you put in this category?
  3 Think about contemporary musicians and bands. Who do you think are the icons of the early 21st century? Why?

6 The nostalgia industry at present focuses on the latter half of the 20th century. Work in groups and discuss what you think people will look back on with nostalgia from the first decade of this century. Think about, for example, music, fashion, TV shows and films, food, and household gadgets and appliances. Present your ideas to the class.

7 You're going to do a role-play. Student A look at page 61. Student B look at page 64.

8 How far did you identify with the opinions and attitude you defended in Ex 7?

Vocabulary **1** In the listening text Shawn Klush uses the phrases *it blew their minds*, and *out of the public eye*. Who or what was he referring to and what do the phrases mean? Check your ideas in the listening script on page 62.

2 Many idiomatic expressions in English use parts of the body. Can you explain the meanings of these idioms?
  1 She loves to be waited on hand and foot.
  2 She turns heads wherever she goes.
  3 He never has a hair out of place.
  4 His outrageous outfits raise a few eyebrows.
  5 He puts his heart and soul into his performances.
  6 She always thanks her fans from the bottom of her heart.
  7 Unfortunately, success has gone to his head.
  8 Her name is on everyone's lips.

3 Work with a partner and discuss these questions.

1 Think of a performer you like or admire. Do any of the expressions in Ex 2 apply to him or her?

2 Which performers can be described by the other expressions?

4 Look at these everyday expressions and match them to the situations below. How else can you state the meaning of these expressions?

a Use your head!

b Keep your fingers crossed!

c Come on, let your hair down!

d Get off my back!

e Keep your eyes open!

f You scratch my back and I'll scratch yours.

1 You've been telling a friend that he doesn't work hard enough and won't pass his exams. What does he say to you?

2 You're at a party and are a bit nervous. Your friend wants you to relax and enjoy yourself. What does she say to you?

3 You need some petrol, but there seem to be no garages for miles around. What do you say to your friend in the car?

4 Your friend is going for an important audition and asks for your support. What does she say to you?

5 You want your boyfriend to help you with some tax forms. He says he'll do it – but wants you to help him with a computer program first. What does he say to you?

6 You've just had four beers and decide to drive to a friend's. Your girlfriend stops you. What does she say?

American English

Pronunciation **1** 🔘 **20** Some sounds are pronounced differently in American English and British English. Look at these words. Listen and tick whether you hear British or American English. The first one has been completed for you.

		British /ɑː/	American /æ/			British /ɜː/	American /ɜːr/
1	last		✓	5	world		
2	chance			6	work		
		/ɒ/	/ɑː/			/eə/	/eər/
3	gosh			7	there		
4	everybody			8	swear		

2 🔘 **21** Here are some words spoken with both British and American English pronunciation. Listen and mark the sound or stress that is different in American English. Then group the words into four American English pronunciation patterns.

1 garage   6 privacy
2 tomato   7 vase
3 ballet   8 café
4 vitamins   9 student
5 new   10 semi-finalist

LANGUAGE STUDY

Spoken phrases with *say* and *speak*

1 Look at these extracts from Listening and speaking Ex 2 on page 42. Match the phrases in **bold** to their uses 1–4.

... going to a different country, (a) ***as they say****, you know, there's different cultures and there's different this and different that.*

For a man to be ... out of the public eye, (b) ***so to speak****, physically, (c)* ***let's say****, but how he still goes on and on ...*

We really try to work hard and er, (d) ***I've said it before and I'll say it again****, he had impact.*

1   to show it's the opinion of a lot of people ☐

2   to give emphasis by referring to something previously stated ☐

3   to show you have expressed something in an unusual way ☐

4   to give an example ☐   *Grammar reference page 59*

2 Complete each sentence using an appropriate phrase in **bold** from Ex 1. Use each phrase once.

1   The best thing about the Internet is that you've always got whatever music you want at your fingertips, _____.

2   I can't stand techno music. I'd rather listen to, _____, folk or jazz.

3   I personally like the album, and, _____, 20 million people can't be wrong.

4   My favourite band? _____, *Snow Patrol* are simply the best band ever.

3 Here are some more common phrases using *say* and *speak*. What are their uses?

1   Anyway, **as I was saying**, we really must swap some music sometime.
2   **Speaking of** great gigs, I saw the *Arctic Monkeys* when they were just starting out.
3   **Personally speaking**, I really don't see the point of tribute bands.
4   I didn't really like it at first, but **I have to say** the album's really grown on me.
5   I don't really like going clubbing. **That said**, I'd rather that than stay in all night.

4 Imagine you are having a discussion about some area of entertainment such as music, film, TV or theatre. Complete the sentences with things you might say.

Example: I'm not a big fan of Elvis. But that said, he did have a great voice.

1   I'm not a big fan of ... But that said ...   4   I have to say ...
2   I've said it before and I'll say it again, ...   5   Personally speaking, ...
3   Speaking of great shows, ...   6   Music, as they say, ...

5 Work in groups of three. Each student writes down any five of these phrases on a piece of paper.

> As I was saying ...   As they say ...   I have to say ...
> I've said it before and I'll say it again ...   Let's say ...   Personally speaking ...
> ... so to speak   Speaking of ...   That said ...

Choose one of these topics, or a topic of your choice, to discuss. As you discuss the topic, use your phrases in an appropriate way. As you use each phrase, cross it off. The first person to use all their phrases is the winner.

> celebrity   computer games   Elvis Presley   marriage   money
> music   nostalgia   the Internet   tribute bands   work

6 *-speak* is used with some nouns to describe the type of language associated with a certain field. Give examples of language which could be described as:

1 business-speak   2 computer-speak   3 football-speak   4 music-speak

Example: business-speak downsize   overheads   parent company

How star-struck are you?

Reading and Speaking

1 Celebrity culture (adulation and emulation of the rich and famous) has been the subject of numerous scientific studies by psychologists. Discuss these questions.

1 Why do you think psychologists are interested in this topic? What do you think they hope to find out?

2 What dangers do you think there are in people taking an interest in celebrities to extremes?

3 To what extent do you think celebrity culture is a global phenomenon? Is star gazing a popular pastime in your country?

2 Do the celebrity culture quiz. Answer 'yes' or 'no' to each question. Then look at page 64 to work out your score and to read the analysis. Do you agree with it?

How Star-struck are you?

*D*o you spend all your time on the Internet reading about famous people? Are you convinced your favourite celebrity is your ideal partner? Or couldn't you care less what famous people get up to in their private lives? Take this test and find out how star-struck you are.

1 I often buy tabloid newspapers or glossy magazines if there's an interesting story about a celebrity on the cover. ____

2 I'd consider plastic surgery to emulate my favourite celebrity. ____

3 I often gossip about the exploits of celebrities with my friends. ____

4 I can't believe the stupid antics of some celebrities and the way they chuck their money about. These people have got more money than sense! ____

5 I've posted a comment to a celebrity on their website or written them a fan letter. ____

6 I'm sick of stars hanging out their dirty laundry in the media. Who cares about their endless stories of drug and alcohol abuse? ____

7 If I got a fleeting glimpse of my favourite star, I'd be in seventh heaven. ____

8 I would do something illegal for my favourite celebrity if he or she asked me. ____

9 I think most celebrities are a bunch of freeloaders. ____

10 If my favourite star died, I wouldn't think life was worth living. ____

11 I would be more inclined to buy a product if it were endorsed by a celebrity I think highly of. ____

12 I think my favourite celebrity is my soul mate. ____

13 I'm counting the days until the Oscars – I love all that red-carpet glamour. ____

14 I think some celebrities are role models; they can inspire you to realise your own potential. ____

15 A lot of so-called celebrities are not talented in the least. They're purely marketing products or the result of trashy reality TV. ____

16 I've contributed to a chatroom discussion about a celebrity that I really admire or really despise. ____

3 What's the difference between being interested in a celebrity and having an obsession with them? Give examples from the quiz. Why and how do you think interest turns to obsession?

Speaking and writing

1 Work in groups. You are going to give a presentation on the effect on celebrities of being stalked by their obsessive fans. First brainstorm ideas about what happens, and what celebrities might do in response. Include any particular cases that come to mind and make notes.

2 In your group decide on the information you are going to use for your presentation and who is going to present it. Organise your notes.

3 Make a group presentation to the rest of the class. Encourage other groups to comment on or discuss your presentation.

 CD-ROM For more activities go to **Pairs Unit 3**

4 Safe and sound?

Identity theft

Lead-in

1 Work with a partner. What do you think is private information and what should be publicly available – to authorities and companies, for example? Make two lists using the ideas in the box and your own ideas. Then compare your ideas with the class.

> club membership   credit history   criminal record   date of birth
> email address   medical history   political affiliation   profession
> qualifications   religion   salary   school records and reports
> value of your flat or house   what you read   where you shop

Reading and vocabulary

1 What exactly is identity theft? Think about why and how it happens. Write a class definition.

2 🔊 **22** Read the information on page 47 and check your ideas from Ex 1.

3 Are these sentences true or false? Correct the false ones.
1 Financial fraud is the main reason people commit identity theft.
2 Identity theft is an online phenomenon.
3 Victims hardly ever know the people who steal their identity.
4 It's fairly easy for criminals to get hold of your personal details.

4 Choose the correct name: Rose, Scott or both. Who …
1 had their <u>credit card details</u> stolen?
2 got lots of <u>bills</u>?
3 had their <u>current account</u> cleaned out?
4 had a demand for a large sum of <u>interest</u>?
5 uses <u>online banking</u>?
6 checks their <u>bank balance</u> regularly?

5 Explain the meaning of the <u>underlined</u> phrases in Ex 4.

6 Match the verbs in the box to the correct nouns. Which word can go with two nouns?

> clean out   close   default on   deposit   open   pay off   take out
> transfer   withdraw

_____ a bank account	_____ money	_____ a loan
_____	_____	_____
_____		

7 Work with a partner. Discuss these questions.
1 Have you or anyone you know ever had your credit card details stolen and used by another person?
2 Have you ever considered using or do you use online banking? What security precautions would you / do you take?
3 What do you do with old bank statements and credit card receipts?

Protect your identity

Identity theft is the world's fastest growing crime. Identity theft is when somebody steals your personal information in order to use your bank account or credit card to withdraw money, or to open new accounts or take out loans in your name. Stealing somebody's identity can also have other motives, for example, drug trafficking or illegal immigration, but these cases are less common. Fraudsters can steal personal information in various ways:

- by phishing: counterfeiting real websites (such as a bank's) and sending people to other illegitimate websites where they have to fill in personal information

- by posing as telemarketers or bank personnel on the phone and asking for personal information

- through the use of cash machines: by noting PIN codes or by using attachments to the machines

- by hacking into commercial databases of personal information or your own personal computer

- by stealing mail or stealing bank statements and credit card receipts from your rubbish bins

- by memorizing your details in their work as shop assistants or waiters

- by being related to you! Frighteningly, 10% of fraudsters are family members.

Identity theft can happen to anybody. These two stories had happy endings – but others haven't been so lucky.

Rose's story

I was a victim of identity theft because I used a free music file-sharing program. Suddenly I was getting bills for all sorts of things and being asked to pay huge amounts of interest on a credit card I didn't even have! I was just about to start college and it couldn't have happened at a worse time. Later I found out that when I downloaded the file-sharing software, I must have also downloaded a spyware program that allowed the person access to the personal information on my computer. I use online banking so all the information they needed was there. I just never imagined something like this would happen to me. I got it all sorted out in the end, but it was a complete nightmare!

Scott's story

I had my personal information stolen by a guy in our pizza delivery place. I go there quite a lot and so they've got my address and telephone number in their customer database. A few months ago some friends and I went there. I had to pay by credit card, and it turns out this guy had a skimmer – one of those gadgets which you can use to take credit card data off the magnetic strip. He downloaded the information onto his PC and used that and the customer database information to make a counterfeit credit card and then clean out my current account. It could have been worse – I haven't got much credit at the bank so he couldn't get that much money. And luckily I check my balance regularly or the whole thing might have gone undetected for weeks.

Speaking and writing

1 Look at these tips about property theft from college accommodation. The phrases in bold are used for giving formal advice and warning. Can you think of other phrases that can be used?

1 **It is recommended that you** report any crimes to the main office immediately.
2 **One simple way to prevent** things being stolen is by locking your room at all times – even when in the immediate vicinity.
3 **Avoid** leaving valuables or documents such as passports in your room.
4 **Consider** purchasing a small room safe or leave valuables at the office.
5 **Take care not to** let unknown people into the building, especially at night.
6 **Beware of** people you do not know purporting to be cleaners or other maintenance staff who require entry to your room.

2 You are going to write some tips about protecting yourself from crime for a college website. Work in two groups. One group is going to write tips about preventing being mugged and the other group is going to write tips about avoiding car crime. First brainstorm ideas in your group.

3 As a group, write your information for the website using the phrases in Ex 1 and a dictionary. Give your tips to the other group.

4 Discuss the other group's work. Comment on their ideas and language and suggest other tips if necessary.

LANGUAGE STUDY

Using modals to express real and unreal past situations

1 Look at these sentences and answer the questions.

1 Which of the modal verbs in **bold** express:
(a) 'real' situations that actually existed or happened ☐ ☐

(b) 'unreal' ideas such as speculation or deduction ☐*1* ☐ ☐ ☐

*I was just about to start college and it (1) **couldn't have** happened at a worse time.*

*... when I downloaded the file-sharing software, I (2) **must have** also downloaded a spyware program ...*

*I (3) **should have** been more careful but I never imagined something like this would happen to me.*

*I (4) **had to** pay by credit card, but didn't think anything about it.*

*It (5) **could have** been worse – I haven't got much credit so he (6) **couldn't** get that much money.*

*I check my balance regularly online or the whole thing (7) **might have** gone undetected for weeks.*

2 Complete the rules with *real* and *unreal*.

When you express _____ situations in the past, you use modal verb + *have* + past participle.

When you express _____ situations in the past, the modal changes form (*can→could, will→would, must /have to→had to*)

Note: *Can* only expresses real situations. Therefore its past form is *could*, and never *can have* + past participle.

Grammar reference page 59

3 Complete these identity-related news stories using the past form of the modal verbs in the box and the verbs in brackets.

could	have to	must	should

Who's the dummy?

A motorist has been fined $250 for driving in a high-occupancy vehicle lane with a life-size inflatable doll, which he hoped would pass as a passenger. The court heard that as there was only one 'human' in the car it (1 be) _____ in a different lane. The court was also told that the mannequin (2 burst) _____ at any time, 'endangering the lives of other road users.' The arresting officer also said that the driver, Jim Evans, from Richmond, Kentucky '(3 pull) _____ the stunt on more than one occasion' as he remembered seeing the same vehicle and 'passenger' before. As well as the fine, Evans (4 hand over) _____ the doll.

could	might	must

A lesson in law

A con-artist (5 not / pick) _____ a worse building to target when a stranger he tried to scam turned out to be a senior police officer. Roberto Cubillas tried to pass himself off as an impoverished student and according to police, he (6 get away with) _____ it had his story not been so far-fetched. Cubillas told the officer that he (7 not / pay) _____ his university fees as he had spent the money on a family funeral. 'He (8 think) _____ I was born yesterday,' said the officer. There was no way that Cubillas (9 know) _____ that the building was home to several high-ranking police officers. While Cubillas (10 look) _____ like a student, he certainly hadn't done his homework!

4 Think about a time in the past when you made a wrong decision or when things didn't work out as hoped. Work with a partner and say what you should or could have done differently and what then might have happened.

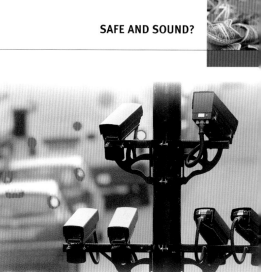

Caught on camera

Listening and vocabulary

1 The use of CCTV (closed-circuit television) cameras is being hotly debated in Britain. Are CCTV cameras used in your country? In what places do you usually find them?

2 🔘 **23** Listen to the radio phone-in and match the viewpoints to the callers. Make notes on the evidence the speakers give to support their opinions.

a It's about privacy. These cameras are just spying on us.

b CCTV surveillance is harassment. People are often misidentified.

c Cameras can help detect the people who commit crimes.

d Cameras prevent people from committing crimes.

Caller 1, Jody: _____ Caller 2, Naseem: _____ Caller 3, Lily: _____
Caller 4, Alvin: _____

3 Listen again. Note down the phrases the speakers use to express opinions. What other phrases do you know for expressing opinions?

1 I _____ having cameras everywhere.

2 I _____ they help stop people from committing crimes.

3 Most people _____ that video surveillance has made them feel safer.

4 I _____ privacy ought to be the main issue here.

5 I _____ that we can't be expected to have faith in video surveillance.

6 I _____ that we need CCTV.

4 Work with a partner.

1 Tell your partner which viewpoint(s) in Ex 2 you agree most with. Why? What is most important: civil liberties or public protection? Express your opinions using the phrases in Ex 3.

2 Do you think there should be restrictions on cameras in certain places – for example schools, nurseries, swimming pools? Why or why not?

5 Work with a partner. Make a mind map about crime. First use words and phrases from the listening text and the rest of the unit. Then find other important words using a dictionary.

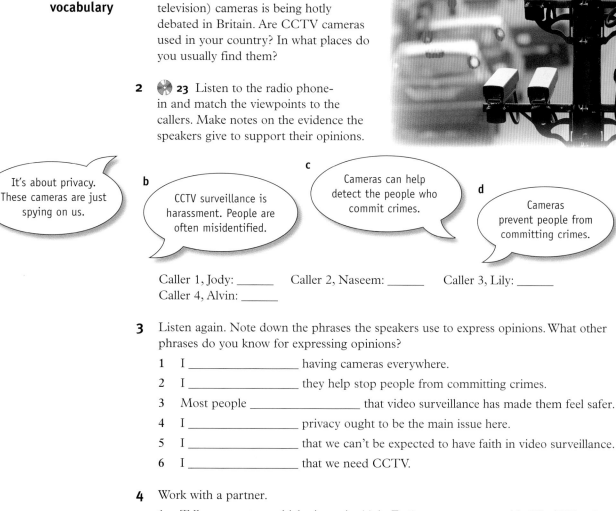

Speaking

1 The council in your town wants to introduce CCTV cameras in a neighbourhood which has had problems with theft, joyriding and mugging. Work in two groups. Group A look at page 61. Group B look at page 64. Follow the instructions.

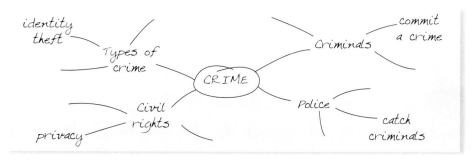

CD-ROM For more activities go to **Pairs Unit 4**

5 Review

Lead-in **1**   1   Can you make four celebrity couples from the people in the photos?
What do you know about them? Are they still together?
2   Are there any famous celebrity couples in your country?
3   Why do you think celebrities are attracted to other celebrities?
4   What do you think are the pros and cons of being a celebrity couple?

The world of celebrity

1   Choose the most natural alternative in the article.

Celebrity splits *under the spotlight*

The recent break-ups of many celebrity couples, including some of
Hollywood's most bankable stars, (1) *have shown / have been showing*
that relationships can and do crack under the pressures of fame and
fortune. Divergent careers which constantly keep the couple apart, and the
strain of heavy work schedules is often to blame. Career jealousy is another
reason, especially when one partner's career (2) *has been taking off / has
taken off* more than the other's. But the most likely reason is that one or the
other (3) *has been meeting / has met* someone else, invariably after falling
for a co-star or someone they (4) *have worked / have been working* with in
some other capacity. It is a wonder how some of today's celebrity couplings
(5) *have lasted / have been lasting* as long as they have.

On the other hand, stars do find it easier to date each other than members
of the public. If you (6) *have drunk / have been drinking* champagne on the
set all day and you come home to someone who (7) *has never lived / has
never been living* in that world and talk about what a hard day you (8) *have
been having / have had*, they won't understand.

2   How do your ideas in Lead-in question 4 compare with those in the article?

3   🔘 **24**   Listen to part of a conversation and answer these questions.
1   Which of the topics are talked about?
2   What opinions are expressed about these topics?

celebrity endorsements ☐   celebrity magazines ☐
celebrity weddings ☐   clothes ☐
earning money ☐   freebies ☐
good causes ☐   self-publicity ☐
spending money ☐   the Oscars ☐

▲ Ben and Anna

4   Complete these extracts from the listening with the correct
form of *say* or *speak*. What is each commenting on?
1   *That* _____, I do agree that it's maybe getting a little out of hand.
2   Yes, *I have to* _____ it can be pretty gross …
3   But *as they* _____, if you've got it, flaunt it.
4   _____ *of* 'flaunting it', did you see those hideous pictures of …
5   They got paid a million, *or so they* _____, by some magazine.
6   The right one on the front cover of, *let's* _____, 'Hello' magazine … can
boost sales massively.
7   *As I was* _____, I suppose any publicity is good publicity.

5 These phrases were used by Anna to focus attention. Complete them to give your own opinions about some of the topics in the box in Ex 1.

Example: *It never ceases to amaze me that anyone should think a product is special just because it's endorsed by a celebrity.*

1 It never ceases to amaze me …
2 Another thing that really annoys me is …
3 What I don't understand is …
4 It's … that gets me.
5 And what I want to know is …

6 Complete these extracts from film reviews with the past form of an appropriate modal verb and the verb in brackets.

Example: The stunning twist at the end (be) <u>*couldn't have been*</u> more surprising.

1 This film (be) _____ great fun to make – the entire cast seems to be relishing every moment and the movie never takes itself too seriously.

2 I wanted to stay to the end, but I just (not / bear) _____ watching this rubbish for a moment longer. I (leave) _____ after 20 minutes.

3 The hype surrounding this film has made seeing it a more desirable night out than it (otherwise / be) _____. It's good, but it isn't a great movie.

4 This film is so badly made that the boom microphone (list) _____ as a supporting character.

5 Watching with a friend we (pause) _____ it every five minutes to check what was going on. The film (not / make) _____ any less sense if we had been watching without sound.

7 Could any of the extracts in Ex 4 describe any films you have seen? Tell a partner.

Example: *Number one could be describing 'Pirates of the Caribbean'. The lead actor …*

8 Imagine you are a film critic. Think of three well-known films and write a short summary for each. Use at least one past modal verb in each summary.

9 Read your summaries to a partner. Can you guess what the films are?

Speaking

1 Work in two groups. You are going to have a debate. Imagine a law has been proposed to ban the paparazzi.

- Each group should choose someone to chair the debate, equal numbers of speakers for and against the proposed law, and an audience to ask questions.

- If you are one of the speakers, prepare your arguments. If you are a member of the audience prepare questions to ask the speakers.

- Hold the debate. If you are chairing the debate make sure you follow the debate procedure and make sure everyone contributes.

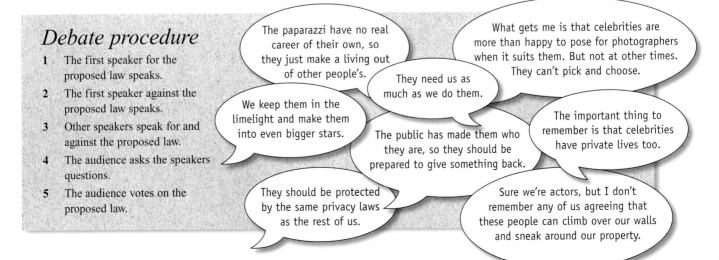

Debate procedure

1 The first speaker for the proposed law speaks.
2 The first speaker against the proposed law speaks.
3 Other speakers speak for and against the proposed law.
4 The audience asks the speakers questions.
5 The audience votes on the proposed law.

The paparazzi have no real career of their own, so they just make a living out of other people's.

They need us as much as we do them.

What gets me is that celebrities are more than happy to pose for photographers when it suits them. But not at other times. They can't pick and choose.

We keep them in the limelight and make them into even bigger stars.

The public has made them who they are, so they should be prepared to give something back.

The important thing to remember is that celebrities have private lives too.

They should be protected by the same privacy laws as the rest of us.

Sure we're actors, but I don't remember any of us agreeing that these people can climb over our walls and sneak around our property.

Song

1 Read the factfile about James Blunt. What connects James Blunt with the following?

> Harrow School   Aerospace engineering   Sandhurst   the British Army
> NATO   the Queen Mother   Los Angeles   Star Wars

2 Work with a partner and discuss these questions.
1 In what way did James Blunt follow in his father's footsteps?
2 What part did music play in his time in the army?

factfile

Singer-songwriter James Blunt was born in Wiltshire, England in 1974 and was educated at Harrow, one of the UK's top public schools. From there he gained an army-sponsored place at Bristol University, where he studied Aerospace Engineering and Sociology before finally completing his education at the Royal Military Academy in Sandhurst. Blunt's father had also been in the British Army and his family has a long history of military service.

Blunt rose to the rank of captain and served as a tank commander in the NATO peacekeeping force in Kosovo, where he carried his guitar around with him strapped to his tank and regularly entertained his fellow troops. Some of the songs from his as yet unwritten debut album were inspired by his experiences there. One of his final duties in the army was as part of the guard of honour at the funeral of the Queen Mother in 2002.

Blunt left the army in 2002 to become a full-time musician. He went to the USA and through a friend of a friend ended up in Los Angeles lodging with the *Star Wars* actress Carrie Fisher. Here he put a band together and soon afterwards he recorded his debut album, *Back to bedlam*. In 2005, the third single from the album, *You're beautiful*, was Blunt's breakthrough hit, reaching number one in several countries.

3 Match each line in the song with its final word or phrase.

4 🔘 **25** Listen and check your answers.

5 Which expressions in the song mean:
1 not worry or get upset about something?   3 pass each other?
2 suddenly notice something?   4 accept the situation?

6 Work with a partner and discuss these questions.
1 What event is he describing?   3 What is his connection with this person?
2 Who is he singing to?   4 How does he feel?

You're beautiful

My life is	subway
My love is	brilliant
I saw an	sure
Of that I'm	pure
She smiled at me on the	plan
She was with another	sleep on that
But I won't lose no	angel
'Cause I've got a	man
Chorus	
You're beautiful, you're	face
You're beautiful, it's	do
I saw your	beautiful
In a crowded	you
And I don't know what to	place
'Cause I'll never be with	true

Yeah, she caught my	moment
As we walked on	face
She could see from my	high
that I was flying	again
And I don't	eye
that I'll see her	think
But we shared a	end
that will last till the	by
Chorus	
You're beautiful, you're	you
You're beautiful, it's	angel
There must be an	beautiful
with a smile on her	true
When she thought	face
that I should be with	up
But it's time to face the	you
I will never be with	truth

Vocabulary

1   Work in groups of three or four. Read how to play 'Talk about it', then play the game.

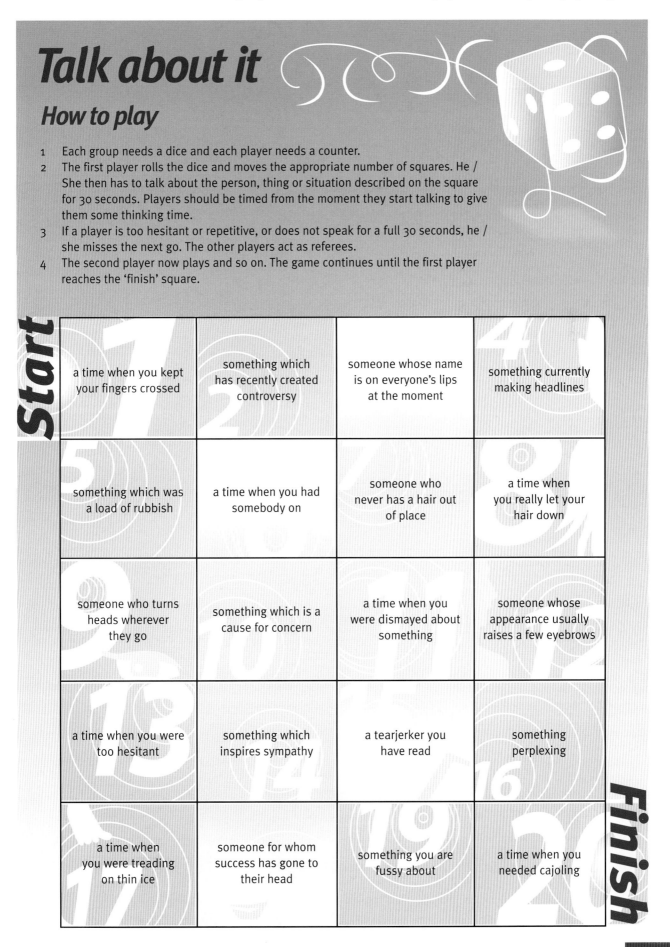

Talk about it

How to play

1   Each group needs a dice and each player needs a counter.
2   The first player rolls the dice and moves the appropriate number of squares. He / She then has to talk about the person, thing or situation described on the square for 30 seconds. Players should be timed from the moment they start talking to give them some thinking time.
3   If a player is too hesitant or repetitive, or does not speak for a full 30 seconds, he / she misses the next go. The other players act as referees.
4   The second player now plays and so on. The game continues until the first player reaches the 'finish' square.

Start

a time when you kept your fingers crossed	something which has recently created controversy	someone whose name is on everyone's lips at the moment	something currently making headlines
something which was a load of rubbish	a time when you had somebody on	someone who never has a hair out of place	a time when you really let your hair down
someone who turns heads wherever they go	something which is a cause for concern	a time when you were dismayed about something	someone whose appearance usually raises a few eyebrows
a time when you were too hesitant	something which inspires sympathy	a tearjerker you have read	something perplexing
a time when you were treading on thin ice	someone for whom success has gone to their head	something you are fussy about	a time when you needed cajoling

Finish

Extra practice

Unit 1

1 Complete the novel extracts with an appropriate form of the word in *italics*.

1 On turning the corner, Molly was _____ to see that the damage to the house was far greater than she had expected. *dismay*

2 She turned as the car drew to a halt. The passenger door opened and she walked _____ towards it. *hesitate*

3 'What on earth do you want to move to England for?' asked Marek in _____. *astonish*

4 'Please, somebody must have seen it happen,' she pleaded with more than a note of _____ in her voice. *desperate*

5 Alfie then shut the gate and ambled off to the house, shaking his head in _____, to complain to a _____ Dora in the kitchen. *perplex* *sympathy*

6 Jean-Luc's head was tilted to the side, and his face was wearing an expression of _____ and _____. *annoy* *confuse*

2 Complete the first part of the text with an appropriate perfect tense of the verbs in brackets.

Bed sharing
'drains men's brains'

A recent study (1 find) _____ that when a man shares a bed, his sleep is disturbed and by morning his stress hormone levels (2 rise) _____ significantly. Women who share a bed, on the other hand, are more likely to sleep more deeply and be mentally sharper in the morning.

The study involved couples who (3 live) _____ together for at least a year. Each couple spent some nights sleeping together and some apart. The couples decided when they slept together, as long as by the end of the research period they (4 spend) _____ ten nights together and ten apart. The couples performed mental agility tests each morning.

Although the men reported they (5 sleep) _____ better with a partner, they actually fared worse in the tests when they (6 do) _____ so.

'It's not surprising that people are disturbed by sleeping together and it is actually quite bizarre that sleeping together (7 evolve) _____ as a habit, because sleep is vital for good physical and mental health,' says Dr Neil Stanley, a sleep expert at the University of Surrey.

3 In the second part of the text, choose the most natural alternative. If both are possible, what is the difference in emphasis?

'Even though both sexes report a more disturbed night's sleep when they (1) *have shared / have been sharing* their bed, women apparently manage to sleep more deeply when they do eventually drop off, and by morning their stress hormone levels on the whole (2) *will not have increased / will not have been increasing* anything like a man's,' explained Dr Stanley. 'There is a suggestion that women (3) *have evolved / have been evolving* to cope better with broken sleep. The female brain (4) *has evolved / has been evolving* for thousands of years to cope with natural life events that involve disturbed sleep – bringing up children and tending to them in the middle of the night being one of the most obvious.'

But Dr Stanley, who (5) *has studied / has been studying* people's sleeping habits for over 20 years, added that people do get used to sharing a bed over time. 'If they (6) *have shared / have been sharing* their bed with their partner for a long time, they miss them when they are not there and that disturbs their sleep.'

4 Write about four books you have read or films you have seen that can be described by the words in the box.

a slow-starter a tearjerker controversial monotonous moving superficial trashy unputdownable

Example: *In my opinion, the Da Vinci Code was good, but a bit superficial.*

1 _____

_____

2 _____

_____

3 _____

_____

4 _____

_____

Unit 2

1 Complete the text with an appropriate form of the verbs in the box.

| ban | cause | create | govern | make | modify |
| rekindle | set | | | | |

GM food – a quick guide

Genetically modified food is constantly (1)_____ the headlines and each latest newsworthy development (2)_____ the debate for and against it. But what exactly is GM food?

In a word, it is food that comes from plants which have had their genetic make-up (3)_____ in order to improve the yield or to enable the plant to exist in more extreme environments than non-GM crops.

The precedent for GM food was actually (4)_____ thousands of years ago when farmers first crossed similar species. However, modern GM crops (5)_____ concern because critics say these crops could cross-pollinate with wild plants, with unknown consequences.

GM supporters claim the regulations that (6)_____ GM foods are stricter than for non-GM foods and that there is no evidence that GM crops are a danger to human health. They say the benefits are that GM crops produce higher yields and therefore they are more efficient in terms of land use, and use fewer pesticides.

However, GM foods have had so much bad publicity that supermarkets in several countries have (7)_____ them. And until the scientists can agree, the only thing we can be totally sure of about GM food is that it will continue (8)_____ controversy.

2 Replace the underlined phrases in these news extracts with the correct form of the phrasal verbs in the box.

| come about | die down | pan out | play down |
| rule out | spell out | touch on | |

1 The official line on further investment remains the same, but in reality the government is waiting to see how things develop before making a decision. _____

2 Ministers close to the president have minimised the importance of any rift between him and the home secretary. _____

3 Professor Wood will talk endlessly about his pioneering research, but when questions mention the political implications, however, he changes the subject. _____

4 The decline in the number of people living in rural areas has primarily happened because of drastic changes in farming methods over the last 20 years. _____

5 The furore over the nuclear programme will surely become less intense with time. _____

6 The government has explained clearly its policy on cloning, and while it hasn't dismissed a total ban, it has said that stricter regulations would be enforced. _____ _____

3 Rewrite these sentences to focus attention more.

1 Not knowing the long-term effects of GM food concerns me.
What concerns me _____

2 The feeling of helplessness really frustrates me.
It's _____

3 I don't understand why on earth anyone would want to live here.
What _____

4 Not knowing who has got access to all your personal details on the Internet worries me.
It's _____

5 Crick and Watson discovered the structure of DNA, didn't they?
Wasn't _____?

4 Rearrange these sentence beginnings.

1 is / about / thing / the / the weekend / best ... *The best thing about the weekend is ...*

2 about / the / thing / is / worst / being my age ...
_____

3 is / that / thing / one / really / me / annoys / about the media ...
_____

4 advantage / the / of / being able to / biggest / is/ speak English ...
_____

5 Complete the sentences in Ex 4 so they are true for you.

Example: *The best thing about the weekend is not having to do any work.*

1 _____
2 _____
3 _____
4 _____

Unit 3

1 Complete the sentences by joining them to the correct feature.

1 He / She really gets up my …

2 He / She never has a … out of place.

3 His / Her antics always raise a few …

4 Success has really gone to his / her …

5 He / She's never out of the public …

6 His / Her name is on everyone's …

2 Match the 'body' idioms in Ex 1 with the definitions.

a always in the press and other media ☐

b made him / her arrogant ☐

c people are talking about him / her ☐

d looks very neat and tidy ☐

e annoys and irritates ☐

f shock, surprise or annoy people ☐

3 Rephrase the sentences replacing the underlined words with an expression that includes the words in *italics*.

Example:
Just <u>show determination</u> and get on with it. *grit / teeth*

Just grit your teeth and get on with it.

1 <u>I'll be wishing you good luck.</u> *keep / fingers*

_____

2 You should <u>relax and enjoy yourself</u> once in a while. *let / hair*

_____

3 I want to thank you <u>very, very much</u>. *bottom / heart*

_____

4 <u>Stop criticising me!</u> *get off / back*

_____!

5 It <u>impressed me very much</u>. *blew / mind*

_____

4 Complete the mini-dialogues with the *say* or *speak* phrases.

> as we were saying   I have to say   speaking of
> that said

1 **A:** We're going to see that *Pink Floyd* tribute band next month. Fancy it?

B: Maybe, I'll see. And _____ _____ tribute bands, have you heard Sam's getting a *Coldplay* one together. I think they're calling it *Oldplay* or something.

2 **A:** What do you think of their new album?

B: Not that great, to be honest. _____, it does have a couple of decent tracks on it. And, _____ earlier, their albums do tend to grow on you.

A: Yeah, not their best, but _____ I still quite like it.

> as they say   don't say
> I've said it before and I'll say it again
> let's say   personally speaking   so to speak

3 **A:** I thought you were a big *Radiohead* fan.

B: Well, like millions, I was. But, _____, when bands start making those awful self-indulgent albums, they deserve exactly what they get if their popularity takes a dive.

4 **A:** I got *The very best of Nashville country* the other day.

B: _____ you're a secret country fan. Surely!

A: Well, variety is the spice of life, _____. And yes, I am a bit of a fan – I can't stand all that commercial 'back home' stuff, _____, but the real, proper country isn't a million miles from, _____, early blues or folk.

B: _____, I'd rather listen to my daughter's TV themes CD.

5 Match words on the left to the terms on the right.

1 URL, P2P, upload   a football-speak
2 gig, riff, jam   b music-speak
3 offside, dive, 4-4-2   c business-speak
4 downsize, turnover, overheads   d computer-speak

Unit 4

1 Complete the crossword.

Across

5 You give these to pay for something over the phone or the Internet (4, 7)

7 You can *take out*, *pay off* or *default* on this

8 You can have a *current* or *deposit* one of these

9 Deposit = pay _____

10 Another way of saying cash machine

11 You can *deposit*, *transfer* or *withdraw* this

14 This kind of banking means you can make some 1 downs at home

15 This is a record of your recent 1 downs

Down

1 11 across are different kinds of this *transaction*

2 This is the amount of money you have in, or owe, the bank

3 You can *open*, *close* or *clean out* this (4, 7)

4 This is one of the world's fastest growing crimes (8, 5)

6 You pay this each month when you borrow money

12 Short for Personal Identification Number

13 Withdraw = take _____

2 Put the words in *italics* in the correct order to complete the advice about money matters when travelling abroad.

1 *is | that | recommended | it* _____ you keep at least one credit or debit card in the hotel safe at all times and don't ever keep all your money and cards in one place when you are travelling.

2 *not | take | to | care* _____ let your credit and debit cards out of your sight.

3 *also | to | want | may | you* _____ take some travellers cheques with you.

4 *idea | is | good | it | to | a* _____ wear a concealed money-belt when you are out and about.

5 *beware | of | always* _____ unofficial money-changers and *sure | always | make* _____ you count your money in front of them before you leave.

6 *do, | you | don't | whatever* _____ accept damaged notes from anyone – in many countries these are not legal.

3 Choose one or more of the topics in the box and use some of the phrases in Ex 2 to give some good advice.

Example: *When selling something on the Internet, always make sure the payment to you has cleared before you send the item.*

buying or selling things on the Internet
studying   organising a party
attending an interview

1 _____

2 _____

3 _____

4 _____

4 Complete these quotes with the correct past form of the verbs in brackets.

1 'In Biblical times, a man (can / have) *could have* as many wives as he (can / afford) _____. Just like today.' (Abigail Van Buren, US advice columnist, 1918 –)

2 'The worst thing you can possibly do is worry and think about what you (can / be) _____.' (Georg Christoph Lichtenberg, German scientist, 1742–1799)

3 'It's never too late to be who you (might / be) _____.' (George Eliot, UK novelist, 1819–1880)

4 'The hardest work in the world is that which (should / do) _____ yesterday.' (Anonymous)

5 'It seems to me probable that anyone who has a series of intolerable positions to put up with (must / be) _____ responsible for them to some extent.' (Robert Hugh Benson, UK priest and author, 1871–1914)

5 Look at this quote and write a few sentences about your life using *could have*, *might have* and *should have*.

'Don't fear failure so much that you refuse to try new things. The saddest summary of a life contains three descriptions: could have, might have and should have.' (Louis E. Boone, US Author, 1941–)

Grammar reference

Unit 1

The perfect

Form

You form the perfect simple with an appropriate form of *have* + past participle.

Present perfect simple:
*He's **been** here for hours.*
***Have** you **spoken** to him yet?*
*I **haven't been** there.*

Past perfect simple:
*She **had** just **left**.*

Future perfect simple:
*I'**ll have been** here for two years next week.*

You form the perfect continuous with an appropriate form of *have + been + -ing*.

Present perfect continuous:
*He'**s been working** hard.*
***Have** you **been waiting** long?*

Past perfect continuous:
*We'**d been travelling** for days.*

Future perfect continuous:
*We'**ll have been going** out together for exactly a year on Friday.*

Use

You use the perfect to talk about a present, past or future situation that is connected in some way with something that happened or started before it.

This connection could be (1) that there is an important consequence or relevance of a previous action or (2) that the action or situation continues to the time referred to.

But what is important is that the situation at the time referred to is the focus, and details (such as when and how etc) of what happened before it are generally of secondary importance.

She's lost her keys. (She doesn't have her keys now because she lost them.)

We've been waiting for ages. (We're still waiting and we started waiting ages ago.)

I'd been driving all day. (At the end of the day I was tired because I was driving all day.)

She'd already left when we got there. (She wasn't there when we got there because she left earlier.)

The perfect is also sometimes explained as being used to express an action in a particular time period that continues to the time referred to.

I've never been to Egypt. (in the period of my lifetime)

I'd never seen anything like it. (in the period up to the time when I saw it)

I'll have had a look at it by then. (in the period between now and 'then')

The simple generally emphasises completion and result and considers the action or situation as a whole.

The continuous generally emphasises continuous or repeated activity and duration.
I've been to New York a couple of times.
I've been going to New York a lot recently.
At last, I've fixed it.
I'd been trying to fix it for about an hour.

Unit 2

Focusing attention

You can focus attention on what you are saying in a variety of ways. One of the most useful ways is to use the following structures.

It is / was ... that / who ...

Whereas in most sentences the new information and / or the information that you want to focus attention on comes at the end, with this structure you put it immediately after *It is / was*.
*It was David **who** came up with the idea.*
***It is** the precedent that this sets **that** is causing concern.*

What ... is / was ...

With *What ... is / was ...* the information you want to focus attention on comes at the end.
***What** was different about their idea was that it made use of recycled material.*
***What** gets me is the money they are paid.*

You can use the structure to focus on either the subject or the object of a sentence.
*I don't understand **why he's so popular**.*
*What I don't understand is **why he's so popular**.*
Her ambition and drive impresses me.
*What impresses me is **her ambition and drive**.*

You can also use other question words in this structure.
***How long** you stay **is** up to you.*
***Who** you see **is** none of my business.*

Noun phrase + is / was ...

The information you want to emphasise comes at the end. The noun phrase helps introduce it.
***The main problem is** how to accommodate so many people.*
***The key issue is** does it actually work?*

Unit 3

Spoken phrases with *say* and *speak*

English has many spoken phrases that include a form of *say* or *speak*. Here are some of the more common ones.

As they say… (to show it's the opinion of a lot of people)
As they say, if you've got it flaunt it.

I've said it before and I'll say it again, … (to give emphasis by referring to something previously stated)
I've said it before and I'll say it again, the money that top footballers are paid is a disgrace.

Let's say … (to give an example)
I can't stand busy pubs. I'd rather go to, let's say, a quiet bar or café or something.

As I was saying … (to refer back to something you have previously said)
As I was saying, shall we get together sometime next week?

I have to say … (to emphasise a statement, often when it may seem to contradict something)
It was a long way up, but I have to say, the view from the top was well worth the effort.

That said, … (to add an opinion that seems to be the opposite of what you have just said, although you think both are true)
It's very expensive. That said, the food is very good.

…, so to speak (to show you have expressed something in an unusual way)
Members of parliament were back in school today, so to speak.

Speaking of … (to introduce something new that you are going to say relating to a subject that someone has just mentioned)
Speaking of money, have we paid those bills yet?

Unit 4

Using modals to express real and unreal past situations

Real past situations

Modal verbs that express 'real' situations that actually existed or happened change their form:

can → could
will → would
must / have to → had to
I couldn't phone you – the battery was dead.
We had to wear a uniform at school.
He said he would be there at about 8.30.

Unreal past situations

The past form of modal verbs that express 'unreal' ideas such as speculation, deduction or hypothesis is:

modal verb + *have* + past participle
Do you think she might have left already?
It must have been Sara who told them.
I couldn't have got there any earlier.

Can only expresses real situations. Therefore its past form is *could*, and not *can have* + past participle.

However, *can't* + *have* + past participle is possible, and is used to make a deduction that something is impossible.
She can have worked harder.
She could have worked harder.
She can't have worked harder.

Wordlist

*** the 2,500 most common English words, ** very common words, * fairly common words

Unit 1

a load of rubbish *expr* /ə ˌləʊd əv ˈrʌbɪʃ/
alarmed *adj* /əˈlɑːmd/
alliteration *n* /əˌlɪtəˈreɪʃn/
annoyed *adj* /əˈnɔɪd/ **
astonished *adj* /əˈstɒnɪʃt/ *
badly written *adj* /ˌbædli ˈrɪtn/
behavioural *adj* /bɪˈheɪvjərəl/ *
bicker *v* /ˈbɪkə/
blissfully *adv* /ˈblɪsfəli/
blurt out *v* /ˌblɜːt ˈaʊt/
cajole *v* /kəˈdʒəʊl/
clench *v* /klentʃ/
controversial *adj* /ˌkɒntrəˈvɜːʃl/ **
curse *v* /kɜːs/ *
delve *v* /delv/ *
desperate *adj* /ˈdespərət/ **
dismayed *adj* /dɪsˈmeɪd/
fiddle with *v* /ˈfɪdl wɪð/ *
gesticulate *v* /dʒeˈstɪkjuleɪt/
give sb / sth a wide berth *expr* /ɡɪv ... ə ˌwaɪd ˈbɜːθ/
hesitant *adj* /ˈhezɪtənt/
hilarious *adj* /hɪˈleərɪəs/
hopeful *adj* /ˈhəʊpfl/ *
in-depth *adj* /ˌɪn ˈdepθ/
informative *adj* /ɪnˈfɔːmətɪv/ *
inspiring *adj* /ɪnˈspaɪərɪŋ/
interpose (my)self *v* /ˌɪntəˈpəʊz (maɪ)self/
irritation *n* /ˌɪrɪˈteɪʃn/ *
lose count of the number of times *phr* /ˌluːz ˈkaʊnt əv ðə ˌnʌmbər əv ˌtaɪmz/
metaphor *n* /ˈmetəfə, -fɔː/ *
monotonous *adj* /məˈnɒtənəs/
moving *adj* /ˈmuːvɪŋ/ **
mystified *adj* /ˈmɪstɪfaɪd/
other half *expr* /ˌʌðə ˈhɑːf/
perplexed *adj* /pəˈplekst/
plead *v* /pliːd/ **
poetic *adj* /pəʊˈetɪk/ *
pound *v* /paʊnd/ *
proportion *n* /prəˈpɔːʃn/ ***
quirk *n* /kwɜːk/
refer to sb / sth as *phr* /rɪˈfɜː tə ... əz ...,/ ***
simile *n* /ˈsɪməli/ *
slow-starter *n* /ˌsləʊ ˈstɑːtə/ *
static *n* /ˈstætɪk/ *
strimmer *n* /ˈstrɪmə/
superficial *adj* /ˌsuːpəˈfɪʃl/ *
tearjerker *n* /ˈtɪəˌdʒɜːkə/
trashy *adj* /ˈtræʃi/
tread on thin ice *expr* /ˌtred ɒn ˌθɪn ˈaɪs/
unmanageable *adj* /ʌnˈmænɪdʒəbl/
unputdownable *adj* /ˌʌnpʊtˈdaʊnəbl/

Unit 2

Are you having me on? *expr* /ə ˌjuː ˈhævɪŋ miː ˌɒn/
arouse *v* /əˈraʊz/ **
attribute *n* /ˈætrɪbjuːt/ *
blood transfusion *n* /ˈblʌd trænsˌfjuːʒn/
bring it home *expr* /ˌbrɪŋ ɪt ˈhəʊm/
cause concern *phr* /ˌkɔːz kənˈsɜːn/
cell *n* /sel/ ***
come about *v* /ˌkʌm əˈbaʊt/
commodity *n* /kəˈmɒdəti/ **
deep down *adv* /ˌdiːp ˈdaʊn/
die down *v* /ˌdaɪ ˈdaʊn/
donor *n* /ˈdəʊnə/ *
echo *v* /ˈekəʊ/ *
embryo *n* /ˈembriəʊ/
fatal *adj* /ˈfeɪtl/ **
genetic *adj* /dʒəˈnetɪk/ **
get (my) head around sth *expr* /ˌget (maɪ) ˈhed əˌraʊnd/
give rise to *expr* /ɡɪv ˈraɪz tuː/
inspire sympathy *phr* /ɪnˌspaɪə ˈsɪmpəθi/

intrinsically *adv* /ɪnˈtrɪnsɪkli/
It doesn't matter *expr* /ɪt ˈdʌzənt ˌmætə/
live up to sb's standards *expr* /ˌlɪv ʌp tə ... ˈstændədz/
make headlines *phr* /ˌmeɪk ˈhedlaɪnz/
never cease to amaze (me) *phr* /ˌnevə ˌsiːs tu əˈmeɪz miː/
offspring *n* /ˈɒfsprɪŋ/ *
one thing I (really) object to *phr* /ˌwʌn θɪŋ (aɪ) (ˈrɪəli) əbˌdʒekt tuː/
perfectionist *n* /pəˈfekʃnɪst/
play down *v* /ˌpleɪ ˈdaʊn/
rekindle debate *expr* /riːˌkɪndl dɪˈbeɪt/
revolutionary *adj* /ˌrevəˈluːʃnri/ **
rule out *v* /ˌruːl ˈaʊt/
screening *n* /ˈskriːnɪŋ/ *
set a precedent *phr* /ˌset ə ˈpresɪdənt/ *
spell out *v* /ˌspel ˈaʊt/
touch on *v* /ˈtʌtʃ ˌɒn/
Whatever *expr* /wɒtˈevə/
Who cares? *expr* /ˌhuː ˈkeəz/
You're kidding me, aren't you? *expr* /jɔː ˈkɪdɪŋ miː ˌɑːnt juː/

Unit 3

a bunch of *expr* /ə ˈbʌntʃ əv/
a fleeting glimpse *phr* /ə ˌfliːtɪŋ ˈɡlɪmps/
antics *n pl* /ˈæntɪks/
as I was saying *expr* /æz aɪ wəz ˈseɪɪŋ/
as they say *expr* /əz ˌðeɪ ˈseɪ/
blow (your) mind *expr* /ˌbləʊ (jɔː) ˈmaɪnd/
chuck (your) money about *phr* /ˌtʃʌk (jɔː) ˈmʌni əˌbaʊt/
Come on, let your hair down! *expr* /ˈkʌm ɒn ˌlet jɔː ˌheə ˈdaʊn/
couldn't care less *phr* /ˌkʊdnt keə ˈles/
emulate *v* /ˈemjuleɪt/ *
endorse *v* /ɪnˈdɔːs/ **
exploits *n pl* /ˈeksplɔɪts/
freeloader *n* /ˈfriːləʊdə/
Get off my back! *expr* /ˌget ɒf maɪ ˈbæk/
glossy *adj* /ˈɡlɒsi/ *
hang out (your) dirty laundry *expr* /ˌhæŋ aʊt (jɔː) ˌdɜːti ˈlɔːndri/
(success) has gone to (your) head *expr* /(səkˌses) həz ˌɡɒn tə (jɔː) ˈhed/
have got more money than sense *expr* /həv ˌɡɒt mɔː ˌmʌni ðən ˈsens/
I have to say *expr* /aɪ ˈhæf tə ˌseɪ/
I've said it before and I'll say it again *expr* /aɪv ˈsed ɪt bɪˌfɔː ənd ˌaɪl ˈseɪ ɪt əˌgen/
Keep your eyes open! *phr* /ˌkiːp jɔː ˈaɪz ˌəʊpən/
Keep your fingers crossed! *expr* /ˌkiːp jɔː ˈfɪŋɡəz ˌkrɒst/
let's say *expr* /ˌlets ˈseɪ/
never have a hair out of place *expr* /ˌnevə ˌhæv ə ˌheər aʊt əv ˈpleɪs/
nostalgia *n* /nɒˈstældʒə/
on everyone's lips *expr* /ɒn ˌevriwʌnz ˈlɪps/
Personally speaking *phr* /ˌpɜːsnəli ˈspiːkɪŋ/
put (your) heart and soul into sth *expr* /ˌpʊt (jɔː) ˌhɑːt ən ˈsəʊl ˌɪntə/
raise eyebrows *expr* /ˌreɪz ˈaɪbraʊz/
seventh heaven *expr* /ˌsevnθ ˈhevn/
so to speak *phr* /ˌsəʊ tə ˈspiːk/
so-called *adj* /ˌsəʊ ˈkɔːld/
soul mate *n* /ˈsəʊl ˌmeɪt/
Speaking of *expr* /ˈspiːkɪŋ əv/
star-struck *adj* /ˈstɑː ˌstrʌk/
tabloid *adj* /ˈtæblɔɪd/
thank sb from the bottom of (your) heart *expr* /ˈθæŋk ... frəm ðə ˌbɒtəm əv (jɔː) ˈhɑːt/
That said *expr* /ˌðæt ˈsed/
(in / out of) the public eye *expr* /ˌ(ɪn, aʊt) əv ðə ˌpʌblɪk ˈaɪ/
turn heads *expr* /ˌtɜːn ˈhedz/

Use your head! *expr* /ˈjuːz jɔː ˈhed/
wait on sb hand and foot *expr* /ˌweɪt ɒn ... ˌhænd ən ˈfʊt/
You scratch my back and I'll scratch yours *expr* /juː ˌskrætʃ ˈmaɪ ˌbæk ən ˌaɪl ˈskrætʃ ˈjɔːz/

Unit 4

a complete nightmare *expr* /ə kəmˌpliːt ˈnaɪtmeə/
affiliation *n* /əˌfɪliˈeɪʃn/
bank balance *n* /ˈbæŋk ˌbæləns/
beware of sb (+ -ing) *phr* /bɪˈweər əv .../ *
bill *n* /bɪl/ ***
burst *v* /bɜːst/ **
clean out *v* /ˌkliːn ˈaʊt/
close *v* /kləʊz/ ***
con-artist *n* /ˈkɒn ˌɑːtɪst/
consider (+ -ing) *phr* /kənˈsɪdə/ ***
counterfeit *adj* /ˈkaʊntəfɪt/
criminal record *n* /ˌkrɪmɪnl ˈrekɔːd/
current account *n* /ˌkʌrənt əˈkaʊnt/
default on *v* /dɪˈfɒlt ˌɒn/
deposit *v* /dɪˈpɒzɪt/ **
endanger *v* /ɪnˈdeɪndʒə/
file-sharing program *n* /ˈfaɪl ˌʃeərɪŋ ˌprəʊɡræm/
financial fraud *n* /faɪˌnænʃl ˈfrɔːd/
get sth (all) sorted out *phr* /ˌget ... (ˌɔːl) ˌsɔːtɪd ˈaʊt/
go undetected *phr* /ˌɡəʊ ˌʌndɪˈtektɪd/
hack (into) *v* /ˈhæk (ˌɪntə)/ *
high-occupancy *adj* /ˌhaɪ ˈɒkjʊpənsi/
high-ranking *adj* /ˌhaɪ ˈræŋkɪŋ/
I should have thought (that) *phr* /aɪ ˈʃʊd həv ˌθɔːt (ðət)/
I'm convinced (that) *phr* /aɪm kənˈvɪnst (ðət)/
I've come to the conclusion (that) *phr* /aɪv ˌkʌm tə ðə kənˌkluːʒn (ðət)/
I've no doubt at all (that) *phr* /aɪv ˌnəʊ ˌdaʊt ət ˌɔːl (ðət)/
identity theft *n* /aɪˈdentəti ˌθeft/
illegitimate *adj* /ˌɪləˈdʒɪtəmət/
impoverished *adj* /ɪmˈpɒvərɪʃt/
inflatable *adj* /ɪnˈfleɪtəbl/
interest *n* /ˈɪntrəst/ ***
it is recommended (that) *phr* /ˌɪt ɪz rekəˈmendɪd (ðət)/
lane *n* /leɪn/ **
loan *n* /ləʊn/ ***
motive *n* /ˈməʊtɪv/ **
one simple way to prevent sb / sth (+ -ing / being + past part) *phr* /ˌwʌn ˌsɪmpl ˌweɪ tə prɪˌvent/
online banking *n* /ˌɒnlaɪn ˈbæŋkɪŋ/
pass (sb / sth / yourself) (off) as (sb / sth) *expr* /ˌpɑːs ... (ˈɒf) əz/
pay off *v* /ˌpeɪ ˈɒf/
phishing *n* /ˈfɪʃɪŋ/
pose as *v* /ˈpəʊz əz/
precaution *n* /prɪˈkɔːʃn/ *
pull off the stunt *expr* /ˌpʊl ɒf ðə ˌstʌnt/
purport *v* /pəˈpɔːt/
safe *n* /seɪf/ *
security *n* /sɪˈkjʊərəti/ ***
spyware *n* /ˈspaɪweə/
take care (not) to (+ inf) *phr* /teɪk ˌkeə (nɒt) tə/
take out *v* /ˌteɪk ˈaʊt/
telemarketer *n* /ˈteliˌmɑːkətə/
transfer *v* /trænsˈfɜː/ ***
valuables *n pl* /ˈvæljʊblz/
(I) wasn't / weren't born yesterday *expr* /(aɪ) ˌwɒznt, ˈwɜːnt ˌbɔːn ˈjestədeɪ/
withdraw *v* /wɪðˈdrɔː/ **

Communication activities

Unit 1, Language study Ex 5 page 36

Top ten annoying habits that can get nasty.

1 Fabricating anecdotes
2 Public use of pet names
3 Taking excessive volumes of luggage on holiday
4 Making your partner spend far longer than they want shopping
5 Laughing at your own jokes when others do not
6 Complaining about or not being interested in your partner's clothes
7 Changing the controls on the car stereo
8 Stealing chips from your partner's plate
9 Spending too long on the computer or playing computer games
10 Leaving clothes lying around

(Based on research by Louisville University, Kentucky)

Unit 2, Lead-in Ex 2 page 38

Dolly the sheep was the first mammal to be cloned. She was cloned from adult cells at a research institute in Scotland in 1996. Dolly later reproduced several offspring of her own through normal means. Scientists claimed cloning animals would allow them to reliably reproduce genetically modified animals for farming purposes and even to provide organs for use in humans. However, it was claimed that Dolly suffered from premature ageing and arthritis, and although many other animals have since been cloned, the process is risky and can lead to deformity. Dolly died in 2003.

Unit 2, Vocabulary and pronunciation Ex 4 page 41

Student A

Look at these conversation openers. Choose one and role-play a conversation with student B. Continue the conversation as long as possible. If the conversation runs out, pick another opener – or think of your own.

a I got a phone call today from somebody I haven't seen for five years.
b I saw your boyfriend / girlfriend kissing somebody else.
c We haven't got any milk.
d Real Madrid have won the Champion's League.

Unit 3, Listening and speaking Ex 7 page 42

Read the rolecard and act out the role-play.

Rolecard

You feel very nostalgic for your childhood and school years. In your room you have lots of momentos and photos that remind you of happy days in the past. You like to watch DVDs of TV programmes and films that you grew up with, and you keep in touch with lots of friends from school, although you have moved to a new city to go to college.

You share a flat with another student who has also moved away from home but is very happy to make a clean break. This evening your flatmate wants to go to a film with you, but you'd rather stay in with your DVDs and your photos.

First make a list of reasons why nostalgia and reminiscing are a good thing. Then answer your flatmate's accusations.

Unit 4, Speaking Ex 1 page 49

Group A

You are members of your town council. You have decided to introduce CCTV cameras in the town centre in an attempt to reduce the high crime rate.

1 First decide how many cameras you need, where you will place the cameras and what result you hope this will have.
2 You are at a meeting with the Town Centre Residents' Association. Role-play the meeting. Start off by presenting your ideas, then listen to and respond to the concerns of the residents.
3 Come to an agreement with the Residents' Association.

Listening scripts

Unit 1 Telling tales

🔘 Listening script 13
Reading text from page 35

💿 Listening script 14

He survived the minute only to find that the clock had begun another. And then he knew, with a sense of furious sadness, that this would be followed by another minute, and another, and throughout each one he would be like he was now, only worse.

He wrote to Catherine. *Please come back to me. I want you. I am sober.*

He dropped the letter off in Corrloch and went into O'Malley's bar and bought a bottle of vodka. He walked across the fields with the dog and lay down on the old bed.

The skipper met him on the road as he was setting off for Corrloch.

'Jack,' he said. 'Have you finished with the writing?'

'I think so.'

'Good, I need you out on the blue.'

'When?'

'Tomorrow. We could get in a couple of weeks before the storms. The forecast is good.'

He would have refused but could not. De Largey came for him in a car. They drove down the valley in silence. They went to sea for two weeks after the flatfish. It was a sober, spiritual time.

💿 Listening script 15

He was standing one morning by the skipper in the wheelhouse. On the radio, various voices of other fishermen were cajoling, complaining, cursing, talking of the forthcoming storms. Their voices were always in the background, and sometimes the sound of the radio would drown out the sound of the sea. Then suddenly Jack heard Catherine's voice.

'Calling the *Blue Cormorant*.'

The strange feeling of her personality at the end of the radio unnerved him. Each nuance was hers and yet not hers. She was present in the small engine room in a disembodied way, full of tact, irony, and sounding genteel.

'That's for you, I'll warrant,' said the skipper.

'That's Catherine,' said Jack, disbelievingly.

'Jack,' she said. 'Are you there?'

'Jack Ferris here. Over.'

'When will you be coming in?'

'Friday at eight. Over.'

'Oh, that's a pity. Did you get my letters?'

Jack looked around and whispered into the mike: 'No. Over.'

'That's strange. You should have had them by now.'

'They haven't arrived, Catherine. Over.'

'You don't sound like yourself.'

'Neither do you. Over.'

'Have you been drinking?'

'No,' he lied. 'Over.'

'Well, that's wonderful. You sound very business-like. Over.'

'Under the circumstances, so would you. Over.'

'Am I embarrassing you?'

Her voice, filled with static, cut through the quiet, while the boat drifted in a calm east wind on a sea that was suddenly without landmarks, on a day that could have belonged to any of the seasons, in a sea that could have been any sea.

'I've made my mind up what to do. I'm sure you'll be glad to know.'

'You have? Tell me. Over.'

The radio gave a hoarse crackle. A whistle blew. A sound like a strimmer went through the airwaves.

'What did you say? Can you please repeat the message, Catherine? Over.'

'I'll be down next weekend. I'll leave a letter in the house.'

'See you then. Over.'

'Goodbye, Jack. Over.'

'Goodbye, Catherine. Over.'

He threw open the door of the light-keeper's house. He stepped into the hallway and found the letter for which he had prepared himself waiting inside the hall door. Then his heart began its furious beat. He kissed the damp envelope and tore it open. *It was good to hear your voice. I hope you remember your promise to me. We must stay sober. And I have to admit I'm also fighting off wretched imaginings that someone else will be enjoying you in my place – but I'm trusting you, treading thin ice in the hope that someday we'll be skating along without fear.*

I love you.

His world had been magically restored. The nightmare was over.

Jack, she had written. *I love you and want to be with you. We have a break this weekend and I'll be down to see you. There are other people and we could be with them. But we know we want to be with each other. Let's grow old and sober together.*

He saw himself waiting on the bridge the following afternoon. He saw her alight from the car and begin running towards him. Overcome with happiness he sat there in the December dusk. The bark of a dog flew by.

Unit 2 A perfect world

🔘 Listening script 16
Reading text from page 39

💿 Listening script 17
(Z = Zoe, E = Ellie)

Z: What's all that noise? ... Ellie, it's 2 o'clock in the morning. Why on earth are you hoovering the living room now?

E: Oh, sorry Zoe. I didn't mean to wake you up. It's just, well, you know my mum's coming tomorrow and I want everything to look tidy.

Z: You're kidding me, aren't you? You're hoovering at 2 o'clock in the morning just because your mum's coming. Who cares if there's a bit of dust?

E: You haven't met my mum yet, have you? She's got a thing about cleaning and everything being tidy. As soon as she gets through the door, she'll look how clean everywhere is. She'll be peering in the fridge and the oven and checking out the bathroom ...

Z: Yeah, but so what? I mean we're students, she won't expect everything to be perfect.

E: Well, actually that's where you're wrong. My mum's a perfectionist, she likes everything to be in its proper place and she's really fussy about everything she does. She even irons socks!

Z: Are you having me on? How can you iron socks? ... It certainly sounds like she expects a lot from people! But it doesn't mean you have to worry about it. You've left home now, this is your place, not hers.

E: Yeah, I know, it's stupid. Perhaps I'm more like my mum than I imagined. What a horrible thought!

Z: Mm, now I think about it, you're a bit of a perfectionist yourself. I mean, you're totally organised. All your CDs are in alphabetic order and your shoes together in neat rows.

E: OK, OK, I know I'm strange like that. But at least I'm not as bad as my mum. She can't stand other people not living up to her standards and when people do things wrong – well!

Z: Mm. Your mum sounds lovely, I'm really looking forward to meeting her!

E: Oh, she's OK deep down. ... Listen, sorry, I woke you. I know you've got to get up early tomorrow.

Z: Oh, it doesn't matter, I'll put the alarm on ... see you in the morning.

E: Yeah, 'night. ... I think I'll just clean the fridge before I go to bed ...

Z: Whatever. Just do it quietly!

💿 Listening script 18
Vocabulary and pronunciation Ex 3 from page 41.

Unit 3 Modern-day icons

💿 Listening script 19
(I = interviewer, S = Shawn)

I: Oh my gosh, Shawn, you know, it's been about a year since we saw each other last and you were on your way to perform in Switzerland. Yeah, I want you to tell me about that experience. Did you know you would be singing for thirty-six thousand screaming fans before you got there?

S: Had no idea. You know, a lot of us were ... we didn't even know what to expect, you know what I mean, going to a different country, as they say, you know, there's different cultures and there's different this and there's different that, I think that the strongest thing that we found out is that music is ... is a powerful tool. And it's funny how you can go over there and throw this music at kids who are, you know, 12, 14, 18 years old and it just, you know, blew their minds, and it blew our minds because it just goes to show how strong and universal music really is, and you know it's a tool that is very, very, powerful and ...

I: And how universal Elvis is ...

S: That's ... yeah that was my next point. For a man to be away and out of the public eye, so to speak, physically, let's say, but how he still goes on and on and on, and it's funny. We brought that show over there and we were backstage and we'd gotten there and, you know, we were nervous to begin with, so we kinda peeked out at the crowd and boy, I looked out at that crowd and my knees liked to buckle, I just went, whoa, wait a minute, it was something to be sought after, something I'll never forget. Hopefully I'll get a chance to go back there. The people in Switzerland are incredible.

I: They love this. You're bringing them closer to the king, it … really… you were there, if you missed it the first time round, you're getting it the second time around. You know, it's wonderful.

S: I really appreciate that. We really try to work hard and, I've said it before and I'll say it again, he had impact, impact, impact. And again for a guy like that to have an effect on the world, and I mean that, the world. When you go over to Switzerland and, you know, they're singing stuff like *In the Ghetto* back to you and, it's like, man, you know, we're how many thousands of miles away from the States and … just amazing, amazing. You know, I'm not necessarily saying I'm filling anybody's shoes, because Lord knows I couldn't do that. God puts special individuals on this earth for a certain reason. He put both hands on Elvis, I swear, you know, unbelievable.

I: Well, you're an inspiration to everyone who wants to pay tribute to him, no matter what their capacity.

S: I appreciate that, to everybody out there who feels that way, you know, I'm trying everything to uphold it, you know, an image is a hard thing to keep up.

🔘 Listening script 20

1 last
2 chance
3 gosh
4 everybody
5 world
6 work
7 there
8 swear

🔘 Listening script 21

Pronunciation Ex 2 from page 43

Unit 4 Safe and sound?

🔘 Listening script 22

Reading text from page 47

🔘 Listening script 23

(P = presenter, J = Jody, N = Naseem, L = Lily, A = Alvin)

P: Hello and welcome to *Young Britain*. Today we're looking at the question of video surveillance. According to statistics from Liberty, the UK human rights and civil liberties organisation, Britain is monitored by over 4 million CCTV cameras, making us the most-watched nation in the world. The government claims CCTV prevents crime and helps detect criminals after crimes have taken place. However, some people object to constantly being caught on camera. They think it's an infringement of their civil liberties. So, let's hear what you think. Let's take our first caller … Jody from Sheffield. Hello, Jody.

J: Hello, …er, well, I just want to say that I definitely support having cameras everywhere. I've felt a lot safer in my area, particularly at night, since we've had cameras … and er I'm convinced they help stop people from committing crimes. You know, if their faces are gonna be on camera, then people think twice about doing something illegal. There used to be a lot of problems on our estate, you know,

like drug dealing and mugging, and now the situation's got a lot better. I don't think that could have happened without CCTV.

P: OK, thanks Jody. And I have to say Jody's opinion does reflect that of the public at large. Most people firmly believe that video surveillance has made them feel safer. … Right, on to our next caller. And it's Naseem from Birmingham.

N: Hi, … you know, what I don't understand is why everyone is so positive about these cameras. I mean, it's just harassment, right? … My mate was charged with a crime he didn't commit when there was a break-in at our local supermarket. The CCTV images were so unclear it could have been anybody. But they marched my mate off to the police station because he's got a police record and said he matched the person on the film.

P: And what happened then?

N: Well, it turned out he was at work when the break-in happened, didn't it? Just like he'd been saying all along. People are supposed to be innocent until proved guilty, aren't they?

P: OK, Naseem, thanks for that. Well, looking at the statistics, there have been a considerable number of misidentifications due to poor-quality images but the technology is improving all the time. Our next caller is Lily from Oxford. Hello Lily.

L: Hello. Well, I should have thought privacy ought to be the main issue here. These cameras are totally in-your-face everywhere you go. You don't know who's watching through these cameras and what they do with the film they take. Remember the case last week? The camera operators were using a camera to spy on a woman in her bathroom, taking pictures of her in the shower. I've come to the conclusion that we can't be expected to have faith in video surveillance, you know, when things like that happen.

P: Well to be quite honest, Lily, how often does something like that happen? I mean, isn't it the case that if you've got nothing to fear, then why let the cameras bother you?

L: Well, I've got nothing to hide, but it's the basic principle, isn't it? Why should we accept people spying on us?

P: OK, Lily, let's turn that question over to the next caller and that's Alvin from London. Hello Alvin. How would you answer Lily's question?

A: Well, she's obviously never been in a situation like I have. I was mugged last month in broad daylight, out on the street, you know, on a Saturday afternoon. This guy just hit me in the face and took my mobile. The streets were packed but there no witnesses because there was so much going on and it was all over so quickly.

P: But the crime was caught on camera?

A: That's right. And two weeks later, they got the guy that did it. So I've no doubt at all that we need CCTV.

P: OK, thanks Alvin. We'll take a break now and then be right back. And if you want to call in with your opinion, remember our number is 021 …

Unit 5 Review

🔘 Listening script 24

(B = Ben, A = Anna)

B: … and I think she's fantastic. All her films have been just brilliant.

A: You know it never ceases to amaze me just how much all these Hollywood stars get paid

for a film. I think it's disgusting. I mean, 20 or 30 million dollars for just a few weeks' work. It just seems to be getting more and more ridiculous. Don't you think?

B: Well, yes, but the films do earn a vast amount, so as a percentage of the earnings the star's fee is probably not that great. And without a big name, the film wouldn't do nearly as well. That said, I do agree that it's maybe getting a little out of hand. And footballers too, getting, like, £150,000 a week! Now that *is* crazy.

A: Yeah. And another thing that really annoys me is all the ludicrous things that these stars spend their money on. You know, stuff like gold-plated bathroom taps, million-dollar barbecue sets, bottles of wine that cost thousands, diamond-studded collars for their irritating little pet dogs and so on.

B: Yes, I have to say it can be pretty gross. But as they say, if you've got it, flaunt it.

A: Speaking of 'flaunting it', did you see those hideous pictures the other day of what's-her-name from that girl band's wedding, you know, the one that's just married that footballer. They got paid a million, or so they say, by some celebrity magazine, just for a few wedding snaps. It's madness. And I read that Elton John actually turned down $6 million to have his wedding televised in the States. But what I don't understand is who on earth is remotely interested enough in all that stuff to warrant the magazines paying such an obscene amount. After all, they're just pictures.

B: I agree, but the right one on the front cover of, let's say, *Hello!* magazine, or something like that, can boost sales massively. I think I remember reading somewhere that the issue with David Beckham's wedding sold three times the normal amount.

A: And the paparazzi – they're just as bad. They've got no real career of their own, so they just make a living out of other people's success. It's the fact that they can get tens of thousands of pounds just for taking dodgy snaps of someone doing their shopping or walking down the street that gets me. And if you ask me, I think the celebrities themselves are behind all this paparazzi stuff a lot of the time. You know, as a way of keeping themselves in the spotlight and on their terms. They might pretend they don't like it, but I wouldn't be surprised if most of the tip-offs come from the celebs themselves.

B: Mm, not sure about that. But as I was saying, I suppose any publicity is good publicity.

A: Well, I suppose so, but what I'd really like to know is who on earth buys these magazines. You always see them in dentists' waiting rooms and such places, but who is actually sad enough to go to the shops to buy a copy?

B: Erm, well …

A: Don't say you buy them, please. … Erm, well if you do, you wouldn't happen to have the latest issue of *Hello!* would you? Apparently, there's a really good feature on ….

🔘 Listening script 25

Song from page 52

Communication activities

Unit 2, Vocabulary and pronunciation Ex 4 page 41

Student B

Look at these conversation openers. Choose one and role-play a conversation with student A. Continue the conversation as long as possible. If the conversation runs out, pick another opener – or think of your own.

a   It's going to rain later.
b   I've put on a kilo.
c   The TV is broken.
d   I'm moving to Argentina.

Unit 3, Listening and speaking Ex 7 page 42

Read the rolecard and act out the role-play.

Rolecard

You are very forward-looking. You prefer to turn your back on the old and get on with the new. As soon as your possessions have outworn practical importance, you throw them away – no point in keeping useless clutter, and you certainly don't keep photo albums.

You are getting increasingly irritated with your flatmate who tends to dwell on the past. This evening you wanted to go to a new film but your flatmate has just said he / she wants to stay in and watch DVDs of old TV series.

First make a list of arguments against nostalgia and living in the past. Role-play the conversation with your flatmate, letting out all your frustration about his / her backward-looking tendencies.

Start like this:

You're not going to watch those old series again? How many times have you seen them now? If I were you ...

Unit 3, Reading and speaking Ex 2 page 45

Quiz score and analysis

Score:

–1 point if you answered 'yes' to questions 4, 6, 9, 15
+1 point if you answered 'yes' to questions 1, 3, 13, 14
+3 points if you answered 'yes' to questions 5, 7, 11, 16
+5 points if you answered 'yes' to questions 2, 8, 10, 12

Analysis:

–4 to 0   You don't give a damn about famous people.

1–10   You find celebrities entertaining, a harmless diversion from dreary everyday reality. This is a harmless level and a healthy emotion.

11–19   Identifying with famous people is natural. But you are overly preoccupied with the lives of the stars and it is probably starting to impinge on your own social life and other interests. Watch out.

20+   You're obsessed with celebrity culture and perhaps overidentify with a single famous person. This could be harmful to your own health – and perhaps to others.

Unit 4, Speaking Ex 1 page 49

Group B

You are the Town Centre Residents' Association for your town. You would like to see crime reduced in your neighbourhood but are sceptical that cameras will achieve this and worried about residents' privacy.

1   First formulate your worries and arguments against cameras.
2   You are at a meeting with members of the council to hear about the CCTV scheme. Listen to the arguments of the council, then ask questions and present your counter-arguments.
3   Come to an agreement with the town council.

Module 3
Groups

Unit	Topic	Language study	Vocabulary	Main skills
1 Living together pages 66–69	• Happy families (Britain's biggest family) • A social experiment (living in an alternative community)	• Ellipsis and substitution	• Family relationships • Community organisation	• **Reading:** understanding gist; understanding vocabulary in context • **Speaking:** discussing cultural values and family relationships; discussing the aims of non-traditional living communities • **Listening:** identifying key information • **Writing:** an online advert
2 Talk talk pages 70–73	• World languages (Are fewer languages better?) • Language learning (attitudes to learning English and other foreign languages)	• Forming adjectives from verbs and nouns (adjective suffixes)	• Sensitive language (euphemisms)	• **Reading:** predicting; understanding main information and vocabulary in context • **Speaking:** evaluating the cultural and practical value of languages; using sensitive language and softeners to avoid offence • **Listening:** identifying key information • **Pronunciation:** sentence stress
3 Net value pages 74–77	• Is the Internet a good thing? • Are you addicted to email? (survey report)	• Using vague language	• Phrasal verbs: communication • Surveys	• **Listening:** understanding gist and key information; understanding vocabulary in context • **Speaking:** discussing the Internet; clarifying information and checking understanding; talking about email addiction; conducting a survey • **Pronunciation:** stress and weak forms • **Reading:** understanding key information • **Writing:** a survey report
4 Team spirit pages 78–81	• Team building • Are you a team player?	• Dependent prepositions	• World of work	• **Reading:** predicting information; checking key information and vocabulary in context • **Speaking:** discussing work practices and leadership styles; describing college- or work-related problems and giving advice • **Listening:** identifying key information; understanding vocabulary in context • **Writing:** a programme script

1 Living together

> **LEARNING AIMS**
>
> - Can use ellipsis and substitution
> - Can discuss cultural values and family relationships
> - Can discuss the aims of non-traditional living communities

Lead-in **1** Discuss these questions with your class.

1 What do you associate with the word 'family'? Brainstorm ideas.
2 What different types of 'family' are there?
3 Is it possible to be a 'family' without having children?

Happy families

Reading and vocabulary

1 Work with a partner and discuss these questions.

1 What do you think the fertility rate (the average number of births per woman) is in your country? Is there a tendency towards having more or fewer children?
2 Do you think small or large families are the norm in Britain? Compare your ideas with the fertility rate on page 93.

2 🔊 **01** Read the article on page 67. Answer these questions.

1 How do Sue and Ian Povey feel about having so many children?
2 How do they feel about having even more children?
3 How do their daughters Becky and Charlotte feel about having children?

3 Find the following sentences in paragraphs 4 and 6 of the article and discuss the meaning of the expressions in **bold**.

1 We're very **close**.
2 All the children **muck in**.
3 We both **devote our lives to** the children.
4 As soon as he walks through the door he is **hands on**.
5 He **suffers in silence**.
6 If anybody is **out of line**, she doesn't need to **lose her temper** – she just **gives them a look**.

4 Work with a partner. Which of the words and phrases in Ex 3 have very positive / positive / rather negative / very negative meanings? Make lists.

5 Add these words and phrases to your lists. Use a dictionary to help you.

1 he really **resents** his little brother
2 they never stop **squabbling**
3 she has **the patience of a saint**
4 they **get on like a house on fire**
5 he **neglects** his children
6 she's always **nagging** us
7 we **stick up for** each other
8 there's a lot of **give and take**

6 Work with a partner. Talk about your family or a family you know well.

1 Are you a close family?

2 As children did you have to muck in and help out? In what ways?

3 Was your father a hands-on parent or more of an authority figure?

4 What did your parents do when you were out of line?

5 Do you ever lose your temper in family situations? When?

Britain's biggest brood

SUPERMUM Sue Povey smiled after giving birth to her 15th baby and said: 'I'm not finished yet – I'm already looking forward to sweet sixteen.' Sue, 43, was speaking after taking baby Isabelle home from hospital. She said: 'I just feel so happy and elated. I think having babies keeps me young. It's like a drug. I'm a babyaholic. I definitely want another one – I knew that in my heart the moment the midwife gave me Isabelle to hold.'

Since Sue first gave birth 23 years ago she has never gone more than two years and three months without doing so. She and husband Ian, 45, now have nine girls and six boys. The couple celebrate their 25th wedding anniversary later this year and live with 13 of their children.

Ian, a systems analyst, said, 'Sue said she wanted six children soon after we were married. I thought she was being a bit ambitious and put it down to wishful thinking. We started off with a six-a-side team, then a football 11 and now we have a rugby 15. But I'm really pleased. Even after having 15 children you still experience the same strength of feeling – a new birth is always exciting. The children were thrilled. They all wanted to be the first to see Isabelle and hold her. If nature has its way I'm sure Sue will have another baby. When you've had 15 I don't think another one makes much difference.'

The former hairdresser was determined that her children should have lots of brothers and sisters, simply because she herself didn't. She felt lonely as a child with just one sister, Barbara, who is 13 years older. Sue said, 'I hated being on my own all the time. I was very shy and couldn't make friends easily. I didn't want my children to feel like that. Some people don't approve of large families but I will never change my mind. We're very close. All the children muck in and help each other out. We both devote our lives to the children so they're never short of love. Ian works all day but as soon as he walks through the door he is hands on. He suffers in silence. He's a saint, as well as being a great taxi driver.'

Sue had wanted to have another baby but had almost given up hope of being able to when doctors confirmed she was expecting Isabelle. Sue said, 'I was beginning to feel my biological clock had run out of batteries. It will be absolutely awful when I can no longer have babies. It will feel like a bereavement – like part of me has died. Twins would be the icing on the cake. There's still time.'

Eldest daughter Becky, 22, said, 'Isabelle's beautiful. I'm getting broody. Fair play to mum. She's incredible.' Hairdresser Charlotte, 19, said, 'Originally I said I wasn't going to have any children but now I think I'd like two. But I'm nowhere near as patient as mum. If anybody is out of line she doesn't need to lose her temper – she just gives them a look.'

Speaking

1 Discuss these questions in groups. Then compare your opinions with another group.

1 How do people feel about large families in your country?

2 Why are women in most European countries having fewer children? What are the demographic consequences of this?

3 How should governments encourage families to have more children?

4 Read the text in the panel. What do you think are the advantages and disadvantages of very young and very old mothers? (Consider medical, economic, social and cultural factors.)

> In some countries it is usual and preferable to have children at an early age. In other countries such as the UK, there is a high rate of unwanted teenage pregnancies and many women put off having children until their thirties or forties. Due to scientific advances it is now also possible to have children past the usual childbearing age. For example, a 66-year-old Romanian woman gave birth to a child.

LANGUAGE STUDY

Ellipsis and substitution

1 Ellipsis (omitting words and phrases) and substitution (replacing words and phrases) are two ways of avoiding repeating what has been said. Which of these extracts from the text on page 67 contain examples of:

a ellipsis ☐ ☐   b substitution ☐

1 *Since Sue first gave birth 23 years ago she has never gone more than two years and three months without **doing so**.*

2 *The former hairdresser was determined that her children should have lots of brothers and sisters, simply because she herself **didn't**.*

3 *Sue had wanted to have another baby but had almost given up hope of **being able to** when doctors confirmed she was expecting Isabelle.*

2 What has been omitted or substituted in each of the extracts?

Grammar reference page 90

3 Complete these findings from a recent UK survey on marriage and the family with the verbs and phrases in the box.

> are doing so   do   not to   to do so   were

1 Despite having taken marriage vows that they will remain together for life, over a third of newly-married couples do not think it is realistic _____.

2 Almost a fifth of women say they expect to be less involved in raising their children than their mothers _____.

3 Fewer people are getting married for religious reasons, but _____ as a way of demonstrating commitment, stability and security.

4 Compared to previous generations there is less pressure to get married in your 20s, and as a result many of today's young adults are choosing _____.

5 Mothers who don't work while their children are growing up tend to get on better with their children later in life than mothers who _____.

4 Do you think the findings in Ex 3 would be similar in your country?

5 Read the text and explain what information has been omitted or substituted.

Example: (1) *take time out to go travelling* is omitted.

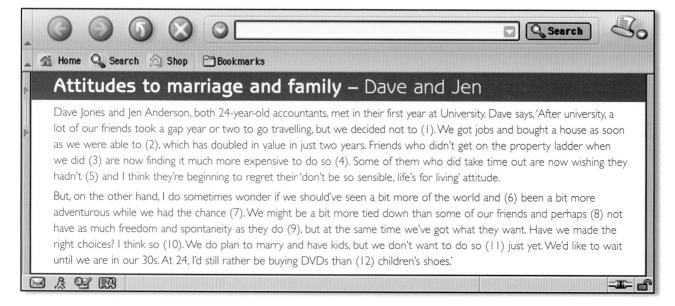

Attitudes to marriage and family – Dave and Jen

Dave Jones and Jen Anderson, both 24-year-old accountants, met in their first year at University. Dave says, 'After university, a lot of our friends took a gap year or two to go travelling, but we decided not to (1). We got jobs and bought a house as soon as we were able to (2), which has doubled in value in just two years. Friends who didn't get on the property ladder when we did (3) are now finding it much more expensive to do so (4). Some of them who did take time out are now wishing they hadn't (5) and I think they're beginning to regret their 'don't be so sensible, life's for living' attitude.

But, on the other hand, I do sometimes wonder if we should've seen a bit more of the world and (6) been a bit more adventurous while we had the chance (7). We might be a bit more tied down than some of our friends and perhaps (8) not have as much freedom and spontaneity as they do (9), but at the same time we've got what they want. Have we made the right choices? I think so (10). We do plan to marry and have kids, but we don't want to do so (11) just yet. We'd like to wait until we are in our 30s. At 24, I'd still rather be buying DVDs than (12) children's shoes.'

6 How is your attitude similar to or different from Dave and Jen's?

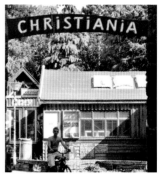

A social experiment

Listening and speaking

1 Some people choose not to live in 'mainstream' society and instead choose to live in alternative communities such as communes or housing cooperatives. Why do you think some people make this choice?

2 🔊 **02** Listen to a report on Christiania, an alternative living community in Copenhagen. As you listen, tick the things that form a part of Christiania's way of life.

art ☐   common childcare and healthcare ☐   common mealtimes ☐

common ownership of property ☐   democracy ☐   eco-friendly practices ☐

independence from Danish laws ☐   no cars ☐   no electricity or running water ☐

prayer and meditation ☐   unconventional housing ☐

3 Work with a partner and discuss these questions.

1 Opponents of Christiania see the community as 'a scourge on the city'. Why?
2 What problem was Christiania facing at the time of the report?
3 According to the report, nearly a million tourists a year visit Christiania. Why do you think so many people are interested in this alternative community?
4 The report asks the question: *Lawless, elitist and dirty? Or progressive, inventive and free?* What do you think?

Vocabulary

1 Listen to the report again and complete these sentences. Then check your answers in the listening script on page 94.

1 A motley group of hippies, artists and misfits have founded a home that **shuns** _____, _____ and _____.
2 Christiania has been **conducting** _____ for more than thirty years.
3 They have even **established** _____.
4 A group of drug-smoking criminals **trespassing** _____ and **ignoring** _____ the rest of Denmark have to obey.
5 Liberal governments in the past **adopted** _____.
6 Residents will have to **register** _____.
7 The plan seeks to **preserve** _____.
8 All the things that have made the area so special are rooted in the unique way they **administer** _____ and **prohibit** the _____.

2 Work in a group. Imagine you are setting up your own alternative community.
First brainstorm ideas you will establish:

Think about:
1 where you will establish your community and the type of housing;
2 how many people and the sort of people you want to attract;
3 your main principles (rules, prohibitions);
4 whether your community will be self-supporting or have outside financial help?

3 Write an online advert to recruit people for your community, using your ideas in Ex 1 and 2. Start like this: *We are a group of … planning to establish … . We are seeking …*

4 Read the adverts of the other groups. Comment on whether you would be attracted to their community or not, explaining your reasons.

CD-ROM   For more activities go to **Groups Unit 1**

2 Talk talk

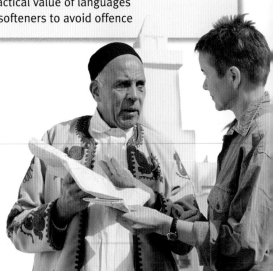

LEARNING AIMS

- Can form adjectives from verbs and nouns using suffixes
- Can evaluate the cultural and practical value of languages
- Can use sensitive language and softeners to avoid offence

World languages

Lead-in **1** Work with a partner and talk about your first language. Discuss these questions:

  1. Where is your first language spoken?
  2. What do you know about the history and development of your language?
  3. Is there a big difference between the written and spoken forms of your language?
  4. How easy or difficult is it for foreign students to learn your language?

Reading and speaking **1** How many languages are spoken in the world today? Agree on an approximate figure as a class. Then read the first two paragraphs of the article on page 71 and find out.

2 03 Read the article in full. Match these summaries to the correct paragraphs.

  a. Speaking a majority language is considered desirable by many people.
  b. Documenting endangered languages is the best way to deal with them.
  c. The number of languages spoken in a country is linked to its degree of isolation.
  d. The end of a life means the end of a language.
  e. There has been a significant change in the ratio of the world's population and the number of languages spoken, aided by communication technology.
  f. People who want to preserve languages seem unaware of the needs of their speakers in the modern world.
  g. The fact that many of the world's languages are dying is of immense concern.

3 Make a list of minority languages that you know are being used less than in the past. Where are they spoken? In what way has their usage changed?

4 Discuss these issues with the class.

  1. What do you think are the advantages of reviving a minority language? Think about issues such as culture, tourism, business, and intellectual gain.
  2. What are the problems associated with reviving a minority language? Think about organisation, finance, speakers' way of life, and national unity.
  3. On balance, do you agree with the author of the article that saving dying languages isn't actually worth all the effort?

Vocabulary **1** Look at the <u>underlined</u> phrases in these sentences from the article. How would we usually express these sentences more directly? Why do we use euphemisms like these?

  When Marie Smith-Jones <u>passes away</u> …
  It's only a matter of time before their current speakers <u>fall silent</u>.

2 Work with a partner. Rewrite these euphemisms in more direct language.
  Example: Her company had to let her go. *Her company fired her.*

  1. He's getting on a bit.
  2. She's very careful with money.
  3. His shoes have seen better days.
  4. I need to go to the bathroom.
  5. She's on the large side.
  6. They're on a low income.
  7. She's between jobs right now.
  8. He likes a tipple.

3 Match the words in Box A with the euphemisms in box B.

A	bald	dishonest	lazy	short	stupid

B	morally different	motivationally deficient	mentally challenged
	hair disadvantaged	vertically challenged	

4 What other euphemisms have you heard in English / your own language?

Example: *In English people say 'senior citizens' instead of 'old people'. In my language we say 'people in the third age' for old people.*

Are fewer languages better?

1 When Marie Smith-Jones passes away, she will take with her a small but irreplaceable piece of human culture. That's because the octogenarian from Anchorage is the last speaker of Eyak, the traditional language of her Alaskan people.

2 To Unesco – the United Nations Educational, Scientific and Cultural Organisation – language extinction is a disaster of, well, unspeakable proportions. It warns of a 'catastrophic reduction in the number of languages spoken in the world' and estimates 3,000 are 'endangered, seriously endangered, or dying.' In other words, children have stopped learning half the world's languages, and it's only a matter of time before their current speakers fall silent. Unesco calls this an 'irretrievable and tragic' development because 'language diversity' is 'one of humanity's most precious commodities.'

3 But is it really? A growing number of people are speaking a smaller number of languages, meaning that age-old obstacles to communication are collapsing. Surely this is a good thing. Michael Krauss of the University of Alaska believes that 10,000 years ago there may have been as many as 20,000 languages spoken by a total human population of perhaps 10 million. Assuming this is true, it would suggest a connection between more people and fewer languages, and between language and the technology that lets people communicate over distance.

4 That makes sense, because geographic isolation promotes linguistic diversity. A language doesn't require more than a few hundred people to sustain it, assuming they keep to themselves. Papua New Guinea is home to the highest concentration of languages anywhere – at least 820 different tongues. Unesco's report describes Papua New Guinea as 'a fitting example for other civilisations to follow.'

5 That's an odd thing to say about a country where a sizeable proportion of the population doesn't own a phone, but it's typical of the language preservationists, who apparently would like to see tribal members live in primitive bliss, preserving their exotic customs. David Crystal makes the point unwittingly in his book *Language Death* when he describes an Australian aboriginal language 'whose vocabulary provides different names for grubs (an important food source) according to the types of bush where they're found.' He's trying to say that we may become more knowledgeable about biology if we preserve and study obscure languages – but he seems oblivious to the reality that most people would rather eat a Big Mac than a fistful of beetle larvae.

6 The most important reason some languages are disappearing is precisely that their native speakers don't regard them as quite so precious. They view linguistic adaptation as a key to getting ahead. This is understandable when about half the world's population speaks one of only 10 languages and when speaking English in particular is a profitable skill.

7 Each language captures something about a way of life, and when one goes mute, it is hard not to feel a sense of loss. But maybe linguists should try to learn as much as they can about 'dying' languages before they vanish completely, rather than engage in an impracticable attempt to save them.

LANGUAGE STUDY

Forming adjectives from verbs and nouns (adjective suffixes)

1   Look at these extracts from the text on page 71. Match the examples of the suffix *-able* with the uses.

a   with verbs to make adjectives describing something that can or can't be done. ☐ ☐ ☐ ☐

b   with nouns to make adjectives describing a quality that something has. ☐ ☐

1   *When Marie Smith-Jones passes away, she will take with her a small but **irreplaceable** piece of human culture.*

2   *Language extinction is a disaster of, well, **unspeakable** proportions.*

3   *Unesco calls this an '**irretrievable** and tragic' development.*

4   *A **sizeable** proportion of the population doesn't own a phone.*

5   *We may become more **knowledgeable** about biology if we preserve and study obscure languages.*

6   *This is **understandable** when about half the world's population speaks one of only 10 languages.*

2   Which negative prefixes are used with the adjectives in the extracts? What other common negative prefixes can you use with adjectives?

Grammar reference page 90

3   Complete these sentences with an adjective ending in *-able* formed from the words in the box. You may need to use a negative prefix or change the spelling.

Example: Today, exposure to the English language is largely *unavoidable*.

advise   appreciate   ~~avoid~~   download   escape   reputation   size   value

1   It is an _____ fact, that English has become *the* language to learn.

2   English-speaking personnel are absolutely _____ for companies doing business in the UK and US as a _____ proportion of the population of these countries speaks no second language at all.

3   When travelling abroad on business, any attempt to speak in your host's language should make an _____ difference to any business relationship.

4   When choosing where to study, it is _____ to make sure the school is _____ and the teachers have recognised qualifications.

5   Another very useful way of learning a language is via the Internet, which may offer a self-study programme via _____ lessons.

4   Rephrase these sentences using an adjective ending in *-able* formed from the verb.

Example: You can't describe it. *It's indescribable.*

1   No-one could have stopped it.   4   It can't be replaced.
2   It can be justified in some cases.   5   It's difficult, but you can do it.
3   It can't be cured.   6   It can't be explained.

5   Work with a partner. Think of people and things that can be described by the adjectives in Ex 4.

6   You can also add other suffixes to nouns to form adjectives describing a quality that something or someone has. Copy the table and add each group of words to the appropriate column according to which suffix they take.

1   colour / care / meaning / use / thought / harm

2   child / snob / slug / sheep / style / fool

3   rock / dust / mist / rain / salt / room / mood / hair

4   adventure / danger / fame / number / advantage

-able	-y	-ful	-ish	-ous
sizeable				
reputable				
knowledgeable				

7   Work with a partner and add more adjectives to each group in the table. Share your ideas with the class.

Language learning

The reading material for the subject I want to study is published mainly in English so I can't get round learning the language.

I'd like to improve my employment potential.

Listening 1 What is your motivation to learn English?

2 🔘 **04** Listen to three students talking about learning English and the role of English in the world. Make notes on:
- their motivation for learning English
- their attitude to English as a *lingua franca*

> **NOTE**
>
> *lingua franca*
> a language people use to communicate when they have different first languages

▲ Tatyana   ▲ Lars   ▲ Paolo

3 Who do you agree with most? Why?

Speaking and pronunciation

1 The three speakers express strong opinions but they use particular expressions to soften those opinions in order to be polite. Listen again and complete the notes with their 'softeners'.

Tatyana: I _____ some people don't like that, but _____, I _____ think it's unavoidable.

_____ all countries should teach children English when they are small, so they find it easy to learn.

Lars: _____ I think it's sad that English has become a *lingua franca* and that other languages, you know, are dying out because English is getting more important. _____, it's practical to have one language you can speak wherever you go.

_____ that English doesn't belong to certain countries anymore. It's just everybody's world language.

Paolo: I've got _____ a problem with English as a *lingua franca*. I know English is important, _____ you can't get by without it nowadays, but I _____ think it would be better if everybody learnt more foreign languages.

But they're _____ imposing their way of life and their view of the world on other people through their language and a lot of people oppose that.

2 Check the sentences in listening script 04 on page 94. Then listen and read the sentences. Mark the sentence stress in the script by underlining the stressed words. Which of the softeners are stressed in these sentences?

3 Work with a partner. Student A look at page 93. Student B look at page 96.

CD-ROM For more activities go to **Groups Unit 2**

3 Net value

- Can use vague language in informal communication
- Can evaluate the importance and dangers of electronic media
- Can clarify information and check understanding

Lead-in

1   Work with a partner and talk about the way you use the Internet.

  1   How often do you use the Internet for communication with other people (email, chat rooms, internet telephoning, blogging)? How much do you use the Internet on your own (for example, for research, surfing, downloading podcasts)?

*spam = unwanted emails sent to large numbers of people

  2   How much spam* do you get? How much of it do you actually read?

  3   What precautions do you take to protect your computer from viruses, spyware and other downloadable threats? What tips do you have for other users?

  4   How helpful are your search results when you use a search engine?

Is the Internet a good thing?

Listening and speaking

1   Look at the photos from two adverts about the Internet. What aspects of the Internet do they represent?

2   ⊙ **05** Listen to the two adverts and check your ideas in Ex1.

Is the Internet a
good **thing**?

Is the Internet a
bad **thing**?

3   Listen again. What other good and bad aspects of the Internet do the adverts mention?

4   The adverts ask *What do you think?* Debate this question in your class.

Divide into two groups. Group A: you think the Internet is a good thing. Group B: you think the Internet is a bad thing.

- In your group, think of more arguments for your debate.
- Hold the debate in class.
- Vote to decide which opinion your class agrees with.

Listening and vocabulary

1 🔘 **06** Listen to Graham and Layla talking about the internet adverts. Summarise their views about the Internet.

2 Work with a partner. Answer these questions.

1 What does Layla think about the way the adverts <u>get</u> their message <u>across</u>?
2 Why couldn't Graham <u>figure out</u> the adverts at first?
3 What aspects of searching for information on the Internet does Graham <u>point out</u>?
4 According to Layla what does using the Internet <u>boil down to</u>?
5 What is Layla <u>getting at</u> when she summarises her view of the Internet?
6 What was Graham <u>on about</u> when he referred to the information society?

3 Listen again and check your answers in Ex 2.

4 Match the <u>underlined</u> verbs in Ex 2 with the verbs in the box. What is the difference in style between the verbs in Ex 2 and these verbs?

amount to	convey	focus on	talking about	trying to say	understand

5 Complete the sentences. Then read your sentences to a partner and comment on his / her statements.

1 I think that being successful in today's world boils down to …
2 People today are always on about …
3 What nobody has pointed out about the Internet is that …
4 What I can't figure out about computers is …
5 Getting at the truth …
6 I sometimes find it difficult to get across …

Speaking and pronunciation

1 Look at these phrases from the listening text, used to clarify or check understanding. Copy the table and put the phrases in the correct column.

~~What do you mean by …?~~   In other words, you …   Do you know what I mean? What I'm getting at is …   Are you with me?   What I mean is, …

Speaker clarification	**Speaker checking**	**Listener checking**
		What do you mean by …?

2 Add these phrases to the table in Ex 1.

So what you're trying to say is …   I suppose I'm really saying …
Do you follow?   Do you get me?
If I've understood you correctly …   To put it a different way …

3 🔘 **07** Listen to the phrases and check your answers. Then listen again and repeat. Pay attention to weak forms and stress.

4 Discuss aspects of computer and internet technology.

• Note down an opinion about three of the things in the box.
• Work with a partner. Take it in turns to give your opinion, clarifying things if necessary using the appropriate phrases in Ex 1 and 2.
• Respond to your partner's opinion, checking that you have understood by using the appropriate phrases in Ex 1 and 2.

blogging   chat rooms   internet dating   live webcams   music file sharing reliability of computer software and hardware the rapid pace of computer technology   Wikipedia and other wikis

LANGUAGE STUDY

Using vague language

1 Look at these extracts from Listening Ex 1 on page 75. What is the function of the language in **bold**?

1 *All that information **and stuff** – and it's free!*

2 *I can't imagine not having the Internet for downloading music, shopping **and whatever**.*

3 *Well, what about credit card fraud and identity theft **and that sort of thing**?*

4 *I think I read that 75% **or so** of websites are in English.*

5 *Not true. It's 50%, or 50-**ish**, anyway.*

6 *I think the Internet actually helps countries with few resources because it gives them, you know, **a kind of** platform to make their problems known.*

7 *Yeah, that's the rose-tinted view, the Internet strengthens social bonds **and all that**.*

Grammar reference page 91

2 Complete these statements about the Internet by putting the words and phrases in *italics* in an appropriate position.

Example: The computer screen has become a ∧ window into a world where reality and
unreality are getting more and more confused. *kind of* [*kind of* written above the caret]

1 I really do wonder about privacy on the Internet. When you're chatting or sending emails, how anonymous actually are you? *or whatever*

2 The danger of the Net is that you can become trapped in a vicious cycle of webpages based on webpages with reliable information becoming more and more difficult to find. *kind of*

3 Sites such as ebay are just fantastic. I get stuff from them all the time. *and the like*

4 I just love getting all those email funnies, you know, jokes, quizzes, funny pictures. *and that sort of thing*

5 It's just the best thing ever – information, people, gaming, music, shopping, and all without having to leave the room. *and so on*

6 The best thing is P2P. It's made the Net a global music collection – you think of a song and two minutes later it's on your hard drive, or MP3 player. And it doesn't cost you a cent. *sort of   or however long   or whatever*

3 Complete these sentences using an appropriate question word combined with the suffix *-ever*.

Example: I just love going out – pubs, clubs, bars, *wherever*.

1 I'll happily listen to anything – rock, pop, classical, country, opera, _____.

2 I'd love to have the chance to live abroad – the UK, USA, Japan, _____.

3 I don't care who wins the cup – Chelsea, Barcelona, AC Milan, _____.

4 I'm always up for going for a drink – afternoon, early evening, _____.

5 I'm happy studying anything in English lessons – grammar, vocabulary, reading, _____.

4 Are any of the sentences in Ex 3 true for you?

5 Work in groups. Ask and answer questions beginning with *How much / How many …? How long …? How far …?* etc and answer them using the phrases in the box.

Example:
A: *How many CDs have you got?*   **B:** *I'd say about 100 give or take.*

about   around   getting on for   give or take   -ish   in the region of
more or less   or so   or thereabouts

Reading and vocabulary

1 Look at the title of the article. What's your answer?

Are you addicted to email?

U.S. residents are so hooked on email that some check for messages in the bathroom, in church, and while driving, a survey sponsored by America Online has found. The average email user in the U.S. has (1) _____ email accounts and spends approximately (2) _____ a day reading, sending, and replying to messages, according to the survey, conducted by Opinion Research.

Email dependency is so strong for (3) _____ of survey respondents that they check their email inbox right after getting out of bed in the morning. The average user checks their inbox (4) _____ times per day, according to the survey.

(5) _____ of respondents acknowledged being so emailaholic that they can't go more than two or three days without checking for messages. That includes vacations, during which (6) _____ of respondents admitted logging in to their inbox.

Unsurprisingly, all that email activity sometimes leads to regrets. (7) _____ of the respondents indicated they would like to have the ability to retrieve a message they have sent but that hasn't been read yet.

There is as well, it seems, some attachment anxiety to sent messages. (8) _____ favoured being able to track where their messages get forwarded.

2 Work with a partner. Read the article and predict what statistics were in spaces 1–8.

3 08 Check your answers for Ex 2 on page 96. What findings surprised you the most?

4 Look at the language used in the answers to Ex 2. What other phrases do you know for referring to statistics in a survey?   Examples: *1 in 10   just over …*

5 Explain the meaning of these words and phrases from the article.

1 hooked on   2 conducted   3 average   4 respondents   5 retrieve   6 track

6 Work with a partner and discuss these questions.

1 What are you hooked on?
2 Looking at the information in the article, would you say you are an 'average' internet user?
3 How do you usually react when asked to be a respondent in a survey being conducted online or in the street?
4 What are the benefits of being able to retrieve and track email messages?

Speaking and writing

1 Work in groups and conduct your own survey about addiction. First choose one of these questions or think of your own question. Are you addicted to …

… your computer?   … text messaging?   … your MP3 player?
… shopping?   … computer games?

2 In your group, formulate your survey questions.

3 Each person in the group interviews two or three people and notes down their answers.

4 Pool your findings and write a group survey report. Use the phrases in Reading and vocabulary Ex 4 to help you, and words to express the opinions of respondents such as *approved of, agreed with*.

5 Read your report to the class. Which survey had the most interesting findings?

CD-ROM   For more activities go to **Groups Unit 3**

4 Team spirit

LEARNING AIMS

- Can use dependent prepositions
- Can discuss work practices and leadership styles
- Can describe college or work-related problems and give advice to others

Lead-in **1** What jobs can you think of where you usually work in a team? In what jobs do you often work alone? Do you prefer working in a team or working alone? Why?

Team building

Reading **1** Look at the activities in the photos on page 79. What are the people doing? Why do you think companies pay a lot of money for employees to do things like this?

2 🔊 **09** Read the article on page 79. Work with a partner and decide if the statements are true or false. Find evidence in the text to support your answers.

1 Working in a team often means working with people you wouldn't normally socialise with.

2 Team-building events usually take place at regular intervals throughout the year.

3 The most important goal of team-building events is to have a fun day out.

4 Employees should take an active part in team events.

5 It's beneficial if employees have no expectations of team events.

6 Companies usually stick to tried and tested types of activities.

7 Companies like E3 pay for the cost of team trips.

8 The effects of team-building trips are usually short-lived.

Vocabulary and speaking **1** Work with a partner. Find these phrases in the text and work out their meaning.

1 **face up to** the challenge
2 **utilise** skills
3 go in **with an open mind**
4 **participate** in tasks
5 **tackle** problems
6 **enhance** performance
7 learn to **delegate**
8 **bond** as a team

2 Put an appropriate form of the words or phrases in Ex 1 in these sentences.

1 I was determined to enjoy my new job and went in on the first day _____ .

2 I _____ really well with the other people in the office right from the start.

3 I've _____ in lots of social events with my colleagues outside work.

4 I try to _____ my experience from holiday jobs as much as possible.

5 I focus on things I find hard and then make an effort to _____ them.

6 As I'm the most junior office member everybody _____ the most menial jobs to me.

7 I've _____ the fact that I'll be making the coffee for a while!

8 The whole experience of starting work has _____ my life in lots of ways.

> Why delegate? I can do everything faster and better myself.

> I think participating in a team-building event would be great fun.

> Bonding with work colleagues isn't necessary – competition among colleagues is a good thing.

> The sort of skills you acquire while tackling problems like learning the drums are not really ones you can utilise later in your work.

3 Rate the statements in the speech bubbles: 5 for strongly agree to 1 for strongly disagree. Then explain and discuss your ratings with a partner.

4 Discuss these questions with your class.

1 Are team-building courses common in your country?
2 Is it usual to socialise with colleagues or other students outside work / study?
3 Do companies or colleges have other ways of creating team spirit in your country?

Get together

Getting up close and personal with a bunch of folks you may never be seen dead with outside work might not be what you bargained for in your career, but it's something you will probably find yourself doing – and possibly enjoying. Many employers see the annual team-building event as the makings of a tight ship in their organisation.

Normally aiming for an eclectic mixture of fun, focus and forward-vision, team awaydays are intended to be more than splattering your colleagues in paint and listening to management-speak, which has little impact on your role once back in the workplace. But can you really expect to gain more from the event than some embarrassing memories?

Well, yes, according to David Evans, chief executive of a company which specialises in improving the performance of other organisations. He feels the image of such events as an excuse for having a knees-up is outdated. 'To be frank we just don't see it today,' says Evans. 'An element of socialising and having fun is part of it, but the management team has to show a return on the investment.'

It is the employee's responsibility, of course, to contribute proactively and face up to the challenge. Caroline Barber recently completed her company's graduate management development programme. She suggests leaving your preconceptions at the door before embarking on any team event. 'Think about what you want to take back into the workplace and how you will utilise the skills learned. Go in with an open mind.'

Team-building days are great for those interested in trying something new. One of the many tasks Barber participated in was a tandem biking exercise around a forest, designed to enhance performance and expose new employees to other people across the business.

And if paint-balling is your preconceived notion of what team-building events are all about, forget it. Employees can anticipate increasingly innovative programmes which force them to tackle unusual problems. Lizzie Barrett is an accounts executive. African drumming was one activity she enjoyed with her team, but not the only one. She says, 'We did circus training last year, which meant we had to learn literally how to juggle, as well as spin plates. It made us aware of timing, control, and ultimately how to delegate, and say no!'

Digital media agency E3 is going a few hundred thousand steps further, taking its entire workforce of 30 on an all-expenses trip to Dubai. Joint managing director Mike Bennett says, 'We give people their own time and space to do with whatever they want but plan several team activities around them. For example, we try to make sure we all eat together of an evening, go on a tour together and, in the case of Dubai, go sea-fishing together.'

Joe Thorne was on E3's last event to Las Vegas. 'As a recent graduate I found the whole experience extremely beneficial,' he says. 'We all partied together and recovered with hangovers from hell around the pool. We bonded massively as a team. But this didn't stop after we touched down at Heathrow Airport. Far from it – the buzz, the memories and the experience lasted for months.'

LANGUAGE STUDY

Dependent prepositions

1 You need to use a particular preposition after many verbs, nouns and adjectives. Look at these extracts from the text on page 79 and identify which of the phrases in bold are:

1 verb + preposition 2 noun + preposition 3 adjective + preposition

a Many employers see the annual team-building event as the (1) **makings of** a tight ship in their organisation.

b Normally (2) **aiming for** an eclectic (3) **mixture of** fun, focus and forward-vision, team awaydays are intended to be more than (4) **splattering** your colleagues **in** paint and listening to management-speak, which has little (5) **impact on** your role once back in the workplace.

c Well, yes, according to David Evans, chief executive of a company which (6) **specialises in** improving the performance of other organisations.

d Team bonding exercises are not just an (7) **excuse for** having a company knees-up.

e One of the many tasks Barber (8) **participated in** was a tandem biking exercise.

f It made us (9) **aware of** timing, control, and ultimately how to delegate, and say no!

g Team-building days are great for those (10) **interested in** trying something new.

2 When a verb, noun or adjective + preposition is followed by a verb, what form does that verb usually take?

Grammar reference page 91

3 Complete these questions using the correct preposition from those given.

Example: *What are you responsible for at work?*

1	What are you responsible		at work?
2	Do you specialise	about	anything at work?
3	How much holiday are you entitled	for	each year?
4	Did you find it difficult to adapt	from	your job when you first started?
5	Is your job in any way different	in	how you imagined it would be?
6	Is your work compatible	into	studying?
7	Do you ever have to translate things	of	or from English at work?
8	Do you ever get fed up	to	your job?
9	What aspects	with	your job are the most difficult?
10	What are the best and worst things		your job?

4 Think about your job or a job you've had (this could be a part-time or weekend job). Work in groups and discuss some of the questions in Ex 3. If you have never had a job, find someone who has and ask them the questions.

5 Complete these newspaper headlines by adding the correct preposition.

1 New search engine to focus _____ teenage market

2 Eligibility _____ citizenship depends _____ wealth says report

3 FIFA suspicious _____ nil-nil draw

4 Area equivalent _____ that of UK destroyed every year

5 Moonbase agreement _____ US and Europe reached

6 Software giant split _____ two separate entities

7 Car manufacturers forced to comply _____ new emission rules

8 Lack _____ support blamed _____ club's bankruptcy

Are you a team player?

Listening

1 What happens if somebody has a problem at your place of work or study? What problems are common? How can they be tackled?

2 🔘 **10** Listen to the radio programme. Where do Maria and Ethan work? What are their problems?

3 Listen again. How do Maria and Ethan introduce their problem? What phrases do they use to express dissatisfaction? Complete the extracts from the programme.

Maria:

1 _____ I work with someone who is always really rude when I ask a question or make a suggestion.

2 Her whole attitude is one of non-cooperation and I've _____ of it.

3 I'm _____ all the friction. It's really _____.

Ethan:

1 I'd like _____ with my new supervisor. She's determined to _____.

2 She constantly has to know my whereabouts … I think she's _____.

3 It's put me _____. I can't afford to leave … but I _____.

4 Which of these things are advice to Maria and which to Ethan? Look at listening script 10 on page 95 and decide. Then underline the phrases Liz uses to give advice.

1 Have you tried approaching your colleague directly?

2 Then if nothing changes, you should think about going to the company's legal department.

3 And rather than making assumptions or placing blame, I recommend you begin the conversation by asking questions.

4 You don't have to meet with her alone; ask her manager or someone from the personnel department to be present.

5 If you're willing to talk with this person – and I think you should do so – then, it's a good idea to consider an approach that won't put your colleague on the defensive.

6 Talking away from your work environment might help.

7 My advice is, speak to her and ask her about the issues she has with you.

5 What do you think of Liz's advice? What would you have suggested? Tell the class.

Writing

1 Work in groups. Write your own 'Dear Liz' phone-in about difficult colleagues. Make up characters and problems. Use the language in Listening Ex 3 and 4.

2 Give your programme to another group to act out to the class. Which programme was most interesting / entertaining / useful / …?

Speaking

1 Are you a team player or a leader? Do the quiz on page 93. Then ask and answer the questions with a partner and note down your partner's answers.

2 Check your partner's score on page 96. Then discuss the results with your partner.

3 Look at the phrases in **bold** from the quiz analysis. Discuss their meaning with the class. Then work with a partner and answer the questions.

1 Do you like to **take the initiative** or prefer others to take it?

2 Is it important for you to **seek approval**?

3 Do you **confront conflict** or avoid it?

4 Do you **have high expectations** of yourself?

5 Do you think it's important that people **realise their potential**?

6 Do you prefer to **implement decisions** or make them?

CD-ROM For more activities go to **Groups Unit 4**

5 Review

Lead-in   1   Discuss these questions.

1   What type of music is coming into fashion and going out of fashion?

2   What are the most popular types of music among people of different ages, such as teenagers, 30-somethings, your parents' generation?

3   Who is your favourite music group or artist? Work in pairs and tell each other about the following:

- the kind of music they play
- the group's line-up
- when you first heard them
- why you like them
- if you have ever seen them or if you think you ever will
- how often and when you tend to listen to them
- your favourite song or album by them
- if they remind you of a particular person, place or time

Speaking

I'd say …

What it boils down to …

I suppose you can say …

What I mean is …

What do you mean by …?

As far as I'm concerned …

So what you're saying is …

1   Look at the attributes of a music group in Box A. Match them with adjectives in Box B that can be used to describe them.

A

- appearance and image
- lifestyle and attitude
- live performance
- lyrics
- voice / singing
- music
- musicians and musicianship

B

captivating, charismatic, colourful, danceable, dynamic, emotive, extravagant, glamourous, inimitable, inspirational, irreplaceable, meaningful, mellow, memorable, noisy, obscure, original, outlandish, outrageous, relatable, reputable, skilful, soulful, talented, unpredictable, upbeat

2   Work in groups. Discuss what makes a good music group and rank the attributes in Ex 1 in order of importance. Add your own ideas if you wish.

- Use examples of groups you know and the adjectives above to illustrate your ideas.
- You can use the phrases in the speech bubbles in your discussion to explain your viewpoint and to clarify understanding of other people's ideas.

3   Present and explain the final ranking of your group to the class.

You are what you listen to

1 Work with a partner and discuss these questions.

1 What kinds of music do you think the people in the pictures listen to?
2 Does your appearance reflect the kind of music you listen to? Has it ever done so?
3 What do you think a person's taste in music says about them?

2 **11** Research has shown a connection between the music someone likes and their personality type. Listen to the first part of a radio programme and answer these questions.

1 Who was the research conducted by?
2 How many people participated in the survey?
3 What was the key element of the research?
4 What did the research reveal about people who listen to:
   a classical music?   b pop and chart music?   c rap and hip-hop?
5 In what way is there more to listening to music than just enjoying it?
6 What can be central to many people's way of life?

3 **12** Listen to the second part of the radio programme. What does the interviewer say about:
a people who organise their CDs carefully?
b people who organise their CDs randomly?
c new couples?

4 Listen again and complete these extracts with the phrases in the box.

| and so on   and that sort of thing   or thereabouts   or so   or whatever   sort of |

1 Some are alphabeticised or divided into genre _____, or, and this is more common we found, more randomly arranged.
2 They have a _____ music room, which has two walls totally filled with shelves of CDs.
3 I think they must have about a thousand between them, _____.
4 Now, she is clearly an extremely organised and reliable person, the kind who doesn't get parking tickets _____.
5 It would be interesting … to see where they, and their CDs, are in another two years _____.
6 They used music to 'check each other out' nearly twice as much as books, television, sport _____.

5 In each of these extracts from the radio programme identify examples of ellipsis and substitution and say what has been omitted or substituted.

1 If you want to assess a person's character, a quick look through their music collection is one of the most reliable ways of doing so.
2 For some young people, music …is why they dress, have their hair and generally look the way they do.
3 Presenter: But isn't that … just a way of asserting your identity?
   Researcher: Well, to a certain extent, yes, I think it is.
4 She and her boyfriend … have not yet combined their collections. Why they haven't done so, I don't know.

6 Work with a partner and discuss these questions.

1 How do you organise your music?
2 What does this say about you?
3 Do you agree with the research findings?

7 What would be on your ten-track CD of favourite songs? Compare your ideas with a partner and explain why you have chosen the tracks.

Song

1 Read the factfile about the *Dandy Warhols* and answer these questions.

1 What is the significance of the following dates?
  a 1995 **b** 1997 **c** 2000 **d** 2001
2 How has the band's line-up changed?
3 Where do the band throw their parties and how did they end up with this place?
4 How was their 2003 album different from their other albums?
5 How well-known are they?

factfile

Formed in Portland, Oregon in 1994 the *Dandy Warhols* consist of members Courtney Taylor-Taylor (vocals, guitar), Zia McCabe (keyboards), Peter Loew (guitar), and Brent DeBoer (drums). They released their debut album, *Dandy's rule OK?*, in 1995, but it wasn't until the release of their second album, *Dandy Warhols come down* in 1997, which included their first hit single, that the group attained more widespread success, especially in Europe. After DeBoer replaced the band's original drummer, who left to pursue a DJ-ing career, the group released their third album, *Thirteen tales from urban Bohemia* to much acclaim in 2000. The track *Bohemian like you* received massive radio play and became a hit in several countries. The song appeared on numerous film and television soundtracks and was used to great effect in television advertising campaigns for Chrysler and Vodafone in 2001. With the money earned from these adverts the band bought part of an apartment block in their hometown, which they converted for use as film and music studios, as well as being somewhere for the band to throw parties. 2003 saw the release of the group's synth-heavy, 80s-influenced fourth album, after which the group returned to more guitar-driven songs with subsequent releases. Though worldwide recognition and commercial success still eludes the band, they have garnered a large cult following in many countries.

2 🔘 **13** Listen to the song and answer these questions.

1 Who do you think the singer is talking to?
2 What do we learn about this person's:
  a car **b** hair **c** job **d** interest in music **e** diet **f** living arrangements

3 What things do the singer and the person he's talking to have in common?

Bohemian* like you

You got a great car
Yeah what's wrong with it today?
I used to have one too
Maybe I'll come and have a look
I really love your hairdo yeah
I'm glad you like mine too
See we're looking pretty cool
Will get ya

So what do you do?
Oh yeah I wait tables too
No I haven't heard your band
'Cos you guys are pretty new
But if you dig on vegan food
Well, come over to my work
I'll have 'em cook you something
That you'll really love

'Cos I like you
Yeah I like you
And I'm feeling so bohemian like you
Yeah I like you
Yeah I like you
And I feel whoa ooo

Wait
Who's that guy just hangin' at your pad
He's lookin' kinda bummed
Yeah you broke up that's too bad
I guess it's fair if he always pays the rent
And he doesn't get bent about
Sleeping on the couch when I'm there

Chorus

I'm getting wise and I'm feeling
so bohemian like you
It's you that I want so please
Just a casual, casual easy thing
Is it, it is for me
And I like you
Yeah I like you
I like you, I like you …
And I feel

* Bohemian = living or
behaving in an informal way
considered typical of artists
and writers.

4 Would you describe any aspect of your lifestyle or behaviour as bohemian?

Vocabulary

1 Read How to play 'Question time' and play the game.

Question time

How to play

1 Play in two teams. You need a coin and each team needs a counter.
2 Each team puts its counter on the 'start' square. Team A tosses the coin and moves one square for heads and two squares for tails. Team B chooses one of the alternatives from the square and asks Team A the question for that colour category. Example for square 1: Name something you can shun.
3 Team A gives their answer. If Team B agrees the answer is correct, Team A can play next time. If the answer is incorrect, Team A misses a turn.
4 Team B now plays and so on.

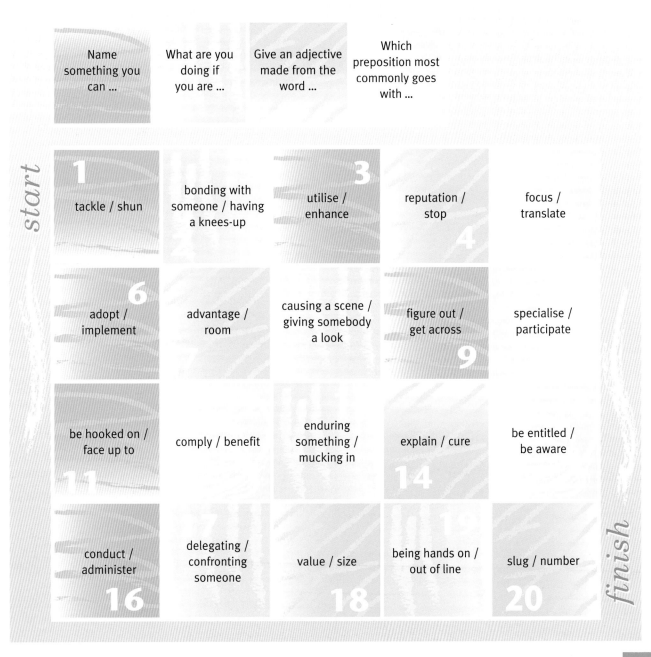

Name something you can …

What are you doing if you are …

Give an adjective made from the word …

Which preposition most commonly goes with …

1 tackle / shun	bonding with someone / having a knees-up	**3** utilise / enhance	reputation / stop	focus / translate **4**
6 adopt / implement	advantage / room	causing a scene / giving somebody a look	figure out / get across	specialise / participate **9**
be hooked on / face up to **11**	comply / benefit	enduring something / mucking in	explain / cure **14**	be entitled / be aware
conduct / administer **16**	delegating / confronting someone	value / size **18**	being hands on / out of line	slug / number **20**

start

finish

Extra practice

Unit 1

1 Complete the phrases in *italics*. The first letter of the missing word is given.

1 We all do our fair share of housework. Everyone has to *m_____ in*.

2 Mum does an awful lot and never complains. She really does *suffer in s_____* some of the time.

3 Mum doesn't really *lose her t_____*, but you know when you're *out of l_____* 'cos she'll *give you a l_____*.

4 Dad looked after us all loads when we were babies. He was very *h_____ on*.

2 Look at this data about the family in Europe. Examples of ellipsis are numbered 1–9. What information has been omitted in each case?

1 *birth rate*   6 _____

2 _____   7 _____

3 _____   8 _____

4 _____   9 _____

5 _____

> The European country with the highest birth rate is Ireland while Germany has the lowest (1).
>
> There are about 5 million babies born in Europe each year, with around one third (2) born outside marriage. The largest proportions of births outside marriage (over 50%) are found in Estonia and Sweden, and the lowest (3) in Cyprus and Greece.
>
> Two thirds of European households are without children. The proportion of households with one child is 16%, 13% (4) have two children and 4% (5) 3 or more (6).
>
> Single-parent households represent 13% of all households in Europe. At 24%, the United Kingdom has the highest rate (7) in Europe.
>
> Cyprus and Denmark have the highest marriage rates in Europe while Slovenia has the lowest (8). The European countries with the highest divorce rates are the Czech Republic and Lithuania, while the lowest (9) are found in Ireland, Italy and Greece.

3 The following sentences contain examples of ellipsis and substitution. Complete them so they are true for you.

Example: I'd love to *be able to take a few days off*, but I just can't at the moment.

1 I'd love to _____, but I just can't at the moment.

2 I've never _____, but I'd like to one day.

3 Most of my friends _____, but I don't.

4 I _____, but I wish I hadn't.

5 I once _____, but I'll never do so again.

6 I didn't _____, but I should have.

4 What has been substituted in each quote? Which quote do you like the best? [ ]

Example:

Any American who is prepared to run for president should automatically, by definition, be disqualified from ever *doing so*. (Gore Vidal, US author & dramatist, 1925–) *running for president*

1 Human beings, who are almost unique in having the ability to learn from the experience of others, are also remarkable for their apparent disinclination to *do so*. (Douglas Adams British science fiction novelist, 1952–2001) _____

2 The definition of genius is that it acts unconsciously; and those who have produced immortal works, have *done so* without knowing how or why. (William Hazlitt, English essayist, 1778–1830) _____

3 The wise man thinks about his troubles only when there is some purpose in *doing so*; at other times he thinks about other things. (Bertrand Russell, British author and philosopher, 1872–1970) _____

5 Complete these headlines with the verbs in the box.

| adopt | conduct | establish |
| preserve | prohibit | register |

1 **All countries to _____ single currency**

2 **US military to _____ human cloning tests**

3 **Scientists _____ direct link between diet and longevity**

4 **EU to _____ all cigarette advertising**

5 **All nations agree to _____ existing rainforest**

6 **All adults to _____ their religion according to new law**

Unit 2

1 Replace the <u>underlined</u> words by completing the euphemisms.

1 He's really <u>mean</u>.

c_____ w_____ m_____

2 My parents are <u>really old</u>.

g_____ o_____ a b_____

3 She's <u>poor</u>. She struggles to pay the bills.

o_____ a l_____ i_____

4 He's really <u>fat</u>.

o_____ t_____ l_____ s_____

5 My friend's car <u>is falling to bits</u>.

h_____ s_____ b_____ d_____

6 He <u>drinks a lot</u> when he goes out.

l_____ a t_____

2 Look at these definitions of adjectives ending in *-able* that are made from the words in the box. Write each adjective in the appropriate space. You will need to add a negative prefix in some cases.

> admire   change   ~~imagine~~   knowledge
> laugh   question   replace   understand

1 Very difficult to imagine: *an agreement between the two countries is <u>unimaginable</u>*

2 Possibly not true, accurate or complete: *the results of the test seem highly* _____

3 Normal and reasonable in a particular situation: *their reaction is perfectly* _____ *in the circumstances*

4 Valuable or rare and impossible to replace if used, lost or destroyed: *an* _____ *collection of jewellery*

5 Very silly or unreasonable: *his claims are* _____

6 Knowing a lot about many different subjects or about one particular subject: *he's extremely* _____ *about business and finance*

7 Tending to change suddenly and often: *a period of rather* _____ *weather*

8 Deserving to be admired or respected: *an* _____ *objective*

3 Complete these news report extracts with an adjective ending in *-able* formed from the words in *italics*. You will need to use a negative prefix in some cases.

1 The law now demands a total ban in all public places, something which was _____ only a few years ago.   *think*

2 The contribution made by every member is _____ and this is the key to their phenomenal chart success.   *value*

3 It does not live up to the hype by any means, but is pleasantly _____ nevertheless.   *watch*

4 His is one of the most _____ faces on the planet.   *recognise*

5 An _____ return of service clinched the game and the second set.   *stop*

6 You are angry that you have lost your money and two hours out of your life watching this _____ horror.   *speak*

7 The assertion that the attacks were not _____ remains _____.   *prevent question*

8 There is no doubt that _____ sums of undeclared money are regularly changing hands between clubs and agents, a situation that FIFA has condemned as '_____ and _____'. The governing body has also made it clear that such illegal dealings are not by any means confined to the less _____ agents.   *size   accept   excuse   reputation*

4 What or who do you think each of the news extracts in Ex 3 is about?

1 Example: *smoking*   5 _____
2 _____   6 _____
3 _____   7 _____
4 _____   8 _____

5 Put an appropriate ending on these words to make them into adjectives.

1 colour*ful*   8 mist___
2 child___   9 meaning___
3 harm___   10 fool___
4 care___   11 hair___
5 advantage___   12 snob___
6 use___   13 mood___
7 dust___   14 rock___

6 Complete these sentences with an adjective formed from the words in the box.

> danger   room   slug   thought

1 Don't worry, he isn't _____.

2 My computer is a bit _____ today.

3 Thank you. That's very _____ of you.

4 It's very _____ in the back.

Unit 3

1 Complete these email extracts with an appropriate form of the phrasal verbs in the box.

be on about   boil down to   figure out
get across   point out

1 As well as the problems with the computer already mentioned, I would also like to _____ the extremely poor customer service on your help-line.

2 I couldn't _____ what your 'agents' were saying. To be honest, most of the time I just didn't have a clue what they _____.

3 I just didn't seem to be able to _____ to them that I'd already tried the things they were suggesting and that they didn't seem to understand my problem. I guess it just _____ the fact that they're not actually that knowledgeable or well-trained.

2 Match the phrases to the correct endings in both groups.

1 What I'm   **a** mean by …?
2 What do you   **b** saying is …
3 If I've understood you **c** getting at is …
4 What I'm trying to   **d** say is …
5 So, what you're   **e** correctly, …

6 To put it   **f** me?
7 Are you with   **g** follow?
8 Do you   **h** a different way
9 Do you see what I   **i** saying?
10 What are you   **j** mean?

3 Which of the phrases in Ex 2 would be used by

1 the speaker [1] [ ] [ ] [ ] [ ] [ ]

2 the listener [ ] [ ] [ ] [ ]

4 Complete the sentences using an appropriate question word combined with the suffix *-ever*, for example *whatever*.

1 I like all computer games – races, shoot 'em ups, role-play, _____.

2 We can go anywhere you like – Fifth Avenue, Central Park, the Statue of Liberty, _____.

3 I don't mind how we get there – taxi, car, walk, _____.

4 Invite who you like – friends, colleagues, classmates, _____.

5 Call round anytime – seven, eight, _____.

6 Stay as long as you like – a couple of days, a week, _____.

5 Rewrite these email extracts by putting the words and phrases in *italics* in an appropriate position.

Example:

So, how's it going now you've moved in together, settling down? We really must meet up and have a good catch up.   *and all that   sometime*

So, how's it going now you've moved in together, settling down <u>and all that</u>? We really must meet up <u>sometime</u> and have a good catch up.

1 | Mel from the London office has sent me an attachment in a compressed format. She said I needed some 'unzipper' program and emailed it to me, but I just don't know what I'm doing with this. Can you have a look at it for me?   *sort of   kind of thing*

2 | I really like the new job. Most of the time it's sorting out error messages. It's just the challenge I really enjoy.   *and the like   kind of*

3 | You're welcome to come and stay one or two nights anytime you like. We've got a spare room-cum-study you can stay in.   *or whatever   sort of*

4 | Maria's away at the moment, so I'm spending my time eating take-away pizza and watching all my old favourite DVDs, you know, 101 Best World Cup goals, 101 Funniest TV moments. You should come round before she's back.   *and that sort of thing   sometime*

6 Answer these questions about yourself with the phrases in the box.

Example: *three years more or less   1 metre 70-ish*

getting on for   give or take   -ish
more or less   or so   or thereabouts

1 How long have you been learning English?

    _____

2 How long have you lived in your house?

    _____

3 How long have you had a computer?

    _____

4 What time do you generally go to bed?

    _____

5 How tall are you?

    _____

6 How much money have you got on you?

    _____

Unit 4

1 Complete the following article about leadership with an appropriate form of the verbs in the boxes.

I'm in charge

implement   run

At it's most basic level leadership involves
(1) _____ meetings effectively, keeping the team informed and (2) _____ and explaining decisions.

bond   enhance   realise   utilise

At mid-level, it includes ensuring that a team
(3) _____ and (4) _____ team performance. This is done by creating the right conditions to (5) _____ team members' individual skills and to enable the team to
(6) _____ its potential fully.

face up to   perform   set   tackle   take

Top-level leaders (7) _____ challenges,
(8) _____ problems head on and
(9) _____ initiative. In doing so they act as role models and inspire confidence in the team. At the top level, leadership is about (10) _____ standards and making sure that people
(11) _____ to that level.

2 Which preposition goes with each set of words and phrases? Use a different preposition for each set.

specialise participate believe be lacking be fluent	*in*	adapt be equivalent be entitled be related be similar		be aware be typical be envious a mixture a lack	
worry reminisce have doubts be nervous		have impact depend concentrate put the blame		translate split divide change	
comply be fed up be compatible be popular		benefit suffer deviate be different		apologise be eligible be famous be responsible	

3 Complete these sentence beginnings with your own ideas.

Example: I'm envious *of people who can play the piano.*

1   I'm envious _____
2   I'm (not) fluent _____
3   I'm similar _____
4   I'm different _____
5   I often reminisce _____
6   I (don't) have (any) doubts _____
7   I'm (not) eligible _____
8   I (don't) think I have the makings _____

4 Match the halves of these work-related quotes.

1 ___   2 ___   3 ___   4 ___   5 ___   6 ___   7 ___

1   The world is divided
2   To manage a system effectively, you might focus
3   Any corporate policy and plan which is typical
4   Don't worry
5   Everyone is entitled
6   One of the penalties for refusing to participate
7   A young man … should look for the single spark of individuality that makes him different

a   in politics is that you end up being governed by your inferiors. (Plato, Greek philosopher, 427–347 BC)
b   to be stupid, but some abuse the privilege. (Anonymous)
c   of the industry is doomed to mediocrity. (Bruce Henderson, management consultant, 1915–1992)
d   on the interactions of the parts rather than their behaviour taken separately. (Russell L. Ackoff, academic and author, 1919–)
e   from other folks, and develop that for all he is worth. (Henry Ford, automobile industrialist, 1863–1947)
f   into people who do things and people who get the credit. (Dwight Morrow, businessman, politician, and diplomat, 1873–1931)
g   about people stealing an idea. If it's original, you will have to ram it down their throats. (Howard Aiken, computer scientist, 1900–1973)

Grammar reference

Unit 1

Ellipsis and substitution

In speaking and writing we generally provide only as much information as is necessary to convey what we want to express. This involves leaving out or replacing words and phrases to avoid repetition.

Ellipsis

Textual ellipsis occurs in both speaking and writing. Words are missed out in grammatically predictable sentence positions. It often occurs after *and*, *but* and *because* etc.

Most of my friends love going clubbing, but I don't (love going clubbing).
I didn't go out last night because I didn't want to (go out last night).
We'd love to get away for a few days, but we just can't (get away for a few days) *at the moment.*
Pete's got ten pounds and I've got twenty (pounds).

Situational ellipsis occurs mainly in speaking. The context makes it clear what is missing.
Feeling better? (~~Are you~~ feeling better?)
A: *Going to the party?* (~~Are you~~ going to the party?)
B: *Possibly.* (~~I am~~ possibly ~~going to the party~~)
A: *When you back?* (When ~~are~~ you ~~coming~~ back?)
B: *Friday.* (~~We are coming back on~~ Friday)

Substitution

Substitution refers to the words we use (*so*, *do*, *did*, etc) that replace words we have omitted.
Do, does, did etc replaces a verb clause.

It is usually used in conjunction with *so* when referring to voluntary or deliberate actions and when referring to the same subject as previously mentioned.

*We'll get married one day, but we're not planning on **doing so** just yet.* (getting married)

*I once did a bungee jump, but I'll never **do so** again.* (do a bungee jump)

*I didn't see the incident, but it seems that everyone else **did**.* (saw the incident)

*I thought it would rain, and **so** it has* (… and it has rained)

A: *Is Dave coming with us?*
B: *I think **so**.* (I think that Dave is coming with us)
A: *It wasn't Carlos who called.*
B: *I thought **not**.* (I thought it wasn't Carlos who called)

Unit 2

Forming adjectives from verbs and nouns (adjective suffixes)

-able

The suffix *-able* can be added to:
- certain verbs to make adjectives describing something that can or can't be done.
  His reaction was totally predictable.
  Lampard's penalty kick was unstoppable.
- certain nouns to make adjectives describing a quality that something has.
  She's very knowledgeable about art.
  Thanks for your invaluable help.

-ible

-ible is a less common alternative to *-able*. There is no simple rule to tell you which words take *-ible* and you need to learn them individually.
They said that it was indestructible.
His behaviour is indefensible.

There are a few common 'irregular' adjectives that end in *-able* or *-ible*.

inexplicable	(you can't explain it)
appreciable	(enough to be noticed/appreciated)
reputable	(has a good reputation)
(il)legible	(you can('t) read it)
(in)edible	(you can('t) eat it)
(in)visible	(you can('t) see it)
(in)audible	(you can('t) hear it)
(in)credible	(you can('t) believe it)
(im)plausible	(difficult to accept as true)

Negative prefixes

Many adjectives ending in *-able* or *-ible* take negative prefixes. The most common negative prefixes used in this way are *un-*, *in-* and *non-*. You need to learn how to form the negative of words as you come across them.

You generally use *il-* for words beginning with *l*, *im-* for words beginning with *m* and *p*, and *ir-* for those beginning with *r*.
illegible   illegal   immovable   immature   impenetrable   irreplaceable   irregular

-y / -ful / -ish / -ous

You can form adjectives from nouns using the suffixes *-y*, *-ful*, *-ish*, and *-ous*.
The meaning is 'having the quality of'

It's been a bit cloudy over the last few days.
India is such a colourful country.
He's very childish.
Speaking a foreign language can be very advantageous for work.

Unit 3

Using vague language

You can use the following phrases to express the idea of 'similarity' to what you have previously mentioned.

and stuff   and / or whatever   and all that   and the like   and that kind / sort of thing / stuff   and so on

I don't really like rap and hip-hop and that kind of stuff.
I love going out clubbing and all that.
We've got all we need here – shops, bars, convenient public transport and so on.

a / some kind of and *a / some sort of* express 'something similar to'
I've got some kind of virus on my computer.
I've got a sort of office at home where I work.

-ever

The suffix *-ever* can be combined with question words to give the meaning 'It doesn't matter which / who / when' etc.

We can leave whenever you like.
I don't mind what we eat – Indian, Chinese, whatever.
Help yourself to anything – food, there's beer in the fridge, DVDs, whatever you want.

Approximating

You can use the following phrases to give approximations.

about   around   getting on for   give or take   -ish   in the region of   more or less   or so   or thereabouts

It's worth in the region of £250,000.
He must be getting on for 40 I'd say.
I'll be there around six-ish.
I've got about 100 CDs or thereabouts.
I'd say he's about 1 metre 80 or so.

Unit 4

Dependent prepositions with verbs, nouns and adjectives

You need to use a particular preposition after certain verbs, nouns and adjectives. Often this preposition is just a linking word, which contributes no meaning.

There are no rules about which prepositions to use with which words and you need to learn which preposition to use as you come across new words. Try to remember the word and the preposition as one item of language, for example '*aim for*', '*specialise in*' etc.

Here are some of the more common verb, noun or adjective + preposition structures.

verb + preposition

aim for   accuse of   adapt to   apologise for   approve of   believe in   benefit from   blame for   complain to / about   comply with   concentrate on   congratulate on   connect to   consist of   cover in   depend on   divide into   dream about / of   embark on / upon   be entitled to   excuse for   expose to   focus on   forgive for   insist on   look forward to   object to   participate in   prevent from   react to   rely on   specialise in   split into   succeed in   think about / of   translate into   worry about

*The document needs **translating into** English.*
*Don't **worry about** me.*
*Can we **focus on** the facts?*
*He's someone you can always **rely on**.*

noun + preposition

advantage of   agreement between   alternative to   aspect of   attitude towards   cause of   contact with   cost of   damage to   decrease / increase in   demand for   difference between   eligibility for   the equivalent of   example of   excuse for   experience of   exposure to   demand for   impact on   lack of   mixture of   need for   participation in   photograph of   reaction to   reason for   relationship with   rise / fall in   rule about   solution to   trouble with

*Was there much **damage to** the car?*
*Have you made **contact with** anyone yet?*
*The **demand for** CD players is decreasing all the time.*
*Is there any **advantage of** going first?*
*I'm having some **trouble with** my computer.*

adjective + preposition

accustomed to   afraid of   allergic to   angry with   aware of   certain about   compatible with   covered in   dependent on   different from   equivalent to   famous / well-known for   interested in   fed up with   fond of   good / bad / useless / terrible at   keen on   lacking in   late for   optimistic about   proud of   ready for   reliant on   responsible for   serious about   sorry for   superstitious about   suspicious of   used to

*I'm **allergic to** dairy products.*
*One Euro is **equivalent to** about 70 pence.*
*Is it **compatible with** Windows Vista?*
*There have been no problems that I'm **aware of**.*

When a verb directly follows a verb, noun or adjective + preposition, you use the *-ing* form of this verb.

*I'm **thinking of** joining a gym.*
*Are you **serious about** joining the police?*
*What's his **excuse for** being late?*
*I'm not really **used to** driving on the left yet.*

Wordlist

*** the 2,500 most common English words, ** very common words, * fairly common words

Unit 1

administer *v* /əd'mɪnɪstə/
adopt *v* /ə'dɒpt/ ***
bereavement *n* /bɪ'riːvmənt/
broody *adj* /'bruːdi/
close *adj* /kləʊs/ ***
conduct *v* /kən'dʌkt/ ***
devote (your) life to *phr* /dɪˌvəʊt (jɔː) 'laɪf tə/
elated *adj* /ɪ'leɪtɪd/
elitist *adj* /ɪ'liːtɪst/
establish *v* /ɪ'stæblɪʃ/ ***
get on like a house on fire *expr* /get ˌɒn laɪk ə 'haʊs ɒn faɪə/
get on the property ladder *expr* /get ɒn ðə 'prɒpəti ˌlædə/
give and take *phr* /ˌgɪv ən 'teɪk/
give sb a look *phr* /ˌgɪv ... ə 'lʊk/
give up hope *phr* /ˌgɪv ʌp 'həʊp/
hands on *adj* /ˌhændz 'ɒn/
hands off *adj* /ˌhændz 'ɒf/
If nature has its way *expr* /ɪf ˌneɪtʃə ˌhæz ɪts 'weɪ/
ignore *v* /ɪg'nɔː/ **
lawless *adj* /'lɔːləs/
lose (your) temper *expr* /ˌluːz (jɔː) 'tempə/
motley group *n* /ˌmɒtli ˌgruːp/
muck in *v* /ˌmʌk 'ɪn/
nag *v* /næg/
neglect *v* /nɪ'glekt/ **
nowhere near as ... as *expr* /ˌnəʊweə 'nɪər əz ... əz/
order *n* /'ɔːdə/ ***
out of line *adj* /aʊt əv 'laɪn/
preserve *v* /prɪ'zɜːv/ ***
progressive *adj* /prəʊ'gresɪv/ **
prohibit *v* /prəʊ'hɪbɪt/ *
register *v* /'redʒɪstə/ ***
resent *v* /rɪ'zent/
scourge *n* /skɜːdʒ/ *
shun *v* /ʃʌn/
squabble *v* /'skwɒbl/
stick up for sb *expr* /ˌstɪk 'ʌp fə/
suffer in silence *phr* /ˌsʌfər ɪn 'saɪləns/
the icing on the cake *expr* /ði ˌaɪsɪŋ ɒn ðə 'keɪk/
the patience of a saint *phr* /ðə ˌpeɪʃəns əv ə 'seɪnt/
tied down *adj* /ˌtaɪd 'daʊn/
trespass *v* /'trespəs/
uniqueness *n* /juː'niːknəs/
wishful thinking *phr* /ˌwɪʃfl 'θɪŋkɪŋ/

Unit 2

advantageous *adj* /ˌædvən'teɪdʒəs/
adventurous *adj* /əd'ventʃərəs/
advisable *adj* /əd'vaɪzəbl/
appreciable *adj* /ə'priːʃəbl/
at any rate *phr* /ət 'eni ˌreɪt/
be between jobs (right now) *phr* /bi bɪˌtwiːn 'dʒɒbz (raɪt ˌnaʊ)/
be getting on a bit *expr* /bi ˌgetɪŋ 'ɒn ə ˌbɪt/
be on a low income *phr* /bi ˌɒn ə ˌləʊ 'ɪŋkʌm/
be very careful with money *phr* /bi ˌveri ˌkeəfl wɪð 'mʌni/
But on the other hand, *expr* /bət ˌɒn ði ˈʌðə ˌhænd/
childish *adj* /'tʃaɪldɪʃ/ *
doable *adj* /'duːəbl/
downloadable *adj* /ˌdaʊn'ləʊdəbl/
dusty *adj* /'dʌsti/ *
foolish *adj* /'fuːlɪʃ/ *
hairy *adj* /'heəri/ *
harmful *adj* /'hɑːmfl/ *
I suppose you can say (that) ... *phr* /aɪ səˈpəʊz jə kən ˌseɪ (ðət)/
in a way *phr* /ɪn ə 'weɪ/

incurable *adj* /ɪn'kjʊərəbl/
indescribable *adj* /ˌɪndɪ'skraɪbəbl/
inescapable *adj* /ˌɪnɪ'skeɪpəbl/
inexplicable *adj* /ˌɪnɪks'plɪkəbl/
irretrievable *adj* /ˌɪrə'triːvəbl/
justifiable *adj* /ˈdʒʌstɪˌfaɪəbl/ ***
kind of *phr* /'kaɪnd əv/
knowledgeable *adj* /'nɒlɪdʒəbl/
like a tipple *phr* /ˌlaɪk ə 'tɪpl/
mentally challenged *adj* /ˌmentəli 'tʃælɪndʒd/
misty *adj* /'mɪsti/
moody *adj* /'muːdi/
morally different *adj* /ˌmɒrəli 'dɪfrənt/
motivationally deficient *adj* /ˌməʊtɪˌveɪʃnəli dɪ'fɪʃnt/
need to go to the bathroom *phr* /ˌniːd tə ˌgəʊ tə ðə 'bɑːθruːm/
numerous *adj* /'njuːmərəs/ **
on the large side /ɒn ðə 'lɑːdʒ saɪd/
reputable *adj* /'repjʊtəbl/
rocky *adj* /'rɒki/ *
roomy *adj* /'ruːmi/
salty *adj* /'sɔːlti/
sheepish *adj* /'ʃiːpɪʃ/
sizeable *adj* /'saɪzəbl/
sluggish *adj* /'slʌgɪʃ/
snobbish *adj* /'snɒbɪʃ/
sort of *phr* /'sɔːt əv/
sth has seen better days *expr* /... həz ˌsiːn ˌbetə 'deɪz/
unavoidable *adj* /ˌʌnə'vɔɪdəbl/
under the circumstances *phr* /ˌʌndə ðə 'sɜːkəmstənsɪz/
unspeakable *adj* /ʌn'spiːkəbl/
unstoppable *adj* /ʌn'stɒpəbl/
vertically challenged *adj* /ˌvɜːtɪkli 'tʃælɪndʒd/

Unit 3

amount to *v* /ə'maʊnt tə/ **
and all that *phr* /ənd ˌɔːl 'ðæt/
and stuff *phr* /ən 'stʌf/
and that sort of thing *phr* /ən ˌðæt ˌsɔːt əv ˌθɪŋ/
and the like *phr* /ən ðə 'laɪk/
Are you with me? *expr* /ə jə 'wɪð ˌmiː/
average *adj* /'ævərɪdʒ/ ***
be getting at *v* /bi 'getɪŋ ˌæt/
be on about *v* /bi ˈɒn əˌbaʊt/
boil down to *v* /ˌbɔɪl 'daʊn tuː/
convey *v* /kən'veɪ/ **
Do you follow? *phr* /də jə 'fɒləʊ/
Do you get me? *expr* /də jə ˌget 'miː/
figure out *v* /ˌfɪgər 'aʊt/
focus on *v* /'fəʊkəs ˌɒn/ ***
get sth across *v* /ˌget ... ə'krɒs/
getting on for ... *expr* /ˌgetɪŋ ɒn fə (fɔ)/
give or take *expr* /ˌgɪv ɔː ˌteɪk/
hooked on *adj* /'hʊkt ɒn/
however (long) *phr* /haʊ'evə (ˌlɒŋ)/
I suppose I'm really saying ... *phr* /aɪ səˌpəʊz aɪm 'rɪəli ˌseɪɪŋ/
In other words, you ... *phr* /ɪn ˌʌðə ˌwɜːdz juː/
in the region of *phr* /ɪn ðə 'riːdʒn əv/
(50)-ish *adj* /('fɪfti)ˌɪʃ/
more or less *phr* /ˌmɔːr ɔː 'les/
or so *phr* /ˌɔː 'səʊ/
or thereabouts *phr* /ˌɔː ˌðeərə'baʊts/
point out *v* /ˌpɔɪnt 'aʊt/
respondent *n* /rɪ'spɒndənt/
retrieve *v* /rɪ'triːv/ *
So what you're trying to say is ... *phr* /ˌsəʊ ˌwɒt jɔː ˌtraɪɪŋ tə ˌseɪ ɪz/
To put it a different way *phr* /tə ˌpʊt ɪt ə 'dɪfrənt ˌweɪ/
track *v* /træk/ *
What do you mean by ...? *phr* /ˌwɒt də jə ˌmiːn baɪ/

What I'm getting at is ... *expr* /ˌwɒt aɪm 'getɪŋ æt ɪz/
whatever *pron* /wɒt'evə/ ***
whenever *pron* /wen'evə/ **
wherever *pron* /weər'əvə/ **
whoever *pron* /huː'evə/ **

Unit 4

a return on the investment *phr* /ə rɪˌtɜːn ɒn ði ɪn'vestmənt/
a tight ship *expr* /ə ˌtaɪt 'ʃɪp/
adapt to *v* /ə'dæpt tə/ **
aspect of sth *n* /'æspekt əv/ **
awayday *n* /ə'weɪdeɪ/
not be seen dead *expr* /ˌnɒt bɪ ˌsiːn 'ded/
be tired of *expr* /bɪ 'taɪəd əv/
best / worst thing (about sth) *n* /ˌbest, 'wɜːst θɪŋ (əˌbaʊt)/
bond *v* /bɒnd/
chief executive *n* /tʃiːf ɪg'zekjʊtɪv/ *
compatible with *adj* /kəm'pætəbl wɪð/ *
comply *v* /kəm'plaɪ/ *
confront conflict *phr* /kənˌfrʌnt 'kɒnflɪkt/
delegate *v* /'deləgeɪt/ *
eclectic *adj* /ɪ'klektɪk/
enhance *v* /ɪn'hɑːns/ **
entitled to *adj* /ɪn'taɪtld tuː/ ***
entity *n* /'entəti/ **
face up to *v* /ˌfeɪs 'ʌp tə/
fed up with *adj* /ˌfed 'ʌp wɪð/
get sb down *expr* /ˌget ... 'daʊn/
get up close and personal *phr* /ˌget ʌp ˌkləʊs ən 'pɜːsnəl/
hangover *n* /'hæŋəʊvə/
have enough of sth / it *expr* /ˌhæv ɪ'nʌf əv/
have high expectations *phr* /ˌhæv ˌhaɪ ˌekspek'teɪʃnz/
Have you tried (+ -ing)? *phr* /həv jə ˌtraɪd/
I can't stand (+ -ing) *expr* /aɪ ˌkɑːnt 'stænd/
I recommend you (+ inf) *phr* /aɪ ˌrekəmend juː/
I'd like your advice on *phr* /aɪd ˌlaɪk jɔːr əd'vaɪs ɒn/
impact *n* /'ɪmpækt/ ***
implement decisions *phr* /ˌɪmplɪˌment dɪ'sɪʒnz/
leave sth at the door *expr* /ˌliːv ... ət ðə dɔː/
literally *adv* /'lɪtərəli/ **
make sb's life a misery *phr* /ˌmeɪk ... ˌlaɪf ə 'mɪzəri/
menial *adj* /'miːniəl/
(-ing) might help *phr* /... maɪt ˌhelp/
My advice is *phr* /'maɪ ədˌvaɪs ɪs/
out of order *expr* /ˌaʊt əv 'ɔːdə/
participate *v* /pɑː'tɪsɪˌpeɪt/
preconceived notion *n* /ˌpriːkənˌsiːvd 'nəʊʃn/
proactively *adv* /prəʊ'æktɪvli/
put sb in a (real) dilemma *phr* /ˌpʊt ... ɪn ə (ˌrɪəl) dɪ'lemə/
realise (your) potential *phr* /ˌrɪəˌlaɪz (jɔː) pə'tenʃl/
seek approval *phr* /ˌsiːk ə'pruːvl/
socialise with *v* /'səʊʃəˌlaɪz wɪð/
specialise in *v* /'speʃəˌlaɪz ɪn/ *
split *v* /splɪt/ **
tackle *v* /'tækl/ **
take the initiative *phr* /ˌteɪk ði ɪ'nɪʃətɪv/
the makings of *expr* /ðə 'meɪkɪŋz əv/
utilise *v* /'juːtɪlaɪz/
not what (you) bargain for *expr* /ˌnɒt ˌwɒt (juː) 'bɑːgɪn fɔː/
with an open mind *phr* /wɪð ən ˌəʊpən 'maɪnd/
You should think about (+ -ing) *phr* /jə ʃʊd ˌθɪŋk əbaʊt '.../

Communication activities

Unit 1, Reading and vocabulary Ex 1 page 66

In 2004 the fertility rate in the UK was 1.77 children per woman. This was an increase from 1.71 in 2003 and a further increase from the record low of 1.63 in 2001. During the 1960s 'baby boom' the fertility rate peaked in 1964 at 2.95 children per woman. In 2004, the average age of women having their first birth was 27.1 years. Around one in five women currently reaching the end of their fertile life is childless.

(Source: National Statistics, www.statistics.gov.uk)

Unit 2, Speaking and pronunciation Ex 3 page 73

1 Read your rolecard for both situations.

2 Prepare notes to help you with your roles.

3 Do the role-plays with Student B. Include the phrases in Speaking and pronunciation Ex 1 and some of the euphemisms from page 70.

Rolecard 1

You lost your job a couple of months ago and have been holed up in your flat, eating fast food and watching TV. You feel very depressed and see no future for yourself. You have really let yourself go but you don't care. Student B is your friend and has come to visit you but you don't really want to see anybody.

Rolecard 2

Student B is your flatmate. A close friend has recently died and he / she is very upset. You sympathise but you need some money to pay the rent and the telephone bill. It is always a bit difficult getting money from your flatmate and the landlord has threatened to evict you over late payments. You suspect your flatmate is milking the situation to avoid paying but you don't want to lose him / her as a flatmate as you have a good relationship otherwise. Talk about the situation with him / her. Start like this: *Listen, I realise ...*

Unit 4, Speaking Ex 1 page 81

Leadership quiz

1 How important is status to you?
- a Very important. I like to feel like I'm part of the elite.
- b Quite important. It's good to be in with the in-crowd.
- c It's more about the quality of relationships than where you fall within those relationships.
- d Not very important. I just want to get on.

2 In your childhood what was your 'gang rank'?
- a The leader; feared by all.
- b The funny one; adored by all.
- c The thinking one; listened to by all.
- d The geeky one; noticed by none.

3 At college or work do you come up with new ideas?
- a All the time. I let everyone know what I think.
- b Quite often, but not at all if it would mean upsetting someone.
- c Often: being careful of any personal and political issues.
- d Rarely: what if it was the wrong thing?

4 You have just faced some negative feedback. How do you respond?
- a Get angry and defensive.
- b Listen carefully but come away feeling disappointed.
- c Consider what you could change or improve.
- d Sigh and think, 'yeah that's me'.

5 Faced with a problem to solve, what do you do?
- a Come up with one solution and pronounce it correct.
- b Generate a few possible solutions and ask others what they think.
- c Brainstorm with a group of people.
- d Seek your tutor's or your manager's advice.

6 You have been asked to do something that is beyond your abilities. Do you ...?
- a take it on energetically: you're up for anything.
- b give it your best shot, making a passing joke about not blaming you if it all goes wrong.
- c agree to do the task, but ask for further direction.
- d stress out and finally confess that you just don't think you could manage it.

7 Is delegation ...
- a a waste of time: no one else will be able to do it as well as you so you might as well do it yourself.
- b an easy way to share the workload.
- c an effective way of creating new learning opportunities for others.
- d something you're always on the receiving end of.

8 Change to you means ...
- a something to be controlled.
- b an opportunity where anything could happen.
- c a chance to make progress.
- d something to just go along with.

Listening scripts

Unit 1 Living together

🔊 Listening script 01

Reading text from page 67

💿 Listening script 02

(P = presenter, R = Reporter)

P: Today on *Your Travel* Lisa Alexander reports on the colourful and controversial living community of Christiania in Copenhagen.

R: Copenhagen seems to epitomise the modern European capital and in many ways it does so.

But in the Christianshavn district lies a different kind of place – a motley group of hippies, artists and misfits have founded a home that shuns rules and conformity. The "freetown" of Christiania has been conducting a social experiment for more than 30 years. Fiercely independent-minded, the Christianite squatters have established their own holidays, government and rules.

The Christianites were determined to create a place where they could create art, let their children play in overgrown nature and live out untraditional lifestyles – and they did. Strange houses were erected. Cars were banned, and ecological experiments with wind and solar power, garbage recycling and water treatment took place before the rest of the country had even heard of the green movement.

A consensus democracy was formed, wherein no decision could be made without the agreement of all participants. There were no laws, only a few rules – paramount amongst them the prohibition on buying and selling property. Even now, Christianites do not own their homes. They have a close community and place a heavy value on community programs – feeding the homeless, creating their own kindergartens, playgrounds and clinics.

But many outside Christiania see the community as a scourge on the city, a group of drug-smoking criminals trespassing on public land and ignoring the laws the rest of Denmark have to obey. Liberal governments in the past adopted a hands-off policy but now the government is demanding changes. The dirt streets are to receive official names; buildings are to receive house numbers; and, residents will have to register where they live. In their words, the government wants to "normalise" the area.

Government officials claim the plan seeks to preserve the cultural uniqueness of the area, which attracts close to a million tourists a year, but private ownership of the land will need to be arranged. Christianites are demanding that a system of common ownership remains. In their eyes, all the things that have made the area so special are rooted in the unique way they administer the area and prohibit the buying and selling of homes.

No matter what the outcome of the negotiations, no amount of normalisation could ever make Christiania normal. Lawless, elitist and dirty? Or progressive, inventive and free? Whatever your opinion is of Copenhagen's most unique neighbourhood, it always leaves a lasting impression on visitors.

Unit 2 Talk talk

💿 Listening script 03

Reading text from page 71

🔊 Listening script 04

(T = Tatyana, L = Lars, P = Paolo)

T: My name's Tatyana, I'm from Russia and I've been learning English in Oxford for about a year now. I'm planning to study international business and administration at an English university. I think it's difficult to get a good job without English – English is the world's *lingua franca*. I realise that some people don't like that, but under the circumstances, I tend to think it's unavoidable. I can't get a good job in my country if I don't learn English. Perhaps all countries should teach children English when they are small, so they find it easy to learn. I found English easy to learn at first, but then it got harder because the tenses are so difficult.

L: My name's Lars and I'm from Germany. I'm doing a summer course in Oxford and I'm er very lucky because my company – I work for an engineering company – is paying for it. I work in the foreign trade department. We sell machine parts to countries all over the world and I have to go to trade fairs and be able to communicate with people who speak different languages. I have to negotiate deals and also talk to people socially in restaurants and things like that. Sometimes I can use German but usually we speak English to our customers. In a way I think it's sad that English has become a *lingua franca* and that other languages, you know, are dying out because English is getting more important. But on the other hand, it's practical to have one language you can speak wherever you go. English is breaking down a lot of obstacles to communication. I suppose you can say that English doesn't belong to certain countries anymore. It's just everybody's world language.

P: My name's Paolo. I work in an export company in Brazil and I need English for my job, so I'm trying to improve it now. I love learning English. I spend all my free time trying to get better. I watch films in English and go to the pub and talk to people. It's really interesting to meet so many different people and just talk to them. I listen to a lot of music in English too. Often I can't understand the lyrics, but I like the sound of the language. I've got a bit of a problem with English as a *lingua franca*. I know English is important, at any rate you can't get by without it nowadays, but I sort of think it would be better if everybody learnt more foreign languages. Native speakers of English are quite arrogant. They think they don't need to speak anybody else's language. They're kind of imposing their way of life and their view of the world on other people through their language, and a lot of people oppose that.

Unit 3 Net value

💿 Listening script 05

Some people think the Internet is a good thing.

The most powerful educational tool the world has ever known.

It's preserving our history, making sure that in the future we never forget the past.

The Internet is a place that is free from state intervention, censorship, and control. The only place where freedom of speech truly exists.

Orwell was wrong. It is not the state that holds all the power. It is us.

Some people think the Internet is a good thing. What do you think?

Some people think the Internet is a bad thing.

Somewhere your identity can be stolen, your home invaded and your savings robbed without anyone setting foot inside your door.

It is one of the most dangerous weapons ever created. A way for the unhinged to spread evil, free of supervision or censorship. A place for mankind to exercise its darkest desires. An open market where you can purchase anything you want.

Orwell was right. The Internet has taken us to a place where everything we do is watched, monitored and processed without us ever realising.

Some people think the Internet is a bad thing. What do you think?

🔊 Listening script 06

(G = Graham, L = Layla)

G: Have you seen those ads for the Internet? You know the ones about whether the Internet is a good or bad thing?

L: Oh yeah, they're clever, very dramatic. They really get the message across.

G: Yes, they are good, but I couldn't figure out what it was all about at first. Isn't it a bit strange for an internet company to be questioning its own product?

L: They've got everybody talking, though. I think most people will say the Internet is a good thing, on balance. All that information and stuff, and it's free! The Internet's, like, a part of life now. I can't imagine not having the Internet for downloading music, shopping and whatever.

G: Yeah, there's lots of information, as you point out, but how much of that is useable? The Net's like a huge rubbish dump, anybody can chuck things in there. You can search forever and you never know how accurate things are, things disappear as soon as they're not news … and what do you mean by 'it's free'? All the articles I've tried to access recently had to be paid for. Give me a decent library any day!

L: So in other words, you'd rather live in the good old days. Come off it!

G: Well, what about credit card fraud and identity theft and that sort of thing? Do you know what I mean? Don't you worry about things like that?

L: Not really, if people want to er … if they want to take you for a ride, they'll always find a way, they don't need the Internet to do it. What it boils down to is being careful. You can't stop using something because it has a couple of risks.

G: Yeah, fair enough but er … so you're not really bothered about the risks?

L: No, what I'm getting at is that, it isn't an open-and-shut case but the pros definitely outweigh the cons.

G: I'm not sure you're right there. I mean you were on about music and shopping. Yeah, great, but there are so many other aspects. Information equals power nowadays, it's the key to everything – information society and all that … Are you with me?

Most of the Internet is dominated by English-speaking websites and American companies. I think I read that 75% or so of websites are in English and so …

L: Not true. It's 50%, or 50-ish, anyway. People are waking up to the fact that customers want websites in their own language … And the Internet actually helps countries that … er, countries with few resources because it gives them, you know, a kind of platform to make their problems known, and that, well that can lead to increased cooperation and tolerance between countries.

G: Yeah, that's the rose-tinted view, the Internet strengthens social bonds and all that … But the reality is the Net alienates people. What I mean is, look at how many people send emails instead of using the phone. It's so impersonal.

L: Ah, but you can always telephone over the Internet with video. That's even better than the phone!

G: OK, OK … why did I start this?

🔘 Listening script 07

Speaking and pronunciation Ex 3 from page 75

🔘 Listening script 08

Reading text from page 77

Unit 4 Team spirit

🔘 Listening script 09

Reading text from page 79

🔘 Listening script 10

(L = Liz, M = Maria, E = Ethan)

L: Hello and welcome to *Dear Liz*. I'm Liz Cooper, here to help you with all your work problems. Today our topic is difficult colleagues. And our first caller is already on the line. Maria. Hello, Maria. What's your problem?

M: Er well, I started working at an advertising agency a few months ago – it's my first job and I really like the work. The problem is that I work with someone who is always really rude when I ask a question or make a suggestion. Her whole attitude is one of non-cooperation and I've had enough of it.

L: Is this person part of your team?

M: Yes – theoretically anyway. In reality she seems to think her ideas are the best and she completely ignores whatever ideas I put forward. I'm tired of all the friction. It's really getting me down.

L: Hmm, yes, I can see your difficulty. What's interesting is that difficult people rarely see themselves as the difficult one. If you're willing to talk with this person – and I think you should do so – then it's a good idea to consider an approach that won't put your colleague on the defensive.

M: What do you mean?

L: Well, first of all talking away from your work environment might help. And rather than making assumptions or placing blame, I recommend you begin the conversation by asking questions. Ask about ways you may be contributing to the problems you've identified. Perhaps you make too many suggestions or ask questions in a manner that seems impertinent from someone who is new to the company.

M: Mmm, OK, well, I'll give it a try. Thank you.

L: You're welcome, good luck Maria. … Right, on the line now is Ethan. Hi Ethan, how can I help?

E: Hi Liz, well, I'm a student and I work at a call centre at weekends to pay for my studies. Anyway, I'd like your advice on a problem with my new supervisor. She's determined to make my life a misery.

L: What does she do exactly?

E: Well, she talks down to me and she constantly has to know my whereabouts and what I'm doing. I think she's out of order.

L: So you haven't had this problem with other supervisors?

E: Never. It's put me in a real dilemma. I can't afford to leave because like I said, I need the money for my course but I can't stand working there now.

L: Have you tried approaching your colleague directly?

E: No, I haven't. To tell the truth I'm a bit scared of her and I don't want to cause a scene.

L: Hmm, but as long as you fear her, you surrender to her. When you're not afraid of her, the dynamics of your relationship will change. Stand up to her.

E: Right, but how do I do that?

L: My advice is, speak to her and ask her about the issues she has with you. You don't have to meet with her alone; ask her manager or someone from the personnel department to be present. Then if nothing changes, you should think about going to the company's legal department.

E: OK, thank you for your advice.

L: Thank *you* for calling. Ethan. …

Unit 5 Review

🔘 Listening script 11

(P = Presenter, AW = Professor Alistair Watson)

P: A recent survey conducted by psychologists at various universities in the UK and the US has found that a person's taste in music, and how it's organised, may help predict which personality groups he or she belongs to, and that if you want to assess a person's character, a quick look through their music collection is one of the most reliable ways of doing so. With me here today to tell us more is Professor Alistair Watson. Professor Watson.

AW: Hello. Around 5,000 volunteers participated in the research. And, yes, it does seem that taste in music does, broadly speaking, correlate with a person's personality.

P: And how was the research carried out?

AW: The key element was getting the volunteers to create a 10-track CD of their favourite songs. Strangers then judged what the anonymous compilers were like. We found that the CD assessment proved significantly more reliable than any other ways of quickly assessing people such as by looks, clothes, taste in films, and so on. For example, people who listen to classical music are more likely to be, and be seen as, quite reflective, and generally very well-read and knowledgeable people. Looking at more contemporary music, pop and chart music fans tend to be quite straightforward and conventional – they're generally pretty dutiful and reliable sort of people. Whereas rap and hip-hop fans, on the other hand, are likely to be a bit more, let's say, socially liberal, rebellious and more image-conscious.

P: So, do we know why musical likes and dislikes are so closely linked to personality?

AW: Well, it seems there's much more to listening to music than, well, just enjoying it. It's thought that individuals select music to send out signals to establish how they like to be seen. For some, music can be central to their way of life, and is why they dress, have their hair and generally look the way they do.

P: But isn't that, particularly with younger people, just a way of asserting your identity?

AW: Well, to a certain extent, yes, I think it is. But at the same time, and as we were saying, a person's musical likes and dislikes can reveal a lot more about a person.

🔘 Listening script 12

(P = Presenter, AW = Professor Alistair Watson)

P: … And you also found that how a person organises their music is a reflection of their personality.

AW: Yes. People organise their CDs and MP3 files in different ways and this certainly indicates personality types. Some are alphabeticised or divided into genre and so on, or, and this is much more common we found, more randomly arranged. If your CDs are stored in no particular order then you are probably more artistic and open to new experiences and ideas. The opposite - religiously following a strict organisational formula – is a sign of an obsessive-compulsive personality. One of the volunteers in the research springs to mind. She and her fiancé live together and they have a sort of music room, which has two walls totally filled with shelves of CDs. I think they must have about a thousand between them, or thereabouts. Her CDs are very carefully organised by genre and then within this by artist and then alphabeticised yet again by album title within that. Now, she is clearly an extremely organised and reliable person, the kind who doesn't get parking tickets and that sort of thing. But what is really quite interesting is that she and her boyfriend, and I think they've been together for a couple of years now, have not yet combined their collections. Why they haven't done so, I don't know. His CDs are stacked completely randomly, by the way.

P: Mmm, maybe it would be interesting to follow that up – see where they, and their CDs, are in another two years or so. And I understand that some of the research looked at how music plays a part in the way couples interact.

AW: Yes. We monitored 'new' couples first six weeks of conversation, and discovered that they used music to 'check each other out' nearly twice as much as books, television, sport or whatever. Essentially, they were using music to communicate their character types.

P: So, next time you're trying to size somebody up, a quick look through their CD collection really does seem to be as good a place to start as any. Thank you Professor Watson.

🔘 Listening script 13

Song from page 84

Communication activities

Unit 2, Speaking and pronunciation Ex 3 page 73

1 Read your rolecard for both situations.
2 Prepare notes to help you with your roles.
3 Do the role-plays with Student A. Include the phrases in Speaking and pronunciation Ex 1 and some of the euphemisms from page 70.

Rolecard 1

Your friend was fired from his / her job a couple of months ago. He / she has been very depressed, staying at home eating fast food and watching TV. Now he / she looks terrible: pale, overweight and wearing dirty old clothes. You think your friend needs to hear the truth in order to pull himself / herself together and get on with life but given his / her emotional state, you need to tread softly.
Start like this: *Listen, I realise …*

Rolecard 2

A close friend of yours has recently died and you are very upset. Student A is your flatmate. You have been having arguments with him / her the last couple of months about money – he / she looks after the finances and pays the bills and you feel you're always being asked for money. Now you think he / she is being unfair by talking about money at a time like this.

Unit 3, Reading and vocabulary Ex 3 page 77

Answers

1 two or three   2 an hour   3 41%   4 five
5 About a quarter   6 60%   7 About half (45%)
8 43%

Unit 4, Speaking Ex 2 page 81

Analysis

How did you score?

Mostly A's

You're a natural born leader just waiting for the right job to come along. You're strong, decisive, and authoritarian. Everyone around you respects you. At least that's what you'd like to think. In reality, the situation may be rather different. At best your arrogant, autocratic approach is seen as old fashioned. You would be wise to be less punitive to those who do not see the world as you do, and open up more to the talents of those around you.

Mostly B's

You've got good potential. You support people. You listen to others. You take the initiative. All this means you have a good professional future. But only if you overcome what could become a fatal career flaw – wanting to be liked. There is nothing wrong with seeking the approval of others, but you do this to such an extent that you want to be everyone's best friend. Try to learn to confront potential conflicts with sensitivity and honesty – people will respect you more for it.

Mostly C's

Management, here you come! You're creative, assertive and empathetic. You easily draw groups together and enjoy heading them up. Most promising, though, is the importance you give to bringing on the abilities of others. You have high expectations of them, higher possibly than they have of themselves. And you seem prepared to do what you can to help them realise their own potential. Be mindful, however, not to let more superficially forceful characters conquer your position.

Mostly D's

You're smart enough to have figured out by now that your place is more likely to be in, rather than at the head of, the team. You prefer to listen to ideas, not voice them. You prefer to implement decisions rather than make them. You're a solid, reliable, loyal team player. But be cautious that in your acquiescence to others, you don't become sycophantic. At times, be prepared to do things your own way.

REVISE EDEXCEL GCSE (9–1)
French
REVISION WORKBOOK

Series Consultant: Harry Smith

Author: Stuart Glover

A note from the publisher

In order to ensure that this resource offers high-quality support for the associated Pearson qualification, it has been through a review process by the awarding body. This process confirms that this resource fully covers the teaching and learning content of the specification or part of a specification at which it is aimed. It also confirms that it demonstrates an appropriate balance between the development of subject skills, knowledge and understanding, in addition to preparation for assessment.

Endorsement does not cover any guidance on assessment activities or processes (e.g. practice questions or advice on how to answer assessment questions), included in the resource nor does it prescribe any particular approach to the teaching or delivery of a related course.

While the publishers have made every attempt to ensure that advice on the qualification and its assessment is accurate, the official specification and associated assessment guidance materials are the only authoritative source of information and should always be referred to for definitive guidance.

Pearson examiners have not contributed to any sections in this resource relevant to examination papers for which they have responsibility.

Examiners will not use endorsed resources as a source of material for any assessment set by Pearson.

Endorsement of a resource does not mean that the resource is required to achieve this Pearson qualification, nor does it mean that it is the only suitable material available to support the qualification, and any resource lists produced by the awarding body shall include this and other appropriate resources.

Difficulty scale
The scale next to each exam-style question tells you how difficult it is.

Some questions cover a range of difficulties.

The more of the scale that is shaded, the harder the question is.

Some questions are Foundation level.

Some questions are Higher level.

Some questions are applicable to both levels.

For the full range of Pearson revision titles across KS2, KS3, GCSE, Functional Skills, AS/A Level and BTEC visit:
www.pearsonschools.co.uk/revise

Contents

1-to-1 page match with the **French Revision Guide** ISBN 9781292132082

AUDIO

Audio files and transcripts for the listening exercises in this book can be accessed by using the QR codes throughout the book, or going to **www.pearsonschools.co.uk/mflrevisionaudio**

Listen to the recording

A small bit of small print
Edexcel publishes Sample Assessment Material and the Specification on its website. This is the official content and this book should be used in conjunction with it. The questions in this Workbook have been written to help you practise every topic in the book. Remember: the real exam questions may not look like this.

Physical descriptions

Comment est ta famille?

1 Lis ces descriptions des membres de la famille et des copains.

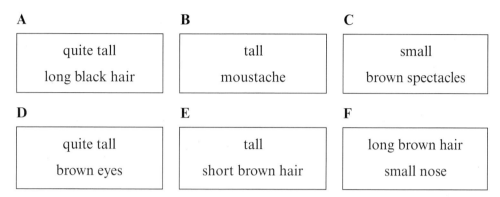

A	B	C
quite tall long black hair	tall moustache	small brown spectacles

D	E	F
quite tall brown eyes	tall short brown hair	long brown hair small nose

C'est quelle personne? Mets une croix [×] dans la case correcte.

	A	B	C	D	E	F
Exemple: Mon cousin est grand et porte la moustache.		×				
(a) Son amie a de longs cheveux marron et un petit nez.						
(b) Notre oncle Pierrot est assez grand. Il a de longs cheveux noirs.						
(c) Ma mère est assez grande et a les yeux marron.						
(d) Sa sœur est petite. Elle porte des lunettes marron.						

(4 marks)

My family's appearance

2 Pierre is describing his family. Which features are mentioned? Listen to the recording and put a cross [×] in each one of the **four** correct boxes.

Example	Body piercing	☒
A	Hair	☐
B	Beard	☐
C	Nose	☐
D	Glasses	☐
E	Feet	☐
F	Eyes	☐
G	Hands	☐

> Look at the words in A–G and think of the French words you are likely to hear. You will be better prepared when you listen!

(4 marks)

Character descriptions

Conversation: Talking about your friends

1 As part of a conversation topic, you might be asked questions about many aspects of yourself, your family and friends. Prepare answers to these questions and then speak for about 30 seconds on each one.

> For all the questions, try to add details and reasons, and use more complex vocabulary if you can. For example, rather than saying *je suis bavard(e)*, why not add complexity by saying *on dit que je suis bavard(e)*?

(a) Tu es quelle sorte de personne?

(b) Décris la personnalité d'un copain / une copine.

> Remember to make any adjective you use agree with the gender of the person whose character you are describing.

(c) Pourquoi est-ce que tu t'entends avec tes amis?

Claire's family

2 Read what Claire says about her family members.

> Mon petit frère s'appelle David. En général, il est sympa, mais s'il est fatigué, il n'est pas très facile. Ma sœur Danielle est toujours optimiste et elle s'entend bien avec toute la famille, sauf notre grand frère, qui s'appelle Marc. Ma mère est un peu plus sévère que mon père, surtout quand nous sommes à table. Mais de temps en temps, mon père peut être très drôle!

Put a cross [×] in each one of the **four** correct boxes.

Example:	Claire's brother is called David.	☒
A	David is usually pleasant.	☐
B	David is always pleasant.	☐
C	Danielle is optimistic.	☐
D	Danielle does not have any brothers.	☐
E	Danielle gets on well with most of the family.	☐
F	The dad is stricter than the mum at meal times.	☐
G	The family never sits around the meal table together.	☐
H	The dad is occasionally funny.	☐

(4 marks)

Describing family

Brothers and sisters

1 Ludovic is talking about his family. Which descriptions are mentioned? Listen to the recording and put a cross [×] in each one of the **four** correct boxes

Example	Doesn't talk to me	☒
A	Is fun to play with	☐
B	Buys me treats	☐
C	Talks too much	☐
D	Is boring	☐
E	Sometimes won't play with me	☐
F	Is sometimes mean	☐
G	Is always kind	☐

Listen out for the key verbs (play, buy, talk).

Think about how you are going to distinguish between two sentences with the same verb. Usually this will be with negatives (*ne ... pas*) and/or adverbs (*quelquefois, souvent*, etc).

(4 marks)

Ma famille

2 Traduis les phrases suivantes **en français**.

Use *mon* (masculine), *ma* (feminine) for 'my'.

(a) I like my family.

.... **(2 marks)**

(b) My brother is annoying.

.... **(2 marks)**

(c) My sister is quite tall.   Remember that the words for 'sister' and 'mother' are feminine.

.... **(2 marks)**

(d) I get on with my mother because she is kind.

....

.... **(3 marks)**

(e) My father gets on my nerves sometimes.   Remember that *m'énerve* means 'gets on my nerves'.

....

.... **(3 marks)**

Friends

Talking about my friends

1   Read these comments relating to friendship.

> **Quelles sont les qualités de vos ami(e)s?**
>
> Mon amie Maryse ne refuse jamais d'aider ses amis.
>
> Suzanne est toujours prête à donner de l'argent aux personnes pauvres.
>
> Mon meilleur ami Robert aime bien écouter les avis de tout le monde.
>
> Lola essaie d'identifier une qualité si on lui demande son avis sur un collègue.
>
> Carla n'est jamais de mauvaise humeur, même si elle est fatiguée.

What is said about each person?

A   Concentrates on people's strengths

B   Never moody

C   Always says 'yes' if a friend needs help

D   Willing to give financial assistance

E   Not tiresome

F   Valuing others' opinions

G   Optimistic

	A	B	C	D	E	F	G
Example: Maryse			×				
Suzanne							
Robert							
Lola							
Carla							

(4 marks)

Picture-based task: My friends

2   Regarde la photo et prépare des réponses aux questions suivantes.

(a) Décris-moi la photo.

> You need to be able to prepare a few sentences about the photo you see. Here you could describe some of the people, and suggest who they might be and where the picture might have been taken.

(b) Je pense qu'un ami devrait être sociable. Quel est ton avis?

> Make sure you know what is being asked. You can ask for a question to be repeated in French.

(c) Mon meilleur ami est gentil et bavard. Comment est ton meilleur ami / ta meilleure amie?

(d) Qu'est-ce que tu as fait récemment avec tes copains?

> This is a good opportunity to use the past tense in both the *je* and the *nous* form.

(e) Qu'est-ce que tu vas faire avec tes copains le week-end prochain?

> At higher level, the last question is 'unpredictable', which means you won't be able to prepare for it. But it will be around the same topic, so take some time to think about relevant vocabulary and phrases that may come in useful.

Role models

Mon oncle

1   Lis cet e-mail de Marcel au sujet de son oncle.

> ✉
>
> Mon oncle m'a toujours inspiré parce qu'il a réussi dans la vie sans avoir beaucoup d'argent. Il a commencé sa propre entreprise à l'âge de seize ans et maintenant il a une grande maison de luxe avec une piscine en plein air dans le sud de la France. Il vient de prendre sa retraite, après avoir gagné plein d'argent.
>
> Cependant, je ne pense pas que l'argent soit la chose la plus importante au monde. Au contraire, je respecte mon grand-père qui a élevé cinq enfants, y compris mon père, après la mort de sa femme. Il est vraiment têtu mais aussi travailleur et responsable.

Trouve les **quatre** bonnes phrases. Mets une croix [×] dans les cases correspondantes.

A	L'oncle de Marcel a toujours été très riche.	☐
B	Son oncle a fondé une entreprise quand il était jeune.	☐
C	Il ne travaille plus.	☐
D	Il a perdu plein d'argent.	☐
E	Marcel pense que l'argent est la chose la plus importante dans la vie.	☐
F	Son grand-père a lutté contre des difficultés.	☐
G	La grand-mère de Marcel est morte.	☐
H	Marcel ne respecte pas ceux qui sont têtus.	☐

> Don't forget to look out for negatives in both the passage and the statements. Don't just assume that because a word is in both, it is the correct answer!

(4 marks)

Les gens qui m'inspirent

2   Écoute Lucie qui parle des gens qui l'inspirent.

Complète les phrases en mettant une croix [×] dans la case correcte.

> If you hear an unfamiliar word, listen very carefully for accompanying words that you do recognise and which may help you to guess the one you don't know.

Listen to the recording

(a) Lucie admire …

☐	A la musique de Carla Bruni
☐	B le look de Carla Bruni
☐	C l'argent de Carla Bruni
☐	D les vêtements de Carla Bruni

(b) Le père de Lucie …

☐	A a trouvé Carla impolie
☐	B n'a jamais rencontré Carla Bruni
☐	C pense que Carla est modeste
☐	D pense que Carla est embêtante

(c) Lucie est impressionnée par …

☐	A le travail bénévole de Carla
☐	B le mariage de Carla
☐	C la famille de Carla
☐	D le mari de Carla

(d) Carla est …

☐	A née en France
☐	B mère de famille
☐	C mécontente
☐	D célibataire

(4 marks)

Relationships

Une photo de famille

1 Ton frère aîné t'a envoyé cette photo de sa famille.

Fais une description de la photo **et** exprime ton opinion sur la famille.

Écris 20–30 mots environ **en français**.

....
....
....
....
....
....
....

> This is a short task so don't be tempted to write more than the suggested number of words.

(12 marks)

Translation

2 Translate this passage **into English**.

> Je m'entends bien avec mon petit frère. Il est compréhensif et amusant, mais je me dispute souvent avec ma sœur. Hier elle a pris ma jupe sans me demander la permission. Elle n'aide jamais à la maison et elle m'énerve tout le temps. Elle m'a dit qu'elle va être moins paresseuse.

> Remember that *je m'entends* and *je me dispute* are reflexive verbs so you won't need to translate *m'* or *me* here, but you will need to translate them later in the passage!
>
> *Sans* is followed by an infinitive in French but you don't use one in English.

....
....
....
....
....
....
....

....   **(7 marks)**

When I was younger

Activities in the past

1   This French teenager is talking about what she did when she was young. Which of the following activities did she do?

Listen to the recording and put a cross [×] in each one of the **four** correct boxes.

Listen to the recording

Example	horse riding	☒
A	swimming	☐
B	judo	☐
C	wind surfing	☐
D	ballet	☐
E	skiing	☐
F	computing	☐
G	cinema	☐

(4 marks)

Conversation: When I was younger

2   As part of a conversation topic, you might talk about what things used to be like when you were younger. Prepare answers to these questions and then speak for about 30 seconds on each one.

> Use the imperfect tense where it is needed to talk about what you used to do.

(a)   Où habitais-tu quand tu étais plus jeune?

(b)   Quels étaient tes passe-temps quand tu étais plus jeune?

(c)   Où allais-tu en vacances quand tu étais plus jeune?

7

Peer group

Peer pressure

1   You hear Mamadou talking about peer pressure.

Listen to the recording and answer the following questions **in English**.

(a) What do members of Mamadou's gang have in common? Give **two** details.

....

....   **(2 marks)**

(b) What happened a few months ago? Give **two** details.

....

....   **(2 marks)**

(c) What happened the next day? Give **two** details.

....

....   **(2 marks)**

(d) How does Mamadou feel?

....   **(1 mark)**

(e) Why did he do what he did?

....   **(1 mark)**

Faire comme les autres

2   Traduis le passage suivant **en français**.

Lots of my friends have tattoos and piercings, but I don't like them because I think that they are ugly. Last week I went into town with my sister and we saw a boy from my school who had a piercing in his nose. My sister has now decided to have a piercing because all her friends have them but in my opinion she is mad.

> 'I don't like them' – Remember that pronouns come before the verb in French.

> 'ugly' – This refers to tattoos and piercings, so it must be plural.

> 'has now decided to have' Remember that it is *décider de* + infinitive.

> 'mad' – Remember that adjectives need to agree with the noun they refer to. In this case, 'she'.

....

....

....

....

....

....

....

....

....   **(12 marks)**

Money

Picture-based task: All about money

1 Regarde la photo et prépare des réponses aux questions suivantes.

(a) Décris-moi la photo.

(b) À mon avis, l'argent ne fait pas le bonheur. Qu'en penses-tu?

> This is a tricky question so keep your answer simple unless you are very confident.

(c) Comment gagnes-tu de l'argent?

(d) Tu aimes faire des économies? Pourquoi (pas)?

> Always give a reason for any opinion if you can.

(e) Comment vas-tu dépenser ton argent la semaine prochaine?

Spending money

2 These three French teenagers are talking about what they are going to buy.

Complete the sentences. Use the correct word or phrase from the box.

Listen to the recording

spend all the pocket money	laptop	buy a cheap one
birthday present	mobile phone	more up to date
cheaper	scarf	desktop computer
blouse	tablet	birthday card

(a) Marthe is going to buy a .... and a

.... **(2 marks)**

(b) Claude would like to buy a .... but does not want to

.... **(2 marks)**

(c) Janine is looking for a .... which is

.... **(2 marks)**

Customs

Different customs

1 Read this email from Kamodou and answer the following questions **in English**.

> ✉
>
> Après être arrivé en France il y a deux mois, j'ai remarqué beaucoup de différences entre la vie au Cameroun et la vie en France. Je pense qu'on est plus formel en France. Par exemple, quand on rencontre quelqu'un on se serre la main, mais il ne faut pas être trop agressif car c'est considéré comme un geste grossier. J'ai été accepté par tous les Français parce que la France a toujours été promotrice de la tolérance raciale et culturelle. En fin de compte, je dirais que tout se passe bien ici!

(a) Where does Kamodou come from?

.... **(1 mark)**

(b) Why does he think cultural life in France is more formal?

.... **(1 mark)**

(c) What is considered to be coarse?

.... **(1 mark)**

(d) What does he say about racial tolerance in France?

.... **(1 mark)**

La vie en France

2 Écoute Marianne qui parle de la vie en France.

Listen to the recording

Trouve les **quatre** bonnes phrases. Mets une croix [×] dans la case correcte.

A	Marianne est française.	☐
B	Elle pense que la vie en Belgique est différente de celle en France.	☐
C	Les Français font attention à ce qu'ils mangent.	☐
D	Les Français mangent trop.	☐
E	En France on ne va pas souvent au cinéma.	☐
F	La France est réputée pour son cinéma.	☐
G	On arrive toujours à l'heure pour une réunion de famille.	☐
H	Il est normal d'arriver à une fête après l'heure convenue.	☐

(4 marks)

Everyday life

Role-play: At the sports centre

1   You are talking to a member of staff at a French sports centre. The teacher will play the role of the employee and will speak first. You must address the employee as *vous*.

You will talk to the teacher using the five prompts below.

- Where you see –? – you must ask a question.
- Where you see –! – you must respond to something you have not prepared.

Vous êtes au centre sportif. Vous parlez à un(e) employé(e).

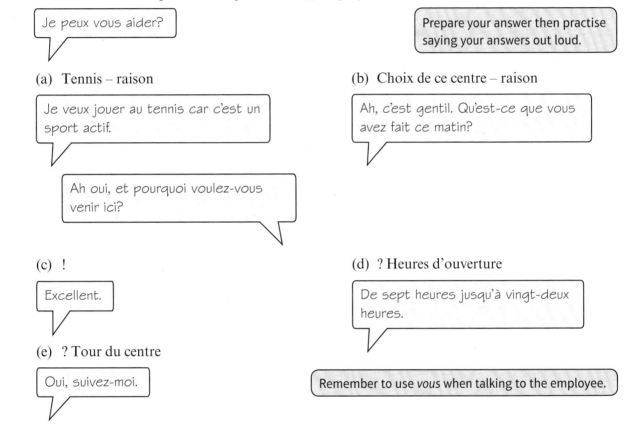

> Je peux vous aider?

> Prepare your answer then practise saying your answers out loud.

Guided

(a) Tennis – raison

> Je veux jouer au tennis car c'est un sport actif.

(b) Choix de ce centre – raison

> Ah, c'est gentil. Qu'est-ce que vous avez fait ce matin?

> Ah oui, et pourquoi voulez-vous venir ici?

(c) !

> Excellent.

(d) ? Heures d'ouverture

> De sept heures jusqu'à vingt-deux heures.

(e) ? Tour du centre

> Oui, suivez-moi.

> Remember to use *vous* when talking to the employee.

La vie quotidienne

2   Écoute Flora qui parle de sa vie quotidienne.

Complète les phrases en choisissant un mot ou des mots de la case. Il y a des mots que tu n'utiliseras pas.

> | travail scolaire | aime | un jour | prend |
> |---|---|---|---|
> | dort | vite | le matin | pas |
> | les sports | beaucoup | fait ses devoirs | les activités |

Listen to the recording

[QR code]

(a) Flora ne .... pas tard.   **(1 mark)**

(b) Flora ne mange .... le matin.   **(1 mark)**

(c) Le soir, elle ....   **(1 mark)**

(d) Elle n'aime pas .... d'équipe.   **(1 mark)**

Meals at home

A birthday celebration

1 Read Sylvestre's account of his mother's birthday.

> Je ne vais jamais oublier le repas extraordinaire que nous avons fait chez nous il y a un mois. C'était pour fêter les soixante-quinze ans de ma mère. Nous lui avions demandé si elle voulait bien inviter ses amis, mais elle a dit qu'elle pourrait trouver ça assez stressant et que son rhume n'était pas complètement parti.
>
> Mon père a tout préparé car il a voulu montrer à toute la famille qu'il était doué pour faire la cuisine et il pensait que Maman méritait de se détendre le jour de son anniversaire. J'ai été très surpris par la qualité supérieure de ce que nous avons mangé, alors que ma sœur n'a rien aimé.
>
> Quand elle a compris que Papa avait préparé ce repas merveilleux, Maman a été très reconnaissante et a trouvé ça incroyable.
>
> Hier, elle m'a dit qu'elle espère qu'il va recommencer avec le repas de Noël!

Answer the following questions in **English**.

You do not need to answer in full sentences.

(a) How long ago was this special meal?

.... **(1 mark)**

(b) Why didn't the mother want to invite lots of other guests?

.... **(1 mark)**

(c) What did the father seek to do by cooking the birthday meal?

.... **(1 mark)**

(d) What did Sylvestre's sister think of the meal? .... **(1 mark)**

(e) What was the mother's initial reaction when she realised who had cooked the meal?

.... **(1 mark)**

Manger en famille

2 Tu postes cette photo sur des médias sociaux pour tes amis.

Fais une description de la photo **et** donne ton opinion sur le petit déjeuner chez toi.

Écris 20–30 mots environ **en français**.

....

....

....

....

....

.... **(12 marks)**

Food and drink

La cuisine régionale

1 Lis cet e-mail de Martin au sujet de la cuisine régionale.

> ✉
>
> Je viens de passer quinze jours en Normandie et la cuisine était superbe. J'ai surtout aimé les produits laitiers qui sont d'une qualité exceptionnelle. Le camembert est sans conteste le fromage français le plus connu au monde. La région est connue aussi pour l'agneau, le bœuf et les fruits de mer dont les moules qui sont les fruits de mer préférés des gens du coin. Les pommes jouent un rôle important dans la cuisine normande, tant dans les desserts que dans la fabrication du cidre.
>
> La semaine dernière, j'ai goûté du porc aux cerises avec des poireaux. C'était délicieux. Mmm!

Mets une croix [×] dans la case correcte.

(a) Martin a préféré …

☐	**A** la viande
☐	**B** les produits laitiers
☐	**C** le poisson
☐	**D** les boissons

(b) Les habitants aiment mieux …

☐	**A** l'agneau
☐	**B** le bœuf
☐	**C** les moules
☐	**D** le porc

(c) On consomme … comme boisson et comme nourriture.

☐	**A** les fruits de mer
☐	**B** les cerises
☐	**C** les pommes
☐	**D** les oranges

(d) Martin a récemment …

☐	**A** mangé un repas délicieux
☐	**B** goûté du cidre
☐	**C** consommé des moules
☐	**D** bu du vin

(4 marks)

À manger et à boire

2 Traduis les phrases suivantes **en français**.

(a) I like eating fish.

> You will have to translate 'eating' as an infinitive in French.

.... **(2 marks)**

(b) I don't like coffee.

.... **(2 marks)**

(c) I have cereal for breakfast.

> Remember – the word for 'cereal' becomes plural in French.

.... **(2 marks)**

(d) We usually have dinner at 6.00 pm.

.... **(3 marks)**

(e) This evening I am going to eat at a smart restaurant with my family.

> The adjective for 'smart' comes after the word it describes.

.... **(3 marks)**

Shopping

Magali's shopping trip

1 Read about Magali's experience of shopping.

> En général, je fais les magasins le week-end avec mon ami Robert. Samedi dernier, nous y sommes arrivés un peu après huit heures et demie car je voulais être en ville avant l'ouverture des magasins. Robert a passé beaucoup de temps à trouver une veste, mais finalement il en a acheté une dans le troisième magasin où nous sommes allés. Après avoir déjeuné, nous avons fait d'autres magasins parce que je voulais vraiment acheter un roman pour l'anniversaire de ma mère. Deux heures plus tard, nous étions trop fatigués pour continuer nos achats. Alors, nous avons pris un petit café. Après ça, il ne me restait que trente minutes pour trouver un deuxième cadeau pour ma mère. Malheureusement, c'était trop tard car le dernier bus de la journée n'allait pas nous attendre! Je n'ai pas envie de retourner en ville demain, mais je n'ai pas le choix.

What does Magali say about shopping? Put a cross [×] in each one of the **four** correct boxes.

Example:	Magali goes shopping on a Saturday morning.	☒
A	Last Saturday, Magali arrived in town just before eight o'clock.	☐
B	Magali wanted to be in town before the shops opened.	☐
C	Robert managed to find a new jacket.	☐
D	They visited just three shops that day.	☐
E	Magali wanted to buy a book for her mother's birthday.	☐
F	By two o'clock, the friends were both very tired.	☐
G	They relaxed for thirty minutes in the café.	☐
H	They had to wait thirty minutes at the bus stop.	☐
I	Magali will need to return to town the following day.	☐

(4 marks)

Shopping plans

2 Listen to these young French people saying what they are going to buy.

Complete the sentences. Use the correct word or phrase from the box.

Listen to the recording

> some earrings   some flowers   some gloves
>
> a bracelet   a bag   a book

(a) Camille is going to buy .... **(1 mark)**

(b) Assiom would like to buy .... **(1 mark)**

(c) Carine is going to buy .... **(1 mark)**

Shopping for food

Buying food

1 Listen to these people buying food.

Complete the sentences. Use the correct word from the box.

> mushrooms   cauliflower   cabbage
>
> eggs   ham   jam

(a) The customer would like some ....   **(1 mark)**

(b) The shopkeeper has no ....   **(1 mark)**

(c) The customer wants to buy ....   **(1 mark)**

Faire les courses

2 Tu es en France et tu postes cette photo sur des médias sociaux pour tes amis.

Fais une description de la photo **et** exprime une opinion sur les magasins en France.

Écris 20–30 mots environ **en français**.

....

....

....

....   **(12 marks)**

Social media

Translation

1 Translate this passage **into English**.

> Je passe beaucoup de temps sur les réseaux sociaux. Je crois que je ne pourrais pas vivre sans mon portable. Je sais qu'il existe plein de dangers, mais c'est un moyen efficace de se renseigner sur les événements mondiaux. Je peux suivre les activités de mes copains et, récemment, une copine a posté une photo de son chien en ligne et tous ses amis l'ont trouvé amusante.

passe – Be careful – this doesn't mean that she is passing something, so find an alternative which makes sense.

pourrais – Be careful with the tense.

il existe – This is just a different way of saying *il y a* in French.

a posté – Remember that this is a past tense.

....

....

....

....

....

....

....

(7 marks)

Role-play: Opinions about social media

2 You are talking to your Belgian penfriend about social media. The teacher will play the role of the penfriend and will speak first. You must address your penfriend as *tu*.

Remember to use *tu* with a friend.

Tu parles avec ton ami(e) belge au sujet des médias sociaux.

Prepare your answer then practise saying your answers aloud.

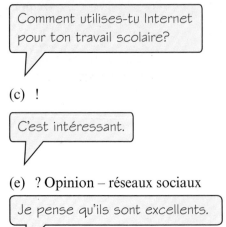

> Je viens de poster une photo en ligne.

(a) Opinion sur Facebook – raison

> Comment utilises-tu Internet pour ton travail scolaire?

(b) Recherches

> Moi aussi. Qu'est-ce que tu as fait en ligne hier soir?

(c) !

> C'est intéressant.

(d) ? Utilisation d'Internet

> Je tchatte avec mes copains.

(e) ? Opinion – réseaux sociaux

> Je pense qu'ils sont excellents.

Technology

Using the internet

1 Read these views on internet use.

> - On peut acheter ses billets de train sur Internet.
> - Pour mes devoirs, Internet est très pratique.
> - Sur Internet, les livres coûtent moins cher.
> - Les parents doivent limiter le temps que leurs enfants passent sur Internet.
> - Je n'imprime pas beaucoup de documents.
> - À mon avis, mon frère passe trop de temps sur Internet.
> - Les sondages sur Internet sont très populaires.
> - Malheureusement, il n'y a pas d'Internet dans notre village.
> - Je trouve que mon clavier est trop petit.

Put a cross [×] next to the **four** ideas mentioned above.

Example:	Using the internet to complete homework	☒
A	Spending too much money on internet purchases	☐
B	Size of keyboard	☐
C	Buying bus tickets online	☐
D	Internet not available locally	☐
E	Cost of printing documents	☐
F	Opinion polls	☐
G	Saving money on the cost of books	☐
H	Parents spending too much time online	☐

> Don't just rely on spotting a word that seems to be related to the answer. Make sure you are really sure it is right before answering.

(4 marks)

Conversation: Using technology

2 As part of a conversation topic, you might talk about your usage of the internet. Prepare answers to these questions and then speak for about 30 seconds on each one.

  (a) Tu aimes faire des achats en ligne? Pourquoi (pas)?

> Remember to add a reason.

  (b) Tu as souvent téléchargé de la musique?

> Refer to a specific example to show that you can use past tenses correctly.

  (c) Comment vas-tu utiliser la technologie la semaine prochaine?

> This gives you the chance to show that you can use future time frames

Internet advantages and disadvantages

Avantages et inconvénients

1 Lis ce passage au sujet d'Internet, écrit par Ruvimbo. Complète chaque phrase en utilisant une phrase de la case. Attention! Il y a des phrases que tu n'utiliseras pas.

> La plupart du temps, je pense qu'Internet est une bonne chose parce que ça nous permet de faire plein de choses qui ne nous semblaient qu'un rêve quand j'avais dix ans. Une fois que j'aurai terminé mes devoirs, je passerai plus d'une heure à chercher des cadeaux sur Internet, sachant que je pourrai trouver les choses que je veux offrir à ma famille à Noël. En plus, ça me coûterait peut-être plus cher de tout acheter dans les magasins. D'habitude, je me débrouille pour tout commander avant le quinze décembre, mais cette année, je n'ai pas l'argent nécessaire pour terminer mes achats car je ne suis jamais payée avant le vingt du mois.
>
> Tout à l'heure, je vais même pouvoir bavarder avec mes cousins au Ghana, sans avoir besoin d'utiliser le téléphone. Mais je vais me dépêcher car je dois éteindre l'ordinateur avant dix heures.
>
> Mais imaginez le sentiment d'horreur d'une de mes collègues le mois dernier! Elle vérifiait que son salaire était bien sur son compte bancaire et a vu que quelqu'un lui avait volé tout l'argent. Au début, la banque n'a pas voulu écouter ma collègue, disant qu'elle aurait dû mieux protéger ses informations personnelles. La banque a mis trois semaines à rembourser l'argent volé et à vérifier qu'elle n'avait pas donné son mot de passe à une autre personne.

Complétez le phrases.

(a) L'Internet donne la possibilité ....

(b) Pour finir ses achats de Noël, Ruvimbo ....

(c) Ruvimbo utilise Internet ....

(d) L'ordinateur de Ruvimbo ne reste pas allumé ....

(e) La collègue de Ruvimbo ....

(f) La banque n'a pas eu très envie de ....

> toute la soirée   aura besoin d'attendre   va vérifier son compte bancaire
>
> a eu une mauvaise surprise   de faire beaucoup de choses
>
> rembourser l'argent volé à Ruvimbo   croire sa cliente
>
> économisera de l'argent dans les magasins   pour parler avec d'autres personnes

(6 marks)

Le pour et le contre

2 Écoute André qui parle des avantages et des inconvénients d'Internet.

Trouve les **quatre** bonnes phrases. Mets une croix [×] dans la case correcte.

A	Rester en contact avec des copains	☒
B	Le cyber harcèlement	☐
C	Faire des achats en ligne	☒
D	Télécharger de la musique	☐

E	Le vol d'identité	☐
F	Favoriser des habitudes malsaines	☒
G	L'addiction et la dépendance	☒
H	La recherche de l'information	☒

(4 marks)

Arranging to go out

Where shall we go?

1 These young people are inviting their friends out. Where do they suggest?

A	**B**	**C**	**D**	**E**	**F**
leisure centre	park	swimming	sports stadium	cinema	shopping centre

Listen to the recording and put a cross [×] in the **four** correct boxes.

	A	**B**	**C**	**D**	**E**	**F**
Example: Jacques					×	
(a) Anna						
(b) Éric						
(c) Bella						
(d) Paul						

(4 marks)

Excuses, excuses!

2 Patrick is inviting friends to go out. Read their replies to his invitation.

- Je suis désolée mais je dois me laver les cheveux.
- Mes parents disent que je dois préparer le repas de ma sœur.
- Je suis malade aujourd'hui.
- Je n'ai pas le temps.
- Je n'aurai pas mon argent de poche avant demain.
- Il va y avoir du brouillard ce soir.
- Je serai trop fatiguée pour y aller.
- Maman dit que je dois me coucher à neuf heures.
- Ce soir, je vais être obligée de faire la cuisine pour mon frère.

Identify the excuses given. Put a cross [×] in each one of the **four** correct boxes.

Example:	I need to wash my hair.	☒
A	I've spent my pocket money.	☐
B	I'm feeling unwell.	☐
C	I'll be too tired.	☐
D	I need to play with my sister.	☐
E	I need to prepare my brother's meal.	☐
F	The weather will be cold.	☐
G	I don't get my pocket money until tomorrow.	☐
H	I must go out with my parents.	☐

(4 marks)

Hobbies

Les passe-temps

1 Ton ami Alain t'a envoyé un e-mail au sujet de ses passe-temps.

Écris une réponse à Alain. Tu **dois** faire référence aux points suivants:
- ce que tu aimes avoir comme passe-temps le week-end et pourquoi
- ce que tu as fait le week-end dernier
- ce que tu vas faire le week-end prochain
- un nouveau passe-temps que tu voudrais essayer.

Écris 80–90 mots environ **en français**.

> Make sure you cover all the bullet points.

Guided

Ma passion c'est ....

....

....

....

....

....

.... **(20 marks)**

Picture-based task: Leisure activities

> To practise speaking activities like this, you can prepare a list of possible answers to questions on certain topics which could be useful here from question (b) onwards. Try to be flexible and adapt what you know or have tried to learn when you are asked questions in response to a photo or as part of a more general conversation.

2 Regarde la photo et prépare des réponses aux questions suivantes.

(a) Décris-moi la photo.

(b) Moi, je n'aime pas les jeux vidéo. Quel est ton avis? Pourquoi?

(c) Parle-moi d'un passe-temps que tu avais quand tu étais plus jeune.

(d) Qu'est-ce que tu vas avoir comme passe-temps la semaine prochaine?

(e) Tu penses que les jeunes devraient être plus actifs? Pourquoi (pas)?

> Try to add some development to your answers, for example by adding opinions and reasons.

Music

Un événement musical

1 Tu participes à un événement musical en France. Tu postes cette photo sur des médias sociaux pour tes amis.

Écris une description de la photo et exprime une opinion sur la musique.

Écris 20–30 mots environ **en français**.

> **Guided**

Sur la photo ....

....

....

....

....

....

> Don't try to describe everyone – there isn't enough space!

(12 marks)

Conversation: Musical activities

2 As part of a conversation topic, you might talk about your musical knowledge. Prepare answers to these questions and then speak for about 30 seconds on each one.

   (a) Tu joues d'un instrument de musique?

   (b) Quelle sorte de musique préfères-tu? Pourquoi?

   (c) Décris un concert auquel tu as assisté.

> Don't just say *Oui/Non*. Add a detail or explain why.

> Don't worry if you have never been to a concert – just make one up.

Sport

A sports fan

1   Read this article about Stéphanie's sport routine.

> Je m'appelle Stéphanie et je m'intéresse à tous les sports. Je pense que le sport est bon pour la santé. Par contre mon père n'est pas d'accord parce qu'il s'est fait très mal à la main pendant qu'il jouait au rugby la semaine dernière. Pendant l'hiver, je joue au rugby au collège, mais ce n'est pas mon sport favori.
>
> Ça fait plus de cinq ans que je fais de la natation. J'essaie d'y aller deux ou trois fois par semaine, mais je n'y vais pas si ma mère ne veut pas m'emmener à la piscine en voiture. Je n'y vais jamais en bus parce que je n'aime pas attendre à l'arrêt d'autobus. La plupart de mes amis aiment bien faire de la natation.
>
> Si j'ai de bonnes notes aux examens en juin, je vais continuer mes études. Ma profession idéale, ce serait professeur d'EPS. Je serais alors obligée de faire trois ans d'études universitaires pour y arriver. Sinon, j'aimerais bien devenir monitrice de ski. Par contre, j'apprécierais moins l'idée de travailler dans un centre sportif où il y aurait trop d'adultes.

Put a cross [×] in the correct box.

> Know how to spot **relevant** details, not necessarily those which first attract your attention.

(a) Stéphanie's father…

☐	**A** will be playing rugby next week.
☐	**B** recently injured his hand.
☐	**C** has not played rugby for months.

(b) Swimming is a sport Stéphanie began …

☐	**A** two or three weeks ago.
☐	**B** over five years ago.
☐	**C** more than a month ago.

(c) If her mum can't drive her to the pool, Stéphanie …

☐	**A** doesn't go swimming.
☐	**B** visits one of her friends.
☐	**C** takes the bus to the pool.

(d) Stéphanie would really prefer to …

☐	**A** work in an office.
☐	**B** become a teacher.
☐	**C** train to be a skiing instructor.

(4 marks)

C'est quel sport?

2   Écoute ces jeunes qui parlent du sport.

Complète les phrases en mettant une croix [×] dans la case correcte.

(a) Sacha aime …

☐	**A** les sports d'équipe
☐	**B** la natation
☐	**C** jouer au volley
☐	**D** tous les sports

(b) Romelu aime mieux …

☐	**A** le rugby
☐	**B** la boxe
☐	**C** les sports nautiques
☐	**D** le foot

(c) Ariane déteste …

☐	**A** jouer au basket
☐	**B** faire du cheval
☐	**C** faire du vélo
☐	**D** aller à la pêche

(3 marks)

Reading

La lecture

1   Traduis les phrases suivantes **en français**.

(a)   I like reading comics.

> Notice how the present participle, ending in '-ing' in English, is translated by **an infinitive** in French.

J'aime lire des bandes dessinées.   **(2 marks)**

(b)   My brother likes to read.

.... **(2 marks)**

(c)   I don't like to read the newspaper every day.

.... **(2 marks)**

> You could use *on* for 'you', which uses the same part of the verb as *il* or *elle*.

(d)   You can read magazines online.

....

.... **(3 marks)**

(e)   Next weekend I would like to read a detective novel.

> The word for 'detective' is an adjective here – remember that most adjectives come after the word they describe in French.

....

.... **(3 marks)**

Translation

2   Translate this passage **into English**.

> Make sure you read back what you have written to make sure that it sounds natural and makes sense.

Je lisais un roman historique quand ma mère est entrée dans le salon. Puisqu'elle ne lit que des magazines de mode, elle m'a regardée d'un air négatif. Pourtant j'ai continué à lire, car la lecture est ma grande passion. Je lis n'importe quoi mais de préférence des histoires d'amour parce qu'on peut s'échapper de la vie de tous les jours et oublier tous ses soucis.

> *Je lisais* – This is an imperfect tense, so remember how to translate this.

> *ne … que* – This is not really a negative – take care.

> *m'a regardé* – Remember that *m'* is a pronoun so it comes before the verb in French but not in English!

....

....

....

....

....

....

.... **(7 marks)**

Films

At the cinema

1   Read the following article.

> **Si vous aimez le cinéma, profitez de nos offres exceptionnelles pour le mois de janvier**
>
> Tout le monde peut profiter de ces réductions! Mais n'hésitez pas trop avant de réserver vos billets, car les places vont partir très vite.
>
> Dans la salle de cinéma, n'oubliez pas d'être assis à votre place avant le début de la séance et d'éteindre votre portable. Nous vous en remercions d'avance.
>
> Bien entendu, on invite les personnes de tout âge à venir voir les films, mais pensez surtout aux jeunes enfants qui se fatiguent facilement et qui perdent souvent leur concentration pendant les séances du soir.
>
> Rappelez-vous également que nos chers clients peuvent garer leur voiture gratuitement et en toute sécurité dans notre parking souterrain.

Answer the following questions **in English**.

(a) During January, who can take advantage of the reduced-price seats?

.... **(1 mark)**

(b) Why exactly is early booking advised? .... **(1 mark)**

(c) What must spectators not forget to do, once in the screening room?

    (i)   ....

    (ii)   .... **(2 marks)**

(d) Give two reasons why bringing children to evening films may not be advisable.

    (i)   ....

    (ii)   .... **(2 marks)**

(e) Name two advantages of using the cinema's own car park.

    (i)   ....   (ii)   .... **(2 marks)**

An interesting film

2   You hear Romain talking about a film he has seen. Listen to the recording and complete the sentences by putting a cross [×] in the correct box for each question.

Listen to the recording

Example: Romain saw a …

A	documentary	☐
B	horror film	☐
C	crime film	☒
D	romantic comedy	☐

(a) He saw the film in …

A	Britain	☐
B	Bruges	☐
C	Quebec	☐
D	France	☐

(b) The film was …

A	subtitled	☐
B	in black and white	☐
C	in English	☐
D	in Spanish	☐

(c) The main character was the …

A	hired killer	☐
B	victim	☐
C	town of Bruges	☐
D	student	☐

(4 marks)

TV

What's on?

1 Aline and her husband Frédéric are discussing television programmes.

Complete the sentences. Use the correct word or phrase from the box.

Listen to the recording

| factual programmes | ~~films~~ | news |
| cartoons | game shows | soap operas |

> Try to work out what you are going to hear when the French speaker mentions these types of programme.

Example: Aline likes watching films.

(a) Aline is bored by the .... **(1 mark)**

(b) Frédéric recommends the .... **(1 mark)**

(c) Aline likes to watch the .... each evening. **(1 mark)**

(d) For Aline, the .... are on too late. **(1 mark)**

Un article sur la télé

2 Un magazine français cherche un article sur la télé.

Écrivez un article au sujet de vos préférences en ce qui concerne la télé pour intéresser les lecteurs.

Vous **devez** faire référence aux points suivants:
- ce que vous aimez regarder à la télé et pourquoi
- une émission que vous avez vue récemment
- un programme que vous voudriez regarder à l'avenir
- votre lieu préféré pour regarder des films.

> It is important to cover all the points mentioned, and don't forget to give and justify your opinions.

Justifiez vos idées et vos opinions.

Écrivez 130–150 mots environ **en français**.

....

....

....

....

....

....

....

....

....

> Continue on lined paper if you need more space.

.... **(28 marks)**

Celebrations

La fête de Pâques

1 Lis cet article sur Pâques et réponds aux questions **en français**.

> Pâques est avant tout une fête chrétienne très répandue en France, célébrée en souvenir de la résurrection de Jésus. C'est l'occasion de grandes messes et de processions religieuses mais c'est aussi un jour de joie où les familles et les amis se retrouvent et profitent de ce moment de fête pour savourer des plats délicieux, y compris de l'agneau, et bien sûr beaucoup de chocolat!
>
> Les enfants cherchent, dans la maison et le jardin, des œufs en chocolat que, selon une tradition qui date du onzième siècle, les cloches de Rome ont fait tomber du ciel. Naturellement ce sont en fait les parents qui les ont cachés. Puisque les Français sont un peu gourmands, on ne consomme pas que des œufs en chocolat, mais aussi des lapins et des poissons en chocolat (peut-être en référence au poisson d'avril).

(a) Pourquoi est-ce qu'on célèbre Pâques, selon l'article?

.... **(1 mark)**

(b) Comment sait-on que c'est une fête religieuse en France?

.... **(2 marks)**

(c) Selon l'article, qu'est-ce qu'on mange à Pâques à part le chocolat?

.... **(1 mark)**

(d) Selon la tradition, d'où viennent les œufs trouvés dans la maison et le jardin?

.... **(1 mark)**

(e) À part les œufs, quelles autres formes en chocolat est-ce qu'on mange?

.... **(2 marks)**

Picture-based task: Celebrating birthdays

2 Regarde la photo et prépare des réponses aux questions suivantes.

(a) Décris-moi la photo.

(b) Moi, je vais au ciné pour fêter mon anniversaire. Et toi?

(c) Qu'est-ce que tu vas faire pour célébrer ton anniversaire l'année prochaine?

(d) Mon anniversaire, c'est ma fête préférée. Quelle est ton opinion?

(e) Tu crois qu'on mange et boit trop aux fêtes? Pourquoi?

Festivals

Astropolis festival

1 Read this text about a music festival.

> Le festival Astropolis L'hiver a lieu en janvier depuis plus de vingt ans, alors c'est le plus ancien festival de musique électronique en France. Brest, à mi-chemin entre Moscou et New York, est un rendez-vous pratique et animé pour ceux qui adorent ce style de musique. Il y a des ateliers où on peut apprendre à jouer de la batterie, et des spectacles des groupes célèbres du monde entier. Un billet ne coûte que cent euros pour trois jours de joie.
>
> Sur présentation de votre billet d'accès au festival, une jolie gamme d'hôtels partenaires vous propose des tarifs réduits. Au centre commercial et au port, il y a tout ce qu'il faut si on a faim ou soif mais on recommande les crêperies en particulier.
>
> Si vous souhaitez être bénévole sur Astropolis, faites une demande sur notre site Web.

Put a cross [×] next to each one of the **four** correct boxes.

A	Astropolis festival will be 20 years old in January.	☐
B	It is the oldest electronic music festival in France.	☐
C	It takes place in Moscow and New York too.	☐
D	There are workshops at the festival.	☐
E	You can learn to play the drums at the festival.	☐
F	A ticket for the festival costs less than 100 euros for 3 days.	☐
G	Local pancakes are recommended.	☐
H	You can book hotels on the festival website.	☐

(4 marks)

Which festival?

2 Listen to these three young French people talking about festivals.

Which festival are they talking about?

Choose the correct festival from the box.

> New Year's Day   Christmas Eve   14 July
>
> Mother's Day   Saint Valentine's Day   April Fool's Day

(a) .... **(1 mark)**

(b) .... **(1 mark)**

(c) .... **(1 mark)**

Holiday preferences

Partir en vacances

1   Lis cet article.

> **Pierre:** Moi, je serai très content de partir en vacances, après avoir terminé les examens de fin d'année. On ne pourra pas partir avant le dix juin car l'un de mes amis ne passera son dernier examen que la veille. Puisque nous serons six à partir ensemble en vacances, il va falloir être d'accord sur notre choix de destination. Tous les autres veulent choisir la Grèce, alors que moi, je n'opterais jamais pour un pays où il risque de faire trop chaud pour moi en été.
>
> **Marie:** L'idée de partir en vacances entre amis, ça ne m'intéresse guère. Dans trois mois, je vais avoir vingt ans et je ne me sens pas pressée d'abandonner l'idée de partir en voyage avec mes deux sœurs aînées. La semaine prochaine, nous allons toutes les trois dans une agence de voyage pour réserver notre séjour de trois semaines au Maroc. Si on attend trop longtemps pour se décider, les prix vont peut-être flamber, ce qui nous est déjà arrivé il y a deux ans. Ce serait dommage!

Trouve les **quatre** bonnes phrases. Mets une croix [×] dans la case correcte.

Exemple:	Pierre sera content de partir en vacances.	☒
A	Pierre partira en vacances le jour de son dernier examen.	☐
B	L'un des amis de Pierre doit passer un examen le neuf juin.	☐
C	Un seul ami de Pierre a une préférence pour la Grèce.	☐
D	La Grèce, ce n'est pas la destination préférée de Pierre.	☐
E	Marie n'a pas trop envie de partir en vacances avec ses amis.	☐
F	Partir en vacances avec des amis, c'est ce que Marie voudrait surtout faire.	☐
G	Selon Marie, le prix des vacances peut baisser si on attend plus longtemps.	☐
H	Les trois sœurs vont faire des réservations pour les prochaines vacances.	☐

(4 marks)

On discute des vacances

2   Ton ami français, Choudry, t'a envoyé un e-mail au sujet des vacances.

Écris une réponse à Choudry.

Tu **dois** faire référence aux points suivants :

- où tu préfères passer les vacances et pourquoi
- des vacances excellentes dans le passé
- la valeur des vacances
- où tu voudrais voyager à l'avenir.

Écris 80–90 mots environ **en français**.

....

....

....

....

....

....

(20 marks)

Hotels

Role-play: At a hotel reception

1 You are booking accommodation for your family at the reception of a French hotel. The teacher will play the role of the receptionist and will speak first. You must address the receptionist as *vous*.

Vous êtes à la réception d'un hôtel en France. Vous réservez des chambres pour votre famille. Vous parlez avec le/la réceptionniste.

> Bonjour. Je peux vous aider?

(a) Nombre de chambres et de personnes

> Quel type de chambres voulez-vous?

(b) Type de chambres

> Quelles activités préférez-vous faire en vacances?

(c) !

> Que prenez-vous pour le petit déjeuner?

(d) Choix de petit déjeuner

> D'accord.

(e) ? Parking

> Oui.

Un hôtel différent

2 Lis ce texte.

> Read the passage carefully, making sure that you find the exact place for each answer.

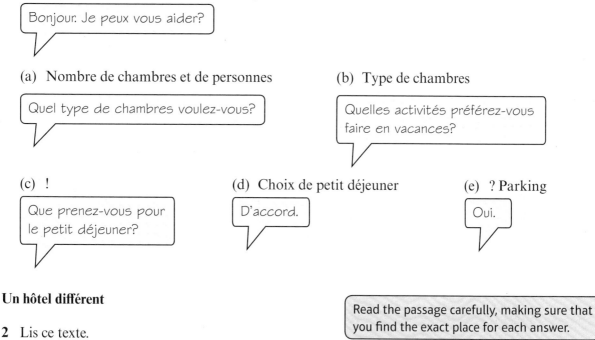

Le palais était un vaste et bel hôtel bâti en pierre au commencement du dix-septième siècle par un docteur en théologie. C'était un vrai logis luxueux où tout avait un grand air, les chambres, les salons, la cour d'honneur, fort large avec des promenoirs à arcades selon l'ancienne mode florentine et les jardins, plantés de magnifiques pommiers. Sur la pelouse devant l'hôtel, il y avait une foule de gens qui bavardaient sans cesse et qui regardaient l'entrée sans jamais tourner les yeux. Dans la salle à manger au premier étage, on prenait le petit déjeuner et le dîner, mais le déjeuner était servi seulement sur la terrasse même quand il faisait froid, ce qui était rare dans cette région.

(Adapted from *Les Misérables* by Victor Hugo)

Mets une croix [×] dans la case correcte.

(a) L'hôtel a été construit …

☐	**A** pour servir d'hôpital
☐	**B** au dix-septième siècle
☐	**C** par un roi
☐	**D** par un médecin

(b) Dans les jardins il y avait …

☐	**A** des arbres
☐	**B** des arcades
☐	**C** des plantes de toutes sortes
☐	**D** des bancs

(c) Les gens devant l'hôtel …

☐	**A** parlaient ensemble
☐	**B** ne regardaient jamais l'entrée
☐	**C** allaient à la salle à manger
☐	**D** avaient mal aux yeux

(d) On servait le déjeuner …

☐	**A** dans le salon
☐	**B** dans la salle à manger
☐	**C** sur la terrasse
☐	**D** à midi

(4 marks)

Campsites

My camping holidays

1   Emma is talking about her camping holidays.

What does she mention? Listen to the recording and put a cross [×] in each one of the **four** correct boxes.

Listen to the recording

Example	The colour of the tents	☒
A	The meals	☐
B	Making the beds	☐
C	Sharing with her sister	☐
D	The beds	☐
E	Eating at a restaurant	☐
F	Doing the washing up	☐
G	Getting on with her parents	☐

(4 marks)

Picture-based task: Camping holidays

2   Regarde la photo et prépare des réponses aux questions suivantes:

(a)   Décris-moi la photo.

(b)   Moi, j'adore faire du camping. Quelle est ton opinion?

(c)   Quels sont les avantages et les inconvénients du camping?

(d)   Tu vas faire du camping l'année prochaine?

(e)   Tu as déjà fait du camping en France?

Accommodation

Holiday accommodation

1   These young people are talking about their holidays.

Where do they stay? Listen to the recording and put a cross [×] in the correct box.

	cousin's house	hotel	city flat	summer camp	rented house	youth hostel
Example: Kevin			×			
(a) Paul						
(b) Isabelle						
(c) Éric						
(d) Éva						

(4 marks)

Mon logement préféré

2   Traduis les phrases suivantes **en français**.

(a) I prefer a hotel.

....   **(2 marks)**

(b) My brother likes a caravan.

....   **(2 marks)**

> Remember that the word for 'parents' will need the *ils* part of the verb and that the definite article ('the') is needed before the word for 'campsites' in French.

(c) My parents don't like campsites.

....

....   **(2 marks)**

> The adjective 'expensive' will need to agree with the word for 'hotels'.

(d) I think that hotels are very expensive.

....

....

....   **(3 marks)**

(e) Last year I stayed in a big hotel at the seaside for two weeks.

....

....

> Use *loger* for 'to stay'.

....   **(3 marks)**

Holiday destinations

Où aller en vacances?

1　Lis ce que dit Amélie sur les choix de vacances.

> Il n'y a rien de plus beau qu'un paysage couvert de neige.
>
> Mon dernier séjour à la montagne, c'était comme un beau rêve! Bien sûr, je n'aurais jamais pu résister à cette gentille invitation de partir la veille de Noël en vacances de neige. Mais on ne peut pas imaginer comme c'est cher de faire du ski! Déjà, la location d'un appartement, ça coûte pas mal d'argent. Puis, il ne faut pas oublier les skis qu'on doit louer, sauf si on décide d'en acheter.
>
> Je suis sûre que je vais être obligée de dépenser moins d'argent pour mes prochaines vacances. Alors, où est-ce que je vais partir cette année? Je n'en sais rien. Moi, passer mes vacances à la plage en train de me faire bronzer? Ce qui est sûr, c'est que je m'y ennuierais énormément. Peut-être que j'aurai envie de passer une petite semaine tranquille à la campagne, car j'en ai marre de faire du tourisme dans les grandes villes.

Trouve les **quatre** bonnes phrases. Mets une croix [×] dans la case correcte.

Example:	Amélie thinks snow-covered landscapes are beautiful.	☒
A	Amélie had a dream about beautiful mountain holidays.	☐
B	The invitation to go skiing was refused by Amélie.	☐
C	The ski trip departed the day before Christmas Day.	☐
D	Skiing costs more than one imagines.	☐
E	Well-located apartments are expensive to rent.	☐
F	The next holiday will cost as much as Amélie's last one.	☐
G	Amélie is not keen on beach holidays.	☐
H	Amélie has already visited some major cities.	☐

(4 marks)

Going on holiday

2　You hear these people talking about where they spend their holidays. Listen to the recording and put a cross [×] in the correct box.

Listen to the recording

A	B
mountains	beach

Put a cross in the correct box.

C	D
big cities	small village

E	F
lake	countryside

	A	B	C	D	E	F
Example:			×			
(a)						
(b)						
(c)						
(d)						

(4 marks)

Travel

Conversation: Travel experiences

1 As part of a conversation topic, you might talk about your opinions on travel. Prepare answers to these questions and then speak for about 30 seconds on each one.

(a) Tu aimes voyager? Pourquoi (pas)?

> **Guided**

Moi, j'aime bien voyager car ...

(b) Tu voudrais visiter quels pays? Pourquoi?

(c) Tu as déjà visité quels pays? Qu'en penses-tu?

> Make sure that you are well prepared for questions about holidays and remember that there is no need to tell the truth. It is better to use words you know or have prepared rather than try to recall words on the spot.

> Try to add a detail to every part of your answer.

Une lettre au maire

2 Vous allez visiter votre ville jumelée en France. Vous écrivez au maire. Écrivez une lettre avec les informations suivantes:

- quand vous allez arriver
- vos activités
- où vous allez logez
- pourquoi vous aimez la France.

Il faut écrire des phrases complètes.

Écrivez 40–50 mots environ **en français**.

> No need to put addresses at the top, just write the letter!

> Make sure that you cover all the points, including a reason in the last bullet point.

> **Guided**

Je vais arriver dans votre ville le 25 juillet pendant les grandes vacances.

J'ai l'intention de ... .

....

....

....

....

....

....

....

.... **(16 marks)**

Holiday activities

Translation

1   Translate this passage **into English**.

> To prepare for this kind of task, be sure to learn and revise vocabulary in topics. Revising 'holiday activities' words as a group will help you remember the difference between *randonnée* and *escalade,* for example.

> Je ne supporte pas les vacances où on ne fait rien car j'aime être toujours actif. L'année dernière je suis allé faire du ski au Canada et cette année j'irai en Allemagne. J'espère y faire de l'escalade et de longues randonnées à la montagne. Par contre, ma sœur préfère s'allonger au soleil, lire un roman policier ou faire les magasins.

> *toujours* – This will need to be translated in a slightly different position in English.

> *y* – This is also in a different position in French than English.

....

....

....

....

....

....

....

....   **(7 marks)**

Discussing holidays

Listen to the
recording

2   Fadela and Paul are looking at holiday brochures. Listen to the recording and answer the following questions **in English**.

(a) Where in Morocco would Fadela like to go?

....   **(1 mark)**

(b) Why would Paul prefer the holiday in Spain to the holiday in Morocco?

....   **(1 mark)**

(c) What sport would Fadela like to do in Italy?

....   **(1 mark)**

(d) For Paul, what is the attraction of cycling in Spain?

....   **(1 mark)**

Holiday plans

Projets pour les vacances

1 Lis cette lettre de Xavier.

> Chère Marianne,
>
> Je vais te parler de ma future visite en Espagne.
>
> L'année dernière, nous y sommes allés en famille, mais cette année, pour changer un peu, je vais y retourner avec mes amis. Je m'ennuie pendant les longs voyages, mais notre vol de nuit ne va durer que deux heures trente. Je n'aimerais pas prendre le bateau pour y aller!
>
> D'habitude, les vacances coûtent cher à Marbella, mais nous allons loger dans l'appartement de ma tante, et donc notre logement sera gratuit. Le soir, nous aurons la possibilité de préparer nos propres repas. Comme activité de vacances, je vais faire de la voile. Moi, je refuse de me faire bronzer sur la plage parce que c'est barbant.
>
> Vive les vacances!   Xavier

Mets une croix [×] dans la case correcte.

(a) Xavier passera ses vacances …

☐	**A** avec des copains
☐	**B** avec sa famille
☐	**C** avec sa famille et ses copains
☐	**D** seul

(b) Le trajet sera …

☐	**A** en train
☐	**B** en avion
☐	**C** en bateau
☐	**D** en car

(c) Ils vont loger …

☐	**A** dans une grande maison
☐	**B** chez un copain
☐	**C** chez sa tante
☐	**D** dans un hôtel

(d) Le logement …

☐	**A** coûtera cher
☐	**B** sera pratique
☐	**C** sera difficile
☐	**D** sera loin du centre-ville

(e) Xavier ne va pas …

☐	**A** faire de la voile
☐	**B** faire de la planche à voile
☐	**C** loger dans un appartement
☐	**D** se faire bronzer

(5 marks)

My next holiday

2 Paul is talking about going on holiday to Morzine. Complete the sentences.
Use the correct word or phrase from the box.

Example: Paul is going with	his whole family
(a) They will stay in …	
(b) In the mornings he will …	
(c) In the afternoons he will …	
(d) In the evening he will …	

> ski   near a cable car
>
> ~~his whole family~~   climb
>
> swim   eat out   eat in
>
> a self-catering chalet
>
> take long walks

(4 marks)

Holiday experiences

Holiday memories

1 Listen to Juliette talking about a holiday.

Put a cross [×] next to the **four** statements which apply **only** to her friend Lucie and not to Juliette herself.

Listen to the recording

Example:	She always spent her holidays in south-east France.	☒
A	She sent a text message to her friend.	☐
B	She went to museums with her parents.	☐
C	She spent a holiday in Bordeaux.	☐
D	She travelled by train.	☐
E	She travelled by car.	☐
F	She went to the beach without her friend.	☐
G	She was bored on the journey.	☐
H	She stayed in a 3-star hotel.	☐

(4 marks)

Les vacances en famille

2 Un magazine français cherche des articles sur les vacances en famille. Écrivez un article sur des vacances récentes que vous avez passées en famille pour intéresser les lecteurs. Vous devez faire référence aux points suivants :

> Try to develop your ideas and make them more interesting by using adverbs and adjectives.

- où vous êtes allés et pourquoi vous avez choisi la destination
- votre opinion sur les vacances en famille
- les activités les plus intéressantes
- des vacances que vous aimeriez avoir à l'avenir.

Justifiez vos idées et vos opinions. Écrivez 130–150 mots environ **en français**.

Guided

Je vais vous raconter les vacances de l'été dernier que j'ai passé avec

ma famille à Menton dans le sud de la France. Nous y sommes allés parce

qu'un ami de mon père venait de passer des vacances merveilleuses là-bas.

....

....

....

....

....

....

....

....

> If you run out of space, continue your answer on lined paper. In the exam you will have more space than this.

(28 marks)

Transport

Conversation: Means of transport

1   As part of a conversation topic, you might talk about modes of transport. Prepare answers to these questions and then speak for about 30 seconds on each one.

(a) Tu aimes voyager en train? Pourquoi (pas)?

Guided

> Je n'aime pas voyager en train parce que je trouve ça ennuyeux, surtout pour les longs voyages. J'écoute de la musique ou je lis, mais à mon avis ce n'est pas agréable.

(b) Tu préfères quel moyen de transport? Pourquoi?

(c) Comment peut-on voyager de l'Angleterre vers la France?

Les inconvénients du voyage

2   Traduis le passage suivant **en français**.

I hate travelling by car because I am often ill. For example, last summer I went to London with my parents and we had to stop as I had a headache. I prefer going everywhere by bike if I can, but for longer journeys I take a coach. Next week my family is going to visit my aunt in Spain but we will not travel by plane because my parents are afraid of flying.

> In French, the present participle in 'I hate travelling' becomes an infinitive after 'I hate' in French.

> 'we had to stop' – Remember this is *s'arrêter* (a reflexive verb).

> Again, like 'travelling' above, 'going' becomes infinitive in French.

> 'my family is going to visit' – Remember how to form the future tense in French.

....

....

....

....

....

....

....

....

....

....

....

....

....

....   **(12 marks)**

Directions

David's email

1   Read these directions to David's house.

> Salut Jeremy! Désolé, mais je ne pourrai pas venir te chercher à la gare. En sortant de la gare, ça te prendra une trentaine de minutes à pied. Pour venir chez moi, tu vas tourner à gauche quand tu quitteras la gare. Il y a une petite colline qui ne prend que cinq minutes à monter – ce sera plus facile demain soir quand tu seras sur le chemin du retour! Tourne à droite en face de la station-service. Puis tu vas aller tout droit, jusqu'à la librairie. Là, si tu regardes bien, tu ne pourras pas rater notre magnifique mairie. Par contre, si tu passes directement devant un grand hôpital sur ta gauche, c'est que tu es allé trop loin!
>
> Fais très attention en traversant toutes les rues parce qu'il faut regarder d'abord à gauche, pas comme en Angleterre. Malheureusement, il n'y a que très peu de zones piétonnes chez nous.

Put a cross [×] next to the **four** correct statements.

Example:	David lives about thirty minutes walk from the station.	☒
A	There is a short hill to walk down.	☐
B	Part of the route is uphill.	☐
C	Turn right opposite a petrol station.	☐
D	There is a library along this route.	☐
E	At one point, the town hall is visible.	☐
F	The route passes in front of a hospital.	☐
G	Jeremy offers road safety advice to David.	☐
H	Pedestrian zones are rare where David lives.	☐

(4 marks)

Getting home

2   Listen. How do these teenagers go home? Put a cross [×] in the correct box in

A	B	C	D	E	F
Turn left	Go straight on	Turn right	Go down a hill	Cross a bridge	Go up a hill

the grid.

	A	B	C	D	E	F
Example:		×				
(a)						
(b)						
(c)						
(d)						

(4 marks)

Listen to the recording

TRACK 23

Holiday problems

Un questionnaire en ligne

1 Un site Internet français pour les jeunes voudrait ton opinion sur les vacances.

Écris à ce site Internet.

Tu **dois** faire référence aux points suivants:

- les problèmes en vacances
- le prix des vacances
- les vacances de rêve
- un exemple de mauvais souvenirs de vacances.

Écris 80–90 mots environ **en français**.

> You do not have lots of space for development, but try to add opinions and details where you can.

Guided

En vacances il y a souvent du stress, par exemple avec les parents.

Il y a aussi les problèmes à l'aéroport ....

....

....

....

....

....

....

....

....

....

.... **(20 marks)**

Les problèmes en vacances

2 Écoute ces jeunes qui parlent des problèmes en vacances.

C'est quelle sorte de problème?

> Listen carefully, but not only for the words in the table. Other words on the same topic will provide the answers you need.

Listen to the recording

Mets une croix [×] dans la case correcte.

		(a) Magali	(b) Jérôme	(c) Louise
A	transport			
B	logement			
C	temps			
D	repas			

(3 marks)

Asking for help

Role-play: Returning an item in a department store

1 You are talking to a shop assistant in a department store. The teacher will play the role of the assistant and will speak first. You must address the assistant as *vous*.

Vous êtes dans un grand magasin. Vous voulez rapporter un article que vous avez acheté.

> Bonjour. Je peux vous aider?

(a) Article rapporté

> Quel est le problème?

(b) Problème – taille, couleur

> Vous cherchez quel article?

(c) !

> Ah bon. Celui-ci vous ira.

(d) ? Pièce d'identité

> Non, ce n'est pas nécessaire.

(e) ? Échanger l'article

> Oui, certainement.

> Putting *Je peux* in front of a verb and making your voice sound the question is a good way of asking questions.

A theft

Listen to the recording

2 You hear a radio report about a theft. Listen to the recording and put a cross [×] in each of the four correct boxes.

Example:	The thief entered the shop at 12.20.	☒
A	The thief wandered round the shop before the theft.	☐
B	The thief stole a football.	☐
C	The thief hid the item in his jacket.	☐
D	A shop assistant alerted the security guard.	☐
E	The shop manager phoned the police.	☐
F	The street outside was busy.	☐
G	The police took 20 minutes to arrive.	☐
H	The thief was caught but escaped.	☐

(4 marks)

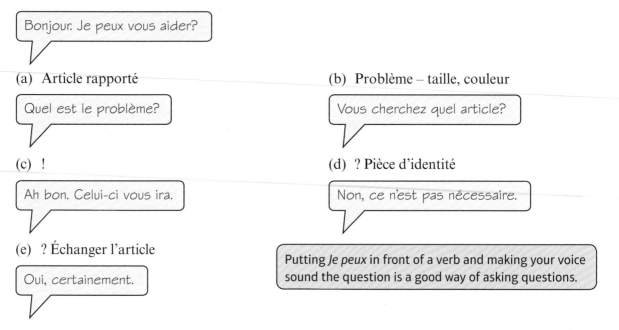

> You will be expected to know a number of different types of pronouns, not only *le, la, les, lui, leur, y* and *en* but also *celui-ci*, etc.

> Are you clear about the difference between *avant de* (before) and *après avoir* (after having)?

Eating out in a café

A café in Nice

1 Read Wolfgang's account of café life in France.

> Manger au café en France, c'est toujours un grand plaisir pour moi. En général, je choisis les croissants, mais toujours sans beurre parce que je trouve que c'est meilleur avec un peu de confiture de fraise. Mais il est essentiel d'arriver dans un café avant dix heures pour en avoir!
>
> Tous les ans, nous allons dans le même petit café à Nice. Presque toute ma famille trouve que leur gâteau au chocolat est délicieux. Je ne résiste jamais à une deuxième part parce qu'il est impossible de trouver ce dessert chez moi en Allemagne. La recette, c'est un grand secret!
>
> Le soir, nous ne mangeons pas souvent dans les cafés parce que nous préférons aller aux restaurants.

Put a cross in the **four** correct boxes.

Example:	Wolfgang always enjoys eating in French cafés.	☒
A	Wolfgang does not have butter on his croissants.	☐
B	In Wolfgang's opinion, raspberry jam improves the taste of the croissants.	☐
C	Wolfgang has found that cafés always sell all their croissants by ten o'clock.	☐
D	Wolfgang visits France at least three times a year.	☐
E	The whole family enjoys the chocolate cake.	☐
F	Wolfgang always has a second portion of cake.	☐
G	Back home in Germany, Wolfgang cannot buy the same dessert.	☐
H	The family never goes to cafés for the evening meal.	☐

(4 marks)

A quick snack

2 Loïc is out with his mother. Listen to him talking about what he would like to eat.

A	B	C	D	E	F
chips	water	cheese	sausage	bread	cakes

Listen to the recording

What does he not want 🙁 and what does he want 🙂 to eat. Put the four correct letters in the boxes

	🙁	🙂
Example:	F	–

(4 marks)

Eating out in a restaurant

Reviewing a restaurant

1 Read Vincent's views about restaurants.

> La plupart des gens aiment bien dîner au restaurant. Pourquoi? Parce que cela évite un tas de travail! On n'a pas à trouver les ingrédients, c'est quelqu'un d'autre qui prépare le repas et on n'a pas besoin de faire la vaisselle. Si vous habitez au cœur de Paris où les parkings sont limités, vous n'avez même pas l'obligation d'aller au restaurant en voiture car les transports en commun sont excellents. Des centaines de restaurants parisiens sont à votre disposition.
>
> Mais n'oubliez pas qu'il faut gagner un bon salaire pour avoir la possibilité de manger au restaurant si on compte y aller plus d'une fois par semaine, surtout à Paris. À part quelques exceptions, mes amis et moi, nous ne pouvons y aller qu'une fois tous les quinze jours. Quel dommage! Nous aimerions bien dépenser plus pour les soirées au restaurant, mais ce n'est pas dans nos habitudes. Un pourcentage important de mon salaire est destiné à payer les factures mensuelles. J'essaie de les payer tout de suite.

Choose the correct ending for each statement, according to the text above.

Example: En général, les gens aiment manger

.... D ....

(a) Dîner au restaurant, cela évite de

....

(b) À Paris, on peut trouver

....

(c) Les gens moins bien payés

....

(d) Vincent et ses amis aimeraient aller

....

A	ne dînent jamais au restaurant.
B	tous les quinze jours au restaurant.
C	plus souvent au restaurant.
D	au restaurant.
E	s'occuper d'autres personnes.
F	faire la vaisselle.
G	des centaines de bons restaurants.
H	énormément de restaurants.
I	ne peuvent pas dîner souvent au restaurant.

(4 marks)

Picture-based task: Eating out

2 Regarde la photo et prépare des réponses aux questions suivantes.

(a) Décris-moi la photo.

> **Guided**

> Sur la photo il y a une famille qui mange dans un restaurant. Je crois qu'il y a le père, la mère, deux enfants et les grands-parents. Les adultes boivent du vin et les petits boivent de l'eau. Tout le monde a l'air content.

(b) Je pense que manger au restaurant, c'est bien. Quel est ton avis?

(c) Quel est ton plat préféré? Pourquoi?

(d) Parle-moi d'un repas récent dans un restaurant.

(e) À quel restaurant aimerais-tu aller à l'avenir?

> Remember to add some details here: *Avec qui? Qu'est-ce que tu as pris? Où es-tu allé(e)? Pourquoi?*

> At higher level, the last question is 'unpredictable' which means you won't be able to prepare for it. But it will be around the same topic, so take some time to think about relevant vocabulary and phrases that may come in useful.

> You could talk about a specific restaurant or a type of restaurant here.

Buying gifts

Shopping lists

1 Listen to these three people talking about what they are buying.

Complete the sentences. Choose the correct word from the box.

> sweets   flowers   earrings   chocolates
>
> gloves   perfume

(a) Louis is buying ....   **(1 mark)**

(b) Ariane is buying ....   **(1 mark)**

(c) Étienne is going to buy ....   **(1 mark)**

Role-play: In the souvenir shop

2 You are talking to a shop assistant in a souvenir shop. The teacher will play the role of the assistant and will speak first. You must address the assistant as *vous*.

Vous êtes dans un magasin de souvenirs.
Vous parlez au vendeur / à la vendeuse.

> Bonjour. Je peux vous aider?

(a) Acheter cadeau

> Bien. Qu'est-ce que vous voulez?

(b) Le cadeau que vous voulez

> Voilà. C'est pour qui?

> Don't go into details, just say what type of gift.

(c) !

> Ah oui, c'est pour une occasion spéciale?

(d) Raison pour l'achat

> Quelle bonne idée!

> Try to think of something simple.

(e) Prix?

> Ça fait 50 euros.

Opinions about food

Who says what?

1 Read the following comments about food.

Avez-vous bien mangé?	
Marianne:	Je ne mange jamais au fast-food, même si je suis pressée.
Patrick:	Qu'est-ce qu'on a bien mangé au restaurant grec hier soir! On va bientôt y retourner.
Freya:	Ce café propose un bon choix de salades au déjeuner.
Sylvestre:	Pour le petit déjeuner, tout était à bas prix, sauf les croissants.
Mara:	Si on va au fast-food, on ne perdra pas de temps.
Thierry:	À mon avis, ce repas indien sera super. J'ai déjà mangé dans ce restaurant l'année dernière.
Ruby:	Ce restaurant ne donnait que rarement des portions généreuses.
Joshua:	On dit que ce petit café sert de bons croissants pour le petit déjeuner.
Ghislaine:	Je n'ai pas pu finir le plat. Quelle énorme portion!

Who mentions the following? Write the correct names in the table below.

Example:	A café which offers a range of salads.	Freya
(a)	A meal enjoyed very recently.	
(b)	One advantage of eating at a fast-food restaurant.	
(c)	A recommendation on where to eat breakfast.	
(d)	The restaurant didn't tend to serve large portions.	

> If you spot an answer which seems to be correct at first glance, check the whole response, to be absolutely sure.

(4 marks)

Opinions about food

2 You hear these people talking about food. What foods do they mention? Listen to the recording and put a cross [×] in each one of the **four** correct boxes.

Listen to the recording

Example	Cereals	☒
A	Fish	☐
B	Meat	☐
C	Crisps	☐
D	Cauliflower	☐
E	Potatoes	☐
F	Cheese	☐
G	Peas	☐

> Remember, this question is not asking you what *you* like and dislike. Listen carefully to the speakers to find out their opinions.

(4 marks)

Weather

Il fait mauvais temps

1 Lis cette conversation.

> «Madame la duchesse est sortie seule» a remarqué François.
>
> «Mais vous ne l'accompagnez pas» a répondu Haudoin. «Pourquoi?»
>
> «Parce qu'il faisait trop froid dehors» s'est exclamé François.
>
> «Trop froid?» a dit le duc, «mais il y avait du soleil hier, n'est-ce pas?»
>
> «Ah oui, mais il ne faisait que deux degrés et le vent était si fort» a répondu Haudoin.
>
> **(Adapted from *La Dame de Monsoreau* by Alexandre Dumas)**

Mets une croix [×] dans la case correcte.

(a) Madame la duchesse est partie …

☐	**A** avec François
☐	**B** accompagnée du duc
☐	**C** toute seule
☐	**D** avec des amies

(b) Selon François …

☐	**A** il faisait très froid
☐	**B** il faisait trop chaud
☐	**C** il faisait beau
☐	**D** le temps était ensoleillé

(c) Selon Haudoin il y avait …

☐	**A** du soleil
☐	**B** un orage
☐	**C** des nuages
☐	**D** du vent

(3 marks)

Today's weather

2 Listen to this weather report.

> Before you listen, make sure you know how to say 'north', 'south', 'east' and 'west' in French.

Choose words from the box to write the correct labels on the map.

sunny	cold	windy	foggy	raining	snowing

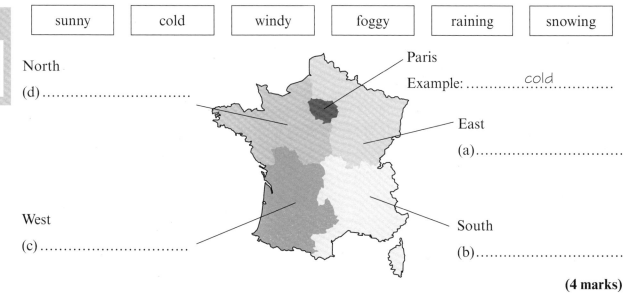

North

(d) ....

Paris

Example: .... *cold* ....

East

(a)...............................

West

(c) ....

South

(b)...............................

(4 marks)

Tourism

Bien préparer le départ en vacances

1 Lis le texte.

> Les préparations de vacances commençaient quinze jours avant le départ. On le savait bien parce que ma mère était comme d'habitude de mauvaise humeur; bien qu'elle soit calme et douce par ailleurs, quand elle fait les préparatifs de voyage, elle est grincheuse. Elle s'occupait des bagages, en se disant ce qu'il ne fallait jamais oublier: vêtements propres, sandales, lunettes de soleil, appareil photo et pièces d'identité. On dirait qu'elle voulait rester à la maison, mais en vérité, elle aimait vraiment partir en vacances.
>
> Une fois arrivée à la destination prévue, elle était la première à sortir en boîte, à regarder de près les bâtiments célèbres ou à organiser des excursions, mais ce qu'elle détestait, c'était faire les valises! Malheureusement elle ne l'a dit à personne.

Mets une croix [×] dans la case correcte.

(a) La mère était de mauvaise humeur …

☐	**A** une semaine avant de partir en vacances
☐	**B** deux semaines avant de partir en vacances
☐	**C** le week-end avant le départ
☐	**D** le jour du départ

(b) La mère parlait toute seule quand elle …

☐	**A** faisait du tourisme
☐	**B** s'habillait
☐	**C** faisait les valises
☐	**D** portait des sandales

(c) Elle ne voulait pas oublier …

☐	**A** les choses nécessaires
☐	**B** les bagages
☐	**C** la famille
☐	**D** son portable

(d) Elle aimait …

☐	**A** s'occuper des valises
☐	**B** rester à la maison
☐	**C** loger dans un hôtel près de la mer
☐	**D** faire beaucoup de choses en vacances

> Read the passage carefully and don't just assume that because a French word is in the passage and in one of the alternatives, that it must be the correct answer.

(4 marks)

Le tourisme au Canada

2 Tu es en vacances au Canada. Tu postes cette photo sur des médias sociaux pour tes amis.

Fais une description de la photo et exprime ton opinion sur les vacances.

Écris 20–30 mots environ **en français**.

Guided Sur la photo ....

....

....

....

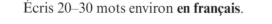

.... **(12 marks)**

Describing a town

Ma ville / mon village

1 Vous écrivez un petit article au sujet de votre ville/village.
Écrivez l'article avec les informations suivantes:

- ce qu'il y a à voir dans votre ville/village et ce qu'il y a à faire
- votre opinion de la ville / du village
- où vous voudriez habiter à l'avenir.

Il faut écrire en phrases complètes.

Écrivez 40–50 mots environ **en français**.

> Remember that the information doesn't have to be true. Use the vocabulary for buildings and towns that you know.

....

....

....

.... **(16 marks)**

Where I grew up

2 Read Marthe's description of the town where she grew up.

> J'ai passé une enfance qui n'avait rien d'extraordinaire dans une petite ville dans le nord-est de la France où je suis née. Je garderai toujours le souvenir de mon père et mon oncle qui rentraient, heureux d'avoir fini leur travail dans les mines et d'anticiper une soirée au cœur de leur famille.
>
> Il y a vingt ans, les mines ont été fermées définitivement et mon père était au chômage, alors un an plus tard ma famille a déménagé à Lyon et, heureusement, le lendemain de notre arrivée dans la ville, mon père a réussi à trouver un emploi comme ingénieur. Quelle chance! Mes parents y sont restés jusqu'à sa retraite quinze ans plus tard, quand ils sont repartis dans le Nord. Moi, j'habite toujours à Lyon mais l'ambiance chaleúreuse de ma ville natale me manque de temps en temps.

Answer the following questions **in English**. You do not need to write in full sentences.

(a) What does Marthe say about her childhood?

 not extraordinary .... **(1 mark)**

(b) Why were her father and uncle happy? Give **two** reasons.

.... **(2 marks)**

(c) What happened 20 years ago?

.... **(2 marks)**

(d) How long did it take Marthe's father to find work in Lyon?

.... **(1 mark)**

(e) What happened 15 years later?

.... **(1 mark)**

(f) What does Marthe miss about the town where she was born?

.... **(1 mark)**

Countries

Listen to the recording

Travelling abroad

1   These young people are discussing foreign travel.

Where are they going?

Complete the sentences. Use the correct word from the box.

Austria	Japan	Germany	Spain
Tunisia	Greece	Switzerland	China

> You might hear more than one country mentioned so listen carefully and check what you are listening for.

(a) Marion is planning to visit ....   **(1 mark)**

(b) Simon likes going to ....   **(1 mark)**

(c) Pauline would like to visit ....   **(1 mark)**

(d) Jean-Marc wants to go to ....   **(1 mark)**

Conversation: Visiting foreign countries

2   As part of a conversation topic, you might talk about foreign travel. Prepare answers to these questions and then speak for about 30 seconds on each one.

(a) Tu as déjà visité quels pays?

(b) Tu voudrais visiter quels pays? Pourquoi?

(c) Quels sont les inconvénients de voyager à l'étranger?

> Try to think of disadvantages from your own experience first, but feel free to make them up. For example, *Si on ne parle pas bien la langue, c'est peut-être un petit problème quand on voyage à l'étranger.*

Places to visit

Une destination touristique

1 Traduis le passage suivant **en français**.

I have already travelled abroad but I would really like to visit Australia because I have never been there. My parents would like to go to the theatre in Sydney and my sister would like to go to the well-known beaches over there because she likes doing water sports and sunbathing. I love nature, so it would be great to see wild animals and people have told me that it's a pretty country.

> 'really' – This will come after 'would like' in French.

> 'I have never been there' – This becomes *ne … jamais* – think about where to place these two words in the sentence.

> 'it would be great' – Remember there is no word for 'would' in French – just use the correct part of the conditional form of the verb.

> 'people' – Use *on*.

J'ai visité à l'étranger mais je voudrais visiter Australie beaucoup car je n'ai jamais été là. mes parents voudraient aller au théatre en Sydney et ma sœur voudrait aller des plages qui sont bien connu car elle aimes des sports nautiques et bain de soleil. J'adore la nature, donc ce sera genial.

(12 marks)

Role-play: At the travel agent's

2 You are staying in Paris on holiday and go to the tourist office for some information. The teacher will play the role of the tourist office employee and will speak first. You must address the employee as *vous*.

À l'agence de voyages. Vous voulez faire une excursion à Rouen.

> Bonjour. Je peux vous aider?

(a) Destination de l'excursion

> Ah bon. Quand voulez-vous partir et pourquoi?

(b) Demain, activité préférée – raison

> Qu'est-ce que vous avez déjà visité à Paris?

(c) !

> C'est intéressant, ça.

(d) ? Restaurants – recommandation

> Ah oui, il y a un bon restaurant italien, rue Beauvoisine.

(e) ? Réduction étudiant

> Non, je regrette.

Describing a region

Trouble in Paris

1 Lis ce passage.

> Un matin du mois de décembre, en se promenant en ville, Frédéric a remarqué dans la rue Saint-Jacques plus d'animation qu'à l'ordinaire. Les étudiants sortaient précipitamment des cafés, ou, par les fenêtres ouvertes, ils s'appelaient d'une maison à l'autre; les boutiquiers*, au milieu du trottoir, regardaient d'un air inquiet; les volets** se fermaient; et, quand il est arrivé dans la rue Soufflot, il voyait un grand rassemblement autour du Panthéon.
>
> Frédéric se trouvait auprès d'un jeune homme blond, et portant moustache et barbe. Il lui a demandé la cause du désordre.
>
> «Je n'en sais rien», a répondu l'autre, «ni eux non plus!» Et il a éclaté de rire.
>
> **(Adapted from L'education sentimentale by Gustave Flaubert)**

*boutiquiers = shopkeepers
**volets = shutters

Trouve les **quatre** bonnes phrases. Mets une croix [×] dans la case correcte.

A	Frédéric faisait une randonné à la campagne.	☐
B	Les étudiants étaient assis au café.	☐
C	La rue n'était pas calme.	☐
D	Il y avait beaucoup de gens au Panthéon.	☐
E	Les boutiquiers ne semblaient pas contents.	☐
F	Frédéric a aidé un homme blond à porter ses bagages.	☐
G	L'homme blond ne savait pas ce qui est passé.	☐
H	L'homme blond semblait être triste.	☐

(4 marks)

Picture-based task: A region of France

2 Regarde la photo et prépare des réponses aux questions suivantes.

> Make sure that you answer the questions using the correct tenses – question (d) will require a conditional and question (e) needs past tenses.

(a) Décris-moi la photo.

> **Guided**
>
> Sur la photo, il y a un vieux bâtiment au milieu d'une rivière. C'est la nuit et ...

(b) Moi, j'aime habiter en ville; et toi, qu'en penses-tu?

(c) Quels sont les désavantages d'habiter à la campagne?

(d) À l'avenir, où voudrais-tu habiter? Pourquoi?

(e) Tu as déjà visité la France?

Subjects

Which subject?

1 Which subject is being discussed? Put a cross [×] in the correct box.

Example: Mon professeur de maths est très sympa.   D

(a) J'aime bien l'histoire.   ....

(b) Ma matière favorite est l'éducation physique.   ....

(c) Mon amie préfère l'informatique.   ....

(d) Le dessin, c'est super!   ....

A	Geography
B	PE
C	Drama
D	Maths
E	French
F	Music
G	History
H	Art
I	IT

> Start with the items
> you can do most easily.

(4 marks)

My lessons

2 Lucas is talking about his lessons at school. What subjects does he mention?
   Listen to the recording and put a cross [×] in each one of the **four** correct boxes.

Listen to the
recording

Example	Maths	☒
A	German	☐
B	Physics	☐
C	English	☐
D	History	☐
E	Chemistry	☐
F	PE	☐
G	ICT	☐

> How well do you know the vocabulary which expresses
> opinion? Can you tell the difference between, for
> example, *ça me fait rire, ça m'est égal* and *ça ne fait
> rien*? These are all common expressions which you can
> find in the Foundation vocabulary list. You need to
> know some of them to be able to fill in the grid.

(4 marks)

School life

La vie au collège

1 Traduis les phrases suivantes **en français**.

(a) I like my school.

J'aime mon collège.   **(2 marks)**

(b) The buildings are old. | Remember that the word for 'building' is masculine in French. |

.... **(2 marks)**

(c) There are a lot of clubs. | Remember which small word follows *beaucoup*. |

.... **(2 marks)**

(d) My favourite subject is music because the teacher is kind.

....

.... **(3 marks)**

(e) Last year I went to Spain with my school.

....

.... **(3 marks)**

Picture-based task: At school

2 Regarde la photo et prépare des réponses aux questions suivantes.

(a) Décris-moi la photo.

> **Guided**
>
> Il y a huit élèves qui travaillent dans une salle de classe. Je crois qu'ils sont en train de faire leurs devoirs.

(b) J'aime mon école. Et toi, que penses-tu de ton collège?

(c) Quelles matières est-ce que tu n'aimes pas? Pourquoi?

(d) Tu étudies le français depuis combien de temps?

(e) Que voudrais-tu faire l'année prochaine? Pourquoi?

| Remember to use the present tense with *depuis* to translate the English phrase 'have been doing'. |

| Don't forget to add a reason for your plans for next year. |

School day

Conversation: School routine

1 As part of a conversation topic, you might talk about your school day. Prepare answers to these questions and then speak for about 30 seconds on each one.

> Try to use connectives and time phrases to add complexity and interest. A possible start might be *Après avoir préparé mes affaires, je vais au collège en car. Une fois arrivé(e) je vais directement à la salle de classe où on a l'appel.*

  (a) Décris ta routine scolaire le matin.

  (b) Qu'est-ce que tu fais pendant l'heure du déjeuner?

  (c) Qu'est-ce que tu as fait au collège hier?

Likes and dislikes

2 Which parts of school life does Anton **dislike**?

Put a cross [×] in each one of the **four** correct boxes.

Example:	Je déteste arriver au collège le lundi matin!	☒
A	Manger à la cantine, c'est sympa.	☐
B	L'éducation physique, c'est trop fatigant.	☐
C	J'aime bien parler avec mes amis en classe.	☐
D	Mon professeur de dessin est amusant.	☐
E	Aller à l'école en autobus, c'est ennuyeux.	☐
F	Je n'aime pas faire la queue à la cantine.	☐
G	J'adore jouer pendant la récréation!	☐
H	Mes cours d'italien sont nuls.	☐

> Take extra care if parts of instructions are in **bold** print.

(4 marks)

Comparing schools

Marie compares schools

1   Read Marie's comparison of schools in Paris and London.

> Ici en France, ma semaine au collège commence à huit heures le lundi matin. En général, les cours durent une heure, mais c'est souvent plus court en Angleterre. Moi, je rentre chez moi à l'heure du déjeuner. Mes cours finissent assez tard l'après-midi, sauf le vendredi. En France, nous avons cours le samedi matin. Quelle horreur!
>
> Mon correspondant anglais s'appelle Danny. Il est content d'être élève en Angleterre, mais il aime bien visiter la France. Il n'aime pas la couleur de l'uniforme qu'il porte, mais il dit que c'est confortable. Danny a des cours de religion, mais ce n'est pas sa matière préférée. Il pense que les professeurs sont plus sévères en France qu'en Angleterre.

Put a cross [×] next to each one of the **four** things mentioned.

Example:	School starting time in France	☒
A	Identical length of lessons in both cities	☐
B	Going home for lunch	☐
C	Very late finish to lessons on Fridays	☐
D	Dislike of Saturday morning lessons	☐
E	Danny's liking of school in the UK	☐
F	Marie's opinions on school uniform	☐
G	Danny's favourite subject	☐
H	Teachers being less strict in England	☐

> Where two or more people are mentioned in a text, make sure that each answer relates to the correct person.

(4 marks)

Adapting to an English school

Listen to the recording

2   Lisa is talking to her mother on the telephone. What does she tell her? Listen to the recording and put a cross [×] in each one of the **four** correct boxes.

Example:	The journey to school is short.	☒
A	School starts earlier than in France.	☐
B	School starts at 8.45 am.	☐
C	School starts later than in France.	☐
D	In France she drinks coffee at break time.	☐
E	The teachers are interesting.	☐
F	She must stay in school all day.	☐
G	She can go to the café at break time.	☐
H	She enjoyed the concert.	☐

> Revise basics! Although this is a higher level question, you must be absolutely sure that you know the difference between all the different ways of telling the time.

(4 marks)

Describing schools

Role-play: My school

1   You are at school talking to a French exchange student. The teacher will play the role of the exchange student and will speak first. You must address the exchange student as *tu*.

Au collège. Tu parles à un étudiant français qui participe à un échange.

> Salut. Les cours commencent à quelle heure?

(a) L'heure du commencement – cours

> Ah bon. Tu as fait beaucoup de devoirs hier?

(b) Devoirs

> D'accord. Il y a quels clubs à ton collège?

(c) !

> C'est bon, ça.

(d) ? Matière préférée

> Moi, je préfère les maths car c'est intéressant.

(e) ? Sports pratiqués – collège français

> On peut faire une gamme de sports mais moi, j'aime bien le badminton.

Un élève français

2   Traduis le passage suivant **en français**.

My friend, Marc, goes to a big mixed school in the north of France. He likes school very much but he has found English very hard. I went to his school last year and it was quite interesting. Lessons start earlier than in England and the students do not wear a school uniform. Marc is going to visit my school next year.

> Remember that in French the translation of 'big' comes before the noun but 'mixed' comes after it.

> If you cannot think of a direct translation of 'hard', try using another English adjective which means the same (e.g. difficult).

....

....

....

....

....

....

....

.... **(12 marks)**

School rules

Mon école

1 Un site Internet français demande ton opinion sur le règlement scolaire.

Écris à ce site Internet. Tu **dois** faire référence aux points suivants:

- le règlement de ton école
- ton opinion sur le règlement
- un incident récent à ton école
- comment tu voudrais changer le règlement.

Écris 80–90 mots environ **en français**.

> Don't try to use words you don't know the French for just to fit in with the school rules. You can make up a rule if you want to.

Guided

Le règlement de mon école est assez strict. ....

....

....

....

....

....

....

....

(20 marks)

Encore de règles!

2 Écoute Lise qui parle de son lycée.

Complète la phrase en mettant une croix [×] dans la case correcte.

Listen to the recording

(a) Lise voudrait …

☐	**A**	porter un uniforme scolaire
☐	**B**	avoir un piercing
☒	**C**	pouvoir se maquiller au lycée
☐	**D**	arriver plus tard le matin

(b) Ses copines …

☐	**A**	ont des tatouages
☐	**B**	portent du maquillage en classe
☐	**C**	respectent le règlement scolaire
☒	**D**	sont souvent en retard

(c) Elle va …

☒	**A**	parler au directeur
☐	**B**	parler à ses parents
☐	**C**	parler avec ses copines
☐	**D**	changer d'école

(3 marks)

Problems and pressures

Les problèmes scolaires

1 Lis cet article.

> L'emploi du temps de Natalie est surchargé. Après sa journée au collège, elle se dépêche de rentrer à la maison pour pouvoir faire ses devoirs et réviser pour les contrôles le lendemain. Ses parents, tous les deux médecins, rentrent tard, mais insistent pour que Natalie leur raconte ce qu'elle a appris pendant la journée avant de se coucher. Le week-end dernier Natalie a dû travailler dur car elle va bientôt passer un examen de violoncelle, sans parler des épreuves scolaires à venir. Elle comprend que ses parents s'inquiètent pour son avenir, pourtant elle voudrait parfois ne rien faire, jouer avec son chat ou inviter ses copines, mais c'est impossible!
>
> Les collégiens ne sont pas les seuls à subir la pression parentale. «Les parents demandent des comptes dès la rentrée» constate Michelle, professeur de chimie dans un grand collège prestigieux. «Ils vérifient que nous travaillons jour et nuit et comparent les résultats avec ceux du collège voisin.»

Réponds aux questions **en français**. Il n'est pas nécessaire d'écrire des phrases complètes.

> When you have questions in French on a longer passage, make sure you read them carefully and understand what you are looking for. Don't just copy chunks of the passage for your answer.

(a) Qu'est-ce que Natalie doit faire ce soir? Donne **deux** détails.

elle doit faire ses devoirs et réviser pour les examens **(2 marks)**

(b) Qu'est-ce qu'elle doit faire avant de se coucher?

elle doit raconter que elle a appris pendant la journée à ses parents **(1 mark)**

(c) Qu'est-ce qu'elle doit faire dans un proche avenir?

elle va passer un examen de violoncelle **(1 mark)**

(d) Qu'est-ce qu'elle aimerait faire de temps en temps? Donne **trois** détails.

elle voudrait ne rien faire, jouer avec son chat ou passer du temps avec ses copains **(3 marks)**

(e) Qui est Michelle?

une prof de chimie dans un grand collège **(1 mark)**

(f) Que font les parents, selon Michelle? Donne **deux** détails.

ils demandent des comptes et comparent les résultats avec ceux du collège voisin **(2 marks)**

Les pressions scolaires

2 Marianne, ton amie belge, t'a envoyé un e-mail sur les problèmes scolaires.

Écris une réponse à Marianne. Tu **dois** faire référence aux points suivants:

- les problèmes à ton collège
- ton opinion sur les pressions
- les pressions scolaires
- ce que tu vas faire pour te relaxer.

Écris 80–90 mots environ **en français**.

....

....

....

....

....

.... **(20 marks)**

Primary school

What did you do at primary school?

1 Read these brief insights into life in a primary school.

A	Chaque cours durait trois quarts d'heure.
B	On jouait dans la cour pendant la récréation.
C	Nous y arrivions à huit heures du matin.
D	Dans la cour de récréation, pas trop de règles à suivre!
E	L'institutrice pensait qu'il était important d'être polie envers tous ses élèves.
F	Il était interdit de jouer pendant les cours.
G	La récréation ne durait que dix minutes.
H	Notre institutrice nous demandait d'être toujours polis.
I	Le dernier cours se terminait à quatre heures.

> Be very careful about words with similar spellings which have very different meanings, e.g. *cours* and *cour*.

Which phrase above best matches each English phrase below? Write the correct letter in the box.

Example: The time pupils arrived at school	C
(a) Teacher showing courtesy towards pupils	E
(b) Length of each lesson	A
(c) What pupils did during breaks	B
(d) Rule applied during lessons	F

(4 marks)

My primary school

2 You hear this man recalling his primary school. Listen to the recording and complete the statements by putting a cross [×] in the correct box for each question.

Listen to the recording

Example: The man's teacher is called …

☐	**A** Mr Tissot
☒	**B** Miss Tissot
☐	**C** Mrs Tissot

(a) The pupils only left the classroom for …

☐	**A** music lessons
☐	**B** science lessons
☐	**C** PE lessons

(b) They went to the football pitch …

☐	**A** if the teacher was in a good mood
☐	**B** when the weather was fine
☐	**C** to play

(c) Playtime lasted …

☐	**A** 15 minutes
☐	**B** 20 minutes
☐	**C** 30 minutes

(d) After lunch he loved …

☐	**A** running races
☐	**B** playing football
☐	**C** chatting with friends

(4 marks)

Success in school

High points at school

1 Read these comments about students succeeding in school.

Ibrahim	J'ai joué pour l'équipe de foot de mon collège et j'ai participé à un concours d'échecs.
Mamadou	Moi, j'ai joué de la batterie dans l'orchestre du collège et j'ai gagné une médaille de bronze en volley.
Sophie	J'ai chanté dans la chorale scolaire et j'ai joué le rôle de Juliette dans une pièce de théâtre.
Régine	Moi, j'ai reçu de bonnes notes dans toutes les matières et j'ai été sélectionnée pour l'équipe régionale de natation.

Enter either **Ibrahim**, **Mamadou**, **Sophie** or **Régine**. You can use each person more than once.

Guided

(a) ....Régine.......... is a good swimmer.

(b) ....Mamadou........ plays drums.

(c) ...Ibrahim.............. enjoys playing chess.

(d) ...Sophie............... has been in the school choir.

(e) ......Régine.............. is good in class.

(f) .....Sophie............... has performed in a school play.

(6 marks)

Conversation: Your school successes

2 As part of a conversation topic, you might talk about what you do well at school.
Prepare answers to these questions and then speak for about 30 seconds on each one.

(a) Tu participes aux clubs scolaires? Lesquels?

(b) Tu fais du sport au collège?

(c) Parle-moi de ta réussite au collège.

> Try to add a few details, however basic.

School trips

Un article de magazine

1 Un magazine français cherche des articles sur les excursions scolaires pour son site Internet.

Écrivez un article sur une excursion scolaire que vous avez faite récemment pour intéresser les lecteurs.

Vous **devez** faire référence aux points suivants:

- pourquoi votre collège avait organisé cette excursion
- votre opinion sur les voyages scolaires en général
- les activités que vous avez faites
- une autre excursion que vous aimeriez faire à l'avenir.

Justifiez vos idées et vos opinions.

Écrivez 130–150 mots environ **en français**.

> In longer questions, try to make sure that you develop the points you make by using adjectives, adverbs and connectives.

Guided

L'année dernière, mon collège a décidé d'organiser une excursion à Londres ....

....

....

....

....

....

....

.... **(28 marks)**

Translation

2 Translate this passage **into English**.

> J'aime les excursions scolaires. Elles sont souvent intéressantes et amusantes parce que mes amis sont avec moi. Je n'aime pas les voyages en car à l'étranger car c'est trop long et je m'ennuie un peu. L'année dernière je suis allé en Espagne avec ma classe d'histoire. C'était génial car j'ai pu pratiquer mon espagnol.

> *car* is seen twice in the text, but it has a different meaning each time. Think carefully about how you will translate *voyages* and *classe d'histoire*.

....

....

....

....

.... **(7 marks)**

School activities

Les événements scolaires

1 Traduis les phrases suivantes **en français**.

(a) I like my school.

.... **(2 marks)**

(b) There are lots of clubs.

> Remember that *beaucoup* is followed by *de*.

.... **(2 marks)**

(c) I go to drama club on Wednesdays.

> This will literally be 'club of drama' when you translate it into French

.... **(2 marks)**

(d) Last week I played football for the school team.

.... **(3 marks)**

(e) We are going to organise a school play next year.

> In French, 'a play' is *une pièce*.

.... **(3 marks)**

What's going on in school?

2 You hear these young people discussing events at their school.

What do they say?

Listen to the recording and put a cross [×] in the correct box.

Listen to the recording

(a) How does Alicia feel about representing her school?

☐	**A** Nervous about it
☒	**B** Looking forward to it
☐	**C** Confident about it
☐	**D** Unhappy about it

(b) Which club does Félix attend?

☐	**A** Swimming
☐	**B** Cookery
☐	**C** Football
☒	**D** Chess

(c) What happened two years ago?

☐	**A** Gaëlle won a school talent show.
☒	**B** Gaëlle took part in a school talent show.
☐	**C** Gaëlle sang very badly.
☐	**D** Gaëlle won a singing competition.

(3 marks)

Exchanges

Role-play: A school trip

1   You are at the home of your French exchange partner, talking about a school trip. The teacher will play the role of your penfriend and will speak first. You must address your penfriend as *tu*.

Tu es chez ton/ta correspondant(e) français(e). Tu parles avec lui/elle.

C'est quoi, comme excursion?

(a) Excursion – description

On voyage comment et à quelle heure?

(b) Transport, heure du départ

Pourquoi est-ce que tu veux faire cette visite?

(c) !

Le voyage dure combien de temps?

(d) Durée

D'accord.

(e) ? Échanges scolaires – opinion

J'aime bien les échanges.

Exchange plans

2   You hear these French students discussing exchanges.

Listen to the recording and answer the following questions **in English**.

(a) How many times has Ariane been to England before?

Guided

Listen to the recording

none .... **(1 mark)**

(b) What is she not looking forward to?

.... **(1 mark)**

(c) What activities are planned for Saturday?

.... **(2 marks)**

(d) What advice does her friend Carine give her?

.... **(1 mark)**

Future plans

A discussion about work

1   Read this discussion between students about their future plans.

FORUM DES JEUNES: Quel talent aimeriez-vous avoir?	
Marie-Flore:	Créer et composer de la musique électronique.
Antonin:	Je joue du piano depuis un an et j'aimerais être un pianiste virtuose, mais malheureusement pour réussir il faut commencer jeune.
Suzanne:	Je voudrais être chanteuse et gagner beaucoup d'argent. Je m'achèterais pas mal de vêtements de luxe!
Dany:	Être créatif, pour devenir un grand styliste et concevoir un nouveau look cool.
Amélie:	Savoir mixer et pouvoir faire danser une salle pleine pendant des heures.
Christophe:	Je voudrais être vedette de cinéma et porter de très beaux vêtements.
Laetitia:	Je voudrais faire de la gymnastique comme une championne. Il faut être souple et ça demande beaucoup d'effort. Il faut s'entraîner cinq ou six heures par jour.
Alice:	J'aimerais devenir chirurgienne. Le corps humain m'intéresse beaucoup et j'aimerais aider les gens.

Who makes the following statements? Write the correct names in the table.

Example: I would like to be a film star.	Christophe
(a) I would like to be a DJ.	Amélie
(b) I started too late to fulfil my ambition.	Antonin
(c) I would like to work in the fashion industry.	Dany
(d) To fulfil my dream I need to be very dedicated.	Laetitia

(4 marks)

Les ambitions

2   Un site Internet français pour les jeunes voudrait ton opinion sur les ambitions.

Écris à ce site Internet.

> Remember to give a reason in bullet point 3.

Tu **dois** faire référence aux points suivants:

- ta personnalité
- le travail que tu as déjà fait
- pourquoi avoir de l'ambition est important pour toi
- tes projets d'avenir.

Écris 80–90 mots environ **en français**.

> **Guided**

On dit que je suis assez travailleur et responsable mais que je suis un

peu timide de temps en temps. ....

....

....

....

....

....

....

....

(20 marks)

Languages beyond the classroom

Role-play: Going to the cinema

1 You are talking to your French friend about going to the cinema. The teacher will play the role of the friend and will speak first. You must address your friend as *tu*.

Tu es en France. Tu vas voir un film au cinéma.
Tu parles avec ton ami(e) français(e).

> C'est quand le film et où?

(a) Film – quand et où

> Qu'est-ce qu'il y a d'autre à faire dans ta ville?

(b) Distractions dans ta ville

> Bon. Parle-moi du dernier film que tu as vu.

(c) !

> C'est intéressant, ça.

(d) ? Films anglais – opinion

> J'aime bien les films anglais.

(e) ? Musique – préférence

> Moi, je préfère la musique rap.

Une Américaine francophone

2 Lis cet article sur Jodie Foster.

> Jodie Foster, l'actrice américaine, parle français presque sans accent et elle se présente facilement dans les médias francophones. De plus, elle se double elle-même dans la version française de certains de ses films! Elle a été scolarisée au Lycée Français de Los Angeles parce que ses parents voulaient qu'elle s'immerge dans la culture francophone. Elle a obtenu son bac en 1980 avant d'étudier la littérature à l'université de Yale. Elle s'intéresse fortement à tout ce qui est français et les films de la Nouvelle Vague n'ont pas de secrets pour elle.
>
> Jeune, elle chantait en français et, de nos jours, bien qu'elle avoue faire des erreurs sur les genres et hésite un peu surtout quand elle parle au téléphone, elle parle français avec une rapidité extraordinaire. «Parler français, ça a changé ma vie» dit-elle, «car celle qui sait parler deux langues vaut deux femmes.»

Réponds aux questions **en français**.

(a) Comment sait-on que Jodie Foster parle couramment français? Donne **deux** détails.

.... **(2 marks)**

(b) Pourquoi est-elle allée au Lycée Français?

.... **(1 mark)**

(c) Qu'est-ce qui s'est passé en 1980?

.... **(1 mark)**

(d) Quels problèmes a-t-elle quand elle parle français maintenant? Donne **deux** détails.

.... **(2 marks)**

(e) Que dit-elle au sujet des personnes bilingues?

.... **(1 mark)**

Relationships in the future

Conversation: Relationships

1 As part of a conversation topic, you might talk about future relationships. Prepare answers to these questions and then speak for about 30 seconds on each one.

> Each one has an introductory sentence or two to get you started.

(a) Tu voudrais te marier un jour? Pourquoi (pas)?

 Guided

> À l'avenir je voudrais me marier car …

(b) À l'avenir, tu voudrais fonder une famille?

 Guided

> J'aime bien les enfants mais je ne sais pas si je voudrais avoir mes propres enfants immédiatement parce que …

(c) Tu penses qu'il sera facile de te faire de nouveaux amis à l'avenir?

Guided

> Je pense que je suis sociable, alors …

My ideal partner

2 You hear these three young French people discussing future relationships.

Complete the sentences. Use the correct word or phrase from the box.

> Remember to listen for negatives.

Listen to the recording

| sporty | reliable | rich |
| good looking | funny | chatty |

(a) Mariette would like to meet someone who is .... **(1 mark)**

(b) Richard's ideal partner would be .... **(1 mark)**

(c) Sonya would like to find someone .... **(1 mark)**

Travel

Mes projets de voyage

1 Traduis le passage suivant **en français**.

People say that I like travelling very much. I have already visited several countries in Europe and next summer I'm going to spend a month in Canada with my family. My dream would be to go to the USA as I am interested in American history. If I save enough money, I'll be able to stay in a five-star hotel in New York.

....

....

....

....

....

....

....

....

....

....

(12 marks)

> 'travelling' – This will be an infinitive in French.

> As Canada is masculine in French, which word translates 'in'?

> 'to the USA' – This is plural in French, so which word translates 'to'?

> 'interested' – The phrase 'to be interested in' is *s'intéresser à*.

> 'to stay' – Use *loger*.

> 'five-star' – This will come after the word for 'hotel' in French.

> As New York is a city, which word translates 'in'?

Les voyages futurs

2 Écoute Yannick qui parle de ses futurs voyages.

Complète les phrases en mettant une croix [×] dans la case correcte.

Listen to the recording

(a) Yannick voudrait aller …

☒	**A**	en Espagne
☐	**B**	aux États-Unis
☐	**C**	en Angleterre
☐	**D**	partout dans le monde

(b) Il aimerait loger …

☐	**A**	dans un hôtel chic et cher
☒	**B**	dans un petit hôtel simple et sympa
☐	**C**	dans un grand hôtel moderne
☐	**D**	dans un vieil hôtel traditionnel

(c) Il n'aimerait pas …

☐	**A**	voyager en avion
☒	**B**	visiter un pays trop froid
☐	**C**	manger des plats épicés
☐	**D**	faire du ski

(3 marks)

Jobs

Picture-based task: Working for a living

1 Regarde la photo et prépare des réponses aux questions suivantes.

(a) Décris-moi la photo.

(b) Je pense qu'il est important de ne pas travailler le week-end. Quel est ton avis?

(c) Parle-moi d'un travail difficile que tu as fait.

> Make sure that the work you talk about was hard. Remember that you can make something up using vocabulary that you already know!

(d) Qu'est-ce que tu vas faire pour choisir le métier que tu voudrais faire?

> This question needs looking at a bit more carefully as it asks you how you are going to decide on your future job, not just which job you'd like to do.

(e) Je pense qu'aller à l'université est une perte de temps. Quelle est ton opinion?

> This will be an unexpected question, so be careful to listen closely when it is asked. Remember that if you do not understand or hear the question, you can ask your teacher to repeat it, but not more than twice.

A working family

2 You hear Christian talking about his family. What does he say? Complete the sentences. Use the correct word or phrase from the box.

> | a driver | a chemist | a cook |
> | ~~an architect~~ | a factory worker | an engineer |

Example: Christian's mother is *an architect*.

(a) His father is ....*engineer*...

(b) His brother is ....*driver*...

(c) His sister is ....*factory worker*...

(d) Christian is ...*a*.....*cook*.. **(4 marks)**

67

Part-time jobs

Gagner un peu plus d'argent

1 Tu as un petit job dans un café. Tu postes cette photo sur des médias sociaux pour tes amis.

Écris une description de la photo et exprime ton opinion sur le travail à temps partiel.

Écris 20–30 mots environ **en français**.

Guided | Sur la photo c'est moi. Je travaille ...

....

....

....

....

....

.... **(12 marks)**

A holiday job

2 Read Karine's account of her part-time job.

> J'habite à Brest, une petite ville au bord de la mer. Je n'aurais jamais pensé que mon petit job cet été allait être si agréable. Tous les matins, j'étais contente d'aller au boulot. Je devais m'occuper des vélos de location et il n'y avait que moi au bureau. Quelle chance!
>
> Les vacanciers avaient l'habitude de louer des vélos tôt le matin et ils ne revenaient que vers six heures du soir, l'heure de fermeture du bureau. Pendant la journée, j'avais peu de travail sauf aux moments rares où il y avait des choses à réparer. Alors, je bronzais sur la plage qui était à dix mètres ou je bavardais avec les passants. Des fois je les conseillais sur les endroits intéressants à visiter.
>
> En fin de journée je devais laver tous les vélos, ce qui était un peu embêtant. Le seul autre inconvénient c'est qu'il fallait être gentille et patiente envers tous les enfants, même les petits gâtés, mais heureusement la plupart des enfants étaient assez sages.

Put a cross [×] next to each one of the **five** correct boxes.

A	Karine always thought her part-time job was going to be pleasant.	☐
B	Karine had to hire bikes to tourists.	☐
C	Karine sometimes had to clean the bikes in the mornings.	☐
D	The tourists usually hired bikes early in the morning.	☐
E	During the day, Karine was not usually very busy.	☐
F	Karine does not seem to know the area well.	☐
G	Karine never needed to repair the bikes.	☐
H	Some tourists asked Karine for information on the area.	☐
I	Karine got on badly with all the children she met.	☐
J	Karine never got angry, even with children who were unbearable.	☐

(5 marks)

Opinions about jobs

Working life

1   Valérie, Édouard and Sacha are talking about their mothers.

Who says the following about their mother? Put a cross in the correct box.

	A Valérie	**B** Édouard	**C** Sacha
Example: She is always tired.	X		
(a) She works full time.			
(b) Her work is difficult.			
(c) She is always busy.			
(d) She works at home.			

(4 marks)

Le métier de professeur

2   Lis ces opinions sur le métier de prof.

C'est qui? Écris le nom correct.

● ● ●	
Être prof, cela vous intéresserait?	
Alain	Les élèves sont parfois bêtes et souvent impolis.
Berthe	Les profs sont assez bien payés à mon avis.
Dominique	Travailler avec les jeunes, c'est un grand plaisir.
Samuel	Je trouve la plupart des élèves paresseux.
Farah	On aurait beaucoup de vacances.
Molly	Le salaire n'est pas important. Je pense qu'il faut vraiment aimer les ados.
Jasmine	Je ne supporterais pas un principal autoritaire.
Paulette	À mon avis les profs ont trop de travail le soir et le week-end.

(a)   En général les élèves ne sont pas travailleurs. ....

(b)   Il y a quelquefois des élèves qui se comportent mal. ....

(c)   Je ne pourrais pas tolérer un patron strict. ....

(d)   On n'a pas assez de temps libre. ....   **(4 marks)**

Workplaces

My job

1 These young French people are talking about where they work.

Complete the sentences. Use the correct word or phrase from the box.

hairdresser's salon	chemist's shop	clothes shop
workshop	town hall	hotel reception

Listen to the recording

(a) Marc works in a .... **(1 mark)**

(b) Alex has a job in a .... **(1 mark)**

(c) Jean-Paul has found a job in a .... **(1 mark)**

Translation

2 Translate this passage **into English**.

> Ma sœur travaille dans un magasin de vêtements en ville. Elle sert les clients et prépare du café pour ses collègues. Elle n'aime pas son emploi parce que c'est assez ennuyeux et qu'elle ne s'entend pas bien avec le patron. Hier elle a dû nettoyer le magasin à la fin de la journée. À l'avenir, elle va chercher un autre emploi dans un centre sportif.

elle a dû – Be careful with the tense here.

journée – Remember that this does not mean 'journey'.

....

....

....

....

....

....

....

....

....

....

.... **(7 marks)**

Applying for jobs

A job interview

1 Jérôme is being interviewed for a job.

What does he say about himself?

Listen to the recording and put a cross [×] in each one of the **four** correct boxes.

> **Guided**

Listen to the recording

A	He has a driving licence.	☒
B	He had a good attendance record at school.	☐
C	He has worked in a team before.	☐
D	He is willing to travel.	☐
E	He has experience working on a supermarket checkout.	☐
F	He has worked abroad.	☐
G	He can start work next week.	☐
H	He is interested in most sports.	☐

(4 marks)

Une lettre de candidature

2 Lis cette lettre de Sophie.

> Madame,
>
> J'ai lu votre annonce sur Internet et je voudrais poser ma candidature pour le poste de secrétaire à votre école maternelle. Je travaille dans le bureau d'une école primaire depuis cinq ans, mais je dois chercher un nouvel emploi parce que j'ai déménagé il y a un mois et que le trajet est trop long.
>
> Je suis très motivée par le poste que vous proposez. Cela me donnerait la possibilité d'apprendre beaucoup de choses sur la routine journalière dans une maternelle, ce qui m'intéresse car mon propre fils va bientôt arriver à l'âge d'entrér à la maternelle. Je pourrais être flexible pour mes heures de travail et serais prête à faire des heures supplémentaires le week-end si vous en aviez besoin.

Mets une croix [×] dans la case correcte.

(a) Sophie a trouvé l'annonce …

☐	**A**	dans un journal
☐	**B**	à la radio
☐	**C**	en ligne
☐	**D**	dans une agence

(b) Elle …

☐	**A**	voudrait travailler dans une école primaire
☐	**B**	travaille dans une école primaire
☐	**C**	travaillait dans une école primaire
☐	**D**	va travailler dans une école primaire

(c) Elle vient de …

☐	**A**	déménager
☐	**B**	trouver un poste dans une école maternelle
☐	**C**	changer d'emploi
☐	**D**	se marier

(d) Le fils de Sophie …

☐	**A**	aime aller à la maternelle
☐	**B**	s'intéresse à la maternelle
☐	**C**	a sa propre routine
☐	**D**	ira bientôt à la maternelle

(4 marks)

Future study

Picture-based task: Going to university

1   Regarde la photo et prépare des réponses aux questions suivantes.

(a) Décris-moi la photo.

 Guided

> Sur la photo il y a un groupe d'étudiants ...

(b) Je pense qu'il n'est pas important d'aller à l'université. Quel est ton avis?

(c) Parle-moi d'un projet scolaire que tu as préparé cette année au collège.

(d) Tu voudrais étudier à l'étranger? Pourquoi (pas)?

(e) Je pense que faire un apprentissage est une bonne idée. Quelle est ton opinion?

> Remember to add a reason when you give your opinion.

Translation: A difficult decision

2   Translate this passage **into English**.

> Je ne sais pas si je vais aller à l'université. Mes parents y sont allés et ils ont de bons emplois, mais je ne suis pas aussi travailleur qu'eux. J'aimerais devenir avocat, c'est vrai, et mes profs disent que je suis assez doué, pourtant je pense que je ne pourrais pas supporter le stress. Je vais prendre une année sabbatique et je voyagerai beaucoup, mais néanmoins il faudra enfin que je décide ce que je voudrais faire dans la vie.

> Pay attention to verbs. Look closely at tenses and the subject of verbs so you don't make a careless error when translating.

....

....

....

....

....

....

....

.... **(7 marks)**

Volunteering

Aidez-moi à aller au Cameroun!

1 Vous voulez travailler comme bénévole dans un collège au Cameroun, mais il y a peu de places disponibles. Écrivez une lettre pour convaincre les organisateurs de vous offrir une place.

Vous **devez** faire référence aux points suivants:

- pourquoi vous voulez participer
- le travail bénévole que vous avez déjà fait
- comment ce travail va vous aider à l'avenir
- pourquoi être volontaire est important pour les jeunes.

Justifiez vos idées et vos opinions.

Écrivez 130–150 mots environ **en français**.

Guided

Madame, Monsieur,

J'ai vu votre annonce dans un magazine que je lisais la semaine dernière

....

....

....

....

....

....

....

....

.... **(28 marks)**

A successful volunteer

2 You hear Marcus talking about his voluntary work.

Listen to the recording and answer the following questions **in English**.

(a) What inspired Marcus to volunteer?

.... **(1 mark)**

(b) What did his group have to do and why did they do it?

.... **(2 marks)**

(c) What specific skills did Marcus have?

.... **(1 mark)**

(d) How does he describe himself and how did he feel at the end of the task?

.... **(2 marks)**

Helping others

Conversation: Offering help

1   As part of a conversation topic, you might talk about how you help people. Prepare answers to these questions and then speak for about 30 seconds on each one.

> When you are asked a question, try to use different tenses, even if not specifically asked to do so. For example, in question (a), you could add an example from the past and/or what you intend to do in the future. This is a good way of showing that you can be spontaneous and can take the initiative in a conversation.

    (a)   Que fais-tu pour aider les autres?

Guided

J'écoute les problèmes de tous mes copains et je leur donne des conseils prudents. Par exemple, hier j'ai dit à ma copine Amanda qu'elle devrait se concentrer sur ses études au lieu de sortir tous les soirs.

    (b)   Qu'est-ce que tu as fait récemment pour aider ta famille?

    (c)   Tu aimes aider les autres? Pourquoi (pas)?

Faire du travail bénévole en ville

2   Tu participes en tant que bénévole au nettoyage de ta ville, avec un groupe. Tu postes cette photo sur des médias sociaux pour tes amis.

    Écris une description de la photo **et** exprime ton opinion sur les volontaires.

    Écris 20–30 mots environ **en français**.

Guided   Sur la photo il y a ....

....

....

....

.... **(12 marks)**

Charities

Travailler pour une organisation caritative

1 Lis ce texte de Raphaël.

> Mon emploi de temps quotidien est surchargé, mais il y a six mois j'ai décidé de faire du travail pour une organisation caritative. Nous vivons dans une société individualiste et j'ai voulu non seulement contrer ce phénomène, mais aussi montrer que les humains sont plus forts quand ils s'unissent.
>
> J'ai choisi d'abord de travailler dans le bureau d'une association qui soutient la recherche contre le cancer puisque j'ai perdu un proche atteint de cette maladie. Je ne fais que téléphoner à des individus afin de les encourager à nous donner de l'argent, mais maintenant je crois que je pourrais faire une différence et que la recherche pourrait apporter quelque chose et aider les autres.

Réponds aux questions en français. Il n'est pas nécessaire d'écrire des phrases complètes.

(a) Quand est-ce que Raphaël a commencé son travail caritatif?

> Guided

il y a six mois ....   **(1 mark)**

(b) Pourquoi est-ce qu'il pense qu'il faut aider les associations caritatives?

....

....   **(2 marks)**

(c) Pourquoi est-ce qu'il a choisi d'abord d'aider la recherche contre le cancer?

....   **(1 mark)**

(d) Que fait-il exactement?

....   **(1 mark)**

(e) Quelle est son opinion sur son travail maintenant?

....   **(1 mark)**

Reasons for helping charities

2 You hear Aicha giving reasons why she helps charities.

Which reasons does she mention?

Listen to the recording and put a cross [×] in each of the **three** correct boxes.

Listen to the recording

A	To make a difference	☐
B	To take part in the local community	☐
C	To meet new people	☐
D	To feel good about herself	☐
E	To meet a challenge	☐
F	To develop new skills	☐

(3 marks)

Training

Listen to the recording

Apprenticeships

1 Amina is talking about her apprenticeship.

Complete the sentences. Use the correct word or phrase from the box.

> | | | | |
> |---|---|---|---|
> | engineering | big | local | difficult |
> | school work | behaviour in school | no problem | cars |

(a) For several years, Amina has been fascinated by .... **(1 mark)**

(b) She finds being the only female .... **(1 mark)**

(c) She gets practical experience in a .... garage. **(1 mark)**

(d) Her apprenticeship has helped her .... **(1 mark)**

Conversation: Being an apprentice

2 As part of a conversation topic, you might talk about your career plans. Prepare answers to these questions and then speak for about 30 seconds on each one.

(a) Quels sont les avantages et les inconvénients des apprentissages?

(b) Aimerais-tu être professeur un jour? Pourquoi (pas)?

(c) Quel serait ton emploi idéal?

> Remember to give positives and negatives when asked about advantages and disadvantages, even if you personally believe there aren't any!

Future professions

Les métiers de l'informatique

1 Lis ce texte.

> Les diplômés en informatique ont du mal à trouver du travail. La croissance de l'informatique a ralenti et il n'y a plus assez d'emplois dans le domaine technique. Les informaticiens doivent être plus spécialisés grâce au développement des téléphones intelligents et des tablettes. On ne peut plus tout apprendre à l'université, donc il faut s'adapter rapidement à de nouveaux outils. Certains sont capables de mieux analyser les besoins de leurs clients avant de concevoir leurs systèmes informatiques. Cela fait d'eux de meilleurs chefs d'équipe et ils réussissent dans leur profession.
>
> Chose bizarre, au Canada on manque d'informaticiens, alors si vous êtes au chômage, mais diplômé en informatique, pourquoi ne pas envoyer un e-mail aux entreprises canadiennes?

Trouve les **quatre** bonnes réponses. Mets une croix [×] dans la case correcte.

A	Les diplômés en informatique peuvent facilement trouver du travail.	☐
B	Il y avait plein d'emplois pour des diplômés en informatique.	☐
C	Il y a plus de chômage au Canada.	☐
D	On peut tout apprendre sur l'informatique à l'université.	☐
E	Il faut se spécialiser pour trouver un emploi en informatique.	☐
F	Si on sait analyser les besoins des clients, on peut réussir.	☐
G	Les universités canadiennes n'offrent pas des cours en informatique.	☐
H	On n'a pas assez d'informaticiens au Canada.	☐

(4 marks)

Future jobs

2 These three French teenagers are discussing future jobs.

What jobs are mentioned?

Listen to the recording and put a cross [×] in each one of the **three** correct boxes.

Listen to the recording

A	lorry driver	☐
B	teacher	☐
C	doctor	☐
D	nurse	☐
E	driver	☐
F	plumber	☐

(3 marks)

Sporting events

Picture-based task: The Tour de France

1 Regarde la photo et prépare des réponses aux questions suivantes.

(a) Décris-moi la photo.

> **Guided**
>
> Sur la photo il y a des cyclistes professionnels qui participent au Tour de France. Les cyclistes sont très proches l'un à l'autre et ça peut être dangereux si un cycliste tombe par exemple. Je crois que je peux voir Chris Froome à l'arrière-plan.

(b) Je pense qu'aller à un événement sportif est formidable. Quel est ton avis?

> When you are describing a photo, you can make assumptions, as shown in this student's answer.

(c) Parle-moi d'un événement sportif auquel tu as assisté.

(d) Quels événements sportifs auront bientôt lieu?

(e) Je pense qu'il faut encourager la compétition sportive pour réunir tous les pays du monde. Quelle est ton opinion?

Translation

2 Traduis les phrases suivantes **en français**.

(a) I like every sport.

> Say 'all the sports'.

.... **(2 marks)**

(b) I watch a rugby match on Saturdays.

> The phrase 'on Saturdays' will have no word in French for 'on' and 'Saturday' will be in the singular.

.... **(2 marks)**

(c) Sporting events are popular.

> You will need to start this sentence with *Les événements*.

.... **(2 marks)**

(d) I would like to go to the Olympic Games.

> Remember that the French word for 'Olympic' is an adjective here.

.... **(3 marks)**

(e) My brother went to a football match yesterday.

> Remember how to form the perfect tense.

.... **(3 marks)**

Music events

A music festival

1   Read this passage about a music festival.

> Chaque printemps, des milliers de spectateurs viennent dans les salles de Bourges pour écouter les artistes les plus connus ou découvrir de jeunes talents musicaux. En mélangeant ainsi les célébrités et les nouveaux venus, le festival offre depuis 1977 une semaine de concerts aux genres musicaux les plus divers. Les sept salles du festival sont toujours bourrées* de gens et il existe aussi quatre scènes gratuites au bord de la rivière où, il y a trois ans, le groupe Indochine a débuté. Il est hors de doute que le festival offre un tremplin pour les jeunes artistes. Cette année, pour la première fois, il y aura des scènes dans une vingtaine de bars en ville.

bourrées = full

Answer the following questions **in English**. You do not need to write in full sentences.

(a) When does this festival take place?

> spring ....   **(1 mark)**

(b) What sort of music can you hear at the festival?

> ....   **(1 mark)**

(c) What are we told about the seven festival halls?

> ....   **(1 mark)**

(d) How much does it cost to watch the performances by the river?

> ....   **(1 mark)**

(e) What will happen for the first time this year?

> ....   **(1 mark)**

A recent music festival

2   Aurore is talking about a music festival she has been to.

Listen to the recording and put a cross [×] in each one of the **three** correct boxes.

A	The festival was in Britain.	☐
B	Aurore heard her favourite group play.	☐
C	The festival took place last year.	☐
D	It was an electronic music festival.	☐
E	Aurore hates electronic music.	☐
F	The festival took place in a field.	☐

(3 marks)

Being green

Helping the environment

1 Read what these three young people do to help the environment.

Denis	Moi, j'achète souvent des produits bio si possible et je réutilise les sacs en plastique plusieurs fois au supermarché. Je vais toujours en ville en vélo, mais je sais que je devrais recycler plus de carton.
Yannick	J'essaie d'économiser l'eau. Par exemple, je prends une douche au lieu d'un bain et je me brosse les dents le robinet fermé. À l'avenir, je vais dire à mes parents de baisser le chauffage central aussi.
Thomas	Pour économiser l'énergie, j'essaie de toujours éteindre toutes les lumières chez moi quand je sors d'une pièce. Hier, j'ai refusé un sac en plastique dans un magasin et je vais recycler tous les articles en verre au lieu de les jeter à la poubelle.

What do they say they do? Enter either **Denis**, **Yannick** or **Thomas**.

You can use each person more than once.

> Remember to look beyond the word. For example, *économiser*, *recycler*, *au lieu de*, *sac en plastique* all appear twice in the texts so you will need to look at the context in order to work out the correct answers.

Guided

(a) ....Yannick............... saves water.

(b) .... recently did not use a plastic bag.

(c) .... tries to use a greener way of travelling.

(d) .... is going to suggest changing the heating arrangements.

(e) .... knows that he should recycle cardboard.

(f) .... already tries to save energy.   **(6 marks)**

Becoming greener

2 You hear these young people talking about what they do to be 'green'.

Listen to the recording and put a cross [×] in each one of the **three** correct boxes.

Listen to the recording

		(a) Noah	**(b) Sophie**	**(c) Didier**
A	Recycling glass			
B	Walking to school			×
C	Taking public transport		×	
D	Saving water			
E	Recycling newspapers	×		
F	Buying organic products			
G	Turning off lights			

(3 marks)

Protecting the environment

Translation

1 Translate this passage **into English**.

> On est en train de détruire la planète. Beaucoup d'animaux sont menacés par les actions de l'homme et il faut essayer de protéger la Terre. Le niveau de la mer monte depuis plusieurs années à cause du réchauffement et du changement climatiques. La pollution a augmenté les risques de santé et on devrait agir afin de résoudre ce problème grave.

> Be careful with cognates like *train* and *menacés* as they can be misleading.

....

....

....

....

....

....

....

....

(7 marks)

Conversation: Problems with the environment

2 As part of a conversation topic, you might talk about environmental issues. Prepare answers to these questions and then speak for about 30 seconds on each one.

(a) À ton avis, quel est le problème environnemental le plus grave?

(b) Qu'est-ce que tu as déjà fait pour essayer de résoudre les problèmes environnementaux dans ta région?

(c) Comment pourrait-on réduire la pollution?

> Here, the three questions require three different tenses, so make sure you practise using verbs associated with the environment in different tenses. For example, *je recycle* (I recycle), *j'ai recyclé* (I recycled) and *je vais recycler* (I'm going to recycle) / *je recyclerai* (I'll recycle).

Environmental issues

Picture-based task: Droughts

1 Regarde la photo et prépare des réponses aux questions suivantes.

(a) Décris-moi la photo.

(b) Je pense qu'il y a assez d'eau partout dans le monde. Quel est ton avis?

(c) Parle-moi de ce que tu as fait pour utiliser moins d'énergie.

(d) Quelle sera la plus grande menace pour le monde à l'avenir?

(e) Je crois qu'on devrait aider les associations caritatives qui protègent l'environnement. Qu'en penses-tu?

> Remember that the final item in this kind of task is an 'unpredictable' question – (e) is an example of this. When preparing the task, try to work out from the photo what sort of question might be asked.

Global problems

2 You hear this discussion about global problems.

Listen to the recording and put a cross [×] in each one of the **four** correct boxes.

Listen to the recording

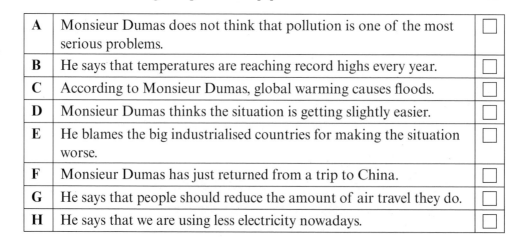

A	Monsieur Dumas does not think that pollution is one of the most serious problems.	☐
B	He says that temperatures are reaching record highs every year.	☐
C	According to Monsieur Dumas, global warming causes floods.	☐
D	Monsieur Dumas thinks the situation is getting slightly easier.	☐
E	He blames the big industrialised countries for making the situation worse.	☐
F	Monsieur Dumas has just returned from a trip to China.	☐
G	He says that people should reduce the amount of air travel they do.	☐
H	He says that we are using less electricity nowadays.	☐

(4 marks)

Natural resources

Listen to the recording

Changing resources in Mali

1 You hear this report about Mali on French radio.

Listen to the recording and answer the following questions **in English**.

(a) What new crop has been harvested in Mali?

...........Cotton.. **(1 mark)**

(b) What are the consequences of this change in production? Give **two** details.

→ lots of space is lost for animals ....

→ .... **(2 marks)**

(c) Why will rivers become polluted?

.........use of pesticides.. **(1 mark)**

(d) What does the report propose?

FIND LAND TO GROW MORE VEGGIES............................... **(1 mark)**

Le commerce équitable

2 Lis ce texte de Marcel.

> Mon oncle achète souvent des produits issus du commerce équitable car il pense que ça vaut la peine, même s'il faut payer un peu plus. Par exemple, le week-end dernier je suis allé en ville avec lui et nous avons acheté du café du Brésil issu du commerce équitable. Malheureusement, mes copains disent que ces produits sont trop chers, mais ils veulent acheter responsable quand-même, alors ils achètent un produit équitable une fois sur deux.

Trouve les **trois** bonnes réponses. Mets une croix [×] dans la case correcte.

A	L'oncle de Marcel n'achète pas souvent des produits issus du commerce équitable.	☐
B	La semaine dernière, Marcel a fait du shopping.	☐
C	On a acheté du chocolat brésilien.	☐
D	Les produits du commerce équitable coûtent plus cher.	☐
E	Les amis de Marcel achètent quelques produits du commerce équitable.	☐
F	Les copains de Marcel n'achètent jamais responsable.	☐

(3 marks)

World problems

Radio headlines

Listen to the recording

1   Listen to these news headlines on French radio and answer the following questions **in English**.

(a)   What has happened in Pakistan?

.... **(1 mark)**

(b)   What has caused damage in the Atlantic Ocean?

.... **(1 mark)**

(c)   Give **two** details about the floods in south-west England.

....

.... **(2 marks)**

(d)   What has happened in Australia and what are people worried about?

....

.... **(2 marks)**

Translation

2   Translate this passage **into English**.

> Dans le monde, il y a beaucoup de gens sans domicile fixe. Il faut donner de l'argent aux organisations qui les aident. Je pense qu'il y a trop de chômage, surtout en Europe, alors les gouvernements devraient faire quelque chose. Je n'aime pas voir la destruction des habitats naturels des animaux sauvages en Afrique. J'ai visité l'Australie le mois dernier et je crois qu'il y avait plein d'animaux qui y vivaient sans problèmes.

> Take care when you are translating object pronouns such as *les aident* here – remember that the pronoun comes before the verb in French but not in English.

....

....

....

....

....

....

.... **(7 marks)**

Articles 1

To say 'the' in French you use *le, la, l'* or *les* in front of the noun. Remember that in French every noun has a gender. Objects are either masculine (m) or feminine (f) and are singular or plural.

A Put in the correct word for 'the' (*le, la, l', les*) in front of these nouns. They are all places around a town.

Example: banque (f) La banque

1 .... commerces (pl)	5 .... cinémas (pl)	9 .... rues (pl)
2 .... pharmacie (f)	6 .... bowling (m)	10 .... appartement (m)
3 .... toilettes (pl)	7 .... gare (f)	
4 .... hôtel (m)	8 .... parking (m)	

B Here is a list of animals. Put the correct word for 'the' in front of the noun.

1 .... chienne (f)	5 .... tortue (f)	9 .... mouche (f)
2 .... serpents (pl)	6 .... éléphant (m)	10 .... cochons d'Inde (pl)
3 .... araignée (f)	7 .... poissons (pl)	11 .... grenouille (f)
4 .... chat (m)	8 .... canard (m)	12 .... singe (m)

To say 'a' or 'an' in French, you use *un* or *une* depending on whether the noun is masculine or feminine.

C Show that you understand when to put *un* or *une* in front of these parts of a house.

1 .... salon (m)	4 .... chambre (f)	7 .... salle à manger (f)
2 .... salle de bains (f)	5 .... sous-sol (m)	
3 .... jardin (m)	6 .... cuisine (f)	

D Fill in the gaps in this table, paying attention to the articles: *un, une, des, le, la, l', les*.

Singular	Plural
	les chiens
un château	
l'animal	
	des voitures
le nez	
le bateau	
un hôtel	
l'arbre	les arbres
	des pages
	les eaux
une araignée	
	les destinations

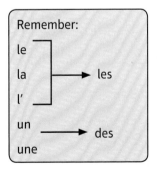

Remember:

le
la ⟶ les
l'
un ⟶ des
une

85

Articles 2

If you want to say 'some' or 'any' in French, you use the partitive article *du*, *de la*, *des* or *de l'*, depending on the gender of the noun you are talking about.

A Put the correct word for 'some' in front of these nouns. Pay attention to the gender given in brackets.

Example: farine (f)   de la farine (some flour)

1 .... œufs (pl)
2 .... confiture (f)
3 .... pain (m)
4 .... haricots verts (pl)

5 .... eau minérale (f)
6 .... jambon (m)
7 .... frites (pl)
8 .... crème (f)

9 .... huile (f)
10 .... riz (m)

B Fill in the gaps below, using *du*, *de la*, *des*, *de l'* in order to ask your friend if they want any of the items:

Tu veux des pâtes, ... abricots, ... fromage, ... chocolat,
.... olives, ... porc, ... pommes de terre, ... ketchup, ... ananas,
.... potage, ... œufs, ... sel et .... poivre?

C Unfortunately, you have nothing left to eat in the house. Using the example below, answer the following questions, then translate into English.

> Always use *de* after a negative in French to say 'some' or 'any'.

Example: Tu as des pommes? Je n'ai pas de pommes. I don't have any apples.

1 Tu as de l'argent? ....
2 Tu as du pain? ....
3 Tu as des céréales? ....
4 Tu as de la pizza? ....

D Re-read all the rules and fill in the gaps with *du*, *de la*, *de l'*, *des* or *de*.

Tu as .... fruits et .... légumes? Oui, j'ai .... fruits mais je n'ai pas .... légumes. Par exemple, j'ai .... pêches et .... cerises mais je n'ai pas .... carottes ni .... pommes de terre. Cependant, j'ai .... pain et .... Nutella, donc on peut manger .... sandwichs.

You use *au*, *à la*, *à l'* or *aux* to translate 'to the'.

E Using *au*, *à la*, *à l'* or *aux*, fill in the gaps to tell your friend where you are going in town this afternoon.

Example: Je vais au cinéma.

1 Je vais .... patinoire.
2 Je vais .... crêperie.
3 Je vais .... théâtre.

4 Je vais .... hôtel de ville.
5 Je vais .... magasins.
6 Je vais .... café-tabac.

F Say what part of the house you are going to, using *Je vais au*, *à la*, *à l'*, *aux* …

1 .... salon
2 .... cuisine
3 .... salle de bains
4 .... chambres
5 .... salle de jeux
6 .... jardin

7 .... atelier
8 .... grenier
9 .... cave
10 .... entrée
11 .... garage
12 .... salle à manger

Adjectives

Adjectives are used to describe nouns. Remember that in French you need to ensure they have the correct endings depending on whether the noun is masculine, feminine, singular or plural.

A Circle the correct form of the adjectives.

1 Ma mère est petit/petite.

2 Mon père est grand/grande.

3 Ma maison est beau/belle.

4 Mon chat est noir/noire.

5 Elle est heureux/heureuse.

6 Les fenêtres sont chère/chères.

B Using the adjectives in the box, complete the sentences below. Don't forget to change them to the feminine or plural form where necessary.

1 Mon chien est .... (sad)

2 Mes crayons sont .... (white)

3 Ma mère est .... (intelligent)

4 Mes frères sont .... (shy)

5 Mes sœurs sont .... (fat)

6 Ma chatte est très .... (cute)

gros
blanc
timide
mignon
triste
intelligent

C Complete this table with all the different forms of the adjectives.

masc. sing.	fem. sing.	masc. plural	fem. plural	English
grand	grande		grandes	big/tall
	petite			
noir		noirs		
	neuve		neuves	
		derniers		last
marron		marron		
triste		tristes		sad
sérieux		sérieux		
	gentille		gentilles	kind
	sèche	secs		
drôle		drôles		funny
	vieille		vieilles	old
	belle	beaux		
ancien		anciens		ancient
blanc		blancs		white
	sportive		sportives	

D Make sentences that use the adjectives in **C** above. Make sure they have the correct form and are in the correct position.

Example: J'ai deux chattes (grand, noir) *J'ai deux grandes chattes noires.*

1 Elle a des yeux (beau, bleu). ....

2 Les fleurs (meilleur, jaune). ....

3 Mes baskets (vieux, blanc). ....

4 Mes parents (pauvre, malade). ....

Most adjectives come *after* the noun but some come *before*, e.g. *grand*.

Possessives

To say something is 'my', 'your', 'his', etc, you use a possessive adjective e.g. *mon, ma, mes*.

A 1 Choose *mon, ma* or *mes* to fill in the gaps.

Dans ma famille, il y a .... père, ... mère, ... sœur et .... deux frères. ....
grand-mère vient souvent nous rendre visite avec .... grand-père. .... amie adore ....
grands-parents et elle vient jouer avec toutes .... affaires quand ils sont là.

2 Use *son / sa / ses* to fill in the gaps.

Dans sa chambre, elle a .... lit, ... livres, ... bureau, ... télévision, ...
bijoux, ... téléphone et .... nounours.

3 Use *notre / notre / nos* to translate 'our' or *votre / votre / vos* to translate 'your'.

Dans notre collège, nous avons .... professeurs, ... bibliothèque,
.... cantine, et .... terrain de sport. Et vous, qu'est-ce que vous avez dans
.... collège et dans .... salles de classe? Vous avez .... tableaux
blancs interactifs et .... gymnase?

4 Your teacher asks you questions about yourself. Insert the correct word for 'your'.

   (a) Comment s'appellent .... père et .... mère?

   (b) Qu'est-ce que tu achètes avec .... argent?

   (c) C'est quand .... anniversaire?

   (d) Qu'est-ce qu'il y a dans .... ville ou .... village?

5 How would you talk about what they have in **their** village?

Dans leur village, ils ont .... mairie, ... cinémas, ...
pharmacie, ... boulangerie, ... cafés, ... parcs, ...
hôpital, ... école et tous .... petits commerces.

B How many grammatically correct but silly sentences can you make from this table?

mon / ma / mes	fromage	est	très	jaune(s)
ton / ta / tes	copines	n'est pas	assez	honnête(s)
son / sa / ses	vélo	sont		moderne(s)
notre / nos	gâteaux	ne sont pas		grand(e)(s)
votre / vos	football			timide(s)
leur / leurs	photos			romantique(s)

....

....

....

....

C These clothes all belong to you. Say so!

Example: La chemise? C'est la mienne!

1 Les pulls? Ce sont ....

2 Les jupes? Ce sont ....

3 Le jogging? C'est ....

To say something is 'mine', use *le, la* or *les* + *mien(ne)(s)*. For example: *La chemise, c'est la mienne.*

Comparisons

> Use the comparative form of the adjective to say 'more than' or 'less than':
>
> *plus* + adjective + *que* or *moins* + adjective + *que*
>
> Use the superlative form of the adjective to say 'the most' or 'the least':
>
> *le / la / les* + *plus / moins* + adjective
>
> The adjective ending must agree with the noun it refers to.

A   Work out who is the most and the least intelligent, Marie, Lydie or Paul.

Marie est intelligente.

Marie est plus intelligente que Paul.

Paul est moins intelligent que Lydie.

Lydie est plus intelligente que Marie.

Paul n'est pas aussi intelligent que Marie.

Qui est le/la plus intelligent(e)? ....

Qui est le/la moins intelligent(e)? ....

B   Using the grades below, make up four sentences about how these students compare in each subject.

Example: En anglais, Anna est meilleure qu'Antoine.

	Antoine	Anna	
Anglais	D	B	....
Français	A	C	....
Géo	C	E	....
Dessin	B	A*	....

C   Put each of these sentences in the correct order, then translate them.

Example: est que courte plus jupe Ma jupe ta   Ma jupe est plus courte que ta jupe.

                                        My skirt is shorter than your skirt.

1   aussi est Sara grand Philippe que ....

2   maths que plus musique Les difficiles sont la ....

3   Les moins sont les sains fruits bonbons que ....

4   Une est moins un confortable cravate qu' jogging ....

5   l' chimie que est intéressante aussi anglais La ....

D   Use the adjective given, with *le / la / les plus* to make a superlative sentence. Make sure the adjective matches the noun.

Example: Le TGV est le train ... (rapide)   Le TGV est le train le plus rapide.

1   Les kiwis sont les fruits ... (sain) ....

2   L'hiver est la saison ... (froid) ....

3   Londres est ... (grand) ville d'Angleterre. ....

Now use the adjective given, with *le / la / les moins* to say 'the least'.

Example: Voilà la cathédrale ... (traditionnel)   Voilà la cathédrale la moins traditionnelle.

4   Où sont les garçons ... (actif)? ....

5   Je prends les vêtements ... (long) ....

6   J'habite dans la région ... (industriel) ....

Other adjectives and pronouns

A Say which clothes you are going to wear on holiday, using *ce*, *cet*, *cette* or *ces*.

Je vais porter …

Example: pull *ce pull*

1 pantalon ....

2 imperméable ....

3 robe ....

4 baskets ....

5 anorak ....

6 sandales ....

7 chaussettes ....

8 jupe ....

> *ce* = this (m)
> *cet* = this (in front of a masculine noun beginning with a vowel)
> *cette* = this (f)
> *ces* = these (plu)

B Say you always prefer the one(s) on the left, using *celui*, *celle*, *ceux* or *celles*.

(You get a clue to the gender by looking at the spelling of 'which' at the beginning.)

Example: Quelle jupe préfères-tu?   Je préfère *celle* à gauche.

1 Quel livre préfères-tu?   Je préfère .... à gauche.

2 Quels garçons préfères-tu?   Je préfère .... à gauche.

3 Quelle salle préfères-tu?   Je préfère .... à gauche.

4 Quelles cartes postales préfères-tu?   Je préfère .... à gauche.

> *celui* (m) / *celle* (f) = the one
> *ceux* (m) / *celles* (f) = those

C Complete the question by asking your friend if they prefer this one here, that one there, these or those.

Example: Quels bateaux préfères-tu? *Ceux-ci ou ceux-là?*

1 Quel stylo préfères-tu? ....

2 Quelle station balnéaire préfères-tu? ....

3 Quelles ceintures préfères-tu? ....

4 Quels hôtels préfères-tu? ....

> You add on *-ci* when you want to say' here'. You add *-là* when you want to say 'there'.

D You don't hear what they say, so you have to ask your friend which one(s) they prefer yet again. Use *lequel*, *laquelle*, *lesquels* or *lesquelles* to repeat each question in exercise C.

Example: Quels bateaux préfères-tu? *Lesquels?*

1 Quel stylo préfères-tu? ....

2 Quelle station balnéaire préfères-tu? ....

3 Quelles ceintures préfères-tu? ....

4 Quels hôtels préfères-tu? ....

> *lequel* (m) / *laquelle* (f) = which one?

E Fill in the missing words as shown in the example.

Example: Quel appartement préfères-tu? Celui-ci ou celui-là? Lequel?

1 .... cuisine préfères-tu? Celle-ci ou ....? Laquelle?

2 Quelles cravates préfères-tu? .... ou celles-là? ....?

3 .... jardin préfères-tu? .... ou ....? Lequel?

4 .... gants préfères-tu? .... ou ....? ....?

Had a go ☐ Nearly there ☐ Nailed it! ☐

Adverbs

> Adverbs are used to describe the verb. In French a lot of adverbs end in *-ment*.

A Form adverbs from these adjectives.

Example: heureux heureusement

1 doux ....   5 attentif ....

2 naturel ....   6 vrai ....

3 absolu ....   7 lent ....

4 général ....   8 gentil ....

B Underline all the adverbs in this paragraph, then translate it. Use the English translations in the box if you are stuck.

first
often
then
finally
in the future

Le matin, <u>d'abord</u>, je me lève à sept heures, puis d'habitude je prends mon petit déjeuner. Ensuite, je quitte la maison et finalement j'arrive au collège à huit heures et demie. Mais c'est souvent trop tôt. Alors, à l'avenir, je vais rester au lit plus longtemps.

In the morning, ...

....

....

C Fill in the gaps from this passage with the best adverb from the box. There may be more than one answer. The first letter of the adverb has been given for you.

> absolument, d'abord, de temps en temps, ~~généralement~~, par conséquent, régulièrement, sans doute, seulement, souvent, toujours, vraiment

Généralement je vais en France avec mes parents et mon petit frère pour les grandes vacances. S........................ mes grands-parents viennent avec nous, et d'........................ c'est v........................... pratique car ils font r........................ du baby-sitting. Cependant, de ...., ils se sentent v........................ fatigués et ils ne sont pas t........................ confortables. P........................ ils ne viendront pas l'année prochaine. À l'avenir, ils viendront s........................ s'ils sont a........................ en bonne forme!

D Complete these sentences using adverbs from the box.

Example: Je conduis (always) très (carefully).

~~attentivement~~
d'habitude
~~toujours~~
doucement
dedans
tout de suite
naturellement
de temps en temps

Je conduis toujours très attentivement.

1 (Usually) il fait la vaisselle (straight away).

....

2 (From time to time) elle écoute de la musique (quietly).

....

3 Ma valise? (Naturally) j'avais laissé mes vêtements (inside).

....

E Write four sentences of your own with at least one adverb in each.

....

....

....

....

Object pronouns

Direct object pronouns are words like 'it', 'me', 'him', 'us', etc. You use them when you don't want to keep repeating a noun or a name.

A Translate these sentences.

Example: Il me regarde. He watches me.

1 Nous te voyons. ....
2 Tu le connais? ....
3 Je veux la voir. ....

4 Vous nous rencontrez. ....
5 Elle vous oubliera. ....
6 Je les perdrai. ....

You use **indirect** object pronouns to replace a noun which has *à* (*au, aux*, etc) in front of it.

B Translate the following sentences. Notice that in English we sometimes omit the 'to'.

Example: Il me donne un billet. He gives me a ticket. / He gives a ticket to me.

1 Je te passe mes bonbons. ....

2 Ne lui dis pas la vérité. ....

3 Nous lui offrirons un bateau. ....

4 Il va nous envoyer un cadeau. ....

5 Tu leur raconteras l'histoire. ....

> Translate 'him' and 'her' as *lui* and 'them' as *leur*.

C Put the words in the correct order to answer the question.

Example: Tu aimes les pommes? je beaucoup aime les Oui Oui, je les aime beaucoup.

1 Vous comprenez le professeur?   le souvent comprenons Nous

....

2 Elle aime les sports nautiques?   pas aime Elle ne du tout les

....

3 Tu vas vendre ton vélo?   vendre vais le Oui je demain

....

4 Il veut acheter la maison?   veut pas il acheter ne Non l'

....

D Replace the underlined noun with a pronoun and move it to the correct position in the sentence.

Example: J'ai mangé le gâteau. Je l'ai mangé.

1 Il cherche les clefs. ....

2 Nous envoyons un cadeau à Jeanne. ....

3 Il a donné des bonbons aux enfants. ....

4 Tu as téléphoné à tes amis? ....

5 Elle dit toujours la vérité à papa. ....

E Complete the following sentences.

Example: I'm sending it to you. Je vous l'envoie.

1 She offered them to us. Elle .... a offerts.

2 Don't sell them to him/her! Ne .... vends pas!

3 I am going to pass it (m) to you. Je vais .... passer.

4 He gave them to you on Saturday. Il .... a donnés samedi.

More pronouns: *y* and *en*

You use *y* to refer to a place which has already been mentioned. It often means 'there': *Il adore Paris. Il **y** est allé hier.* You also use it with verbs that take *à*.

A Replace the nouns with the pronoun *y*.

Example: Tu vas au cinéma ce soir? Tu y vas ce soir?

1 Il va habiter **au Canada**. ....

2 Elle a vu ses amis **en France**. ....

3 Vous jouez **au tennis**? ....

4 Je suis arrivé au collège avant les autres. ....

5 Tu es allée **au travail** ce matin? ....

You use *en* to replace a noun. It often means 'of it', 'of them' or 'some':
J'aime le chocolat. J'en mange beaucoup.

B Unjumble these sentences with *en* in order to answer the questions.

Example: Tu as de l'argent? ai j' Oui en Oui j'en ai

1 Tu fais beaucoup de sport? en beaucoup J' fais ....

2 Elle fait du ski? pas en fait n'Elle ....

3 Vous avez deux frères? trois ai Non en j' ....

4 Ils mangent de la pizza tous les jours? les en samedis Ils tous mangent ....

5 Il y a des bouteilles dans la cave? y en Il a plusieurs ....

C Replace the nouns in brackets with either *y* or *en*.

> Using pronouns makes your work more interesting and for your GCSE, if you are aiming for higher grades, you should try and use them.

1 Je vais [au restaurant] de temps en temps.

....

2 J'adore les fruits et je mange beaucoup [de fruits].

....

3 Ma faiblesse, c'est le chocolat, mais je ne mange jamais [de chocolat] parce que je ne veux pas grossir.

....

4 Je suis allé [au théâtre] la semaine dernière, avec mon frère.

....

5 On va au concert ce soir. Tu veux aller [au concert]?

....

6 Moi, j'adore le poulet, mais mon frère ne mange pas [de poulet] parce qu'il est végétarien.

....

Other pronouns

Relative pronouns are used when you want to link statements together to avoid repetition and to make your French more fluent.

A Fill in the gaps with *qui* (followed by a verb), or *que / qu'* (followed by a subject/person).

Example: C'est le bruit *que* je n'aime pas.

1   Le repas .... j'ai pris était excellent.

2   C'est Claude .... est le plus beau.

3   Ce sont mes parents .... adorent la viande.

4   Voilà le chapeau .... il a perdu.

5   Où sont les robes .... sont déchirées?

6   L'église .... j'ai visitée était vieille.

7   L'homme .... monte dans le train est gros.

8   Ma copine .... s'appelle Mathilde a seize ans.

9   Quel est le film .... tu veux voir?

> *Qui* means 'which', 'who' or 'that' and replaces the subject in a sentence.
> *Que* means 'whom', 'which' or 'that' and replaces the object in the sentence.

> *Dont* replaces 'whose' or 'of whom/which' for example:
> *Je veux voir le film **dont** j'ai vu la bande-annonce.*
> I want to see the film whose trailer I saw.

B Translate the following sentences carefully once you have inserted *dont*.

Example: La personne *dont* je parlais n'est plus là.

The person I was talking about is no longer there.

1   La vie .... vous rêvez n'existe pas.

....

2   Les papiers .... j'ai besoin sont dans le tiroir.

....

3   Je ne connais pas la maladie .... tu souffres.

....

4   Ce garçon .... je te parlais a quitté le collège.

....

C Which would you use: *y, en, où, qui, que* or *dont*? Insert the correct pronoun and translate into English.

1   Le repas .... nous avons mangé était excellent.

....

2   Le stylo .... vous avez besoin est cassé.

....

3   Des bonbons? J'...................... ai mangé beaucoup.

....

4   Le café .... je vais le samedi est fermé.

....

5   Le cinéma Gaumont? J'...................... suis allée pour voir 'Amélie'.

....

Present tense: -er verbs

A Give the *je*, *nous* and *ils* forms of each of these verbs.

Verb	je (j')	nous	ils
aimer	j'aime	nous aimons	ils aiment
jouer			
habiter			
regarder			
donner			
inviter			
marcher			
trouver			
voler			
garder			

B Use the verbs above to write how you would say:

Example: he likes il aime

1 you (pl) keep ....
2 she invites ....
3 you (s) live ....
4 we find ....
5 he looks at ....

6 you (pl) walk ....
7 you (s) give ....
8 she steals ....
9 he plays ....
10 they look at ....

Although the verbs below are *-er* verbs, they are slightly irregular in that the spelling often changes. For example, *manger* becomes *mangeons* in the *nous* form.

C Put the verbs in brackets in the correct form and watch out for the spelling.

-ger verbs

1 ils (ranger) ....
2 nous (plonger) ....
3 nous (nager) ....
4 je (manger) ....

-ler / *-ter* verbs

1 je (s'appeler) ....
2 ils (jeter) ....
3 nous (se rappeler) ....
4 elle (projeter) ....

-yer verbs

5 tu (envoyer) ....
6 vous (payer) ....
7 j' (essayer) ....
8 nous (nettoyer) ....

acheter-type verbs

5 tu (acheter) ....
6 elles (préférer) ....
7 vous (se lever) ....
8 il (geler) ....

D Fill in the correct part of the verb in these questions and translate them.

Example: Tu (parler) français? Tu parles français?...Do you speak French?

1 Ils (habiter) en France? ....
2 Marie (ranger) sa chambre? ....
3 Vous (préférer) les sciences? ....
4 Les sœurs (jeter) les fruits? ....
5 Mon copain et moi (acheter) des frites? ....

Present tense: *-ir* and *-re* verbs

-ir and *-re* verbs are another set of verbs which follow a regular pattern. It is important to learn the most common verbs.

A What do these *-ir* verbs mean? Match the English to the French.

choisir	to warn
ralentir	to slow down
réfléchir	to punish
rougir	to finish
finir	to blush
atterrir	to reflect / think about
punir	to land
avertir	to choose

> Remember, both *-ir* and *-re* verbs can be either regular or irregular. Be careful to learn how each group behaves (*Revision Guide* page 96). On this page, the **irregular** verbs have stars. Keep them separate in your vocabulary lists to help you remember which is which.

B Fill in the gaps in this table. (The verbs are irregular.)

	dormir*	sortir*
je		sors
tu	dors	
il/elle		sort
nous		
vous		sortez
ils/elles	dorment	

> Be careful, many of the regular *-ir* verbs, such as *choisir* and *finir*, add -is, -is, -it, -issons, -issez, -issent.

C Put the correct ending on these *-ir* verbs to make them match their subjects.

Example: Ils (avertir) les garçons. Ils avertissent les garçons.

1 L'ami (choisir) un cadeau. ....

2 Vous (courir*) aux magasins. ....

3 Nous (finir) nos devoirs. ....

4 Je (remplir) le verre de vin. ....

D Complete the table below.

	vendre	prendre*	dire*
je			
tu	vends		
il/elle			
nous		prenons	disons
vous		prenez	
ils/elles	vendent		

E Give the correct present tense of the verb in brackets.

1 nous (vendre) ....

2 ils (répondre) ....

3 je (descendre) ....

4 tu (prendre*) ....

5 vous (boire*) ....

6 elle (lire*) ....

7 j' (écrire*) ....

8 il (comprendre*) ....

Avoir and *être*

A Give the correct part of *avoir* in these sentences.

Example: Tu as un frère?

1 Elle .... un hamster.

2 J'............... les cheveux blonds.

3 Ils .... une grande maison.

4 Il .... onze ans.

5 Nous .... un petit gymnase.

6 Vous .... un beau chien.

7 Ma sœur .... une jupe rouge.

8 Les filles .... un piercing.

9 Tu .... deux guitares.

10 Vous .... une nouvelle maison.

B Translate the following sentences into French.

Example: We have a house in Angers.   Nous avons une maison à Angers.

1 They have a dog and three hamsters.   ....

2 Do you (s) have a sister?   ....

3 She has black hair.   ....

4 We have a big kitchen.   ....

5 I have three children.   ....

6 I am sixteen years old.   ....

7 He has a car.   ....

C Fill in the gaps with the correct part of *être*.

Example: Il est très amusant.

1 Je .... français.

2 Nous .... paresseux.

3 Ma tante .... assez petite.

4 Vous .... sportif mais timide.

5 Mes yeux .... bleus.

6 Tu .... célibataire?

7 Les chiens .... mignons.

8 Je .... au chômage.

9 Nous .... mariés.

10 Il .... paresseux.

D Write six sentences using *être* or *avoir* and words from the grid below.

Je	maison	bouclés	petit
Tu	yeux	bleu	professeur
L'homme	grand	amusant	court
Nos chiens	mariés	cheveux	piercing
Vos parents	rouge	voiture	marron
Les filles	triste	long	gros

....

....

....

....

....

....

Remember, when you are using the verb *être* you need to make sure the adjective agrees with the noun!

Reflexive verbs

A Add the correct reflexive pronoun to this verse, do the actions, then try and learn it.

Je .... lève.

Tu .... laves.

Il .... brosse les dents.

Je .... habille et après je prends mon petit déjeuner.

> ***se laver* – to wash oneself**
> je me lave
> tu te laves
> *il/elle/on* se lave
> nous nous lavons
> vous vous lavez
> ils/elles se lavent

B Add the correct reflexive pronoun.

Mes parents se réveillent tôt le matin. Je .... appelle Lydie. Le matin

je .... réveille à 7 heures et demie mais je ne .... lève pas tout de suite.

Normalement ma sœur .... lève à 8 heures. Nous .... lavons dans la salle de

bains et nous .... habillons vite. Après le petit déjeuner, nous .... dépêchons

pour prendre le bus pour aller au collège. On .... approche du collège et on est très

contentes.

Vous .... amusez bien à votre collège?

C Write the numbers of these sentences in the correct order to match your morning routine.

1 Je me douche et je m'habille.

2 Je me réveille et je me lève.

3 J'arrive au collège et je m'amuse bien.

4 Je me dépêche pour prendre mon petit déjeuner et quitter la maison.

....

D Complete the table with verbs in the present and perfect tense. Remember to use *être* with reflexive verbs.

Present	Perfect
1 je	je me suis reposé(e)
2 elle se douche	elle
3 nous	nous nous sommes amusé(e)s
4 elles s'étonnent	elles
5 vous	vous vous êtes dépêché(e)(s)

E Circle the correct part of the verb to complete the sentence.

1 Je me *est / suis / es* reposée à 8 heures ce matin.

2 Nous nous *êtes / sont / sommes* dépêchés pour aller au match.

3 Ma sœur ne s'est pas *douché / douchée / douchées* hier soir.

4 Mes deux frères se *ont / sont / était* bien entendus en vacances.

5 Vous vous êtes *couchée / couchés / couché* tôt samedi, mes amis?

6 Les garçons se sont *disputé / disputées / disputés*.

Other important verbs

> The verbs *devoir* (to have to / must), *pouvoir* (to be able to / can), *vouloir* (to want to) and *savoir* (to know) are known as **modal verbs**.

A   Complete this table with the correct part of the modal verb.

	devoir	**pouvoir**	**vouloir**	**savoir**
je	dois			sais
tu		peux		
il/elle/on			veut	
nous	devons			savons
vous			voulez	
ils/elles		peuvent		

B   Rearrange the words to make correct sentences.

Example: la dois prendre Je première rue *Je dois prendre la première rue.*

1   mon -vous Pouvez père aider? ....

2   nager -tu Sais? ....

3   maison acheter parents une veulent Mes nouvelle ....
....

4   s'arrêter feux On toujours doit aux rouges ....
....

5   moi avec ce Voulez danser soir -vous? ....
....

6   sais allemand français Je et parler ....

C   Change the verb to match the new subject given in italics.

Example: Il doit travailler dur et moi aussi, *je dois travailler dur.*

1   Elle veut trouver une chambre avec un balcon et nous aussi, *nous* ....

2   Les élèves peuvent louer un vélo et toi aussi, *tu* ....

3   Le pilote doit tout vérifier et vous aussi, *vous* ....

4   Elle sait faire la cuisine, et eux aussi, *ils* ....

5   Je peux faire un pique-nique et elles aussi, *elles* ....

6   Il ne peut jamais comprendre les règles et vous non plus, *vous* ....

7   Nous savons préparer le dîner et moi aussi, *je* ....

D   Make up six sentences about school from this table.

	(ne) doit (pas)	manger en classe.
		porter ses propres vêtements.
	(ne) peut (pas)	courir dans les couloirs.
On		répondre aux professeurs.
	(ne) veut (pas)	dormir en classe.
		lancer les cahiers en l'air.
	(ne) sait (pas)	faire des piercings aux autres élèves.
		envoyer des textos.

Had a go ☐ Nearly there ☐ Nailed it! ☐

The perfect tense 1

> You use the perfect tense to talk about single events in the past. It is formed by using the present tense of *avoir* + past participle.

A Create your own sentences using a word or words from each column.

J' ai	fini	le gâteau
Tu as	détesté	le bateau
Il a	vendu	les devoirs
Elle a	regardé	l'argent
Nous avons	lavé	la maison
Vous avez	attendu	l'autobus
Ils ont	choisi	les chiens
Elles ont	perdu	le pain

....
....
....
....
....
....
....
....

B Add the correct part of *avoir* to complete these sentences.

Example: J'ai regardé la télé samedi soir.

1 Mme Blanc............... invité sa copine au match.

2 Vous............... terminé le repas?

3 Ils............... fumé une cigarette.

4 Il............... beaucoup neigé ce matin.

5 Tu n'............... pas mangé de légumes?

6 Nous............... choisi un bon restaurant.

7 Elle n'............... pas rougi.

8 Ils............... atterri à l'aéroport d'Orly.

9 J'............... rendu visite à ma tante.

10 Nous n'............... pas entendu.

C Did you notice the position of the *ne ... pas* in exercise B to say that they did **not** do something? Using the table in exercise A to help you, how would you say the following?

Example: You (s) did not sell the house. Tu n'as pas vendu la maison.

1 We did not lose the money. ....

2 They did not wash the bus. ....

3 You (pl) did not wait for the dogs. ....

4 I did not finish the bread. ....

5 She did not sell the boat. ....

6 He did not hate the homework. ....

D Revise the irregular past participles, then fill in the gaps in these sentences.

Example: Il a vu la voiture. (voir)

1 J'ai............... le pique-nique par terre. (mettre)

2 Elle a............... à son frère. (écrire)

3 Tu n'as rien............... au collège? (faire)

4 Il n'a pas............... ma lettre. (lire)

5 Nous avons............... acheter une Renault. (pouvoir)

E Complete these sentences with the correct part of *avoir* and the past participle of the verb given.

1 J'...........................la situation. (comprendre)

2 Il...............................de rentrer vite. (promettre)

3 Tu...............................un taxi à la gare? (prendre)

4 Qu'est-ce que tu...............................? (faire)

The perfect tense 2

> The perfect tense can also be formed using the verb *être* + past participle, when the verb is reflexive and with 14 verbs of movement

A Add the correct part of the verb *être* to complete these sentences.

Example: Tu *es* né en 2000?

1 Elle .... tombée.

2 Mes copains .... arrivés trop tard.

3 Les chats .... montés sur le toit.

4 Marie n'............... pas descendue vite.

5 Mme Lebrun .... allée à la piscine.

6 Vous .... retournés en France?

7 Je ne .... pas parti tôt.

8 Elles .... mortes l'année dernière.

B Make the past participle match the subject of these *être* verbs, by adding agreements (-, -e, -s, -es) to those that need it.

Example: Mes cousines sont (resté) à l'hôtel. Mes cousines sont restées à l'hôtel.

1 Élise est arrivé......... à 11 heures.

2 Jim est mort......... il y a 20 ans.

3 Nous sommes entré........., tous les garçons, dans l'épicerie.

4 Marie n'est rentré......... qu'à minuit.

5 Mes stylos ne sont pas tombé.........

6 Il est sorti......... avec sa sœur jumelle.

C Complete the sentences.

Example: Je suis allé au collège et elle aussi, elle *est allée au collège.*

1 Tu es monté très vite et les filles aussi, elles ....

2 Les vendeurs sont arrivés et moi aussi, je ....

3 Nous ne sommes pas tombés et eux non plus, ils ....

4 Monsieur Dasse est mort et sa femme aussi, elle ....

D Complete this table to show a reflexive verb in the perfect tense.

je	me	suis	lavé
tu		es	
il			
elle			lavée
nous		sommes	
vous			
ils	se		lavés
elles			

Reflexive pronouns:

me	nous
te	vous
se	se

E Form the perfect tense of these reflexive verbs.

Example: Nous (se promener) *Nous nous sommes promenés.*

1 Ils (se coucher) ....

2 Elle (s'ennuyer) ....

3 Vous (se disputer) ....

4 Je (s'endormir) ....

The imperfect tense

> The imperfect is another tense that you use to talk about the past. You use it to describe what happened over a period of time, what something was like and ongoing actions which were interrupted.

A Give the imperfect (*je*, *nous* and *ils* forms) of these verbs.

1	jouer	**je jouais**	**nous jouions**	**ils jouaient**
2	finir	**je finissais**	**nous finissions**	**ils finissaient**
3	perdre	....	....	....
4	avoir	....	....	....
5	être	....	....	....
6	boire	....	....	....
7	aller	....	....	....
8	partir	....	....	....
9	faire	....	....	....
10	lire	....	....	....
11	savoir	....	....	....
12	prendre	....	....	....

B Change the ending of the imperfect tense to match the new subject.

Example: Il fumait et nous aussi, nous fumions.

1 J'attendais et elle aussi, elle ....

2 Vous écriviez et eux aussi, ils ....

3 Tu dormais et le chien aussi, il ....

4 Mes parents regardaient et moi aussi, je ....

5 Mon ami était poli et mes sœurs aussi, elles ....

> All verbs except *être* are regular in the imperfect tense.
> **1** Take the *nous* form of the present tense and take off the *-ons* ending: *nous habit(ons)*.
> **2** Add the imperfect endings:
> | | |
> |---|---|
> | j'habitais | nous habitions |
> | tu habitais | vous habitiez |
> | il/elle habitait | ils/elles habitaient |

C Put the verbs into the imperfect tense, then translate the sentences.

Example: Tu visitais beaucoup de monuments (visiter).

You used to visit lots of monuments.

1 Je .... avec mon petit frère sur la plage. (jouer) ....

2 Nous .... très souvent ensemble. (manger) ....

3 Le serveur .... dur pour nous. (travailler) ....

4 On .... beaucoup de glaces. (vendre) ....

5 Papa et Marc .... du ski nautique. (faire) ....

6 Tu .... très content. (être) ....

D When you are talking or writing about the past, you often need to use a mixture of perfect tense and imperfect tense verbs. Put the following verbs in the correct past tense.

J' [aller] au collège quand j' [voir] l'accident. Il y [avoir] beaucoup de monde. J' [appeler] «au secours!».

....

....

....

....

....

The future tense

The **near future** is used to say what is going to happen. It is formed using *aller* + infinitive.

A Use the correct part of *aller* to say what you are going to do in the near future and say what these sentences mean.

Example: Je vais regarder un film. I am going to watch a film.

1 Il .... sortir ce soir. ....

2 Nous .... vendre la maison. ....

3 Vous .... comprendre bientôt. ....

4 Tu .... partir en vacances. ....

5 Maman .... voir un concert. ....

6 Les garçons .... arriver en retard. ....

B Unjumble these sentences in the near future tense.

Example: ta Je à question vais répondre   Je vais répondre à ta question.

1 aller allons en Nous ville demain ....

2 partir Quand vas-tu? ....

3 vont leurs Ils devoirs faire ....

4 tennis allez au jouer Vous? ....

5 Lydie cuisine faire la va ....

6 aider Ses vont sœurs ....

The **future** is used to say what you **will** do. To form the future, add the future endings to the infinitive of the verb: *-ai, -as, -a, -ons, -ez, -ont.*

C Say what everyone will do at the weekend. Put the verb into the future tense.

Example: Je prendrai un bon petit déjeuner. (prendre)

1 Il .... sa nouvelle voiture. (laver)

2 Tu .... ta copine à manger. (inviter)

3 Nous .... nos devoirs. (finir)

4 Vous .... les nouvelles. (attendre)

5 Elle .... visite à sa tante. (rendre)

6 Ils .... en France. (arriver)

7 Elles .... beaucoup. (bavarder)

8 Je .... une nouvelle robe. (choisir)

D Now try these irregular verbs. Check you know the irregular stem.

Example: vous (pouvoir) vous pourrez

1 ils (devoir) ....

2 nous (savoir) ....

3 je (faire) ....

4 elle (être) ....

5 tu (avoir) ....

6 elles (venir) ....

7 il (voir) ....

8 tu (aller) ....

E Now translate all of exercise D into English.

Example: You will be able to

1 ....

2 ....

3 ....

4 ....

5 ....

6 ....

7 ....

8 ....

The conditional tense

The conditional is used to say what you **would** do. It is formed like the future but has different endings. The conditional endings are: *-ais, -ais, -ait, -ions, -iez, -aient.*

A Complete the gaps in this table.

	-er verbs	-ir verbs	-re verbs
	jouer	choisir	vendre
je	jouerais		
tu		choisirais	
il/elle			vendrait
nous		choisirions	
vous	joueriez		vendriez
ils/elles		choisiraient	

B What would these people do if they won the lottery? Add the correct part of the verb in brackets and say what the sentence means in English.

Example: Je partirais en vacances avec ma famille. (partir)

I would go on holiday with my family.

1 Ma mère .... une belle maison. (habiter) ....

2 Vous ne .... plus. (travailler) ....

3 Nous .... beaucoup de pays. (visiter) ....

4 Tu .... de l'argent aux autres. (offrir) ....

5 Ils .... de l'argent à la banque. (mettre) ....

6 Je .... ma vieille voiture. (vendre) ....

Some verbs are irregular in the conditional: *aller: j'irais   faire: je ferais   voir: je verrais*

C Complete these sentences using the conditional of the verb in brackets. They all have irregular stems, but they keep the same endings as above.

Example: Nous ferions une promenade. (faire)

1 Je .... très riche. (être)

2 Vous .... le monde entier. (voir)

3 Ils .... beaucoup d'amis. (avoir)

4 Elle .... épouser son fiancé. (vouloir)

D Write four 'si' sentences of your own, using either the future or conditional tense.

....

....

....

....

....

....

....

....

....

Be careful with 'if' clauses!

si + present tense + future tense:
*Si tu **viens**, moi aussi j'**irai**.*
If you come, I will go too.

si + imperfect tense + conditional:
*Si tu **mangeais** correctement, tu n'**aurais** pas faim.*
If you ate properly, you wouldn't be hungry.

The pluperfect tense

> You use the pluperfect to talk about an event which happened one step further back than another past event: 'I **had done** something'.

A Translate these sentences into English.

Example: Si seulement j'avais écouté tes conseils. If only I had listened to your advice.

1 Tu avais déjà fini ton déjeuner. ....

2 Nous avions entendu les informations. ....

3 Ils avaient promis de rentrer avant minuit. ....

4 Vous aviez déjà bu toute la bouteille. ....

5 Elle n'avait jamais lu ce livre. ....

6 Ils étaient déjà partis. ....

7 Elle était venue toute seule. ....

8 Les enfants s'étaient couchés de bonne heure. ....

> Like the perfect tense, you form the pluperfect by using an auxiliary (*avoir* or *être*) + a past participle. The difference is that you use the **imperfect tense** of the auxiliary. The verbs which take *être* are the same ones that take *être* in the perfect tense.

B Change these verbs from the perfect into the pluperfect.

Example: J'ai joué. J'avais joué.

1 Elle a fini ....

2 Nous avons lu ....

3 Elles sont arrivées ....

4 Vous êtes partis ....

5 Tu es tombé? ....

C Match the sentence halves, then translate the sentences.

1 J'avais toujours voulu

2 Il était

3 Elles étaient

4 Heureusement, nous

5 Ma sœur était

6 Mes parents

7 Si tu avais

8 J'avais laissé

a parti en vacances quand on est arrivés a la maison.

b ma voiture dans le parking.

c aller à Bordeaux, mais mes parents ont décidé d'aller en Alsace.

d partie de bonne heure, mais il y avait beaucoup de circulation.

e avions acheté des sandwichs.

f parties quand il a commencé à pleuvoir.

g avaient loué un appartement au bord de la mer.

h gagné au loto, qu'est-ce que tu aurais fait?

1 ....

2 ....

3 ....

4 ....

5 ....

6 ....

7 ....

8 ....

Negatives

You use negatives when you want to say 'not', 'never', 'no longer', 'none', etc. French negatives almost always have two parts: *ne* before the verb and *pas*, etc, after the verb, making a 'sandwich'.

A Match the French to the English translations.

ne ... pas	neither ... nor
ne ... jamais	not any, none
ne ... plus	nobody, not anybody
ne ... rien	not yet
ne ... personne	no longer, no more
ne ... aucun	never
ne ... que	nothing, not anything
ne ... ni ... ni...	not
ne ... pas encore	only

B Translate these sentences.

Example: Il ne parle pas de son accident.   He doesn't talk about his accident.

1 Nous n'aimons ni la géo ni l'histoire. ....

2 Je ne mangerai plus de viande. ....

3 Il n'est jamais arrivé. ....

4 Ils n'ont rien trouvé. ....

5 Je n'envoie aucune carte postale. ....

6 Elle ne fait que deux heures par mois. ....

7 Il ne retournera plus jamais en Italie. ....

C Rearrange the words to make correct sentences.

Example: ne vaisselle fais la Je jamais. Je ne fais jamais la vaisselle.

1 aucune Nous idée avons n' ....

2 n'a dix Paul euros que ....

3 fête n' Personne ma venu à est ....

4 bu Ils n'ont café rien au ....

5 achèterez n' de chocolat plus Vous? ....

D Make these sentences negative by inserting the given words. Remember that *du, de la, des, un* and *une* all change to *de (d')* and mean 'any' if they appear after the negative.

Example: Je vois un nuage dans le ciel (ne ... pas) Je ne vois pas de nuage dans le ciel.

1 Nous fumerons des cigarettes (ne ... plus) ....

2 Elle a dit bonjour (ne ... jamais) ....

3 Tu rencontres deux amies en ville (ne ... que) ....

4 Il a compris (ne ... rien) ....

E Answer these questions in the perfect tense with the negative given.

Example: Il est sorti? (ne ... pas) Non, il n'est pas sorti.

1 Ils ont acheté une maison? (ne ... jamais) Non, ils ....

2 Elle a fait de la lecture? (ne ... pas) ....

3 Elles sont venues? (ne ... jamais) ....

The perfect infinitive and present participles

The perfect infinitive

A Give the perfect infinitive of the following verbs.
e.g. Manger = avoir mangé

> Be careful as you will need to remember if the verb uses *avoir* or *être* in the perfect tense

1 faire ....
2 aller ....
3 jouer ....
4 finir ....
5 arriver ....

6 mettre ....
7 vouloir ....
8 sortir ....
9 écrire ....
10 partir ....

B Match up the French and English

1	Après avoir joué au foot	A	After having left
2	Après être arrivé à la gare	B	After having eaten
3	Après avoir mangé	C	After having got up
4	Après avoir pris une douche	D	After having played football
5	Après s'être levé	E	After having had a shower
6	Après être entré dans la cuisine	F	After having done my homework
7	Après avoir fait mes devoirs	G	After having entered the kitchen
8	Après être parti	H	After having arrived at the station

C Translate these sentences into French

> Remember that with *être* verbs, the past participle must agree with the subject

1 After having gone into town, she had lunch.
2 After having eaten, he went to the cinema.
3 After having arrived at the station, the girls bought their tickets.
4 After having chatted to his friends, Paul went home.

The present participle

A Put these infinitives into present participles

1 finir ....
2 acheter ....
3 aller ....
4 dire ....
5 manger ....

6 faire ....
7 prendre ....
8 vouloir ....
9 partir ....
10 venir ....

B Complete the sentences by changing the verb in brackets into the present participle

1 J'ai lu un livre en (écouter) de la musique. ....
2 Elle lui a expliqué la situation en (rire). ....
3 Nous avons réussi en (travailler) dur. ....
4 Ils sont entrés dans la maison en (courir). ....
5 Ma mère a tricoté en (regarder) la télé. ....

The passive and the subjunctive

The passive

A Match up the correct English and French.

1	La lettre a été écrite par mon grand-père.	A	The biscuits are made by my mother.
2	Les biscuits sont faits par ma mère.	B	The castle was ruined.
3	Les animaux ne sont pas admis.	C	The film was watched by everyone.
4	Le château a été ruiné.	D	The letters will be sent tomorrow.
5	Le film a été regardé par tout le monde.	E	The letter was written by my grandfather.
6	Les lettres seront envoyées demain.	F	Pets are not allowed.

B Translate the following into French

Example: The results will be published. Les résultats seront publiés.

1   The boys were found by the police. ....

2   She will be injured if she does not pay attention to the traffic. ....

3   The apples are washed by the children. ....

4   He has been invited to a party. ....

5   The house will be sold. ....

6   The castle was built a hundred years ago. ....

> Remember that the past participle agrees with the subject when the passive is used.

The subjunctive

A Match up the English and French

1	Il faut qu'on parte.	A	It's a pity that she cannot come.
2	Bien qu'il soit travailleur.	B	It's possible that pollution will be reduced.
3	Avant qu'ils arrivent.	C	We must leave.
4	À condition que tu travailles bien.	D	Before they arrive.
5	C'est dommage qu'elle ne puisse pas venir.	E	Although he is hard-working.
6	Il est possible qu'on réduise la pollution.	F	Provided that you work well.

B Translate the following sentences into English.

1   Il semble qu'ils aient peur. ....

2   Je veux que tu m'accompagnes. ....

3   Il faut que tout le monde vienne chez nous. ....

4   Bien qu'elle travaille bien, elle n'est pas très douée. ....

5   Je la vois chaque matin avant qu'elle aille au travail. ....

6   Je vais beaucoup réviser pour que mes parents soient fiers. ....

Questions

In French you can make something a question by raising your voice at the end of a sentence. However, if you are aiming at a higher grade you need to use question words.

A Make these sentences into questions by using *est-ce que*.

Example: Tu manges des bonbons.   Est-ce que tu manges des bonbons?

1 Il peut venir lundi.   ....

2 Vous avez une carte de la ville.   ....

3 Les élèves ont fini leurs devoirs.   ....

4 Elle veut aller en ville.   ....

5 Vous êtes vendeuse.   ....

6 Nous arriverons au collège à l'heure.   ....

B Find the five pairs of questions which mean the same.

1 Est-ce que tu aimes le français?   A Fait-il du français le mardi?

2 Est-ce qu'elle est française?   B As-tu français le mardi?

3 Est-ce qu'il adore le français?   C Aimes-tu le français?

4 Est-ce que tu as français le mardi?   D Est-elle française?

5 Est-ce qu'il fait du français le mardi?   E Adore-t-il le français?

C Separate into ten questions.

Est-cequetuvasenvilledemainmatinest-cequ'iljoueautennisest-cequ'ellepartiraen vacancesenjuilletest-cequetuasperdutaclefest-cequetuasréservéunechambreest-ce quetupréfèresvoyagerenavionouentrainest-cequelesportablessontutilesest-ceque lechienestmignonest-cequetuveuxalleraucinémaavecmoiest-cequetusaisfairedelavoile

D Match the question word with the rest of the sentence.

1 Qu'   A es-tu venu?

2 Combien de   B est-ce que tu aimes faire?

3 Où   C est-ce que tu vas aider les pauvres?

4 Comment   D habites-tu?

5 Pourquoi   E préférez-vous voyager en France? En train?

6 À quelle heure   F parles-tu le français?

7 Depuis quand   G est-ce que tu te réveilles le matin?

8 Quand   H personnes habitent à Londres?

E Imagine you get the chance to interview your favourite celebrity. Prepare a list of six questions for them.

....

....

....

....

....

....

Prepositions, conjunctions and intensifiers

A Match up opposite pairs of prepositions.

1	sur	A	à la fin
2	devant	B	partout
3	loin de	C	sans
4	nulle part	D	contre
5	pour	E	après
6	avec	F	sous
7	avant	G	derrière
8	au début	H	près de

B How many of these prepositions do you recognise?

Loin de, près de, en face de,

devant, derrière, à côté,

nulle part, partout, pour ou contre,

à droite, à gauche, environ.

C Fill the gaps with the words in the box. The first letter is given in the text as a clue for some of them. Then translate it into English. You may use some words more than once.

à   À la fin   Après   D'abord   dans   de   et   mais   nulle part   parmi
partout   près de   puis

D ...., je me suis levée à 7 heures, p...............je me suis lavée. Je suis entrée
d............... la salle de bains située p............... ma chambre et j'ai décidé ....
prendre une douche .... me brosser les dents aussi. A............... ma
douche, j'ai cherché ma serviette p............... m...............je ne l'ai trouvée n...............
À ....j'ai réussi .... retrouver mon pyjama p............... mes affaires
...............je suis rentrée .... ma chambre.

First of all, I got up at 7 o'clock ....

....

....

....

....

....

D All these prepositions, conjunctions and intensifiers have been jumbled up. How quickly can you write them correctly?

1	cnod	6	etdapnn	11	nvdtae ....
2	etesiun	7	tvnaa	12	spèr ed ....
3	ssaui	8	ne eacf ed	13	oervnni ....
4	ttrpuao	9	zceh	14	ssna ....
5	sima	10	mpria	15	rsev ....

Test: listening

Edexcel publishes official Sample Assessment Material on its website. This test has been written to help you practise what you have learned across the four skills, and may not be representative of a real exam paper.

At the tourist office

1   What do these people want to do?

Listen to the recording and put a cross [×] in each one of the **three** correct boxes.

Listen to the recording

Example	Watch a football match	☒
A	Go to the cinema	☐
B	Go shopping	☐
C	Catch a train	☐
D	Go to a theme park	☐
E	Visit the castle	☐
F	See a play	☐
G	Find a good hotel	☐

(3 marks)

School studies

2   Marc is talking about his school with a friend.

Listen to the recording and answer the following questions **in English**.

Example: What is Marc studying in history?

> Guided

the First World War ....

Listen to the recording

(a) Why does Marc like history so much?

.... **(1 mark)**

(b) Which subject does he hate?

.... **(1 mark)**

(c) What does Marc do at break time?

.... **(1 mark)**

The environment

3 Alice and Robert are talking about what they do to protect the environment.

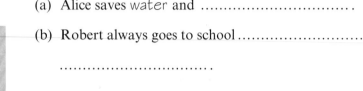

recycles glass	recycles paper	recycles metal	electricity
~~water~~	by public transport	on foot	by car

Complete the sentences. Use the correct word or phrase from the box.

> **Guided**

Listen to the recording

(a) Alice saves water and .... **(2 marks)**

(b) Robert always goes to school .... and

.... **(2 marks)**

Les rapports personnels

4 Lucas parle de sa famille et de ses amis.

Comment sont ces personnes? Choisis entre: **bavard**, **timide**, **intelligent**, **paresseux** et **amusant**.

Listen to the recording

Exemple: Son père est intelligent.

(a) Son frère est .... **(1 mark)**

(b) Mohammed est .... **(1 mark)**

(c) Yvon n'est jamais .... **(1 mark)**

Mes vacances

5 Écoute Margot qui parle des vacances.

Complète les phrases en choisissant un mot ou des mots dans la case. Il y a des mots que tu n'utiliseras pas.

Listen to the recording

les magasins	~~la natation~~	quinze jours	une semaine
avec sa famille	en ville	sans ses parents	chez sa meilleure copine
à la campagne	dans une auberge de jeunesse	dans un petit camping	un mois

Exemple: Margot aime faire de la natation.

(a) Sa mère aime passer les vacances .... **(1 mark)**

(b) L'année dernière, la famille a passé .... en Italie. **(1 mark)**

(c) Cette année, Margot va loger .... **(1 mark)**

(d) Ses vacances de rêve seraient .... **(1 mark)**

Social media

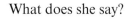

6 You hear Muriel talking about social media.

What does she say?

Listen to the recording and complete these statements by putting a cross [×] in the correct box for each question.

Example: Muriel uses social media …

×	**A**	every day
☐	**B**	once a fortnight
☐	**C**	once a week
☐	**D**	twice a week

(a) She says that she could not live without …

☐	**A**	her laptop
☐	**B**	her mobile phone
☐	**C**	her tablet
☐	**D**	her desktop computer

(b) Muriel never …

☐	**A**	gives her personal details online
☐	**B**	posts photos on social networking sites
☐	**C**	worries about cyber bullying
☐	**D**	uses chatrooms

(c) Muriel's cousin …

☐	**A**	was bullied online
☐	**B**	was the victim of identity theft
☐	**C**	has received lots of compliments online
☐	**D**	has never used social networking sites

(d) Muriel …

☐	**A**	has recently bought a new mobile
☐	**B**	has recently lost her mobile
☐	**C**	is going to buy a new mobile
☐	**D**	hopes to buy a new computer

(4 marks)

Where I live

7 Jamel is talking about where he lives.

Put a cross [×] in each one of the **two** correct boxes for each question.

(a) What does Jamel say about the village where he lives?

Example	He doesn't like it.	×
A	The people who live there are friendly.	☐
B	There is a cinema there.	☐
C	There are no shops there.	☐
D	There are not many young people.	☐
E	It's a 30-minute journey to get to the shops.	☐

(b) What does he say about where he used to live?

A	It was a small town.	☐
B	His family left there 12 years ago.	☐
C	It was a lively place.	☐
D	Everything there was better than in his village.	☐
E	Jamel often goes back there.	☐

(4 marks)

Volunteering

8 You hear Corinne talking about her recent visit to Africa.

Listen to the recording and answer the following questions **in English**.

(a) Why did Corinne volunteer in a school?

.... **(1 mark)**

(b) How do we know that the children wanted to go to school?

.... **(1 mark)**

(c) Why did school start early?

.... **(1 mark)**

(d) How did the school manage to have enough books?

.... **(1 mark)**

(e) What **two** problems are mentioned?

.... **(2 marks)**

....

World problems

9 You hear this extract on French radio about dangers to the environment.

Listen to the recording and put a cross [×] in each one of the **three** correct boxes.

Example	Our planet is in danger.	☒
A	We have started to reduce carbon dioxide emissions.	☐
B	Big waves have already started to threaten many small islands.	☐
C	More glaciers have started to melt.	☐
D	There are more storms and winds.	☐
E	More species will be threatened in the future.	☐
F	Record levels of rainfall have been noted globally.	☐
G	Sea levels have stabilised a little recently.	☐

(3 marks)

Test: reading

Leisure activities

1 Read these comments about leisure activities on a website.

Aline:	J'aime bien faire de la plongée car c'est passionnant. Je vais au ciné de temps en temps.
Barbara:	Quand je suis libre, j'adore faire du VTT avec mes meilleures copines. Des fois je joue aussi au hockey.
Caroline:	La lecture me plaît énormément, mais j'aime également faire du cheval à la campagne.
Delphine:	Mon passe-temps préféré, c'est dessiner car j'aime être créative, mais j'aime aussi l'art dramatique.

Who says the following? Enter either **Aline**, **Barbara**, **Caroline** or **Delphine**.

You can use each person more than once.

Example: Aline likes going to the cinema.

(a) .... reads a lot.

(b) .... likes drawing.

(c) .... sometimes participates in a team sport.

(d) .... likes diving.

(e) .... goes horse-riding.   **(5 marks)**

Technology at school

2 Read what Paul says about technology at his school.

J'apprends à un lycée moderne où il y a une douzaine de salles d'informatique qui disposent d'ordinateurs portables. Il y a un écran tactile dans la plupart des classes et dans certaines classes on a aussi accès aux tablettes. Je trouve donc ridicule qu'il soit interdit d'apporter nos portables à l'école. J'aimerais bien utiliser Internet sur mon propre portable afin de faire des recherches pour mon travail scolaire.

Put a cross [×] in the correct box.

Example: Paul's school is …

☐	**A**	old
☒	**B**	modern
☐	**C**	very small
☐	**D**	mixed

(a) In his school there are a dozen …

☐	**A**	classrooms
☐	**B**	computers
☐	**C**	computer rooms
☐	**D**	IT teachers

(b) You can use tablets in …

☐	**A**	some classrooms
☐	**B**	every classroom
☐	**C**	maths lessons
☐	**D**	no classrooms

(c) Paul thinks it is ridiculous that …

☐	**A**	there are not enough tablets
☐	**B**	there are not enough touch screens in school
☐	**C**	you are not allowed to bring mobiles to school
☐	**D**	you need to do lots of research at home

(3 marks)

Un emploi à temps partiel

3 Lis cet e-mail de Roxanne.

> ✉
>
> Cet été, pendant les grandes vacances, je vais travailler dans un petit supermarché tout près de chez moi pour avoir un peu d'argent supplémentaire. Je vais passer la plupart du temps à la caisse et mes copains me disent que c'est un emploi monotone et ennuyeux. Je vais faire des économies car je voudrais acheter un vélo comme cadeau d'anniversaire pour mon petit ami.

Complète chaque phrase en utilisant un mot de la case. Attention! Il y a des mots que tu n'utiliseras pas.

> ~~supermarché~~   loin   être   barbant
>
> facile   offrir   près   gagner

Exemple: Roxanne va travailler dans un supermarché.

(a) Le supermarché se trouve ………………………… de la maison de Roxanne.   **(1 mark)**

(b) Elle va ………………………… de l'argent.   **(1 mark)**

(c) Les copains de Roxanne pensent que le travail va être …………………………. **(1 mark)**

(d) Roxanne va ………………………… un cadeau d'anniversaire à son copain.   **(1 mark)**

A music event

4 Read the blog post below.

> Chaque année en août, le festival international des jeunes musiciens a lieu à Marseille. Le festival a commencé il y a huit ans avec une dizaine de groupes et de chanteurs européens, mais cette année les organisateurs ont invité plus de soixante-dix concurrents, y compris deux groupes asiatiques et cinq chanteurs africains. Naturellement, le festival attire plein de spectateurs des quatre coins du monde et cette année il y aura trois énormes campings dédiés au festival, mais il faut faire attention, car même en été, le beau temps n'est pas assuré.

Answer the following questions **in English**.

Example: When does the festival take place? August.

(a) How do you know that the festival is bigger than when it started?

……………………………………………………………………………   **(1 mark)**

(b) What special arrangements have been made for spectators?

……………………………………………………………………………   **(1 mark)**

(c) What are spectators warned about?

……………………………………………………………………………   **(1 mark)**

Translation

5 Translate this passage **into English**.

> Je vais à l'école en car. Les cours commencent à huit heures et demie et à mon avis c'est trop tôt. Ma matière préférée c'est le dessin car je m'entends bien avec le prof. Je n'aime pas les maths car on nous donne beaucoup de devoirs. Hier j'ai passé un examen d'histoire et c'était vraiment difficile. Le collège me plaît parce que j'ai plein de copains et la plupart des profs sont sympas.

....

....

....

....

....

....

....

.... **(7 marks)**

La télé-réalité

6 Lis ce texte.

> Quinze ans après le début de *Loft Story*, la télé-réalité en France marche toujours aussi bien auprès des jeunes qui restent devant le petit écran. Cette génération consomme différemment la télé, sur les tablettes ou sur un ordinateur, mais les jeunes sont quand même accros aux émissions de télé-réalité. L'émission culte, ce sont *Les Anges de la télé-réalité* dont la sixième saison vient de débuter avec près de 2 millions de téléspectateurs parmi les 15–22 ans. Il s'agit de faire cohabiter d'anciens candidats de télé-réalité française dans une villa en Floride. Chaque personne doit s'accomplir dans la chanson, la comédie et la mode afin de récolter de l'argent pour une association caritative qui veut construire une école au Sénégal. Les recettes de l'audience ne varient jamais: des corps bronzés, de belles filles, de la passion, des disputes et des amitiés.

Mets une croix [×] dans la case correcte.

Exemple: *Loft Story* a débuté …

☐	**A** il y a cinq ans
☒	**B** il y a quinze ans
☐	**C** il y a huit ans
☐	**D** en 2014

(a) La télé-réalité reste populaire auprès …

☐	**A** des jeunes
☐	**B** des femmes
☐	**C** des petits
☐	**A** de tout le monde

(b) *Les Anges de la télé-réalité* …

☐	**A** n'est plus populaire
☐	**B** est une émission qui vient de se terminer
☐	**C** passe actuellement en France
☐	**D** attire moins de 2 millions de téléspectateurs

(c)   Les candidats doivent …

☐	**A** aller en Italie
☐	**B** voyager au Sénégal
☐	**C** préparer beaucoup de recettes
☐	**D** vivre ensemble

(d) L'émission …

☐	**A** se passe dans une école
☐	**B** aide une organisation caritative
☐	**C** a lieu au Sénégal
☐	**D** est diffusée en Afrique

(4 marks)

A tourist destination

7   Read this extract from a tourism website.

> ● ● ●
>
> **La Corse, une destination dont tout le monde rêve!**
>
> Surnommée l'île de beauté, la Corse possède un climat méditerranéen qui assure dès le printemps des conditions climatiques impeccables pour les vacances. Les loisirs marins sont nombreux, surtout la voile, et on peut louer un bateau à prix raisonnable ou on peut également se détendre sur des plages sablonneuses où le ciel bleu est accompagné par un soleil radieux. Les marcheurs auront de quoi faire avec de belles randonnées à travers la montagne ou sur les chemins côtiers. On ne se lasse pas non plus de goûter aux spécialités culinaires, surtout pour les végétariens.
>
> Attention cependant, la Corse est une destination chère, particulièrement pendant la haute saison. Pourquoi ne pas essayer un gîte rural ou une maison d'hôtes. Et les campings, sans être spécialement bon marché, restent une des solutions les plus économiques. Un séjour en Corse peut donc revêtir un visage différent selon le budget dont on dispose, mais surtout selon les envies que l'on a.

Put a cross [×] next to each one of the **three** correct boxes.

Example:	Corsica is nicknamed Beauty Island.	☒
A	The weather in Corsica is perfect for holidays all year round.	☐
B	You can hire boats quite cheaply in Corsica.	☐
C	There are sandy beaches in Corsica.	☐
D	Corsica is good for those who like walking by the coast.	☐
E	Vegetarians are not especially well catered for in Corsica.	☐
F	Campsites in Corsica are particularly cheap.	☐
G	Every holiday in Corsica is more or less the same.	☐

(3 marks)

Le médecin arrive

8   Lis le passage et trouve les **quatre** bonnes phrases. Mets une croix [×] dans la case correcte.

> Charles est monté au premier étage voir le malade. Il le trouvait dans son lit, suant* sous ses couvertures. C'était un gros petit homme de cinquante ans, à la peau blanche, à l'œil bleu, chauve sur le devant de la tête, et qui portait des boucles d'oreilles. Il avait à ses côtés, sur une chaise, une grande carafe d'eau ce qu'il versait de temps en temps dans un verre, disant qu'il avait toujours vraiment soif. On avait entendu les cris de douleur de loin, mais dès qu'il a vu le médecin, il a commencé à geindre** faiblement.
>
> **(Adapted from *Madame Bovary* by Gustave Flaubert)**

suant = sweating
**geindre = groan*

A	Le malade était au premier étage.	☐
B	Le malade était au lit.	☐
C	L'homme n'était pas mince.	☐
D	L'homme était très jeune.	☐
E	L'homme voulait manger une baguette.	☐
F	Il y avait des yeux bleus.	☐
G	L'homme ne souffrait pas.	☐
H	L'homme a crié dès que Charles est entré.	☐

Translation

9 Translate this passage **into English**.

> La ville de Bamako est dans le sud du Mali. Il n'y pleut presque jamais et on ne peut pas facilement cultiver assez de nourriture parce qu'il y fait chaud. Il y existe une grande pauvreté malgré les efforts des organisations caritatives. Le chômage est un problème grave partout et de plus en plus de jeunes sont en train de quitter le pays afin de trouver un emploi.

....

....

....

....

....

....

....

.... **(7 marks)**

Test: speaking (Foundation)

Role-play: Travel and tourism

SPEAKING
TRACK
61

Listen to the
recording

1   You are going to eat at a restaurant in France with your English friend. The teacher will play the part of the waiter/waitress and will speak first.

You must address the waiter/waitress as *vous*.

You will talk to the teacher using the five prompts below.

- Where you see –? – you must ask a question.
- Where you see –! – you must respond to something you have not prepared.

Task:

Vous êtes dans un restaurant en France avec un(e) ami(e) britannique. Vous parlez au serveur / à la serveuse.

1   Table et nombre de personnes
2   Boissons désirées
3   !
4   Dessert préféré – pourquoi
5   ? Toilettes

> After you have prepared your answer, play the audio file of the teacher part and give your answers in the pauses.

Picture-based task: School

SPEAKING
TRACK
62

Listen to the
recording

2   Regarde la photo et prépare des réponses sur les points suivants:

- la description de la photo
- ton opinion sur les études universitaires
- un projet que tu as fait
- ce que tu veux faire comme études l'année prochaine
- ton opinion sur l'apprentissage.

> After you have prepared your answer, play the audio file of the teacher part and give your answers in the pauses. If you need more time, pause the recording.

Test: speaking (Higher)

Role-play: The environment

1 You are talking about the environment with a Belgian penfriend. The teacher will play the part of the penfriend and will speak first.

You must address your penfriend as *tu*.

You will talk to the teacher using the five prompts below.

- Where you see –? – you must ask a question.
- Where you see –! – you must respond to something you have not prepared.

Task:

Tu parles de l'environnement avec ton ami(e) belge.

1 Actions pour protéger l'environnement

2 Recyclage dans ta région – opinion

3 !

4 ? Transports en commun – opinion

5 ? Solutions possibles

> After you have prepared your answer, play the audio file of the teacher part and give your answers in the pauses.

Picture-based task: Town, region and country

2 Regarde la photo et prépare des réponses sur les points suivants:

- la description de la photo
- ton opinion sur l'importance du tourisme dans ta ville / ton village
- les changements récents dans ta ville / ton village
- où tu voudrais habiter plus tard dans la vie
- !

> After you have prepared your answer, play the audio file of the teacher part and give your answers in the pauses. If you need more time, pause the recording.

Test: writing (Foundation)

Un festival de musique

1 Tu participes à un festival de musique en France. Tu postes cette photo sur des médias sociaux pour tes amis.

Fais une description de la photo **et** exprime ton opinion sur la musique.

Écris environ 20–30 mots **en français**.

....

....

....

.... **(12 marks)**

Études en France

2 Vous allez faire des études en France. Vous écrivez au principal du collège où vous allez.

Écrivez un e-mail avec les informations suivantes:

• quand vous allez commencer les études

• vos matières préférées

• vos projets pour l'année prochaine

• pourquoi vous voulez étudier en France.

Écrivez 40–50 mots environ **en français**.

....

....

....

....

....

....

....

....   **(16 marks)**

Les fêtes

3   Joël, ton ami belge, t'a envoyé un e-mail sur ce qu'il a fait pour fêter son anniversaire.

Écris une réponse à Joël. Tu dois faire référence aux points suivants:
- comment tu as fêté ton dernier anniversaire
- ta fête préférée et pourquoi
- comment tu vas célébrer le Nouvel An cette année
- pourquoi les fêtes sont importantes.

Écris 80–90 mots environ **en français**.

....

....

....

....

....

....

....

....

....

....   **(20 marks)**

Le collège

4   Traduis les phrases suivantes en français.

(a) I don't like my school.

....   **(2 marks)**

(b) There are lots of classrooms.

....   **(2 marks)**

(c) There are five lessons per day.

....   **(2 marks)**

(d) Usually at break I chat with my friend in the canteen.

....   **(3 marks)**

(e) Last year I played football for the school team. It was great.

....   **(3 marks)**

Test: writing (Higher)

L'avenir

1   Un site Internet français cherche tes opinions sur l'avenir.

Écris à ce site Internet.

Tu **dois** faire référence aux points suivants:
*   ta personnalité
*   tes rêves et tes projets quand tu étais jeune
*   ton travail / tes voyages possibles à l'avenir
*   pourquoi il est important d'avoir des rêves.

Écris 80–90 mots environ **en français**.

....

....

....

....

....

....

....

....

....

.... **(20 marks)**

Les vacances

2   Un magazine français cherche des articles sur les vacances pour son site Internet.

Écrivez un article sur vos dernières vacances pour intéresser les lecteurs.

Vous **devez** faire référence aux points suivants:
*   ce que vous avez fait l'année dernière pendant les vacances
*   pourquoi vous avez choisi cette destination
*   ce que vous pensez des vacances en général
*   vos vacances idéales.

Justifiez vos idées et vos opinions.

Écrivez 130–150 mots environ **en français**.

....

....

....

....
....
....
....
....
....
....
....
....
....
....
....
....

(28 marks)

Une ville en France

3 Traduis le passage suivant **en français**.

> My friend Marc lives in a big house in Rennes in the west of France. He loves living there because there are lots of things for young people to do. He used to live in the east in a little village in the countryside but he moved two years ago. In the future he would like to live abroad, perhaps in England as he has several friends there.

Mon ami s'appelle Marc habite dans
une grande maison à Rennes en de
l'ouest de la france. Il adore habite
ça car il y a beaucoup à choses à
faire pour les jeunes. Il habitait dans
l'est en une petite ville à la
campagne mais il change de place
il y a deux ans. À l'avenir il voudrait habiter
à l'étranger, peut-être en Angleterre
car il a pleusier amies là-bas

(12 marks)

Answers

The answers to the Speaking and Writing activities below are sample answers – there are many ways you could answer these questions.

Identity and culture

1. Physical descriptions

Reading

1 (a) F (b) A (c) D (d) C

Listening

2 B, E, D, C

2. Character descriptions

Speaking

Listen to the recording

1 Sample answers:
   (a) On dit que je suis assez timide et vraiment travailleur, mais je ne suis pas d'accord parce que je suis sociable, surtout quand je sors avec mes copains. Je pense que je suis assez sérieux en classe, mais quand j'ai du temps libre je suis plutôt marrant et un peu bizarre de temps en temps. Par exemple, le week-end dernier je me suis habillé en fantôme et je suis sorti avec mes copains!
   (b) Ma meilleure copine, Lucy, est très amusante et elle me fait toujours rire. Tout le monde dit qu'elle est sympa et généreuse et elle est toujours prête à aider ses copains et sa famille, ce qui m'impressionne. Elle va m'aider avec mes devoirs ce soir.
   (c) Je m'entends bien avec mes amis parce qu'on a les mêmes personnalités et qu'on partage les mêmes centres d'intérêt aussi. Je pense que tous mes copains sont géniaux et drôles comme moi.

Reading

2 A, C, E, H

3. Describing family

Listening

1 A, B, C, F

Writing

2 (a) J'aime ma famille.
   (b) Mon frère est embêtant.
   (c) Ma sœur est assez grande.
   (d) Je m'entends avec ma mère parce qu'elle est gentille.
   (e) Mon père m'énerve quelquefois.

4. Friends

Reading

1 Suzanne – D; Robert – F; Lola – A; Carla – B

Speaking

Listen to the recording

2 Sample answers:
   (a) Il y a sept jeunes, quatre filles et trois garçons. Ils sont en train de regarder leurs portables. Je pense qu'ils s'amusent bien car ils sourient. À mon avis, ce sont des copains en vacances ensemble, peut-être en France.
   (b) À mon avis, un bon ami devrait être fidèle et sympa, et mes copains ont les mêmes loisirs que moi. Il faut pouvoir écouter les problèmes de ses amis aussi.
   (c) Mon meilleur copain est très gentil. Il s'appelle Luke et je le connais depuis cinq ans. Il va au même collège que moi. On s'amuse bien ensemble et il me fait tout le temps rire.

   (d) La semaine dernière, je suis allé au cinéma avec plusieurs copains et nous avons vu un film comique qui était vraiment marrant. Après avoir mangé dans un petit café en ville, nous sommes rentrés chez moi où nous avons joué sur ma console de jeux.
   (e) Le week-end prochain, je vais faire de la natation avec mes amis au centre sportif dans une ville voisine, ensuite nous irons au stade regarder un match de rugby.

5. Role models

Reading

1 B, C, F, G

Listening

2 (a) A (b) C (c) A (d) B

6. Relationships

Writing

1 Sample answer:
Voilà une photo de Marc, mon frère aîné, sa femme qui s'appelle Alice et ses deux enfants, Kevin, qui a six ans, et Melissa qui a neuf ans. J'aime toute la famille.

Reading

2 I get on well with my little brother. He is understanding and funny, but I often argue with my sister. Yesterday she took my skirt without asking my permission. She never helps at home and she gets on my nerves all the time. She has told me that she is going to be less lazy.

7. When I was younger

Listening

1 C, D, E, G

Speaking

Listen to the recording

2 Sample answers:
   (a) J'habitais dans une grande maison individuelle au bord de la mer dans le sud de l'Écosse, mais maintenant nous habitons dans une grande ville moderne dans l'est de l'Angleterre. Je crois que je préfère l'Écosse car c'était très pittoresque, mais il faisait trop froid en hiver.
   (b) Quand j'étais jeune, je faisais du vélo presque tous les jours, mais maintenant je n'en fais plus car je suis trop occupé. Je jouais sur mon ordinateur et je jouais aussi de la flûte, ce qui me plaît toujours.
   (c) Nous allions toujours faire du camping au pays de Galles et il pleuvait sans cesse. Une année, nous sommes allés en France, mais mes parents ne parlent pas français et ils avaient des difficultés à s'exprimer, alors nous n'y sommes pas retournés.

8. Peer group

Listening

1 (a) They are about the same age / they like the same rap music.
   (b) Two of the gang stole bottles of alcohol / from a shop in the area.
   (c) Mamadou and his friends stole clothes / from a department store.
   (d) Ashamed
   (e) Peer pressure / people said it would be cool.

Writing

2 Beaucoup de mes amis ont des tatouages et des piercings, mais je n'aime pas ça car je pense que c'est moche. La semaine dernière je suis allé(e) en ville avec ma sœur et nous avons vu un garçon de mon école qui avait un piercing au nez. Maintenant ma sœur a décidé d'avoir un piercing parce que tous ses amis en ont mais à mon avis elle est folle.

9. Money

Speaking

1 Sample answers:

(a) Sur la photo il y a une femme qui a plein d'argent à la main. Elle est heureuse car elle vient d'acheter beaucoup de cadeaux.

Listen to the recording

(b) Je crois que l'argent est essentiel mais pas très important dans la vie, car à mon avis être heureux, c'est plus important.

(c) La semaine dernière, j'ai rangé ma chambre et mes parents m'ont donné de l'argent. J'ai aussi trouvé un petit job dans un centre sportif en ville où je travaille six heures le samedi.

(d) Je n'aime pas faire des économies car je suis très impulsif, mais je fais des économies pour un nouveau portable.

(e) Je vais acheter un jean et des baskets et j'irai aussi au cinéma.

Listening

2 (a) birthday present / scarf
(b) laptop / spend all the pocket money
(c) tablet / more up to date

10. Customs

Reading

1 (a) Cameroon
(b) People shake hands when they meet.
(c) Shaking the hand too aggressively.
(d) France promotes racial tolerance / he has been accepted.

Listening

2 B, C, F, H

11. Everyday life

Speaking

1 Teacher transcript and sample answers:

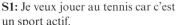

Listen to the recording

T: Je peux vous aider?
S1: Je veux jouer au tennis car c'est un sport actif.
T: Ah oui, et pourquoi voulez-vous venir ici?
S2: C'est bien équipé et le personnel est poli.
T: Ah, c'est gentil. Qu'est-ce que vous avez fait ce matin?
S3: J'ai joué au badminton.
T: Excellent.
S4: Quelles sont vos heures d'ouverture?
T: De sept heures jusqu'à vingt-deux heures.
S5: D'accord. Je peux faire un tour du centre?
T: Oui, suivez-moi.

Listening

2 (a) dort (b) pas (c) fait ses devoirs (d) les sports

12. Meals at home

Reading

1 (a) One month
(b) One of the following: could be stressful / still had a cold
(c) One of the following: show cooking skills / Mother could relax
(d) She disliked everything
(e) One of the following: grateful / found it unbelievable

Writing

2 Sample answer:

Voilà mon père qui aide mon frère avec ses devoirs. On mange des céréales et on boit un jus d'orange. Je n'aime pas le petit déjeuner car je suis pressé le matin.

13. Food and drink

Reading

1 (a) B (b) C (c) C (d) A

Writing

2 (a) J'aime manger du poisson.
(b) Je n'aime pas le café.
(c) Je prends des céréales au petit déjeuner.
(d) D'habitude on dîne à six heures du soir.
(e) Ce soir je vais manger dans un restaurant chic avec ma famille.

14. Shopping

Reading

1 B, C, E, I

Listening

2 (a) some flowers (b) a book (c) a bag

15. Shopping for food

Listening

1 (a) mushrooms (b) cabbage (c) eggs

Writing

2 Sample answer:

Sur la photo il y a deux boulangers français qui sourient. Ils vendent des croissants et des baguettes. J'adore les magasins français car ils sont intéressants.

16. Social media

Reading

1 I spend lots of time on social network sites. I think that I would not be able to live without my mobile. I know that there are many dangers but it's an efficient way of keeping up with world events. I can follow my friends' activities and recently a friend posted a photo of her dog online and all her friends found it amusing.

Speaking

2 Teacher transcript and sample answers:

Listen to the recording

T: Je viens de poster une photo en ligne.
S1: Moi, je déteste Facebook car c'est barbant.
T: Comment utilises-tu Internet pour ton travail scolaire?
S2: Je fais des recherches en ligne.
T: Moi aussi. Qu'est-ce que tu as fait en ligne hier soir?
S3: J'ai téléchargé de la musique.
T: C'est intéressant.
S4: Et toi, comment utilises-tu Internet?
T: Je tchatte avec mes copains.
S5: Que penses-tu des réseaux sociaux?
T: Je pense qu'ils sont excellents.

17. Technology

Reading

1 B, D, F, G

Speaking

2 Sample answers:

Listen to the recording

(a) Moi, je fais presque tous mes achats en ligne, surtout à Noël ou si je dois acheter un cadeau, parce que c'est moins cher. De plus, on n'a pas besoin de quitter la maison, donc c'est un moyen efficace et pratique de tout acheter. Je viens d'acheter un collier pour ma meilleure amie et tout s'est bien passé, mais un copain m'a dit qu'il avait acheté un DVD qui n'est pas arrivé. La seule chose que je n'achète pas en ligne, ce sont les vêtements car on doit les essayer avant des acheter.

(b) J'ai téléchargé beaucoup de musique parce que je trouve ça pratique: on n'a pas besoin d'acheter tout un album si on n'aime que quelques chansons. Il y a des sites où on peut télécharger à des prix raisonnables, mais il existe aussi des sites où certaines chansons sont gratuites.

(c) La semaine prochaine, je vais tchatter avec plusieurs amis en ligne, ce qui sera intéressant car un de mes meilleurs copains vient de déménager en Corse et grâce à la technologie, je pourrai non seulement lui parler facilement mais aussi le voir sur mon écran!

18. Internet advantages and disadvantages

Reading

1 (a) de faire beaucoup de choses
(b) aura besoin d'attendre
(c) pour parler avec d'autres personnes
(d) toute la soirée
(e) a eu une mauvaise surprise
(f) rembourser l'argent volé à Ruvimbo

Listening

2 A, F, G, H

19. Arranging to go out

Listening

1 (a) C (b) A (c) D (d) F

Reading

2 B, C, E, G

20. Hobbies

Writing

1 Sample answer:

Ma passion c'est le foot. J'y joue tous les week-ends pour mon club car c'est un sport actif qui me garde en forme et en plus je joue bien.
Samedi dernier, après avoir joué au foot, je suis allé au centre sportif avec quelques copains et nous y avons passé une heure à nager. J'ai trouvé ça très divertissant.
Le week-end prochain, je vais aller au bord de la mer avec ma famille et s'il fait beau, nous ferons de la planche à voile.
À l'avenir, je voudrais faire de l'escalade car c'est un sport physique et un peu dangereux.

Speaking

2 Sample answers:

Listen to the recording

(a) Il y a deux amis qui jouent sur une console de jeux et leurs amis les regardent. Il me semble que tout le monde s'amuse très bien.
(b) Moi, j'aime bien les jeux vidéo car ils sont stimulants et marrants, mais j'ai beaucoup de travail scolaire à faire, alors je joue moins sur mon ordinateur et ma console.
(c) Quand j'étais plus jeune, je jouais au rugby, mais je me suis cassé le bras, donc j'ai arrêté d'y jouer et maintenant je préfère jouer au tennis car c'est moins dangereux.
(d) La semaine prochaine je vais faire de la natation à la piscine qui se trouve tout près de ma maison. J'irai là-bas avec mes copains et nous prendrons un repas ensemble avant de rentrer. Ce sera génial.
(e) À mon avis les jeunes devraient être plus actifs car c'est bon pour la santé. C'est pourquoi je fais du sport régulièrement.

21. Music

Writing

1 Sample answer:

Sur la photo on voit mon orchestre. Nous allons jouer dans un festival de musique à Rouen. Au milieu, c'est Monsieur Richards, notre chef d'orchestre. J'adore la musique classique et je joue de la flûte.

Speaking

2 Sample answers:

Listen to the recording

(a) Je jouais de la flûte mais je n'en joue plus car je n'ai pas le temps.
(b) Je préfère la musique rock car c'est rythmé, mais je déteste la musique rap car c'est très barbant.
(c) Il y a un mois je suis allée voir Beyoncé en concert à Londres avec un groupe de copains. Elle a chanté toutes mes chansons favorites et j'étais très contente.

22. Sport

Reading

1 (a) B (b) B (c) A (d) B

Listening

2 (a) A (b) C (c) B

23. Reading

Writing

1 (a) *J'aime lire des bandes dessinées.*
(b) Mon frère aime lire.
(c) Je n'aime pas lire le journal tous les jours.
(d) On peut lire des magazines en ligne.
(e) Le week-end prochain je voudrais lire un roman policier.

Reading

2 I was reading an historical novel when my mother entered the living room. Since she only reads fashion magazines, she looked at me in a negative way. However, I continued reading, because reading is my big passion. I read anything, but I prefer love stories because you can escape from daily life and forget your worries.

24. Films

Reading

1 (a) Everyone
(b) Tickets sell quickly
(c) (i) Take seat promptly
(ii) Switch off mobile
(d) (i) They tire easily
(ii) They lose concentration
(e) (i) Free
(ii) Safe

Listening

2 (a) C (b) C (c) A

25. TV

Listening

1 (a) soap operas (b) factual programmes (c) news (d) cartoons

Writing

2 Sample answer:

Je regarde la télé tous les jours, normalement après être rentré de l'école. Ce que j'aime le mieux, ce sont les documentaires parce que la nature me plaît énormément et je suis fasciné par les animaux. J'aime aussi les feuilletons car je les trouve divertissants et quelquefois drôles.
La semaine dernière, j'ai regardé un documentaire sur les animaux sauvages en Australie et j'étais ravi de voir les kangourous et les koalas dans leur habitat naturel. J'ai trouvé les images sensationnelles et on les a regardé en famille chez nous.
Le week-end prochain, on va passer une émission comique à la télé et j'aimerais le regarder avec mes copains car on aime bien rigoler ensemble. Il s'agit de deux jeunes hommes qui n'ont pas de chance et qui sont toujours en train de faire des bêtises.
Je préfère regarder des films au ciné car j'aime bien le grand écran, même si on doit se taire pendant la séance!

26. Celebrations

Reading

1. (a) En souvenir de la résurrection de Jésus.
   (b) Il y a de grandes messes et processions religieuses.
   (c) l'agneau / des plats délicieux
   (d) du ciel
   (e) lapin/poisson

Speaking

2. Sample answers:

Listen to the recording

   (a) C'est l'anniversaire d'un petit garçon qui a six ans. Il y a un gâteau d'anniversaire en chocolat et toute sa famille est là. On applaudit.
   (b) Mes parents organisent une soirée pour moi ou de temps en temps je sors avec mes copains.
   (c) Je vais passer la journée avec mes amis au centre sportif puis, le soir, j'irai dans un restaurant en ville avec ma famille et nous dînerons ensemble.
   (d) Moi, je préfère Noël parce que je reçois plein de cadeaux et de cartes et qu'on fait un grand repas. Tout le monde est content et j'aime ça.
   (e) Oui, on mange trop, surtout à Noël, et certaines personnes boivent trop d'alcool. À mon avis, c'est dommage parce que ce n'est pas bon pour la santé.

27. Festivals

Reading

1. B, D, E, G

Listening

2. (a) New Year's Day
   (b) Saint Valentine's Day
   (c) Mother's Day

Local area, holiday and travel

28. Holiday preferences

Reading

1. B, D, E, H

Writing

2. Sample answer:

Moi, je préfère aller en vacances au bord de la mer parce que j'adore bronzer et pratiquer des sports nautiques comme la voile et le ski nautique. J'aime aussi nager et faire de la plongée.
Il y a deux ans je suis allé dans le sud de la France avec ma famille et on a passé des vacances formidables sur la côte dans un gîte. Il a fait beau presque tous les jours, alors j'ai nagé dans la mer et mes parents ont pu se faire bronzer.
À mon avis, les vacances sont essentielles pour éviter le stress quotidien.
Un jour, j'aimerais aller en Grèce car c'est un pays pittoresque.

29. Hotels

Speaking

1. Teacher transcript and sample answers:

Listen to the recording

   T: Bonjour. Je peux vous aider?
   S1: Je voudrais deux chambres pour quatre personnes.
   T: Quel type de chambres voulez-vous?
   S2: Je voudrais deux chambres à deux lits avec douche, s'il vous plaît.
   T: Quelles activités préférez-vous faire en vacances?
   S3: J'aime me faire bronzer et faire de la natation.
   T: Que prenez-vous au petit déjeuner?
   S4: Je prends un croissant et du café.
   T: D'accord.
   S5: Il y a un parking à l'hôtel?
   T: Oui.

Reading

2. (a) B (b) A (c) A (d) C

30. Campsites

Listening

1. A, C, D, F

Speaking

2. Sample answers:

Listen to the recording

   (a) Il y a des jeunes dans des tentes dans un camping. À l'arrière-plan, il y a un champ et des arbres.
   (b) J'aime assez faire du camping parce que c'est relaxant à la campagne.
   (c) Ce n'est pas cher et on est en plein air, mais un hôtel est plus confortable, surtout quand il pleut ou qu'il fait du vent. Il y a aussi le problème des insectes!
   (d) Je vais faire du camping au pays de Galles avec mes copains et j'espère qu'il ne va pas pleuvoir.
   (e) Oui, j'ai passé une semaine dans un camping en Bretagne avec ma famille il y a deux ans. Je me suis bien amusé.

31. Accommodation

Listening

1. (a) Paul = hotel
   (b) Isabelle = cousin's house
   (c) Éric = youth hostel
   (d) Éva = rented house

Writing

2. (a) Je préfère un hôtel.
   (b) Mon frère aime une caravane.
   (c) Mes parents n'aiment pas les campings.
   (d) Je pense que les hôtels sont chers.
   (e) L'année dernière j'ai logé dans un grand hôtel au bord de la mer pendant deux semaines.

32. Holiday destinations

Reading

1. C, D, G, H

Listening

2. (a) B (b) A (c) F (d) D

33. Travel

Speaking

1. Sample answers:

Listen to the recording

   (a) *Moi, j'aime bien voyager car* il est important d'élargir ses horizons et j'adore découvrir la culture et les traditions d'autres régions. J'aime également essayer les plats locaux et les spécialités du pays.
   (b) J'aimerais voyager en Afrique car c'est un continent mystérieux à mon avis. J'ai envie de visiter le Maroc en particulier, car on m'a dit que les marchés sont magnifiques et que les habitants sont chaleureux et aimables. À l'avenir, je voudrais aussi faire un safari afin de découvrir les animaux dans leur habitat naturel.
   (c) J'ai visité quelques pays en Europe, comme l'Espagne et l'Allemagne, mais mon pays préféré c'est la France. J'y suis allé quatre fois et les vacances que j'ai passées à Biarritz étaient superbes. J'y ai fait de la planche à voile et nous avons logé dans un hôtel cinq étoiles tout près de la mer.

Writing

2. Sample answer:

Je vais arriver dans votre ville le 25 juillet pendant les grandes vacances. J'ai l'intention de visiter les monuments historiques et de pratiquer beaucoup de sports. Je vais loger dans l'auberge de jeunesse en ville. J'aime la France car c'est un pays pittoresque.

34. Holiday activities

Reading

1   I cannot stand holidays where you do nothing as I always like to be active. Last year I went skiing in Canada and this year I will go to Germany. I hope to go rock climbing there and have long walks in the mountains. On the other hand, my sister prefers stretching out in the sun, reading a detective novel or going shopping.

Listening

2   (a) by the sea / on the coast
    (b) longer (c) (rock) climbing
    (d) likes the sun / likes to get a tan

35. Holiday plans

Reading

1   (a) A (b) B (c) C (d) B (e) D

Listening

2   (a) a self-catering chalet
    (b) ski
    (c) swim
    (d) eat out

36. Holiday experiences

Listening

1   A, B, E, G

Writing

2   Sample answer:
Je vais vous raconter les vacances de l'été dernier que j'ai passé avec ma famille à Menton dans le sud de la France. Nous y sommes allés parce qu'un ami de mon père venait de passer des vacances merveilleuses là-bas.
En général, j'aime passer mes vacances avec ma famille parce que mes parents paient tout et que je n'ai pas besoin de dépenser mon propre argent, mais, malheureusement, il y a moins de liberté, surtout quand je voudrais sortir le soir.
J'ai surtout aimé nager dans la mer, l'eau était chaude, et un jour on a fait une excursion à Nice où j'ai pu acheter des cadeaux superbes dans des grands magasins luxueux, mais tout était si cher!
À l'avenir je voudrais passer mes vacances au pays de Galles dans un camping avec mes copains parce que nous aurons plus de liberté et que la nature me plaît beaucoup.

37. Transport

Speaking

1   Sample answers:

Listen to the recording

(a) *Je n'aime pas voyager en train parce que je trouve ça ennuyeux, surtout pour les longs voyages. J'écoute de la musique ou je lis, mais à mon avis ce n'est pas agréable.*
(b) Je préfère voyager en avion car c'est très rapide. Je n'ai pas peur en avion mais je sais que c'est un moyen dangereux de voyager. Néanmoins, j'aime prendre l'avion.
(c) On peut prendre l'Eurostar, y aller en avion ou en bateau. La dernière fois que je suis allé en France, nous sommes allés jusqu'à la côte anglaise en voiture, puis on a pris le ferry pour Calais, mais la mer était agitée et j'étais assez malade.

Writing

2   Je déteste voyager en voiture parce que je suis souvent malade. Par exemple, l'été dernier je suis allé à Londres avec mes parents et on a dû s'arrêter car j'avais mal à la tête. Je préfère aller partout en vélo si je peux, mais pour les plus longs voyages je prends le car. La semaine prochaine ma famille va aller voir ma tante en Espagne, mais nous n'allons pas voyager en avion car mes parents ont peur de prendre l'avion.

38. Directions

Reading

1   B, C, E, H

Listening

2   (a) E (b) A (c) D (d) C

39. Holiday problems

Writing

1   Sample answer:
En vacances il y a souvent du stress, par exemple avec les parents.
Il y a aussi les problèmes à l'aéroport si le vol est retardé.
Naturellement, il peut également y avoir des problèmes de logement et de transport comme des hôtels sales ou une voiture qui tombe en panne.
Les vacances, c'est souvent trop cher aussi, surtout quand on voyage.
Mes vacances de rêve seraient en Grèce car l'histoire ancienne me plaît.
L'année dernière en Espagne, les employés de notre hôtel étaient impolis et les repas dans le restaurant n'étaient pas bons, donc on ne va pas y retourner.

Listening

2   (a) C (b) A (c) D

40. Asking for help

Speaking

1   Teacher transcript and sample answers:

Listen to the recording

T: Bonjour. Je peux vous aider?
S1: Bonjour. Je rapporte ce pantalon.
T: Quel est le problème?
S2: Il est trop petit et la couleur ne me va pas.
T: Vous cherchez quel article?
S3: Je voudrais un pantalon noir.
T: Ah bon. Celui-ci vous ira.
S4: Merci. Vous voulez une pièce d'identité?
T: Non, ce n'est pas nécessaire.
S5: Je peux échanger le pantalon?
T: Oui, certainement.

Listening

2   A, C, E, F

41. Eating out in a café

Reading

1   A, C, F, G

Listening

2   ☹ C, E   ☺ A, B

42. Eating out in a restaurant

Reading

1   (a) F (b) H (c) I (d) C

Speaking

2   Sample answers:

Listen to the recording

(a) *Sur la photo il y a une famille qui mange dans un restaurant. Je crois qu'il y a le père, la mère, deux enfants et les grands-parents. Les adultes boivent du vin et les petits boivent de l'eau. Tout le monde a l'air content.*
(b) Manger au restaurant, ça me plaît parce que j'adore essayer des plats différents et que je suis assez gourmand. Je préfère les restaurants chics où la cuisine est d'une qualité exceptionnelle.
(c) Quand je vais au restaurant, j'aime mieux prendre des pâtes à la sauce piquante car je trouve les repas épicés délicieux. J'aime aussi l'agneau mais je n'aime pas le porc car le goût me déplaît.

(d) La semaine dernière je suis allé dans un restaurant italien avec ma famille. Nous avons pris une pizza délicieuse et j'ai bu du coca, mais mes parents ont commandé une bouteille de vin rouge car nous avons fêté l'anniversaire de ma mère.

(e) Je voudrais bien aller dans un restaurant indien qui se trouve assez près de chez moi, car mes amis disent qu'on y sert des plats vraiment savoureux.

43. Buying gifts

Listening

1   (a) gloves (b) earrings (c) sweets

Speaking

2   Teacher transcript and sample answers:

Listen to the recording

T: Bonjour. Je peux vous aider?
S1: Bonjour madame. Je voudrais acheter un cadeau.
T: Bien. Qu'est-ce que vous voulez?
S2: Je voudrais acheter un sac à main.
T: Voilà. C'est pour qui?
S3: C'est pour ma mère.
T: Ah oui, c'est pour une occasion spéciale?
S4: C'est pour son anniversaire.
T: Quelle bonne idée!
S5: C'est combien, ça?
T: Ça fait 50 euros.

44. Opinions about food

Reading

1   (a) Patrick (b) Mara (c) Joshua (d) Ruby

Listening

2   A, C, D, F

45. Weather

Reading

1   (a) C (b) A (c) D

Listening

2   (a) East = snowing
    (b) South = sunny
    (c) West = windy
    (d) North = raining

46. Tourism

Reading

1   (a) B (b) C (c) A (d) D

Writing

2   Sample answer:
Sur la photo on voit mes deux sœurs et moi. Nous mangeons des glaces devant un musée près de Montréal. J'adore les vacances car on peut visiter des monuments.

47. Describing a town

Writing

1   Sample answer:
J'habite dans une petite ville dans le sud de l'Angleterre. On peut y visiter la cathédrale. Il y a un centre commercial et un cinéma et on peut aussi aller au centre sportif. J'aime ma ville parce qu'elle est animée et que j'ai des copains ici. Cependant, je voudrais habiter en Espagne.

Reading

2   (a) *not extraordinary*
    (b) to finish work / to look forward to an evening with family
    (c) mines closed / Dad unemployed
    (d) one day
    (e) he retired / he and Mum returned to the north
    (f) warm atmosphere

48. Countries

Listening

1   (a) Switzerland (b) Austria (c) Tunisia
    (d) China

Speaking

2   Sample answers:

Listen to the recording

(a) J'ai déjà visité l'Espagne et la Belgique avec ma famille. Je les ai trouvées très différentes. J'ai passé une semaine au bord de la mer dans le sud de l'Espagne et il faisait très chaud, même trop chaud, mais je me suis bien amusé à bronzer et à nager dans la mer. Cependant, mes vacances en Belgique étaient plus culturelles puisque j'ai visité les monuments historiques, quelques musées et des champs de bataille de la Première et de la Deuxième Guerres mondiales.

(b) Je voudrais aller au Brésil car il y fait très chaud et j'ai envie de bronzer et de jouer au foot sur les plages célèbres de Rio. On dit que c'est un beau pays pittoresque et j'aimerais également regarder un match de foot dans un des stades de la région.

(c) Naturellement il y a des problèmes de transport, surtout si on voyage en avion, mais si on ne parle pas la langue, il sera peut-être difficile de communiquer avec les gens du pays. De plus, la cuisine peut être trop épicée ou trop différente, ce qui est un inconvénient si on tombe malade.

49. Places to visit

Writing

1   J'ai déjà voyagé à l'étranger mais j'aimerais vraiment visiter l'Australie parce que je n'y suis jamais allé. Mes parents voudraient aller au théâtre à Sydney et ma sœur aimerait aller sur les plages connues car elle aime faire des sports nautiques et se faire bronzer. J'adore la nature, alors ce serait super de voir des animaux sauvages et on m'a dit que c'est un joli pays.

Speaking

2   Teacher transcript and sample answers:

Listen to the recording

T: Bonjour. Je peux vous aider?
S1: Bonjour. Je voudrais faire une excursion à Rouen.
T: Ah bon. Quand voulez-vous y aller et pourquoi?
S2: Je voudrais y aller demain et visiter un musée car j'adore l'histoire.
T: Qu'est-ce que vous avez déjà visité à Paris?
S3: J'ai visité la tour Eiffel.
T: C'est intéressant, ça.
S4: Vous pouvez me recommander un restaurant?
T: Ah oui, il y a un bon restaurant italien, rue Beauvoisine.
S5: Merci. Il y a un tarif réduit pour les étudiants?
T: Non, je regrette.

50. Describing a region

Reading

1   C, D, E, G

Speaking

2   Sample answers:

Listen to the recording

(a) *Sur la photo il y a un vieux bâtiment au milieu d'une rivière. C'est la nuit et* il y a des cafés et des bars au bord de la rivière.

(b) Moi, j'aime aussi habiter en ville car c'est plus animé. On peut facilement faire les magasins et on peut aller au ciné ou au centre sportif aussi.

(c) À mon avis, la campagne est trop tranquille et il n'y a rien à faire, à part les promenades. On ne peut pas sortir le soir.

(d) Je voudrais habiter en Espagne dans une maison énorme au bord de la mer avec une piscine en plein air, donc je pourrais nager tous les jours.

(e) Oui, je suis allé à Paris avec un groupe de mes copains du collège et j'ai aussi visité Rouen avec ma famille. Je me suis très bien amusé car la France me plaît bien.

School

51. Subjects

Reading

1 (a) G (b) B (c) I (d) H
2 C, E F, G

Listening

2 A, D, F, G

52. School life

Writing

1 (a) *J'aime mon collège.*
(b) Les bâtiments sont anciens.
(c) Il y a beaucoup de clubs.
(d) Ma matière préférée c'est la musique car le prof est gentil.
(e) L'année dernière je suis allé en Espagne avec mon collège.

Speaking

2 Sample answers:

 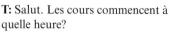

(a) *Il y a huit élèves qui travaillent dans une salle de classe. Je crois qu'ils sont en train de faire leurs devoirs.*
(b) J'aime mon collège car les profs sont compréhensifs et travailleurs et j'ai beaucoup de bons copains ici.
(c) Je n'aime pas les maths car c'est une matière difficile et compliquée.
(d) J'étudie le français depuis quatre ans mais je trouve ça difficile.
(e) Je voudrais continuer mes études parce que j'aimerais avoir le bac.

53. School day

Speaking

1 Sample answers:

(a) Après avoir préparé mes affaires, je vais au collège en car. Une fois arrivé(e) je vais directement à la salle de classe où on a l'appel. Le matin il y a quatre cours et chaque cours dure une heure. À dix heures et demie on a une récré de vingt minutes, ce qui me plaît car je peux bavarder avec mes amis ou jouer au foot s'il fait beau. Les cours se terminent à midi et demi.
(b) Naturellement je prends le déjeuner à l'école, normalement un sandwich, des chips et un jus de fruits. Après avoir mangé, je fais du travail scolaire à la bibliothèque avant de parler avec mes copains ou d'aller au club d'échecs.
(c) Hier, c'était une journée fatigante car j'ai eu deux cours d'EPS avant la récré, et avant de déjeuner j'ai passé un examen blanc en maths, qui était difficile à mon avis. Après avoir mangé, je suis allé à l'entraînement de foot. Le dernier cours était sciences et nous avons eu une épreuve. Je suis enfin rentré chez moi vers quatre heures.

Reading

2 B, E, F, H

54. Comparing schools

Reading

1 B, D, E, H

Listening

2 B, C, F, H

55. Describing schools

Speaking

1 Teacher transcript and sample answers:

T: Salut. Les cours commencent à quelle heure?
S1: Les cours commencent à huit heures vingt.
T: Ah bon. Tu as fait beaucoup de devoirs hier?
S2: J'ai eu des devoirs de maths et d'anglais.
T: D'accord. Il y a quels clubs à ton collège?
S3: Il y a un club de musique et un club de théâtre.
T: C'est bon, ça.
S4: Quelle est ta matière préférée?
T: Moi, je préfère les maths car c'est intéressant.
S5: Tu pratiques quels sports à ton collège?
T: On peut faire toute une gamme de sports mais moi, j'aime bien le badminton.

Writing

2 Mon copain, Marc, va à un grand collège mixte dans le nord de la France. Il aime beaucoup le collège mais il a trouvé l'anglais très difficile. Je suis allé à son collège l'année dernière et c'était assez intéressant. Les cours commencent plus tôt qu'en Angleterre et les élèves ne portent pas d'uniforme scolaire. Marc va visiter mon école l'année prochaine.

56. School rules

Writing

1 Sample answer:
Le règlement à mon école est assez strict. Naturellement il faut respecter les professeurs et être à l'heure et ça c'est juste, mais je déteste porter l'uniforme scolaire qui consiste d'un blazer bleu, d'une chemise blanche et d'un pantalon noir. Hier une copine n'a pas porté sa cravate et elle a été punie. Je trouve ça ridicule.
Il ne faut pas porter de bijoux et je trouve ça injuste, alors je changerais cette règle parce que je voudrais pouvoir porter des boucles d'oreilles et une bague.

Listening

2 (a) C (b) D (c) A

57. Problems and pressures

Reading

1 (a) faire ses devoirs / réviser pour les contrôles
(b) discuter de ce qu'elle a appris avec ses parents
(c) examen de violoncelle
(d) rien / jouer avec son chat / inviter ses copines
(e) prof de chimie
(f) vérifient que les profs travaillent / on travaille / tout le monde travaille beaucoup / comparent les résultats des élèves

Writing

2 Sample answer:
Au collège il y a trop de stress causé par les examens à venir. Moi, je suis stressé(e) car j'ai peur de rater mes examens et je travaille dur depuis deux mois. Je me fâche facilement avec mes copains et mes parents et je suis très triste. Je sais que j'ai beaucoup révisé, mais je ne peux pas me relaxer. Après avoir passé mes examens je vais regarder beaucoup de télé, écouter de la musique et aussi sortir avec mes amis.

58. Primary school

Reading

1 (a) E (b) A (c) B (d) F

Listening

2 (a) C (b) B (c) C (d) A

59. Success in school

Reading

1 (a) *Régine* (b) Mamadou (c) Ibrahim (d) Sophie
(e) Régine (f) Sophie

Speaking

2 Sample answers:

Listen to the recording

(a) Je vais au club de théâtre car j'aime l'art dramatique, et je suis membre de l'orchestre scolaire.

(b) Je joue au foot en hiver et au tennis en été, mais je préfère jouer au rugby et je m'entraîne au collège deux fois par semaine.

(c) J'ai fait des progrès en maths et en sciences et j'ai joué au rugby pour l'équipe de mon école.

60. School trips

Writing

1 Sample answer:

L'année dernière, mon collège a décidé d'organiser une excursion à Londres et puisque c'était une visite au théâtre et que je m'intéresse beaucoup à l'art dramatique, j'y ai participé. En général j'aime les voyages scolaires car ils sont stimulants et normalement mes copains sont là, alors on s'amuse bien ensemble.

Cette fois, on a vu une pièce comique dans un vieux théâtre célèbre et c'était vraiment intéressant et marrant. Après avoir quitté le théâtre, j'ai pu passer une heure au centre-ville où j'ai acheté quelques petits souvenirs pour ma famille, ce qui m'a beaucoup plu, avant de rentrer en car.

L'année prochaine, on va organiser une excursion à Stratford pour voir une pièce de Shakespeare et j'aimerais bien y aller parce que je n'y suis jamais allé(e) et que je voudrais voir tous les sites historiques là-bas.

Reading

2 I like school trips. They are often interesting and fun because my friends are with me. I don't like coach journeys abroad because they are too long and I get a bit bored. Last year I went to Spain with my history class. It was great because I could practise my Spanish.

61. School activities

Writing

1 (a) J'aime mon école.
(b) Il y a beaucoup de clubs.
(c) Je participe au club d'art dramatique le mercredi.
(d) La semaine dernière j'ai joué pour l'équipe de football du collège.
(e) On va organiser une pièce scolaire l'année prochaine.

Listening

2 (a) B (b) D (c) B

62. Exchanges

Speaking

1 Teacher transcript and sample answers:

Listen to the recording

T: C'est quoi, comme excursion?
S1: C'est un voyage à Paris et le billet coûte cent euros.
T: On voyage comment et à quelle heure?
S2: On voyage en car et on part à huit heures.
T: Pourquoi est-ce que tu veux faire cette visite?
S3: Je voudrais voir la tour Eiffel.
T: Le voyage dure combien de temps?
S4: Le voyage dure deux heures.
T: D'accord.
S5: Que penses-tu des échanges?
T: J'aime bien les échanges.

Listening

2 (a) *none* (b) coach trip (c) bowling/meal
(d) have a dictionary with her

Future aspirations, study and work

63. Future plans

Reading

1 (a) Amélie (B) Antonin (c) Dany (d) Laetitia

Writing

2 Sample answer:

On dit que je suis assez travailleur et responsable mais que je suis un peu timide de temps en temps. J'ai déjà travaillé dans un petit magasin de mon quartier où je servais les clients et mon patron était très content de moi. Pour moi, avoir de l'ambition est important parce que je voudrais réussir dans la vie. J'aimerais aller à l'université afin de trouver un emploi satisfaisant et bien payé, mais, à mon avis, ce qui importe, c'est le bonheur.

64. Languages beyond the classroom

Speaking

1 Teacher transcript and sample answers:

Listen to the recording

T: C'est quand le film et où?
S1: C'est ce soir à huit heures au cinéma en ville.
T: Qu'est-ce qu'il y a d'autre à faire dans ta ville?
S2: Il y a un stade de foot et on peut aussi aller au théâtre.
T: Bon. Parle-moi du dernier film que tu as vu.
S3: J'ai vu le dernier James Bond et c'était passionnant.
T: C'est intéressant, ça.
S4: Que penses-tu des films anglais?
T: J'aime bien les films anglais.
S5: Quelle sorte de musique préfères-tu?
T: Moi, je préfère la musique rap.

Reading

2 (a) Elle parle presque sans accent / elle se présente facilement dans les médias français / elle se double elle-même dans les versions françaises de ses propres films.
(b) Ses parents voulaient qu'elle s'immerge dans la culture francophone.
(c) Elle a eu son bac.
(d) Elle hésite un peu (au téléphone) / elle se trompe de genre.
(e) Parler le français a changé sa vie / elle dit que celle qui sait parler deux langues vaut deux femmes.

65. Relationships in the future

Speaking

1 Sample answers:

Listen to the recording

(a) *À l'avenir je voudrais me marier car* je pense que le mariage est important pour montrer son amour. Si je rencontre un partenaire avec qui je m'entends bien, ma vie sera heureuse. Pourtant, je voudrais trouver un bon emploi avant de me marier.

(b) *J'aime bien les enfants mais je ne sais pas si je voudrais avoir mes propres enfants immédiatement parce que* j'aimerais avoir assez d'argent avant de commencer à fonder une famille.

(c) *Je pense que je suis sociable, alors* je crois qu'il ne sera pas difficile de me faire de nouveaux amis à l'avenir quand je quitterai l'école. J'espère aller à l'université et il y aura plein de gens avec qui je pourrai m'entendre.

Listening

2 (a) funny (b) rich (c) reliable

66. Travel

Writing

1 On dit que j'aime beaucoup voyager. J'ai déjà visité plusieurs pays en Europe et l'été prochain je vais passer un mois au Canada avec ma famille. Mon rêve serait d'aller aux États-Unis car je m'intéresse à l'histoire américaine. Si j'économise assez d'argent, je pourrai loger dans un hôtel cinq étoiles à New York.

Listening

2 (a) B (b) B (c) B

67. Jobs

Speaking

1 Sample answers:

(a) Il y a un homme d'affaires qui travaille sur un ordinateur portable dans un bureau. Deux collègues lui parlent. Je crois qu'ils travaillent à l'étage le plus élevé parce qu'on ne peut pas voir d'autres bâtiments de la fenêtre.

(b) Moi, je crois qu'il est très important de ne pas travailler le week-end, sauf si on travaille pour des services d'urgences naturellement, parce qu'il faut se détendre un peu.

(c) Je viens de trouver un petit job dans un restaurant et hier j'ai dû nettoyer la cuisine, ce qui était vraiment difficile car il y avait des ordures partout. Ce n'était pas du tout agréable.

(d) Je vais faire un stage afin de découvrir quel métier je voudrais faire à l'avenir. Je vais aussi parler à des personnes qui font plusieurs emplois différents et discuter avec mes parents et mes professeurs.

(e) Je ne suis pas d'accord. Je pense qu'il est important d'aller à l'université. En effet, avec une licence en poche, on pourra trouver un meilleur emploi et être bien payé.

Listening

2 (a) an engineer (b) a taxi driver (c) a factory worker
   (d) a cook

68. Part-time jobs

Writing

1 Sample answer:

Sur la photo c'est moi. Je travaille dans un petit café en ville. J'aime avoir un petit job pour gagner de l'argent supplémentaire, alors je peux acheter des vêtements et payer mon forfait portable.

Reading

2 B, D, E, H, J

69. Opinions about jobs

Listening

1 (a) C (b) A (c) B (d) C

Reading

2 (a) Samuel (b) Alain (c) Jasmine (d) Paulette

70. Workplaces

Listening

1 (a) chemist's shop (b) hairdresser's salon
   (c) town hall

Reading

2 My sister works in a clothes shop in town. She serves the customers and makes coffee for her colleagues. She doesn't like her job because it's quite boring and she does not get on well with her boss. Yesterday she had to clean the shop at the end of the day. In the future she is going to look for another job in a sports centre.

71. Applying for jobs

Listening

1 A (example), F, G, H

Reading

2 (a) C (b) B (c) A (d) D

72. Future study

Speaking

1 Sample answers:

(a) *Sur la photo il y a un groupe d'étudiants* qui viennent de recevoir leur licence à l'université. Ils sont tous très contents.

(b) Moi, je pense qu'il est important d'aller à l'université, surtout si on veut trouver un emploi bien payé.

(c) Le mois dernier j'ai préparé un projet sur l'environnement. C'était intéressant parce que j'ai fait un sondage en ville.

(d) Moi, je ne voudrais pas étudier à l'étranger parce que j'ai beaucoup d'amis en Angleterre, alors j'aimerais aller à l'université ici.

(e) Pour ceux qui voudraient apprendre un métier spécialisé, c'est très important.

Reading

2 I don't know if I'm going to go to university. My parents went and they have good jobs, but I'm not as hard working as they are. I'd like to become a lawyer, that's true, and my teachers insist that I am clever enough; however, I don't think that I would be able to bear the stress. I'm going to take a gap year and I'll travel a lot, but I shall nevertheless finally have to decide what I'd like to do in life.

73. Volunteering

Writing

1 Sample answer:

Madame, Monsieur

J'ai vu votre annonce dans un magazine que je lisais la semaine dernière et j'aimerais poser ma candidature pour un des postes dans le collège au Cameroun. Je m'intéresse à l'éducation des jeunes et je voudrais aider ceux qui sont défavorisés. Naturellement je parle bien le français mais ma langue maternelle c'est l'anglais, alors je pourrais aider les enfants à améliorer leurs compétences en anglais.

J'ai déjà fait du travail bénévole dans ma région où j'ai aidé les personnes âgées. J'ai promené les chiens, j'ai fait les courses et j'ai travaillé dans le jardin. Je sais que travailler en Afrique va élargir mes horizons et je rêve de pouvoir découvrir un nouveau pays différent. Je suis prêt à travailler dur.

Je pense que tous les jeunes devraient essayer de faire quelque chose pour aider les autres, surtout quand ils n'ont pas grand-chose.

Listening

2 (a) a TV programme about poverty
   (b) build a clinic / to help the local people who fall ill
   (c) construction skills
   (d) a citizen of the world / proud

74. Helping others

Speaking

1 Sample answers:

(a) *J'écoute les problèmes de tous mes copains et je leur donne des conseils prudents. Par exemple, hier j'ai dit à ma copine Amanda qu'elle devrait se concentrer sur ses études au lieu de sortir tous les soirs.*

(b) Le week-end dernier, j'ai aidé mon petit frère avec ses devoirs de maths et il était très content. Samedi, j'ai lavé la voiture de mon père et il était étonné quand j'ai refusé d'accepter de l'argent! Demain, je vais nettoyer la cuisine et travailler dans le jardin, s'il fait beau.

(c) Aider les autres m'intéresse beaucoup parce que je pense que c'est juste. Si j'ai un don particulier, je peux aider mes amis ou ma famille, mais si j'ai besoin d'aide, ils m'aideront aussi.

Writing

2 Sample answer:

Sur la photo il y a deux jeunes qui sont en train de ramasser des papiers et des bouteilles vides dans un parc. Une fille met une bouteille dans un sac en plastique noir. J'aime être bénévole.

75. Charities

Reading

1 (a) *il y a six mois*

(b) pour contrer la société individualiste / montrer que les humains sont plus forts quand ils s'unissent

(c) il a perdu un proche à cause de cette maladie

(d) il téléphone aux gens pour demander de l'argent

(e) *either:* il fait une différence, *or:* la recherche apporte quelque chose / aide les autres

Listening

2 B, E, F

76. Training

Listening

1 (a) cars (b) no problem (c) local (d) school work

Speaking

1 Sample answers:

Listen to the recording

(a) Les avantages des apprentissages sont nombreux. Par exemple, on peut gagner de l'expérience et en plus on reçoit un petit salaire. De plus, on peut améliorer ses compétences et ses capacités. Par contre, la formation peut être longue et si on trouve un emploi tout de suite après avoir quitté le collège, on aura peut-être un meilleur salaire.

(b) Non, je n'aimerais pas être professeur car les heures sont longues. Les élèves sont souvent paresseux et ils se comportent mal. Bien sûr les professeurs ont de longues vacances et le salaire est assez bon, mais il faut encore travailler trop le soir et le week-end.

(c) Mon emploi idéal serait comme ingénieur car j'aime bien résoudre les problèmes et je suis fort en technologie et en science.

77. Future professions

Reading

1 B, E, F, H

Listening

2 A, C, D

International and global dimension

78. Sporting events

Speaking

1 Sample answers:

Listen to the recording

(a) *Sur la photo il y a des cyclistes professionnels qui participent au Tour de France. Les cyclistes sont très proches l'un de l'autre et ça peut être dangereux si un cycliste tombe par exemple. Je crois que je peux voir Chris Froome à l'arrière-plan.*

(b) Oui, aller à un événement sportif, c'est passionnant mais c'est cher aussi. Par exemple, j'ai payé presque trente livres pour regarder un match de foot au stade de Manchester City.

(c) Le week-end dernier, je suis allé au stade de rugby de Gloucester où j'ai regardé un match contre le Stade Français. Heureusement, Gloucester a gagné et j'étais content.

(d) Les Jeux Olympiques auront lieu cet été et je les attends avec impatience car j'adore tous les sports, surtout la natation et l'athlétisme.

(e) Je ne suis pas d'accord. À mon avis, il est plus important de participer même si on n'est pas fort en sport parce qu'il faut s'amuser quand on fait du sport.

Writing

2 (a) J'aime tous les sports.

(b) Je regarde un match de rugby le samedi.

(c) Les événements sportifs sont populaires.

(d) Je voudrais aller aux Jeux Olympiques.

(e) Mon frère est allé à un match de foot hier.

79. Music events

Reading

1 (a) *spring*

(b) all sorts / many different

(c) they are full of people

(d) free

(e) stages in about 20 bars in town

Listening

2 B, E, F

80. Being green

Reading

1 (a) *Yannick*   (d) Yannick

(b) Thomas   (e) Denis

(c) Denis   (f) Thomas

Listening

2 (a) E (b) C (c) B

81. Protecting the environment

Reading

1 We are in the process of destroying the planet. Lots of animals are threatened by men's actions and we must protect the Earth. The sea level has been rising for several years because of global warming and climate change. Pollution has increased health risks and we should act in order to resolve this serious problem.

Speaking

2 Sample answers:

Listen to the recording

(a) À mon avis, le problème le plus grave c'est l'effet de serre qui provoque le réchauffement de la Terre. Naturellement, il y a trop de pollution aussi, mais je crois que ce n'est pas si grave.

(b) J'ai recyclé presque tout, y compris le verre et le papier. Le week-end dernier, je suis allé au centre de recyclage avec mes parents et on a recyclé le métal et le carton.

(c) On pourrait interdire aux voitures et aux poids lourds de rouler en centre-ville car ils causent beaucoup de pollution. De plus, on devrait encourager les gens à prendre les transports en commun afin d'économiser l'énergie.

82. Environmental issues

Speaking

1 Sample answers:

Listen to the recording

(a) Il y a un jeune Africain qui boit de l'eau au robinet. Il n'a pas de verre, alors il boit l'eau dans sa main.

(b) Je ne suis pas d'accord. Il y a un manque d'eau dans certains pays du monde, par exemple en Afrique où il ne pleut pas beaucoup.

(c) J'ai baissé le chauffage central chez nous, j'ai aussi dit à mes parents d'éteindre la lumière quand ils quittent une pièce car je crois qu'il faut économiser plus d'énergie.

(d) À mon avis, la plus grande menace c'est le changement climatique qui provoquera plein d'inondations. Comme le niveau de la mer montera, beaucoup d'îles seront en danger de disparition.

(e) Je suis d'accord. Il faut aider les organisations caritatives qui essaient de résoudre les problèmes de l'environnement, comme Greenpeace. À l'avenir, je vais leur donner de l'argent.

Listening

2   B, C, E, G

83. Natural resources

Listening

1   (a) cotton
    (b) deforestation / animal species disappearing
    (c) more pesticides used
    (d) find land for more vegetables to be grown

Reading

2   B, D, E

84. World problems

Listening

1   (a) earthquake
    (b) strong winds
    (c) thousands of inhabitants have had to vacate their homes / they could not take all their belongings / rain still falling (any 2 from 3)
    (d) fire / danger to animals

Reading

2   In the world, there are lots of homeless people. You must give money to the organisations which help them. I think that there is too much unemployment, especially in Europe, so governments should do something. I don't like to see the destruction of the natural habitats of wild animals in Africa. I visited Australia last month and I think there were lots of animals who were living there with no problems.

Grammar

85. Articles 1

A 1   les commerces   2   la pharmacie
       3   les toilettes   4   l'hôtel
       5   les cinémas   6   le bowling
       7   la gare   8   le parking
       9   les rues   10   l'appartement

B 1   la chienne   2   les serpents
       3   l'araignée   4   le chat
       5   la tortue   6   l'éléphant
       7   les poissons   8   le canard
       9   la mouche   10   les cochons d'Inde
      11   la grenouille   12   le singe

C 1   un salon   2   une salle de bains
       3   un jardin   4   une chambre
       5   un sous-sol   6   une cuisine
       7   une salle à manger

D

le chien – les chiens; un château – *des châteaux*; l'animal – *les animaux*; une voiture – des voitures
le nez – *les nez*; le bateau – *les bateaux*; un hôtel – *des hôtels*; l'arbre – les arbres;
une page – des pages; *l'eau* – les eaux; une araignée – *des araignées*; *la destination* – les destinations

86. Articles 2

A 1   des œufs   2   de la confiture
       3   du pain   4   des haricots verts
       5   de l'eau minérale   6   du jambon
       7   des frites   8   de la crème
       9   de l'huile   10   du riz

B Tu veux des pâtes, des abricots, du fromage, du chocolat, des olives, du porc, des pommes de terre, du ketchup, de l'ananas, du potage, des œufs, du sel et du poivre?

C 1   Je n'ai pas d'argent. I don't have any money.
       2   Je n'ai pas de pain. I don't have any bread.
       3   Je n'ai pas de céréales. I don't have any cereal.
       4   Je n'ai pas de pizza. I don't have any pizza.

D Tu as des fruits et des légumes? Oui, j'ai des fruits mais je n'ai pas de légumes. Par exemple, j'ai des pêches et des cerises mais je n'ai pas de carottes ni de pommes de terre. Cependant, j'ai du pain et du Nutella, donc on peut manger des sandwichs.

E 1   à la patinoire   2   à la crêperie
       3   au théâtre   4   à l'hôtel de ville
       5   aux magasins   6   au café-tabac

F 1   au salon   2   à la cuisine
       3   à la salle de bains   4   aux chambres
       5   à la salle de jeux   6   au jardin
       7   à l'atelier   8   au grenier
       9   à la cave   10   à l'entrée
      11   au garage   12   à la salle à manger

87. Adjectives

A 1   Ma mère est petite.   2   Mon père est grand.
       3   Ma maison est belle.   4   Mon chat est noir.
       5   Elle est heureuse.   6   Les fenêtres sont chères.

B 1   Mon chien est triste.   2   Mes crayons sont blancs.
       3   Ma mère est intelligente. 4   Mes frères sont timides.
       5   Mes sœurs sont grosses.   6   Ma chatte est très mignonne.

C

grand	grande	**grands**	grandes	big/tall
petit	petite	**petits**	**petites**	**small**
noir	**noire**	noirs	**noires**	**black**
neuf	neuve	**neufs**	neuves	**new**
dernier	**dernière**	derniers	**dernières**	last
marron	**marron**	marron	**marron**	(chestnut) brown
triste	**triste**	tristes	**tristes**	sad
sérieux	**sérieuse**	sérieux	**sérieuses**	**serious**
gentil	gentille	**gentils**	gentilles	kind
sec	sèche	secs	**sèches**	**dry**
drôle	**drôle**	drôles	**drôles**	funny
vieux	vieille	**vieux**	vieilles	old
beau	belle	beaux	**belles**	**beautiful**
ancien	**ancienne**	anciens	**anciennes**	ancient
blanc	**blanche**	blancs	**blanches**	white
sportif	sportive	**sportifs**	sportives	**sporty**

D 1   Elle a de beaux yeux bleus.
       2   Les meilleures fleurs jaunes
       3   Mes vieilles baskets blanches
       4   Mes pauvres parents malades

88. Possessives

A (1) Dans ma famille, il y a mon père, ma mère, ma sœur et mes deux frères. Ma grand-mère vient souvent nous rendre visite avec mon grand-père. Mon amie adore mes grands-parents et elle vient jouer avec toutes mes affaires quand ils sont là.

(2) Dans sa chambre, elle a son lit, ses livres, son bureau, sa télévision, ses bijoux, son téléphone et son nounours.

(3) Dans notre collège, nous avons nos professeurs, notre bibliothèque, notre cantine et notre terrain de sport. Et vous, qu'est-ce que vous avez dans votre collège et dans vos salles de classe? Vous avez vos tableaux blancs interactifs et votre gymnase?

(4) (a) Comment s'appellent ton père et ta mère?
(b) Qu'est-ce que tu achètes avec ton argent?
(c) C'est quand ton anniversaire?
(d) Qu'est-ce qu'il y a dans ta ville ou ton village?

(5) Dans leur village, ils ont leur mairie, leurs cinémas, leur pharmacie, leur boulangerie, leurs cafés, leurs parcs, leur hôpital, leur école et tous leurs petits commerces.

B *Examples from the table:* Mon fromage est très timide; Nos copines ne sont pas très honnêtes; Leurs photos sont assez jaunes; Vos gâteaux sont très romantiques!

C 1 Les pulls? Ce sont les miens!
2 Les jupes? Ce sont les miennes!
3 Le jogging? C'est le mien!

89. Comparisons

A Lydie est la plus intelligente. Paul est le moins intelligent.

B *Other examples:* Anna est pire qu'Antoine en français. Anna est la meilleure en dessin.

C 1 Philippe est aussi grand que Sara. = Philippe is as tall as Sara.
2 Les maths sont plus difficiles que la musique. = Maths is more difficult than music.
3 Les bonbons sont moins sains que les fruits. = Sweets are not as healthy as fruit.
4 Une cravate est moins confortable qu'un jogging. = A tie is less comfortable than a tracksuit.
5 La chimie est aussi intéressante que l'anglais. = Chemistry is as interesting as English.

D 1 Les kiwis sont les fruits les plus sains.
2 L'hiver est la saison la plus froide.
3 Londres est la plus grande ville d'Angleterre.
4 Où sont les garçons les moins actifs?
5 Je prends les vêtements les moins longs.
6 J'habite dans la région la moins industrielle.

90. Other adjectives and pronouns

A 1 ce pantalon   2 cet imperméable
3 cette robe   4 ces baskets
5 cet anorak   6 ces sandales
7 ces chaussettes   8 cette jupe

B 1 Je préfère celui à gauche.   2 Je préfère ceux à gauche.
3 Je préfère celle à gauche.   4 Je préfère celles à gauche.

C 1 Quel stylo préfères-tu? Celui-ci ou celui-là?
2 Quelle station balnéaire préfères-tu? Celle-ci ou celle-là?
3 Quelles ceintures préfères-tu? Celles-ci ou celles-là?
4 Quels hôtels préfères-tu? Ceux-ci ou ceux-là?

D 1 Lequel?   2 Laquelle?
3 Lesquelles?   4 Lesquels?

E 1 Quelle cuisine préfères-tu? Celle-ci ou celle-là? Laquelle?
2 Quelles cravates préfères-tu? Celles-ci ou celles-là? Lesquelles?
3 Quel jardin préfères-tu? Celui-ci ou celui-là? Lequel?
4 Quels gants préfères-tu? Ceux-ci ou ceux-là? Lesquels?

91. Adverbs

A 1 doucement   2 naturellement
3 absolument   4 généralement
5 attentivement   6 vraiment
7 lentement   8 gentiment

B Le matin, <u>d'abord</u> je me lève à sept heures, <u>puis d'habitude</u> je prends mon petit déjeuner. <u>Ensuite</u>, je quitte la maison et <u>finalement</u> j'arrive au collège à huit heures et demie. Mais c'est <u>souvent</u> trop tôt. <u>Alors</u> <u>à l'avenir</u> je vais rester au lit plus longtemps.

In the morning, first of all I get up at 7 o'clock then usually I have my breakfast. Then I leave the house and finally I arrive at school at half past eight. But it is often too early. So, in future I am going to stay in bed longer.

C Souvent mes grands-parents viennent avec nous, et d'abord c'est vraiment pratique car ils font régulièrement du baby-sitting. Cependant, de temps en temps, ils se sentent vraiment fatigués et ils ne sont pas toujours confortables. Par conséquent ils ne viendront pas l'année prochaine. À l'avenir, ils viendront seulement s'ils sont absolument en bonne forme!

D 1 D'habitude il fait la vaisselle tout de suite.
2 De temps en temps elle écoute de la musique doucement.
3 Ma valise? Naturellement j'avais laissé mes vêtements dedans.

92. Object pronouns

A 1 We see you.   2 Do you know him?
3 I want to see her.   4 You meet us.
5 She will forget you.   6 I will lose them.

B 1 I am passing my sweets to you.
2 Do not tell him/her the truth.
3 We will give him/her a boat.
4 He is going to send us a present.
5 You will tell them the story.

C 1 Vous comprenez le professeur? Nous le comprenons souvent.
2 Elle aime les sports nautiques? Elle ne les aime pas du tout.
3 Tu vas vendre ton vélo? Oui, je vais le vendre demain.
4 Il veut acheter la maison? Non, il ne veut pas l'acheter.

D 1 Il les cherche.
2 Nous lui envoyons un cadeau.
3 Il leur a donné des bonbons.
4 Tu leur as téléphoné?
5 Elle la dit toujours.

E 1 Elle nous les a offerts.
2 Ne les lui vends pas!
3 Je vais te/vous le passer.
4 Il te/vous les a donnés samedi.

93. More pronouns: *y* and *en*

A 1 Il va y habiter.
2 Elle y a vu ses amis.
3 Vous y jouez?
4 J'y suis arrivé avant les autres.
5 Tu y es allée ce matin?

B 1 J'en fais beaucoup.
2 Elle n'en fait pas.
3 Non, j'en ai trois.
4 Ils en mangent tous les samedis.
5 Il y en a plusieurs.

C 1 J'y vais de temps en temps.
2 J'en mange beaucoup.
3 … je n'en mange jamais …
4 … j'y suis allé …
5 … tu veux y aller …?
6 … mon frère n'en mange pas …

94. Other pronouns

A 1 Le repas que j'ai pris était excellent.
2 C'est Claude qui est le plus beau.
3 Ce sont mes parents qui adorent la viande.
4 Voilà le chapeau qu'il a perdu.
5 Où sont les robes qui sont déchirées?
6 L'église que j'ai visitée était vieille.
7 L'homme qui monte dans le train est gros.
8 Ma copine qui s'appelle Mathilde a seize ans.
9 Quel est le film que tu veux voir?

B 1 The life which you are dreaming about does not exist.
2 The papers which I need are in the drawer.

3 I do not know the illness from which you are suffering.

4 This boy who I was talking to you about has left the school.

C 1 Le repas que nous avons mangé était excellent. = The meal which we ate was excellent.

2 Le stylo dont vous avez besoin est cassé. = The pen that you need is broken.

3 Des bonbons? J'en ai mangé beaucoup. = Sweets? I have eaten lots of them.

4 Le café où je vais le samedi est fermé. = The café where I go on Saturdays is closed.

5 Le cinéma Gaumont? J'y suis allée pour voir 'Amélie'. = The Gaumont cinema? I went there to see 'Amélie'.

95. Present tense: -er verbs

A aimer: j'aime, nous aimons, ils aiment
jouer: je joue, nous jouons, ils jouent
habiter: j'habite, nous habitons, ils habitent
regarder: je regarde, nous regardons, ils regardent
donner: je donne, nous donnons, ils donnent
inviter: j'invite, nous invitons, ils invitent
marcher: je marche, nous marchons, ils marchent
trouver: je trouve, nous trouvons, ils trouvent
voler: je vole, nous volons, ils volent
garder: je garde, nous gardons, ils gardent

B 1 vous gardez 2 elle invite
3 tu habites 4 nous trouvons
5 il regarde 6 vous marchez
7 tu donnes 8 elle vole
9 il joue 10 ils/elles regardent

C -ger verbs:
1 ils rangent 2 nous plongeons
3 nous nageons 4 je mange
-yer verbs:
5 tu envoies 6 vous payez
7 j'essaie 8 nous nettoyons
-ler / -ter verbs:
1 je m'appelle 2 ils jettent
3 nous nous rappelons 4 elle projette
acheter-type verbs:
5 tu achètes 6 elles préfèrent
7 vous vous levez 8 il gèle

D 1 Ils habitent en France? Do they live in France?
2 Marie range sa chambre? Does Marie tidy her room?
3 Vous préférez les sciences? Do you prefer science?
4 Les sœurs jettent les fruits? Do the sisters throw out the fruit?
5 Mon copain et moi achetons des frites? Are my friend and I buying chips?

96. Present tense: -ir and -re verbs

A choisir = to choose
ralentir = to slow down
réfléchir = to reflect / think about
rougir = to blush
finir = to finish
atterrir = to land
punir = to punish
avertir = to warn

B
	dormir	sortir
je	dors	sors
tu	dors	sors
il/elle	dort	sort
nous	dormons	sortons
vous	dormez	sortez
ils/elles	dorment	sortent

C 1 L'ami choisit un cadeau.
2 Vous courez aux magasins.
3 Nous finissons nos devoirs.

4 Je remplis le verre de vin.

D
	vendre	prendre	dire
je	vends	prends	dis
tu	vends	prends	dis
il/elle	vend	prend	dit
nous	vendons	prenons	disons
vous	vendez	prenez	dites
ils/elles	vendent	prennent	disent

E 1 nous vendons 2 ils répondent
3 je descends 4 tu prends
5 vous buvez 6 elle lit
7 j'écris 8 il comprend

97. Avoir and être

A 1 Elle a un hamster.
2 J'ai les cheveux blonds.
3 Ils ont une grande maison.
4 Il a onze ans.
5 Nous avons un petit gymnase.
6 Vous avez un beau chien.
7 Ma sœur a une jupe rouge.
8 Les filles ont un piercing.
9 Tu as deux guitares.
10 Vous avez une nouvelle maison.

B 1 Ils/Elles ont un chien et trois hamsters.
2 Tu as une sœur?
3 Elle a les cheveux noirs.
4 Nous avons une grande cuisine.
5 J'ai trois enfants.
6 J'ai seize ans.
7 Il a une voiture.

C 1 Je suis français.
2 Nous sommes paresseux.
3 Ma tante est assez petite.
4 Vous êtes sportif mais timide.
5 Mes yeux sont bleus.
6 Tu es célibataire?
7 Les chiens sont mignons.
8 Je suis au chômage.
9 Nous sommes mariés.
10 Il est paresseux.

98. Reflexive verbs

A Je me lève / Tu te laves / Il se brosse les dents / Je m'habille et après / je prends mon petit déjeuner

B Mes parents se réveillent tôt le matin. Je m'appelle Lydie. Le matin, je me réveille à 7 heures et demie mais je ne me lève pas tout de suite. Normalement ma sœur se lève à 8 heures. Nous nous lavons dans la salle de bains et nous nous habillons vite. Après le petit déjeuner, nous nous dépêchons pour prendre le bus pour aller au collège. On s'approche au collège et on est très contentes. Vous vous amusez bien à votre collège?

C 2, 1, 4, 3

D 1 je me repose je me suis reposé(e)
2 elle se douche elle s'est douchée
3 nous nous amusons nous nous sommes amusé(e)s
4 elles s'étonnent elles se sont étonnées
5 vous vous dépêchez vous vous êtes dépêché(e)(s)

E 1 Je me suis reposée à 8 heures ce matin.
2 Nous nous sommes dépêchés pour aller au match.
3 Ma sœur ne s'est pas douchée hier soir.
4 Mes deux frères se sont bien entendus en vacances.
5 Vous vous êtes couchés tôt samedi, mes amis?
6 Les garçons se sont disputés.

99. Other important verbs

A

	devoir	pouvoir	vouloir	savoir
je	dois	peux	veux	sais
tu	dois	peux	veux	sais
il/elle/on	doit	peut	veut	sait
nous	devons	pouvons	voulons	savons
vous	devez	pouvez	voulez	savez
ils/elles	doivent	peuvent	veulent	savent

B 1 Pouvez-vous aider mon père?
2 Sais-tu nager?
3 Mes parents veulent acheter une nouvelle maison.
4 On doit toujours s'arrêter aux feux rouges.
5 Voulez-vous danser avec moi ce soir?
6 Je sais parler allemand et français.

C 1 nous voulons trouver une chambre avec un balcon
2 tu peux louer un vélo
3 vous devez tout vérifier
4 ils savent faire la cuisine
5 elles peuvent faire un pique-nique
6 vous ne pouvez jamais comprendre les régles
7 je sais préparer le dîner

D *Examples:* On ne doit pas manger en classe. On ne veut pas répondre aux professeurs. On peut dormir en classe. On ne sait pas envoyer des textos.

100. The perfect tense 1

A *Examples:* J'ai vendu la maison. Elle a détesté le bateau. Nous avons fini les devoirs.

B 1 Mme Blanc a invité sa copine au match.
2 Vous avez terminé le repas?
3 Ils/Elles ont fumé une cigarette.
4 Il a beaucoup neigé ce matin.
5 Tu n'as pas mangé de légumes?
6 Nous avons choisi un bon restaurant.
7 Elle n'a pas rougi.
8 Ils ont atterri à l'aéroport d'Orly.
9 J'ai rendu visite à ma tante.
10 Nous n'avons pas entendu.

C 1 Nous n'avons pas perdu l'argent.
2 Ils/Elles n'ont pas lavé le bus.
3 Vous n'avez pas attendu les chiens.
4 Je n'ai pas fini le pain.
5 Elle n'a pas vendu le bateau.
6 Il n'a pas détesté les devoirs.

D 1 J'ai mis le pique-nique par terre.
2 Elle a écrit à son frère.
3 Tu n'as rien fait au collège?
4 Il n'a pas lu ma lettre.
5 Nous avons pu acheter une Renault.

E 1 J'ai compris la situation.
2 Il a promis de rentrer vite.
3 Tu as pris un taxi à la gare?

101. The perfect tense 2

A 1 Elle est tombée.
2 Mes copains sont arrivés trop tard.
3 Les chats sont montés sur le toit.
4 Marie n'est pas descendue vite.
5 Madame Lebrun est allée à la piscine.
6 Vous êtes retournés en France?
7 Je ne suis pas parti tôt.
8 Elles sont mortes l'année dernière.

B 1 Élise est arrivée à 11 heures.
2 Jim est mort il y a 20 ans.
3 Nous sommes entrés dans l'épicerie.
4 Marie n'est rentrée qu'à minuit.
5 Mes stylos ne sont pas tombés.
6 Il est sorti avec sa sœur jumelle.

C 1 elles sont montées très vite
2 je suis arrivé(e)
3 ils ne sont pas tombés
4 elle est morte

D je me suis lavé(e)   tu t'es lavé(e)
il s'est lavé   elle s'est lavée
nous nous sommes lavé(e)s
vous vous êtes lavé(e)(s)
ils se sont lavés   elles se sont lavées

E 1 Ils se sont couchés.
2 Elle s'est ennuyée.
3 Vous vous êtes disputé(e)(s).
4 Je me suis endormi(e).

102. The imperfect tense

A 1 *jouer*   7 aller
  je jouais   j'allais
  nous jouions   nous allions
  ils jouaient   ils allaient
2 *finir*   8 partir
  je finissais   je partais
  nous finissions   nous partions
  ils finissaient   ils partaient
3 perdre   9 faire
  je perdais   je faisais
  nous perdions   nous faisions
  ils perdaient   ils faisaient
4 avoir   10 lire
  j'avais   je lisais
  nous avions   nous lisions
  ils avaient   ils lisaient
5 être   11 savoir
  j'étais   je savais
  nous étions   nous savions
  ils étaient   ils savaient
6 boire   12 prendre
  je buvais   je prenais
  nous buvions   nous prenions
  ils buvaient   ils prenaient

B 1 elle attendait   2 ils écrivaient
3 il dormait   4 je regardais
5 elles étaient polies

C 1 Je jouais avec mon petit frère sur la plage. = I used to play with my little brother on the beach.
2 Nous mangions ensemble très souvent. = We used to eat together very often.
3 Le serveur travaillait dur pour nous. = The waiter used to work hard for us.
4 On vendait beaucoup de glaces. = They used to sell lots of ice-cream.
5 Papa et Marc faisaient du ski nautique. = Papa and Marc used to water ski.
6 Tu étais très content. = You used to be happy.

D J'allais au collège quand j'ai vu l'accident. Il y avait beaucoup de monde. J'ai appelé «au secours!».

103. The future tense

A 1 Il va sortir ce soir. = He is going to go out this evening.
2 Nous allons vendre la maison. = We are going to sell the house.
3 Vous allez comprendre bientôt. = You are going to understand soon.
4 Tu vas partir en vacances. = You are going to go away on holiday.
5 Maman va voir un concert. = Mum is going to see a concert.
6 Les garçons vont arriver en retard. = The boys are going to arrive late.

B 1 Nous allons aller en ville demain.
2 Quand vas-tu partir?
3 Ils vont faire leurs devoirs.
4 Vous allez jouer au tennis?

5   Lydie va faire la cuisine.

    6   Ses sœurs vont aider.

C 1 Il lavera sa nouvelle voiture.

    2   Tu inviteras ta copine à manger.

    3   Nous finirons nos devoirs.

    4   Vous attendrez les nouvelles.

    5   Elle rendra visite à sa tante.

    6   Ils arriveront en France.

    7   Elles bavarderont beaucoup.

    8   Je choisirai une nouvelle robe.

D 1 ils devront   2   nous saurons

    3   je ferai   4   elle sera

    5   tu auras   6   elles viendront

    7   il verra   8   tu iras

E 1 they will have to 2 we will know

    3   I will do   4   she will be

    5   you will have   6   they will come

    7   he will see   8   you will go

104. The conditional tense

A

	-er verbs	-ir verbs	-re verbs
	jouer	choisir	vendre
je	jouerais	choisirais	vendrais
tu	jouerais	choisirais	vendrais
il/elle	jouerait	choisirait	vendrait
nous	jouerions	choisirions	vendrions
vous	joueriez	choisiriez	vendriez
ils/elles	joueraient	choisiraient	vendraient

B 1 Ma mère habiterait une belle maison. = My mother would live in a beautiful house.

    2   Vous ne travailleriez plus. = You would no longer work.

    3   Nous visiterions beaucoup de pays. = We would visit lots of countries.

    4   Tu offrirais de l'argent aux autres. = You would give money to others.

    5   Ils mettraient de l'argent à la banque. = They would put some money in the bank.

    6   Je vendrais ma vieille voiture. = I would sell my old car.

C 1 Je serais très riche.

    2   Vous verriez le monde entier.

    3   Ils auraient beaucoup d'amis.

    4   Elle voudrait épouser son fiancé.

105. The pluperfect tense

A 1 You had already finished your lunch.

    2   We had heard the news.

    3   They had promised to return before midnight.

    4   You had already drunk the whole bottle.

    5   She had never read this book.

    6   They had already left.

    7   She had come on her own.

    8   The children had gone to bed early.

B 1 Elle avait fini.   2 Nous avions lu

    3   Elles étaient arrivées. 4 Vous étiez partis.

    5   Tu étais tombé?

C 1 c: I had always wanted to go to Bordeaux but my parents decided to go to Alsace.

    2   a: He had gone on holiday when we arrived at the house.

    3   f: They had left when it started to rain.

    4   e: Luckily, we had bought some sandwiches.

    5   d: My sister had left early but there was a lot of traffic.

    6   g: My parents had rented a flat by the seaside.

    7   h: If you had won the lottery, what would you have done?

    8   b: I had left my car in the car park.

106. Negatives

A ne … pas = not; ne … jamais = never; ne … plus = no longer, no more; ne … rien = nothing, not anything; ne … personne = nobody, not anybody; ne … aucun = not any, none; ne … que = only; ne … ni … ni = neither … nor; ne … pas encore = not yet

B 1 We like neither geography nor history.

    2   I will no longer eat any meat.

    3   He never arrived.

    4   They found nothing.

    5   I am sending no postcards.

    6   She only does two hours per month.

    7   He will never return to Italy again.

C 1 Nous n'avons aucune idée.

    2   Paul n'a que dix euros.

    3   Personne n'est venu à ma fête.

    4   Ils n'ont rien bu au café.

    5   Vous n'achèterez plus de chocolat?

D 1 Nous ne fumerons plus de cigarettes.

    2   Elle n'a jamais dit bonjour.

    3   Tu ne rencontres que deux amies en ville.

    4   Il n'a rien compris.

E 1 Non, ils n'ont jamais acheté de maison.

    2   Non, elle n'a pas fait de lecture.

    3   Non, elles ne sont jamais venues.

107. The perfect infinitive and present participle

The perfect infinitive

A 1 avoir fait 2 être allé 3 avoir joué 4 avoir fini 5 être arrivé 6 avoir mis 7 avoir voulu 8 être sorti 9 avoir écrit 10 être parti

B 1 D 2 H 3 B 4 E 5 C 6 G 7 F 8 A

C 1 Après être allée en ville, elle a déjeuné.

    2   Après avoir mangé, il est allé au ciné.

    3   Après être arrivées à la gare, les filles ont acheté leurs billets.

    4   Après avoir bavardé avec ses amis, Paul est rentré.

The present participle

A 1 finissant   2 achetant   3 allant   4 disant

    5   mangeant 6 faisant   7 prenant 8 voulant

    9   partant   10 venant

B 1 écoutant   2 riant   3 travaillant

    4   courant   5 regardant

108. The passive and the subjunctive

The passive

A 1 E 2 A 3 F 4 B 5 C 6 D

B 1 Les garçons ont été trouvés par la police.

    2   Elle sera blessée si elle ne fait pas attention à la circulation.

    3   Les pommes sont lavées par les enfants.

    4   Il a été invité à une fête.

    5   La maison sera vendue.

    6   Le château a été construit il y a cent ans.

(If this is better as a receptive task, give the French and request the English.)

The subjunctive

A 1 C 2 E 3 D 4 F 5 A 6 B

B 1 It seems that they are afraid.

    2   I want you to come with me.

    3   Everyone must come to our house.

    4   Although she works well, she is not very talented.

    5   I see her every morning before she goes to work.

    6   I'm going to do lots of revision so that my parents are proud.

109. Questions

A 1 Est-ce qu'il peut venir lundi?

    2   Est-ce que vous avez une carte de la ville?

    3   Est-ce que les élèves ont fini leurs devoirs?

    4   Est-ce qu'elle veut aller en ville?

    5   Est-ce que vous êtes vendeuse?

    6   Est-ce que nous arriverons au collège à l'heure?

B 1 C   2 D   3 E   4 B   5 A

C Est-ce que tu vas en ville demain matin?

    Est-ce qu'il joue au tennis?

    Est-ce qu'elle partira en vacances en juillet?

    Est-ce que tu as perdu ta clef?

    Est-ce que tu as réservé une chambre?

    Est-ce que tu préfères voyager en avion ou en train?

Est-ce que les portables sont utiles?
Est-ce que le chien est mignon?
Est-ce que tu veux aller au cinéma avec moi?
Est-ce que tu sais faire de la voile?

D 1 B 2 H 3 D 4 E 5 A 6 G 7 F 8 C

E *Example questions:* Où habites-tu? À quelle heure est-ce que tu te lèves le matin? Combien de frères est-ce que tu as? Qu'est-ce que tu aimes faire le week-end?

110. Prepositions, conjunctions and intensifiers

A 1 F 2 G 3 H 4 B 5 D 6 C 7 E 8 A

B *Student answers will vary.*

C D'abord, je me suis levée à 7 heures, puis je me suis lavée. Je suis entrée dans la salle de bains située près de ma chambre et j'ai décidé de prendre une douche et de me brosser les dents aussi. Après ma douche, j'ai cherché ma serviette partout, mais je ne l'ai trouvée nulle part. À la fin, j'ai réussi à retrouver mon pyjama parmi mes affaires et je suis rentrée dans ma chambre.
First of all, I got up at 7 o'clock then I had a wash. I went in to the bathroom situated near my bedroom and I decided to take a shower and brush my teeth as well. After my shower, I looked for my towel everywhere. But I couldn't find it anywhere. In the end I managed to find my pyjamas amongst my things and I went back into my bedroom.

D 1 donc 2 ensuite 3 aussi 4 partout 5 mais
6 pendant 7 avant 8 en face de 9 chez
10 parmi 11 devant 12 près de 13 environ
14 sans 15 vers

111. Test: listening

1 B, E, G
2 (a) useful (b) English (c) goes to library
3 (a) *water* / recycles paper
(b) by public transport / recycles glass
4 (a) bavard (b) amusant (c) paresseux
5 (a) à la campagne
(b) quinze jours
(c) dans une auberge de jeunesse
(d) sans ses parents
6 (a) B (b) C (c) D (d) A
7 (a) A, E (b) C, E
8 (a) She wants to become a teacher.
(b) They walked huge distances to get to school.
(c) Because of the heat.
(d) Thanks to charitable organisations.
(e) Only one old computer and electricity often cut off.
9 B, D, E

115. Test: reading

1 (a) Caroline (b) Delphine (c) Barbara (d) Aline
(e) Caroline
2 (a) C (b) A (c) C
3 (a) près (b) gagner (c) barbant (d) offrir
4 (a) more competitors / people from further afield involved
(b) three dedicated campsites
(c) good weather not guaranteed
5 I go to school by bus. Lessons start at 8.30 and in my opinion it's too early. My favourite subject is art as I get on well with the teacher. I don't like maths because they give us lots of homework. Yesterday I took a history exam and it was really difficult. I like school because I have lots of friends and most of the teachers are nice.
6 (a) A (b) C (c) D (d) B
7 B, C, D
8 A, B, C, F

9 Sample answer:
The town of Bamako is in the south of Mali. It hardly ever rains there and it's not easy to grow food because of the hot weather. There is a lot of poverty in spite of all the work by charities. Unemployment is a serious problem everywhere and more and more young people are leaving the country to find work.

120. Test: speaking (Foundation)

1 Teacher transcript and sample answers:

T: Je peux vous aider?
S1: Je voudrais une table pour deux personnes s'il vous plaît.
T: Qu'est-ce que vous voulez comme boisson?
S2: Je voudrais un coca et une limonade.
T: Vous avez choisi votre plat principal?
S3: Nous voudrions un steak-frites et une omelette au fromage.
T: Quel est votre dessert favori et pourquoi?
S4: Je préfère les glaces au chocolat car elles sont délicieuses.
T: Il y a autre chose?
S5: Oui, où sont les toilettes?
T: Les voilà, à gauche.

2 Teacher transcript and sample answers:

T1: Décris-moi la photo.
S: Il y a un étudiant qui travaille dans une bibliothèque, peut-être à l'université. Il écrit dans un cahier et il y a plein de livres autour de lui.
T2: À mon avis, aller à l'université est important. Quel est ton avis?
S: Je pense qu'il est important d'aller à l'université car je voudrais avoir un bon emploi bien payé.
T3: Parle-moi d'un projet que tu as fait au collège.
S: J'ai fait des recherches sur la vie de Nelson Mandela en histoire. J'ai regardé des clips vidéo et j'ai lu des livres sur sa vie. C'est un modèle pour moi.
T4: Qu'est-ce que tu vas faire comme études l'année prochaine?
S: Je vais préparer mon bac au lycée en maths, chimie et biologie car je voudrais être pharmacien un jour.
T5: Je pense qu'il y a beaucoup d'avantages à faire un apprentissage. Quelle est ton opinion?
S: À mon avis, faire un apprentissage est important si on veut trouver un emploi manuel, mais ce n'est pas pour tout le monde.

121. Test: speaking (Higher)

1 Teacher transcript and sample answers:

T: Qu'est-ce que tu fais pour protéger l'environnement?
S1: Je recycle les journaux et j'économise l'eau.
T: Que penses-tu du recyclage dans ta région?
S2: Il n'y a pas assez de centres de recyclage. C'est triste.
T: Qu'est-ce que tu as fait récemment pour protéger l'environnement?
S3: J'ai recyclé toutes les bouteilles vides de notre maison.
T: D'accord.
S4: Que penses-tu des transports en commun dans ta ville?
T: Les bus ne sont pas assez fréquents.
S5: Quelles sont les solutions possibles?
T: Je ne sais pas.

2 Teacher transcript and sample answers:

SPEAKING TRACK 102 — Listen to the recording

T1: Décris-moi la photo.

S: C'est la place du marché dans une ville en France. Les bâtiments sont anciens et il y a plein de cafés. C'est très animé.

T2: Je pense qu'il est important de faire du tourisme. Quel est ton avis?

S: Je pense qu'il est vraiment important de visiter d'autres pays et d'autres régions car on peut découvrir des cultures différentes et des plats différents aussi. Par exemple, l'année dernière je suis allé en Chine et j'ai essayé la cuisine chinoise, ce qui m'a beaucoup plu.

T3: Parle-moi des changements récents dans ta ville ou dans ton village.

S: Autrefois ma ville était moins grande mais on a commencé à fabriquer des chaises et la population a augmenté. Maintenant il y a plus d'industries, et plus de magasins!

T4: Où voudrais-tu habiter plus tard dans la vie?

S: J'aimerais habiter en Espagne car il y fait plus chaud qu'en Angleterre et il y a plein de choses à faire et à visiter. Je rêve d'habiter dans une grande maison au bord de la mer où je pourrais me faire bronzer et faire des sports nautiques tous les jours.

T5: Je pense qu'il y a beaucoup d'activités pour les jeunes qui habitent en ville. Quelle est ton opinion? Pourquoi?

S: Selon moi, il n'y a pas assez d'activités pour les jeunes, surtout dans les petites villes. De plus, la plupart des activités coûtent cher et il est difficile de trouver beaucoup d'activités à faire le soir.

122. Test: writing (Foundation)

Sample answers:

1 Il y a plusieurs personnes qui jouent dans un orchestre. Moi, j'adore la musique car c'est vraiment relaxant. Je préfère la musique classique, mais j'aime aussi le rock.

2 Je vais commencer mes études dans votre collège en septembre. Ma matière préférée, c'est le dessin car c'est créatif, mais j'aime aussi les maths et le français bien sûr. L'année prochaine, je vais étudier pour le bac mais je n'ai pas encore choisi mes matières. Je voudrais étudier en France pour améliorer mon français.

3 Pour mon dernier anniversaire, je suis allé au ciné avec quelques copains et on a vu un film comique. Ma fête favorite c'est certainement Noël, car tout le monde est content et on donne et reçoit des cadeaux. Cette année je vais fêter le Nouvel An en Écosse avec toute ma famille. Nous allons passer une semaine là-bas et j'attends ce séjour avec impatience. À mon avis, il est important de célébrer toutes les fêtes traditionnelles parce qu'on doit respecter les traditions.

4 (a) Je n'aime pas mon collège.

(b) Il y a beaucoup de salles de classe.

(c) Il y a cinq cours par jour.

(d) D'habitude, à la récré, je bavarde avec mes amis dans la cantine.

(e) L'année dernière, j'ai joué au foot pour l'équipe du collège. C'était génial.

125. Test: writing (Higher)

Sample answers:

1 Je suis toujours poli et souvent optimiste et modeste, mais mes copains disent que je suis assez bavard et vraiment généreux. Quand j'étais jeune je voulais déjà voyager. Pour mon futur emploi, je voudrais trouver un poste dans une banque ou dans un bureau, mais ce qui importe c'est que je sois heureux. J'aime bien voyager et je rêve de visiter plusieurs pays étrangers parce que j'aimerais pouvoir élargir mes horizons. Il est très important d'avoir des rêves car à mon avis il faut être ambitieux.

2 L'année dernière, j'ai passé des vacances formidables en Italie. Je suis allé à Rome avec ma famille et on a logé dans un petit hôtel confortable. On a tout visité et j'ai surtout aimé les monuments historiques et, naturellement, les plats de la région!! On a choisi d'y aller car mon père adore l'histoire et il voulait explorer le Colisée. À mon avis, il est essentiel de passer au moins deux semaines en vacances pendant l'été parce qu'il faut se détendre après avoir travaillé dur pendant le reste de l'année. De plus, on doit pouvoir oublier le stress quotidien et les problèmes de la vie quotidienne. Pour mes vacances idéales, je voudrais bien visiter le Japon car j'adore la technologie et j'aimerais prendre le train rapide afin de faire le tour de ce pays fascinant.

3 Mon ami, Marc, habite une grande maison à Rennes, dans l'ouest de la France. Il adore y habiter parce qu'il y a beaucoup de choses à faire pour les jeunes. Il habitait dans l'est dans un petit village de campagne mais il a déménagé il y a deux ans. À l'avenir il aimerait habiter à l'étranger, peut-être en Angleterre car il a plusieurs copains là-bas.